Topographies of Class

Social History, Popular Culture, and Politics in Germany
Geoff Eley, Series Editor

Series Editorial Board
Kathleen Canning, University of Michigan
David F. Crew, University of Texas, Austin
Atina Grossmann, The Cooper Union
Alf Lüdtke, Max-Planck-Institut für Geschichte, Göttingen, Germany
Andrei S. Markovits, University of Michigan

Recent Titles
The German Patient: Crisis and Recovery in Postwar Culture
  Jennifer M. Kapczynski
Topographies of Class: Modern Architecture and Mass Society in Weimar Berlin,
  Sabine Hake
Neither German nor Pole: Catholicism and National Indifference in a Central
  European Borderland, James E. Bjork
Beyond Berlin: Twelve German Cities Confront the Nazi Past, edited by
  Gavriel D. Rosenfeld and Paul B. Jaskot
The Politics of Sociability: Freemasonry and German Civil Society, 1840–1918,
  Stefan-Ludwig Hoffmann
Work and Play: The Production and Consumption of Toys in Germany,
  1870–1914, David D. Hamlin
The Cosmopolitan Screen: German Cinema and the Global Imaginary, 1945 to
  the Present, edited by Stephan K. Schindler and Lutz Koepnick
Germans on Drugs: The Complications of Modernization in Hamburg, Robert P. Stephens
Gender in Transition: Discourse and Practice in German-Speaking Europe, 1750–1830,
  edited by Ulrike Gleixner and Marion W. Gray
Growing Up Female in Nazi Germany, Dagmar Reese
Justice Imperiled: The Anti-Nazi Lawyer Max Hirschberg in Weimar Germany,
  Douglas G. Morris
The Heimat Abroad: The Boundaries of Germanness, edited by Krista O'Donnell,
  Renate Bridenthal, and Nancy Reagin
Modern German Art for Thirties Paris, Prague, and London: Resistance and Acquiescence
  in a Democratic Public Sphere, Keith Holz
The War against Catholicism: Liberalism and the Anti-Catholic Imagination in Nineteenth-
  Century Germany, Michael B. Gross
German Pop Culture: How "American" Is It? edited by Agnes C. Mueller
Character Is Destiny: The Autobiography of Alice Salomon, edited by Andrew Lees
Other Germans: Black Germans and the Politics of Race, Gender, and Memory in the
  Third Reich, Tina M. Campt
State of Virginity: Gender, Religion, and Politics in an Early Modern Catholic State,
  Ulrike Strasser
Worldly Provincialism: German Anthropology in the Age of Empire, edited by
  H. Glenn Penny and Matti Bunzl
Ethnic Drag: Performing Race, Nation, Sexuality in West Germany, Katrin Sieg
Projecting History: German Nonfiction Cinema, 1967–2000, Nora M. Alter
Cities, Sin, and Social Reform in Imperial Germany, Andrew Lees
The Challenge of Modernity: German Social and Cultural Studies, 1890–1960,
  Adelheid von Saldern
Exclusionary Violence: Antisemitic Riots in Modern German History, edited by
  Christhard Hoffman, Werner Bergmann, and Helmut Walser Smith

For a complete list of titles, please see www.press.umich.edu

Topographies of Class

Modern Architecture and
Mass Society in Weimar Berlin

Sabine Hake

THE UNIVERSITY OF MICHIGAN PRESS

Ann Arbor

Copyright © by the University of Michigan 2008
All rights reserved
Published in the United States of America by
The University of Michigan Press
Manufactured in the United States of America
⊛ Printed on acid-free paper

2011   2010   2009   2008   4   3   2   1

A CIP catalog record for this book is available from the British Library.

Library of Congress Cataloging-in-Publication Data

Hake, Sabine, 1956–
    Topographies of class : modern architecture and mass society in
Weimar Berlin / Sabine Hake.
        p.   cm. — (Social history, popular culture, and politics in
Germany)
    Includes bibliographical references and index.
    ISBN-13: 978-0-472-07038-1 (cloth : alk. paper)
    ISBN-10: 0-472-07038-X (cloth : alk. paper)
    ISBN-13: 978-0-472-05038-3 (pbk. : alk. paper)
    ISBN-10: 0-472-05038-9 (pbk. : alk. paper)
    1. Berlin (Germany)—History—1918–1945.   2. Architecture—
Germany—Berlin—20th century.   3. Mass society.   4. Berlin
(Germany)—Buildings, structures, etc.   5. Berlin (Germany)—
Intellectual life—20th century.   I. Title.
DD879.H35   2008
943'.155085—dc22   2008007857

ISBN13 978-0-472-02519-0 (electronic)

Acknowledgments

Research for this book has been supported by grants from the National Endowment for the Humanities, the Rockefeller Foundation, and the German Academic Exchange Service (DAAD). A special thank-you goes to the Dean of the College of Liberal Arts at the University of Texas for awarding me a Dean's Fellowship during the last stage of the project. Initial ideas and first versions were presented to attentive audiences at the German Studies Association annual conferences in Milwaukee and Pittsburgh, and at cultural studies conferences in Manchester, Minneapolis, and Berlin; my thanks are due the organizers and participants for providing an atmosphere of critical exchange. In selecting the illustrations for this book, I have been helped by archivists at the Bauhaus-Archiv, Landesarchiv, Technikmuseum, and Bildarchiv Preußischer Kulturbesitz; Iris Hahn of the Stadtmuseum and Tanja Keppler of the Berlinische Galerie were particularly supportive. I am grateful to Geoff Eley for taking an interest in the project, and to Chris Hebert, Christine Byks-Jazayeri, and Marcia LaBrenz for seeing it through to completion. For their personal encouragement and professional support throughout the years, I would like to thank Marc Silberman, Peter Jelavich, Stephen Brockmann, Alan Marcus, and Janet Ward. Several colleagues and friends have read the manuscript in its entirety, and I am most grateful for their critical comments and helpful suggestions: Barbara McCloskey, Fred Evans, David Crew, and especially Sky Arndt-Briggs. I would like to thank Maeve Cooney for her editorial assistance and Lee Holt for preparing the indexes. Almost every line of the book was written with Minski at my side; he will be greatly missed. This book is dedicated to Annetta Kapon, best friend.

Several parts of chapters have been published in earlier versions, and I thank the editors and anonymous readers who helped me to sharpen my arguments. The section on Hilberseimer in chapter 3 appeared as part of a larger discussion on the historical avant-gardes in "Imagining the New Berlin: Mass Utopia and the Ideology of Form," in Richard McCormick, Patrizia McBride, and Monika Zagar, eds., *Legacies of Modernism: Art and Politics in Northern Europe, 1890–1950* (London: Palgrave, 2007), 110–18. A version of the case study on Mossehaus was published as "Visualizing the Urban Masses: Modern Architecture and Architectural Photography in Weimar Berlin," *Journal of Architecture* 11, no. 5 (2006): 523–30. A few arguments in chapter 6 were first developed in "Urban Paranoia in Döblin's 'Berlin Alexanderplatz,'" *German Quarterly* 67 (1994): 349–70. Several passages from chapter 7 appeared first, though in very different form, in "Urban Spectacle in Walter Ruttmann's 'Berlin, Symphony of the Big City,'" Stephen Brockmann and Thomas Kniesche, eds., *Dancing on the Volcano: Essays on the Culture of the Weimar Republic* (Columbia: Camden House, 1994), 127–42.

Every effort has been made to find the copyright holders of the images reproduced in this book.

Contents

Introduction

Since Berlin's emergence as a major metropolis during the Wilhelmine Empire, its status in the urban imagination has been defined through architecture: built architecture as well as unbuilt architecture, and debates about architecture as well as representations of architecture. This rich architectural culture has contributed to the transformation of Berlin into a key site of German modernity and made possible the displacement of social questions onto spatial registers that partially accounts for the city's continuing hold over the urban imagination. More than in other European cities, the process of building has been accompanied by intense debates over representational strategies, symbolic meanings, and discursive functions. These debates revolve around the capital as the symbol of empire, nation, and statehood, the metropolis as an agent of industrialization and modernization, and Berlin as an icon of German mass culture and modernity.

From the monumental architecture of the Wilhelmine period and Albert Speer's plans for Germania, capital of the Third Reich, to the competing postwar modernisms of West and East Berlin and the ongoing reconstruction of postunification Berlin, spatial interventions have been conceived, perceived, and experienced as both agents and indicators of more fundamental changes in the structure of modern mass society and the organization of urban life. In the process, buildings both ordinary and extraordinary have been enlisted in broader reflections on the relationship between tradition and modernity, the meaning of architectural form and style, the symbolic function of public places and urban spaces, and what this study will examine as spatial manifestations of social conflict and change. In similar ways, traffic squares, shopping boulevards, coffeehouses, amusement centers, train stations, and residential neighborhoods have inspired critics, scholars, writers, filmmakers, and photographers to measure the effects of urbanization on conceptions of modern subjectivity and to map what this book's title refers to as the city's contested topographies of class. Weimar Berlin has played—and continues to play—a key role in organizing these symbolic investments and allegorical readings and in defining the terms under which architecture has emerged as one of the most powerful tropes of mass society and what mass discourse sought to contain: the crisis of traditional class society. Especially the years from the stabilization of the currency in 1924 to the world economic depression in 1929 gave rise to a veritable flood of critical, philosophical, literary, photographic, and filmic texts that approach architecture as a formal expression of modern mass society and that traverse the cityscape to explore, whether with hope, fear, or trepidation, the sites and settings of a future beyond class. Using this so-called stabilization period as a lens through which to examine broader questions of German urbanism and modernity, the chapters that follow retrace the complex relationship between modern architecture and mass society across what initially might appear as familiar terrain: the planning initiatives of Martin Wagner and Martin Mächler, the modernist architecture of Erich Mendelsohn and Ludwig Hilberseimer, the city texts of Siegfried Kracauer and Franz Hessel, the photobooks of Mario von Bucovich, Sasha Stone, and Laszlo Willinger, and, last but not least, the most famous Berlin texts from the period, Alfred Döblin's city novel *Berlin Alexanderplatz* (1929) and Walter Ruttmann's city film *Berlin, die Sinfonie der Großstadt* (Berlin, Symphony of the Big City, 1927).

The relevance of these texts to the making of Weimar urbanism and German modernity, however, cannot be assessed outside their contribution to the reconfiguration and rearticulation of class, a critical category largely missing from the existing scholarship. Relying on a combination of close textual readings and extensive historical contextualization, and taking full advantage of the conceptual challenges of transdisciplinary work, I propose to show how Weimar architectural culture problematized the class-based categories that had sustained urban culture until that point. This process took place primarily through the historical alliance of urban culture with bourgeois culture. Consequently, I read the textual productivity surrounding specific buildings, streets, and squares as a class-specific (i.e., bourgeois) reaction to the erosion of traditional class distinctions and cultural hierarchies and the emergence of a simultaneously more heterogeneous and homogeneous urban culture spearheaded by white-collar workers. Expressed through, and projected on, the most innovative architectural styles available at the time, these spatial fantasies of Weimar

Berlin not only shed light on the crisis of bourgeois subjectivity and the perceived threat of deindividualization, but also grant access to the new forms of collectivity, community, and public life that are an essential, though often overlooked or disregarded, part of the making of the modern masses and the power of the classical metropolis.

This initial description also indicates what this book is not: it is neither a historical assessment of *Neues Bauen* (New Building) nor an account of white-collar class culture in Berlin. Similarly, it does not offer a critique of bourgeois culture as the foundation of the classic metropolis, nor does it advocate the recognition of the working class as its largest social body. Instead, both categories—modern architecture and class society—provide the discursive framework in which I undertake a series of close textual readings on the central role of architectural culture in problematizing issues of space and identity and negotiating contradictory positions on mass culture and modernity. In that regard, these readings are also intended as testimony to the power of aesthetic practices in making meaning through their simultaneous opening toward and containing of otherness and difference, including the kind of differences associated with class.

In reconstructing Weimar Berlin's topographies of class, chapter 1 begins with an overview of urban development from the Wilhelmine to the Weimar years, with special attention paid to mass housing and mass transit. Martin Wagner's ambitious program for the New Berlin is presented as both a continuation of older reform initiatives and a radical departure from the spatial order of the classical metropolis, a point illustrated by his bold proposals for modern traffic squares and Potsdamer Platz in particular. Introducing the modern masses as the main protagonists of Weimar architectural culture, chapter 2 reconstructs the constitutive tension between scholarly inquiry and cultural critique by bringing together three very different but complementary perspectives: a geographical description of the city's central neighborhoods and their spatial organization of social difference, several sociological studies about white-collar workers and white-collar culture, and the polemical debate on the meaning of "Berlin" and "the masses" in the Weimar feuilleton. Building on this mapping of the spatial and the social in the first two chapters, chapter 3 assesses the contribution of New Building and the organization of the modern masses along two lines: the conception of architecture as a radical social intervention, especially in the writings of Adolf Behne, and the role of functionalism and rationalism as competing perspectives on mass society in two Berlin-based projects by Erich Mendelsohn and Ludwig Hilberseimer.

Organized around the Kurfürstendamm as one of the central topoi in the Weimar feuilleton, chapter 4 uses the city texts of Franz Hessel and Siegfried Kracauer to analyze the complex relationship between the act of walking and the crisis of bourgeois subjectivity through their respective strategies of reading the city as text. Kracauer's urban hieroglyphics and Hessel's instructions on flanerie will be presented as two paradigmatic responses to the experience of modernity and the threat of massification. While the former's method of deciphering the spatial image opens up a space for critical interventions, the latter's emphasis on the pleasures of strolling closes off the city text against the reality of loss and dislocation. In recognition of the pivotal role of photography in aligning modern architecture with new visual regimes, chapter 5 considers the photographic representation of New Building in a two-part fashion: a formal analysis of the visual representation of Mendelsohn's Mossehaus and the new Alexanderplatz as two key sites in the New Berlin; and a broader discussion of the conventions of architectural photography in the trade press, the illustrated press, and the Berlin photobooks by Sasha Stone, Mario von Bucovich, and Laszlo Willinger. Chapter 6, on Alfred Döblin's *Berlin Alexanderplatz,* uses the Alexanderplatz project to measure the multilayered resonances of the trope of construction in the author's extensive reflections on modernist writing and the conception of the city novel. In accordance with this study's overarching concern with mass society and the problem of class, the author's narrative deconstruction of spatiotemporal relations and subject-object relations is analyzed from the decentered perspective of the lumpenproletariat, that is, a position equally removed from the educated bourgeoisie and the revolutionary proletariat. Continuing along these lines, chapter 7 offers a close reading of Walter Ruttmann's *Berlin, Symphony of the Big City* that focuses on the contribution of the genre of the city symphony and the aesthetics of New Objectivity to the dream of a metropolis unburdened by the old divisions of class and beholden only to the laws of visual spectacle.

The real and imaginary urban spaces mapped in these seven chapters allow us to reconstruct the provocation of class during a crucial period in the history of modern Germany and its only true metropolis: Berlin. In accordance with the symbolic functions alluded to in the beginning, architecture in this context refers to much more than a theme, motif, or critical trope; it establishes a discursive framework for reflecting on the fundamentally spatial nature of social relations, especially in relation to the question of class, and for analyzing the pivotal role of the metropolis, understood here in the widest sense of physical structures, infrastructure networks, and communication technologies, in dislocating and relocating the modern subject. Moreover, my close attention to the metropolis as a site of social conflicts and divisions complicates the simple oppositions of interior and exterior, subjective and objective, and real and imagined space that have characterized earlier scholarship on the representation of the big city in literature, film, and the visual arts and gives way to a more dynamic understanding of the relationship among spatiality, textuality, and identity.

In developing more sophisticated approaches, scholars of the culture of the metropolis have benefited greatly in recent years from architectural theory, urban geography, critical theory, and what has become known as the spatial turn in cultural studies.[1] One concept will be of particular relevance and serve as a guiding principle in my discussion of Weimar architectural culture: the sociospatial dialectic. Urban geographer Edward Soja introduced the term as an alternative to the bipartite view of space as physical form and mental construct, which is shared by crude applications of reflection theory that assume a physical reality outside discourse and radically textualist readings that reduce all physical space to discursive effects. According to Soja, urban space is to be seen neither as "a separate structure with its own autonomous laws of construction, nor . . . an expression of the class structure emerging from the social (i.e., aspatial) relations of production." Instead, urban space and, by extension, the symbolic practices constituting and sustaining urban space must be thought of as "a dialectically defined component of the general relations of production, relations which are simultaneously social and spatial."[2]

As spatial manifestations of social relations, architectural practices bring into relief the shifting terrain of class relations during the Weimar years and foreground the pivotal significance of urban texts in producing the modern mass subject as an imaginary subject beyond class. However, the contribution of architecture to the sociospatial dialectic can only be assessed if we recognize class as an important category in the making of Weimar culture and the representation of Weimar Berlin. Cultural studies regularly evoke this almost mythical place as a high point of classical modernity, a laboratory of modern mass culture, and a founding site of white-collar society. Yet aside from the growing attention to gender, a category that, because of the extensive scholarship already done on women in the metropolis, will remain marginal to this investigation, the provocation of Weimar Berlin remains tied to a surprisingly undifferentiated and apolitical notion of subjectivity. Mediated through individual perceptions and lived out through interpersonal relationships, urban experience in this context functions primarily as an extension of bourgeois consciousness and, despite the diagnoses of crisis and the phantasmagoria of otherness, ends up reaffirming key features of bourgeois subjectivity such as the belief in autonomy, individuality, and self-determination. Even where the question of subjectivity and identity has been problematized through feminist or poststructuralist categories, the underlying negotiation of subject positions and subject effects rarely extends to a public sphere or social body.

As the chapters that follow will show, modern architecture and design allowed architects, writers, and artists to articulate the crisis of subjectivity in relation to questions of class and to confront, whether explicitly or implicitly, the masses and the problem of massification. A standard element of Weimar debates on the metropolis, the concept of massification captures the contradictory responses to modern mass society in its very conceptual vagueness and ambiguity, a fact that makes it ideally suited as a heuristic device for negotiating the various layers of meanings surrounding the historical constellation of modern architecture and mass society. Suggesting processes of democratization as well as social leveling, assaults on individualism as well as moments of liberalization, massification functioned as a key element in the discourses of modern architecture, consumer culture, and mass society. For the purposes of this study, it will be used—like other elements of contemporaneous mass discourse—to reconstruct the complicated connection between aesthetic practice and social change, or, to phrase it differently, between the imagined and real metropolis, during a period that saw a fundamental transformation of the basic terms defining their relationship.

There are few periods in the history of modern Berlin in which social questions and spatial concerns were debated with greater intensity than during the Weimar Republic, and there is no architectural movement that so influenced subsequent approaches to city planning and urban discourse than that of *Neues Bauen,* to use the German term for modern architecture or architectural modernism.[3] Throughout this study, I will use the term *New Building* to emphasize the uniquely German contribution to modern architecture, which includes a greater openness to traditional, local, and regional styles and a stronger emphasis on the spiritual and communal meanings mobilized by the act of building. Brought to the fore by the proponents of New Building, the inevitable tensions between the urban traditions and class divisions of the prewar years and the utopian designs for a more democratic, if not socialist future made the German capital a highly contested site in the reconfiguration of class society and mass society and endowed architecture with symbolic as well as symptomatic functions. Specifically, it was Wagner's ambitious program of the *Neue Berlin* (New Berlin) and its resonances in criticism, photography, literature, and film that fundamentally changed the urban imaginary at a key moment in the crisis of modern class society and that opened up the present toward an alternatively feared or welcomed future beyond class.

As the quintessential German metropolis, the Berlin of the 1920s and early 1930s continues to inspire a seemingly inexhaustible source of critical rereadings and theoretical appropriations, and this is no coincidence.[4] Berlin was not only the largest German city, the capital of the first German republic, and a metropolis with cosmopolitan tastes and international ambitions; it was also the center of the historical avant-gardes, a highly politicized intelligentsia, and a thriving Americanized mass culture. And unlike other European capitals such as Paris or London, Berlin was home both to the great state bureaucracies and cultural institutions and to the kind of industries and businesses that produced a large working class. The most advanced trends in modern architecture and design found a fertile testing ground in Berlin, as did the newest proposals for the rationalization of labor and leisure and the organization of consumption and entertainment. In short, Weimar Berlin functioned as a veritable laboratory of mass culture and modernity. Thus it should not surprise us that from the beginning, *Weimar culture, urban culture,* and *Weimar Berlin* have functioned as almost interchangeable terms, with the one read as an extension of the other and with all three terms treated as symptomatic expressions of German modernity. The literary, photographic, and filmic texts from the period already took full advantage of the metonymic slippage between two terms, *Weimar Berlin* and *modern metropolis,* and enlisted their imaginary topographies in more general debates on mass culture and mass society. As a discursive construct, the modern metropolis opened up a privileged space for thinking about tradition, innovation, and radical change and for tracing their heterogeneous manifestations in social and spatial practices. Not surprisingly, Weimar Berlin has been studied as a primary site for the urban manifestations of modernity and modernization, and the cityscape been approached as a privileged locus of modern subjectivity, which invariably means as a subjectivity in crisis.

Located at the center of this semiotic surplus, the modern metropolis, on one hand, represents nothing but an abstraction. It is a product of the discourses and disciplines that have analyzed the parallel trajectories of modernization, industrialization, and urbanization with a clear awareness of the resulting losses: of distinct urban traditions and local peculiarities, of clear social hierarchies and spatial divisions, and of a shared sense of home and belonging. On the other hand, the metropolis functions as a continual source of sensory perceptions, affective states, physical sensations, critical insights, social encounters, and aesthetic experiences; it is the site where the terms of subjectivity and identity are continuously defined, expanded, and negotiated. Further complicating matters, the metropolis in this particular case is a historical phenomenon, accessible to us only in the form of texts, whether in the conventional sense of written documents or in the wider sense of architectural and urban practices.

Projecting this conceptual opposition, or rather triangulation, into the history of urbanization, the modern metropolis marks the tension, so central for understanding the dialectic of modernity, between the metropolis as the center of capitalism—that is, the industrial city—and the metropolis as the center of enlightenment—that is, the city of learning and the arts. To rephrase it in terms that resonated deeply with Weimar contemporaries, the fascination of the metropolis brings together the threat of exploitation and oppression, on one hand, and the promise of liberation and emancipation, on the other. In making sense of the conceptual divisions within urban discourse and in locating its ideological dimensions more directly in the social struggles and cultural debates of the Weimar period, we must pay closer attention to the historical conditions under which architecture assumed such overdetermined functions as a symbol of modern mass society. Hence we must ask: How did the New Building movement engage the social and the spatial? How did it provide figures of mediation and tropes of difference? And how did it articulate conflict and change? In order to answer these questions, we must first define architecture in a way that acknowledges these symbolic investments and discursive effects. As a "privileged aesthetic language," to quote Fredric Jameson, architecture combines utilitarian and aesthetic, commercial and artistic, individual and social perspectives in ways that make it ideally suited to the work of cognitive mapping and its goal, "to enable a situational representation on the part of the individual subject to that vaster and properly unrepresentable totality which is the ensemble of society's structure as a whole."[5]

Confirming the formative power of the architectural imagination, this cognitive mapping extends to unbuilt projects and imaginary places and includes architectural theories as well as urban utopias. It might even be argued that the fact that so few projects of the New Berlin were ever realized and that so much of Weimar architectural culture consisted of textual practices has contributed greatly to its enduring appeal as an urban fantasy and social imaginary. For the same reasons that the metropolis as a concept cannot be separated from the effects of time and place—in other words, from history—the discourse of architecture must be analyzed within the ideological constellations at a particular historical juncture. To invoke Jameson again, in the same way that urbanism since the Enlightenment has been conceptualized through two seemingly irreconcilable alternatives, namely, urbanism as the production of social equilibrium and urbanism as the science of sensations, architecture, too, has to be examined through the tension between aesthetic utopia and social engineering that found privileged expression in Weimar architectural culture.[6]

In order to take full advantage of Jameson's notion of cognitive or mental mapping, we must open up the meaning of architecture toward the larger field of architectural culture and include what is commonly described as representations of, reflections on, and responses to architecture in other textual media, forms, and practices. Architectural culture, in the words of Francesco Dal Co, "attempts to spin a 'spider's web' over the difference between knowledge and power, and in its threads, language and knowledge, technics and design, tectonic activity and art, function and meaning, *Zeitgeist* and tradition, culture and civilization, all are intended to be reconciled."[7] Defined in such a way, Weimar architectural culture engaged not only architects and city planners, but also critics, writers, photographers, and filmmakers interested in the textures and tectonics of urban life. Contributions ranged from the discussion of the aesthetic, social, and political aspects of New Building on the cultural pages of daily newspapers to its representation in literary, filmic, and photographic media and its proliferation as an overdetermined signifier and signified across all of Weimar culture. This rich architectural culture organized the relationship between urbanism and architecture, articulated the dynamics of subjectivity and spatiality, and connected artistic visions to social programs. One of the main goals shared by all involved was to bring the competing perspectives on the modern metropolis into one coherent master narrative, complete with a clearly defined past, present, and future. The resultant narrative—or rather, the competing narratives presented under the heading of functionalism and rationalism—invariably confronted the threat of the modern masses and the problem of massification, reason enough to pay closer attention to the role of architectural culture in addressing the problem of class.

All contributions to Weimar architectural culture examined in this book represent direct or indirect responses to phenomena of massification: mass production, mass consumption, mass housing, mass communication, mass transportation, and, of central importance to the politics of urban space, the kind of mass mobilization carried out in the name of a more open, egalitarian, and democratic mass society. In the same way that references to the urban masses in the Wilhelmine period meant the industrial working class, debates on massification during the Weimar years revolved around white-collar workers. As the symbol of both social change and social leveling, they were of particular interest to the cultural and intellectual elites professionally involved in the organization of metropolitan life. These elites included representatives of the established *Bildungsbürgertum* (educated classes), the artistic and literary avant-gardes, and the new cadre of urban managers, entrepreneurs, and technocrats. The rise of the metropolis as the home of the modern masses threatened the self-understanding of those members of the bourgeois public sphere most firmly committed to humanist ideals such as the value of education, the significance of high art, and the primacy of literary culture, and it ultimately forced them to come to terms with the commercialization of literary culture and the democratization of cultural consumption. At the same time, the transition from the literary-based public sphere of the nineteenth century to the visually oriented mass culture of the twentieth century gave those working with new media technologies growing influence both as vocal advocates of modern mass culture and as effective mediators between the old and new middle classes.

A number of historical developments made architectural culture so central to the rearticulation and reconfiguration of class after World War I: the delayed process of urbanization that reached both a high point and a turning point during the republic's various political and economic crises; the provocation of New Building and its concerted efforts to organize the urban masses in accordance with reformist, functionalist, and rationalist principles; the making of a radicalized urban proletariat and of an alternative public sphere around working-class culture; the empowerment of previously oppressed, discriminated, and marginalized social groups, including women, and their active participation in the culture of the metropolis; and the proliferation of an American-style consumer culture that promised economic equality and social mobility through its mass-produced fantasies and attractions. Several additional factors contributed to the ascendancy of architectural culture as an integrative discourse during the 1920s: the major political changes after the collapse of the monarchy and the repeated legitimation crises in a capital shaken by putsches, assassinations, strikes, and corruption scandals; the dramatic expansion of the city economy due to improved mass transportation and communication systems and the internationalization of capitalist production and consumption, including its inflationary cycles; and the ongoing transformation of urban life in response to the rationalization of labor and leisure and the commodification of public and private sphere.

Coming together in the metropolis as the place where everything is multiplied, intensified, and accelerated, all of these forces and developments gave rise to the pervasive mood of disillusionment and resignation after the lost war and the failed revolution, but they also contributed to the simultaneous sense of openness, possibility, confidence, and opportunity, especially during the brief stabilization period. The real and imaginary topographies of Weimar Berlin provided the perfect setting for two closely related developments: the continual deterioration of traditional class society as a result of the successive traumas of war, revolution, and inflation, and the concurrent transformation of this class-based urban culture through the media-based forms of mass entertainment and consumption associated with white-collar culture. As the master narratives of innovation and progress became increasingly difficult to maintain, writers, critics, and theoreticians turned to the spatial tropes provided by architecture and city planning to test their modernist commitments within the changing configurations of modern mass society. Many focused on the spatial interventions of New Building to measure Weimar's promises of social mobility and economic equality against the leveling effects of mechanization, rationalization, and standardization. In their search for viable alternatives, some turned to highly politicized mass utopias, including those associated with various revolutionary movements, such as Bolshevism, while others found a similar utopian element in the self-consciously modern products and mentalities introduced as part of Americanization. With these mass utopias functioning as, in the words of Susan Buck-Morss, "the driving ideological force of industrial modernization in both its capitalist and socialist forms,"[8] architects and city planners consciously set out to harness the revolutionary impulse within New Building and create new urban sites and designs beyond the traditional divisions of class.

In light of this rich textual and visual archive, it is not surprising that Weimar Berlin has played a key role in the emergence of German cultural studies as an interdisciplinary, if not transdisciplinary field of study.[9] This process can be traced from the reclamation in the late 1960s of Weimar Berlin as a laboratory of German modernism and progressive mass culture and the city's canonization in 1987 as a key site of German history and national identity during the 750-year celebrations in East and West Berlin, to the continual enlistment, since German unification in 1989, of the capital of the Berlin Republic in the competing topographies of the local and global. Initially based in *Germanistik* and its interpretative methodologies, studies on the literary representation of the metropolis have greatly expanded the purview of urban representation, from an early thematic approach and focus on literary genres to a radical opening up of the city text, or textual city, toward psychoanalytic, neo-Marxist, feminist, poststructuralist, and postcolonial readings. Similar tendencies have characterized critical scholarship on the filmic representation of Weimar Berlin, with a special emphasis on spectatorship and visual spectacle and the resulting expansion of the city image toward simulation and virtuality as the preferred modes of the postmetropolis.

During the same time period, growing attention to Weimar Berlin as a site of contradictory influences and nonsynchronous developments, distinct local and regional traditions, and diverse social, ethnic, and gendered identities has given rise to numerous studies on working-class culture, youth culture, industrial culture, neighborhood culture, and Jewish culture, all of which have complicated previous accounts of urbanization and modernization and drawn attention to the metropolis as a site of cultural heterogeneity as well as unassimilated difference. Meanwhile, architectural historians have greatly expanded our knowledge of New Building in Berlin (e.g., the public housing estates, the high-rise competitions) and either revisited the work of Bruno Taut, Erich Mendelsohn, Martin Wagner, Ludwig Hilberseimer, and Mies van der Rohe in the larger context of Weimar culture and political life or reassessed the uniquely German project of New Building and social democracy from the perspective of ideology critique and postmodern thought.[10]

Through a transdisciplinary approach involving literary analysis, film studies, photo history, sociology, urban geography, and intellectual history, and through a combination of historical contextualization and close textual analysis, this study proposes to integrate architectural history and criticism more directly and productively in the critical project of German studies, among other things by utilizing recent conceptualizations of spatiality for the reclamation of class as a key category of Weimar urbanism. Studying the profoundly spatial nature of class identity is relevant not only to Weimar Berlin as a case study of German mass culture and modernity but also to contemporary debates on postunification Berlin and, more generally, the social-spatial dialectic of the (post)metropolis. More specifically, the close connection between modern architecture and the problem of class will allow us not only to better understand the social, political, and aesthetic project of New Building but also to look behind the strategies of projection and displacement that define the contemporary obsession with architecture as a master trope of history, memory, and heritage. However, such connections can only be uncovered through an initial recognition of the fundamental otherness of Weimar modernism and architectural culture, an otherness that finds foremost expression in its relationship to the future as the telos of the urban imagination and that is intricately linked to class as a category of social conflict and radical change.

As a contribution to the increasing disciplinary border crossings in German studies, this critical reconstruction of Weimar Berlin's topographies of class can be positioned in relation to three broader areas of concern and their respective sets of difficulties. The first set of concerns involves the status of the city as text and the inherent limitations of textual readings, especially when it comes to the metropolis as a public sphere and a space for social practices and experiences. Much of the recent scholarship has been based on the assumption that, as David Frisby notes, the metropolis possesses features of textuality, that it can be read; but does it also mean that its readers approach the city text "out of a desire to know and to analyze what is new in the modern metropolis"?[11] This statement raises more questions than it answers. Are all readers reading the same text, and are they reading from the same perspective and under similar conditions? How is their perception of the new affected by the material conditions of their reading? What is the role of forgetting in the reading of the city text, what the role of blindness and misrecognition, and what the place of conflict and contradiction? Most important, how can we wrest from the city text that which is contained and controlled by signifying practices and then erased, for a second time, by allegorical rereadings? This question is particularly relevant for understanding the unique power of the metropolis to facilitate experiences of community and solidarity—as well as alienation and anomie—and to make available a space for individual and collective agency—a power theorized best through what this study describes as the sociospatial dialectic.

Ultimately, introducing spatial categories into the study of the metropolis and using the sociospatial dialectic to make sense of Weimar architectural culture means recognizing that, as Henri Lefebvre and others have argued, every society produces its own space and that every space is produced in history.[12] It requires us to acknowledge the centrality of symbolic practices to the production of social space and to regard the naive belief in space as given and intelligible as an integral part of the ideologies of the urban. Moving beyond the conceptual binaries found in conventional readings of the metropolis and the textual universalism prevalent in poststructuralist readings allows us subsequently to develop critical categories, however provisional and imperfect, for opening up urban discourse toward the theoretically sophisticated models developed by Lefebvre and Soja, for such categories allow us to confront the reality of the social through the crisis of traditional class society and the rise of the modern masses.[13] Concretely, this means to approach the dialectics of the social and the spatial through architectural culture as a material practice, discursive force, and heuristic device and to trace their contribution to the reconfiguration and rearticulation of class across the real and imaginary landscapes of Weimar Berlin.

A second set of arguments revolves around the status of modern architecture and the modernist imaginary within the heterogeneous culture of the metropolis and the place of the modern metropolis, whether as horror vision or nostalgic fantasy, within contemporary discourses of the urban. There is no doubt that the poststructuralist critique of modernity and the postmodern rejection of modernism have contributed to the current romance with the classical (i.e., the premodern) metropolis: a preference for works and texts that locate the attractions of the metropolis in the nineteenth century, a concomitant affinity for urban structures, forms, and styles criticized by modernists as products of an architecture of class domination and capitalist exploitation, and an ongoing proliferation of palimpsestic readings, archaeological approaches, and retrospective sensibilities.[14] Denounced as cold, inhospitable, and alienating, modern architecture and urban planning have come to represent the absolute other to the dream world of classical urbanity conjured up by modern and postmodern flaneurs and evoked with nostalgic yearning and sentimental attachment by many scholars working on urban culture. Not surprisingly, memories of the nineteenth century continue to dominate contemporary efforts at urban renewal, from the appropriation of the arcade as a postmodern simulation of urbanity to the preference for historicist forms and styles in the movement of New Urbanism.

As Christine Boyer has shown, the postmodern critique of the modernist movement is predicated on the rejection of planned progress in favor

of a plurality of forms and styles, even if only in its aesthetic manifestation, and committed to the immediacy of experience promised by the simulation of the classical metropolis over the modernist reenactment of rupture and fragmentation. Pointing to the inevitable blind spots produced by
such misreadings, Boyer observes:

> As being "modern" in the early part of the twentieth century meant,
> among other things, being self-consciously new, blowing up the con-
> tinuum of tradition, and breaking with the past, the contemporary art
> of city building, by returning to traditions established in the nine-
> teenth century, explicitly jumps over the city of modernism, hoping to
> drive that representational order out of their sight.[15]

Against this current preoccupation with history, preservation, and
memory work, my study calls for a critical reassessment of the modernist
program of formal innovation and radical change as realized in the social
and political interventions of New Building and its local manifestations in
the New Berlin. Against the conventional view of architectural modernism
as the heroic achievement of a few great individuals, I treat architecture as
an integral part of modern mass culture and the ideologies of the urban
that organized this complicated relationship. Focusing on the productive
qualities of the modernist imagination, including its destructive aspects,
and assessing its utopian ambitions, including those that failed, allow us to
rediscover the unredeemed promises of modern architecture, beginning
with its commitment to social justice and democratic change.

From such a perspective, the inherent tension within modernism between the perfect order of the plan and the fragmentation of modern life
can only be resolved in the concrete terms of urban architecture as social
practice and political intervention. Similarly, the dichotomies that have
haunted the modernist imagination from the start, beginning with the
competing imaginaries of the metropolis as organism and as machine,
must be interpreted as direct manifestations of the changing coordinates of
identity and subjectivity. From such a perspective, modern architecture
represents the most important historical attempt to formulate alternatives
to the foundation of the classical metropolis in the spatial politics of class.
For that reason alone, its social and spatial solutions to the problems of
mass society have to be considered as an integral part of the history of urbanization, and its formal provocations and artistic interventions appreci-
ated as an essential element of metropolitan culture. Even the historical
failure of this ambitious project of mass organization and utopian thought

in the post–World War II modernisms in East and West cannot diminish the original impulses under which architecture was enlisted in the fight for social equality and democracy, nor obviate its importance for current analysis and practice.

What are the broader implications of approaching modern architecture and mass society in Weimar Berlin in this particular fashion? What is at stake in reconceptualizing Weimar culture and German modernity from the largely forgotten perspective of class? These questions bring me to my third and final point, the usefulness of class as a category to contemporary debates in German studies. As should be evident by now, little is to be gained from using class to revive the kind of Marxist orthodoxies that have been rightly criticized for their economic determinism, universalism, and unyielding belief in class as the dominant category of identity. Consequently, this study attempts neither a rediscovery of working-class culture in the capitalist metropolis nor a reevaluation of urban culture from the perspective of bourgeois society. Instead of reconstructing class identity as unified and unambiguous, the following close readings take the overdetermined nature of modern subjectivity and identity as given and, instead, focus on the double crisis of urban space and class as articulated through the sociospatial dialectic as defined here. Consequently, the analysis of the dissolution of traditional class society and the opening up toward other notions of identity, subjectivity, and spatiality allow me to examine how architectural culture dislocates and relocates the modern subject and how it creates a space for the exploration of provisional identities and alternative scenarios.

By using Weimar architectural culture to untangle some questions and concerns shared by mass discourse, class discourse, and urban discourse, I hope to delineate a third way between the class reductionism of Marxist orthodoxy and the equally dogmatic celebration of heterogeneity, hybridity, pluralism, diversity, and multitude in poststructuralist thought.[16] Asserting that there is no more dominant category of identity, whether based on class, gender, or ethnicity, or maintaining that all identities are overdetermined cannot mean turning away from an analysis of the spatial manifestations of power, domination, and hegemony and denying the potential of the metropolis as an agent of human emancipation and political change. On the contrary, insisting that conflict and contradictions are the formative principles of urban life, that the problems of the metropolis can be explained in class terms, and that an analysis of the class structure yields important insights into the ideological functions of architec-

tural culture brings renewed appreciation of the heterogeneous cultures and nonsynchronous developments that have always been part of the capitalist metropolis.

Defined in this way, the diagnosis of the crisis of traditional class society through the lens of Weimar architectural culture allows us also to identify some of the historical trajectories that connect Weimar Berlin to postunification Berlin. Privileging the category of class—not as the dominant category of identity, but the dominant identity in crisis—brings into sharp relief the radical otherness of Weimar Berlin and, in so doing, illuminates contemporary architectural culture and conceptions of the urban across the violent ruptures of the twentieth century. From the perspective of the postindustrial city, the industrial city can therefore be reclaimed as the primary site for the historical shift from production to consumption as the driving force of urban life. From the perspective of post-Fordism, the gradual convergence of labor and leisure, and of public and private spheres, in the Fordist metropolis reveals the compromises between capitalist development and social reform made already under the heading of modernization and rationalization. From the perspective of global capitalism, the spatial politics of late capitalism finds initial expression in the modernist doctrine of a separation of urban functions and the assault on the traditional understanding of space and place. From the perspective of the networked city, with its emphasis on immaterial flows, the Weimar fascination with movement and circulation lays the ground for technological progress and social engineering as the unifying myths behind the modern city economy. From the perspective of the digital city, the arrival of the electrified, illuminated city announces the dissolution of the time-space continuum by new mass media and anticipates the rise of the virtual city and the postmodern simulacrum.[17] Last but not least, from the perspective of the corporate city, the enlistment of architecture and urban planning as instruments of public policy and social activism forces us to confront the profound difference between modern and contemporary conceptions of the urban and to make productive use of that very difference.

With these broader implications, the opening of urban discourse to its social and spatial dimensions is bound to shed new light on the crisis of modern subjectivity and its formally most advanced manifestations in New Building, but this time with a clear view of the historical ruptures that contributed to this historical crisis: the decline of traditional class society and the rise of white-collar society. Reading Weimar Berlin as both a symptom and a cause of this sociospatial dialectic opens up the urban imaginary to

its roots in collective experiences, political imaginaries, and, most important, in social and spatial interventions. To conclude with Lefebvre: "What is an ideology without a space to which it refers, a space which it describes?"[18] As this question inevitably leads us back to Weimar Berlin, a series of others logically follows: Whose city was it? Who designed its public spaces and places, and who defined their meaning and function? How was the relationship between real and imaginary city organized? What kinds of subjects and subjectivities were constituted through these spaces, and how did they contribute to the making of the spatial imagination? What processes of deterritorialization and reterritorialization, of dislocating and relocating subjectivity, and of confronting and containing otherness were inscribed into these spaces? Which technologies, media, and disciplines were involved, and what are the formal registers and discursive practices developed in the process? In attempting to answer some of these questions, I begin this set of inquiries in Berlin, circa 1920, as it became a testing ground for new ideas about modern masses and classes.

Setting the Scene: Weimar Berlin, circa 1920

Despite the modernist office buildings and public housing initiatives for which it has become known, Berlin during the 1920s and early 1930s remained essentially a Wilhelmine city. While its social composition and administrative structure underwent fundamental changes, its external appearance continued to reflect the political ambitions and economic developments of the prewar years. Having left an indelible mark on the layout of the city center and the look of many neighborhoods, the imperial past consequently provided the stage on which modernism and modernity after World War I made their spectacular entry in the form of new media, technologies, and audiovisual attractions. Moreover, the prewar ideologies of the urban established the conditions under which Weimar architectural culture assumed such a key role in the reconfiguration and rearticulation of class.

After the founding of the Wilhelmine Empire in 1871, the German capital experienced a period of exceptional growth, with its population increasing from one million inhabitants during the 1870s and two million around 1900 to four million by 1920. The belated emergence of a world city that, before German unification, had been little more than a Prussian garrison town and royal court produced a unified, homogeneous cityscape that, with the exception of the historic center, lacked the rich layers of medieval, feudal, and imperial history found in other European capitals. The creation of Greater Berlin in 1920 made the German capital the third largest city in the world after London and New York. With rigid class divisions already under attack since the rise of social democracy and working-class movements in the 1870s, and with the political institutions and structures of the Wilhelmine Empire either dismantled or weakened after Germany's defeat in World War I, the city was more than ready to com-

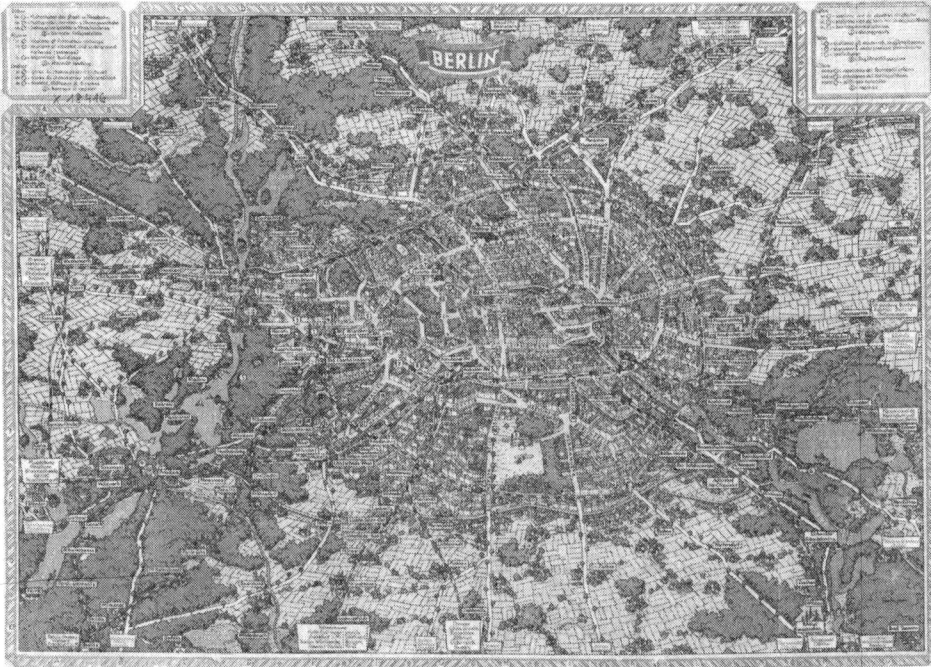

Fig. 1.1. Kurzer Wegweiser und Bildplan von Berlin, Ausstellungs-, Messe- und Fremdenverkehrsamt der Stadt Berlin 1931. Courtesy of Bildarchiv Preußischer Kulturbesitz Berlin.

plete the process of urban reform initiated around the turn of the century and to fully realize the project of modernity under democratic conditions (fig. 1.1).

Born out of the spirit of reform and revolution, Weimar architectural culture came to function as a laboratory for artistic innovation and social change. A politically radicalized generation of architects emphatically rejected the legacies of the Wilhelmine Empire and set out to develop forms and structures more appropriate to the political goals of the Weimar Republic. Because of the lack of available funds and resources, first during the immediate postwar period and then during the world economic crisis after 1929, public and private commissions remained few and far between, prompting many to turn their creative energies toward urban utopias and architectural fantasies. The irreconcilable gap between theory and praxis— and the strong desire to close that gap sometime in the near future—con-

tributed to the emergence of architectural culture as a master discourse bringing together diverse ideas about social reform, technological progress, economic growth, industrial design, and modern life. Key to the resulting synergies was the power of architecture to provide a spatial image of the project of modernity and to make visible the changing dynamics of modern class society.

During an all too brief period after the stabilization of the currency in 1924, these ideas found their clearest articulation in the work of Martin Wagner and the architects associated with the *Neue Berlin* (New Berlin). In terms of measurable accomplishments, the program of the New Berlin remained limited to a few well-known buildings, and many more incomplete or unrealized projects. Even enthusiastic endorsements in the *feuilleton,* the cultural pages of daily newspapers and illustrated magazines, could not distract from the fact that the city's basic structures, beginning with its geometrical layout and unified form, and its eclectic and, more often than not, ostentatious styles were products not of the modern spirit in architecture but of the enormous waves of urbanization, industrialization, and modernization already completed before the outbreak of World War I.[1]

Before and after the war, the oppositions, contradictions, and non-synchronicities of Weimar architectural culture became most apparent in relation to the changing structure of class society. Wilhelmine Berlin had been defined by the old aristocratic and military elites as well as by an influential educated bourgeoisie, a rising entrepreneurial middle class, a small but powerful group of nouveaux riches, and an enormous industrial proletariat and urban underclass. Soon after national unification, technological progress and economic growth brought louder demands for adequate representation from various social and ethnic groups and different political and cultural organizations within this vast agglomeration of independent cities and counties. After the lost war and failed revolution, these unresolved problems culminated in what many architects, city planners, sociologists, philosophers, and urban critics anxiously and persistently evoked as the specter of the urban masses and what it really stood for: the problem of class.

The discrepancies between the ubiquitous architecture of class domination and imperial ambition and new proposals for democratic forms of living and rational models of organization provide the underlying structure for this introductory chapter on city planning in Weimar Berlin. The arrival of New Building produced a surfeit of symbolic activities surrounding the idea of metropolis, a surfeit that required a continuing negotiation of what Ernesto Laclau and Chantal Mouffe describe as the opposition between the "totalitarian myth of the Ideal City" and the "positivist pragmatism of reformists without a project."[2] Bringing together past and future in the present, the real and imaginary spaces of Weimar Berlin will subsequently be approached in a two-part fashion: through a historical overview of the legacies of Wilhelmine architecture in the first part and a critical assessment of the work of Martin Wagner, the most influential city planner of the Weimar years, in the second part. Throughout, I will repeatedly turn to traffic as an overdetermined trope of modernity to tease out its symptomatic functions within the sociospatial dialectic, an approach that concludes with Potsdamer Platz as the first of four case studies presented in the book.

I. Historical Legacies and Reformist Beginnings

If Berlin after 1919 remained largely a Wilhelmine metropolis, how are we to approach the real and imaginary architectures of Weimar Berlin? How are we to envisage the physical environment that gave rise to the program of the New Berlin? And how are we to imagine the city that inspired bold proposals for social change as well as dire pronouncements on the crisis of the metropolis? We could begin by assuming the perspective of visitors arriving from elsewhere. Finding themselves in unfamiliar terrain, tourists and foreigners often turned to the popular Baedeker city guides and tourist maps to make sense of their first impressions. Time and again, the verdict remained the same: Berlin was an ugly city. The 1923 Baedeker complained about the uniform layout of streets, a product of the late-nineteenth-century boom years that made no "distinctions between wide arteries and smaller side streets."[3] Similarly, the 1927 Baedeker concluded: "The overall image of Berlin is that of a young world city that, filled with an ardor for work, began to grow quickly and vigorously only in the mid–nineteenth century. As a result, it lacks the attractions of the organically developed, artistic cityscape characteristic of older big cities."[4]

To a few foreign visitors, including a large number of writers and artists, such shortcomings opened up new and as yet unexplored possibilities. Russian-born Iwan Heilbut praised the "stern, orderly beauty, an order that, in its most beautiful sense, does not aim at monotony but at brightness, conviviality, and health."[5] In *Der Querschnitt,* Parisian Amédé Ozenfant expressed surprise about the absence of street crowds and traffic jams, while Jean Giradoux raved about the many public parks, gardens, and forests, proclaiming that "Berlin is not a garden city, Berlin is a garden."[6] Arriving from Oxford, Stephen Spender was pleasantly surprised by the unified cityscape, a product of the infamous Prussian sense of order and discipline. Yet he admitted that this monotonous layout also deprived Berlin of a discernible identity:

> There were a good many squares, but these had little positive character. They were just places where several streets halted and had a rest before going on with their uniformed march, at the exact opposite side of the square from where they had left. They were more like spaces in time than in place, intervals in which the passerby was able to breathe before resuming the logic of the street.[7]

Used to the rich splendor of Vienna, Stefan Großmann similarly felt a deep sense of spatial alienation: "The brand-new, geometrically laid-out streets in the West, straight and clean, with sixteen and a half square meters of lawn in the middle, all that was practical, useful, sanitary, and bright but, at the same time, foreign, insurmountably foreign."[8]

Many German critics and writers insisted on the benefits of such monotony and uniformity for the ongoing project of urbanization. In 1918, Berlin native Julius Bab noted: "Only one thing is unique to Berlin: the perpendicular, straight, and broad systems of streets that . . . may not make an aesthetically pleasing impression but are well able to accommodate larger traffic volumes without any problems."[9] Equating spatial openness with artistic freedom, Würzburg-born Leonhard Frank observed that "Berlin is flat, and it is wide. Someone leaving Berlin by car might believe that it never ended," and linked the absence of such external boundaries to the city's remarkable susceptibility to "all new and future art and literature in the world."[10] Hermann Kesser from Munich arrived at the opposite conclusion and described

> a layout that almost entirely lacks visual persuasion and represents little more than a network of lines, an order . . . a series, a calculated sum. Points had to be connected with each other according to objective principles. Straight lines were drawn from one point to the other. The space in between was filled with houses. That is how streets developed. Their sole meaning is connection, movement, and traffic—not living, relaxing, and strolling.[11]

Even Curt Behrendt, a strong supporter of New Building who advised municipal agencies on new projects, noted that the German capital had tempo and energy but still lacked "the coherent form that . . . would allow all neighborhoods to showcase the country's economic, intellectual, and artistic accomplishments."[12]

The perceived lack of beauty, history, and tradition, which often found expression in vague pronouncements on Berlin as a city without identity, and the obsession with traffic and movement prompted Egon Erwin Kisch, in his typical matter-of-fact style, to remind his readers of the social and economic inequities behind such critical clichés and to draw attention to the clash of tradition and modernity visible everywhere in the streets of Weimar Berlin:

> At the airport mechanics stand by to repair the engines of incoming transatlantic airplanes, while on the Landwehr Canal an old barge carrying fruit floats by, as it did a hundred years ago. On the Avus racecars pass each other, and drivers get killed in the attempt to generate a little advertisement for businesses, while the mailman trudges up three, four, five flights of stairs day after day, year in and year out. At Gleisdreieck the long distance, underground, and elevated lines meet in the air, yet not far from here the baker's apprentice delivers bread to customers with a dogcart. In the North Harbor cranes unload freight weighing hundreds of tons, activated by the push of a button, but no machine helps the poor woman laborer carry bricks from the Spree barges to the canal's bank.[13]

Taking a highly critical approach to the "iron landscape" of expanded traffic networks, Joseph Roth used Gleisdreieck, a triangular intersection of several train lines near the Anhalter Station, to diagnose the ascendancy of traffic as the new urban paradigm and to measure the destructive effects of technology on the very foundations of urban life. As an allegory of modernity, Gleisdreieck for Roth offered a truly apocalyptic vision: "The future world will be such a Gleisdreieck of powerful dimensions. The earth has lived through several transformations based on natural laws. It is experiencing a new one based on constructive, rational, but no less elementary laws. . . . The 'landscape' acquires an iron mask"[14] (fig. 1.2).

In the same way that Weimar Berlin has been celebrated for its cosmopolitan atmosphere and its openness to artistic experimentation, Wil-

Fig. 1.2. Gleisdreieck. Photograph by Max Missmann, 1927. Courtesy of Stiftung Stadtmuseum Berlin.

helmine Berlin has been denounced for its resistance to cultural innovation and political reform. In light of the extensive continuities between prewar and postwar architectural culture documented by Julius Posener and others, such persistent myths can only be explained through the self-representation of architectural modernism, repeated in much of the early scholarship, as a radical break with tradition and the past. The apotheosis of Weimar Berlin as the founding site of German modernity and the continuing influence of the modernist master narrative have distracted from the strange admixture of liberal, progressive, and conservative politics, of antiurban, nationalist and *völkisch* ideologies, and of traditionalist, regionalist, and modernist sensibilities that informed the prevailing attitudes toward the metropolis in the first decades of the twentieth century. The artificial separation of architecture from other techniques of mass organization has also made it difficult to see the larger ideological configuration in which architectural culture assumed such a unique function in the discourses on class. Adding to these blind spots, scholarly assessments of the prewar metropolis have tended to focus on individual buildings and individual architects. As a result, the sustained efforts by city governments to provide an adequate infrastructure (canalization, electrification, mass transportation), a range of municipal services and facilities (hospitals, schools, public parks), and, most important, affordable housing have until recently been downplayed or ignored.[15]

In the same way that the revisions of modernism in the postmodernism debate have allowed architectural historians to trace the continuities of urban development from Wilhelmine to Weimar Berlin and to situate the modernist movement within the contradictions of twentieth-century architectural culture, historians have used the Weimar Republic as a case study in the making of German modernity. In so doing, they have challenged earlier assumptions about a special German path to modernity that holds the coexistence of premodern, antimodern, and modern tendencies responsible for the partial modernization of German society, with advances in industry and technology not matched by social and political reforms. Rejecting this model of a "normal" path to modernity and identifying nonsynchronicities as an integral part of modernity, Detlev Peukert has diagnosed the pervasiveness of conflict and crisis in what he calls a critical phase in the era of "classical modernity." Most important for our purposes, the paradox of "the hopeful picture of avant-garde cultural achievement and the bleak picture of political breakdown and social misery"[16] moves the assessments beyond the rigid conceptual oppositions that have informed definitions of classical modernity throughout the post–World War II years. The juxtaposition of modern versus traditional, and progressive versus reactionary, which continues to infuse Weimar culture with considerable symbolic currency, is informed by a liberal understanding of progress and democracy that fails to account for the ruptures of dictatorship, war, division, and unification and their profound effect on Berlin architecture and urban planning since the Weimar years. Here the revisions of mass culture and modernity initiated by Peukert and developed further by Adelheid von Saldern and others have shed new light on the complexities of urban development and the dynamics of innovation and tradition from the late nineteenth to the early twentieth century.[17] Among other things, the enduring influence of what David Blackbourn calls the long nineteenth century made itself felt in the persistent belief in social progress and civil society and the embrace of modernity as a force of bourgeois emancipation.[18]

In recognition of such continuities, our historical overview must begin with Berlin's emergence during the 1870s as the nation's undisputed center of political and economic power and the unprecedented building frenzy made possible by new advances in electrification and canalization and a steady expansion of mass transportation and communication networks. This historical moment found privileged expression in the aesthetics and mentality of the so-called *Gründerzeit* (literally, founding period) and its architecture of hegemony. Two interrelated developments were inscribed in its monumental forms and historicist styles: the creation of enormous wealth by new corporations and stock companies and the rise of nationalist sentiment and imperialist ambition after the unification of the Deutsche Reich under Wilhelm I (and Chancellor Bismarck) in 1871. The period's aggressive expansionism and crass materialism found expression in the splendor of its commercial, industrial, and government architecture but also contributed to the inadequacies of mass housing and transportation. The preoccupation with surface effects in public and private life gave rise to a historical eclecticism that borrowed freely from gothic, renaissance, baroque, and classical styles and was loudly denounced by subsequent generations of architects as the clearest manifestation of an oppressive society founded on social and economic inequality and held together by a public culture of ostentation and hypocrisy.

The postwar rejection of Wilhelmine architecture culminated in critical attacks on the Reichstag and the Kaiser Wilhelm Memorial Church as the most visible symbols of the continuities of power. Designed by Paul Wallot and completed in 1894, the Reichstag had been enlisted in the politics of space and place ever since the controversial choice of its location, which many considered peripheral in relation to Wilhelmstraße, the real center of government during the imperial period. The selection of a rather conventional design after two highly publicized architectural competitions, followed by a series of alterations, including the addition of the *Dem deutschen Volke* (To the German People) inscription, further contributed to the building's special place in the urban imagination. Two architectural competitions for several government office buildings on the Platz der Republik, the former Königsplatz—the first held in 1921–22, the second in 1929—took full advantage of the Reichstag's symbolic function by juxtaposing modern and traditional styles, an indication also of persistent anxieties over the most appropriate form of representing the first German republic. Similarly, the Kaiser Wilhelm Memorial Church, completed by Franz Schwechten in 1895 in the then-popular neoromanesque style, served many Weimar critics, including Siegfried Kracauer, as a prime example of the ideologies of form whose analysis yielded important insight into the hold of the past on the present. Located at the beginning of the fashionable Kurfürstendamm, the church not only revealed to them the material excesses and stylistic pretensions of the prewar years but also inspired comparisons to the surface effects achieved by the many storefront renovations in the modernist style (fig. 1.3).

Weimar critics viewed the architecture of the large industries and corporations built in the late nineteenth century much more favorably. After all, Prussian classicism and prewar modernism had forged a highly productive alliance in functional architecture and industrial design, as evidenced by Peter Behrens's influential work for the Berlin-based AEG corporation.[19] Best known for two industrial complexes in the working-class northwest and northeast, the 1909 turbine factory on Hüttenstraße and a large production facility for small engines on Voltastraße, Behrens was the first to achieve the unification of art and industry in the vocabulary of a modernized classicism. His buildings celebrated the beauty of industry and technology, thereby also validating the importance of aesthetic considerations in the workplace and in everyday life. As the house designer for AEG, Behrens promoted the unification of product design, industrial architecture, and corporate identity in the modern *Gesamtkunstwerk* (total work of art) and advocated the reorganization of labor and leisure according to the most advanced management principles, with the corporation assuming functions (housing, health care, education, recreation) until then only performed by the city or the state.[20] During the 1920s, Behrens was widely admired for bringing good design to the masses, factors that may have contributed to his selection as the final winner of the Alexanderplatz competition in 1929.

The main objective of architecture and urban planning in Wilhelmine Berlin had been the effective organization of masses: masses of people, masses of materials, masses of goods, and masses of capital. Yet if Behrens's turbine factory, to quote Fritz Neumeyer, was the "Acropolis of the industrial age,"[21] then the infamous Meyers Hof tenement on Ackerstraße must be described as the catacombs of high capitalism. The seemingly unlimited need of Berlin-based industries for more workers, coupled with ineffectual zoning laws and rampant real estate speculation, had early on produced the so-called *Mietskasernen* (literally, rental barracks), a much-deplored form of mass housing where workers and their families lived under crowded, unhealthy, and dangerous conditions, sometimes lacking even basic utilities. Typically, working-class neighborhoods such as

Fig. 1.3. Kaiser Wilhelm Memorial Church. Photograph by Willy Pragher, ca. 1930. Courtesy of Staatsarchiv Freiburg.

Wedding, Friedrichshain, Kreuzberg, and Prenzlauer Berg consisted of monotonous blocks of apartment buildings, with each building five to six floors high and integrated into the perimeter block through a unified façade adorned in various historicist styles. The so-called *Hinterhöfe* and *Hinterhäuser*, a series of inner courtyards and rear buildings accessible only through the main building, added to the high population density. According to urban geographer Ferdinand Leyden, more than 36 percent of all Berlin neighborhoods had five-story apartment buildings (plus ground floor); in Prenzlauer Berg, the average number of inhabitants per building was ninety-five.[22] The six inner courtyards of the infamous Meyers Hof on Ackerstraße, whose slumlike conditions were regularly showcased in *Berliner Illustrirte Zeitung* (*BIZ*), *Arbeiter-Illustrierte Zeitung* (*AIZ*), and other Weimar illustrated magazines, provided shelter to as many as six hundred people.[23]

Describing Berlin as "the largest tenement city (*Mietskasernenstadt*) in the world," Werner Hegemann, in his controversial history *Das steinere Berlin* (Berlin Built in Stone, 1930), concluded that "every city is the accurate and unfailing expression in stone of the mental forces that contributed to its construction, stone for stone, over the course of centuries."[24] In late-nineteenth-century Berlin that meant the alliance of Prussian militarism and German nationalism with the forces of industrial capitalism, an alliance acknowledged in the derogatory term *rental barracks* and maintained through the oppressive conditions of industrial labor and mass housing. Described, vilified, but also romanticized in numerous milieu studies and reformist treatises since the 1890s, the tenements had been held responsible for a series of social ills: tuberculosis and other infectious diseases, alcoholism and malnutrition, domestic violence and petty crime, sexual abuse and prostitution, and, perhaps most ominous, revolutionary tendencies. Not surprisingly, the areas of highest population density were also the centers of the infamous Red Berlin, reason for some architectural historians during the 1970s to romanticize the tenement as the founding site of an authentic working-class culture. Living up to their reputation as a source of dissent and unrest, the tenements during the world economic crisis saw violent tenants' strikes, political confrontations, and the kind of communist uprisings depicted in Klaus Neukrantz's *Barrikaden am Wedding* (Barricades in Wedding, 1931) about the infamous May Day of 1929.[25]

There is no doubt that the Wilhelmine era had created the problems of mass housing that continued throughout the Weimar period. Yet the dedicated work of early social reformers and political activists, especially on issues such as public health, renters' rights, zoning codes, and real estate tax structure, had also established the institutional and discursive frameworks for the more ambitious reform initiatives of the 1920s. From the beginning, the municipal government approached housing reform with the goal of turning Berlin into a showcase for the progressive social policies of the Weimar Republic. Repeated efforts were made to eliminate the inner courtyards and to permit only block construction, with all buildings accessible from the street. The introduction of a new building code in 1925 prevented the most egregious aspects of the tenement in new construction but had little effect on substandard prewar housing. More long-range proposals for breaking up the tenements included the building of new thoroughfares and the expansion of public transportation systems with the eventual goal of moving skilled workers and employees to the outskirts of the city, to the famous public housing estates (*Großsiedlungen*) discussed in greater detail later.

A rarely mentioned by-product of economic development and urban growth, far removed from the misery of the tenements, was the architecture of wealth and privilege that had produced affluent suburbs such as Dahlem and Wannsee and solidly bourgeois neighborhoods such as Charlottenburg and Wilmersdorf. The westward shift of the commercial center had coincided with the arrival of new professional classes, including the managerial and technocratic elites settling in Schöneberg, Wilmersdorf, and Charlottenburg. These residential neighborhoods also became home to Berlin's assimilated German-Jewish middle class and a growing number of foreigners, exiles, and émigrés arriving from the Soviet Union and elsewhere. The administrative autonomy of these independent cities prior to the incorporation of Greater Berlin contributed to their small-town atmosphere and character. Apartment houses and public buildings displayed the restrained styles of neoclassicism, *Jugendstil,* and Werkbund-inspired precursors of Weimar modernism and served, throughout the 1920s, as bourgeois havens of comfort, safety, and solidity. By contrast, the westernmost suburbs attested to the growing influence of the *Besitzbürgertum* (moneyed middle class) whose members, unlike those of the traditional *Bildungsbürgertum* (educated middle class), displayed their newly found prosperity in spectacular private residences. Unlike the bank presidents and company founders who had built their city palaces close to the Royal Palace in the historic center, this new upper middle class favored the bucolic utopias of the English garden city movement, with building styles ranging from the ever-popular *Jugendstil* and various regionalist modernisms to the classicist modernism perfected by Peter Behrens.

To Weimar contemporaries, the tenements and factories in working-class neighborhoods served as a visible reminder of the close connection between industrialization and proletarization during the Wilhelmine era. Yet the large department stores built around the turn of the century also added an entirely new element: the emergence of consumption as a driving force in the city economy and a key factor in the self-understanding of the new middle classes. Responding to the growing significance both of consumption as a form of popular entertainment and of architecture as an object of aesthetic appreciation, these department stores took full advantage of the latest developments in interior design and product advertising to cultivate new consumerist desires. In the Wertheim store, completed in the neoclassical style by Alfred Messel in 1896 at the corner of Leipziger Straße and Leipziger Platz, goods were displayed on several open floors surrounding an enormous light-flooded atrium. The Tietz department store on Leipziger Straße, completed in 1900 by Bernhard Sehring, featured the first curtain wall, soon to become a defining feature of the modernist high-rise. Confirming Werner Sombart's observation that the modern metropolis had been born out of the spirit of luxury consumption, these early temples of commodity culture marked the beginning of a momentous shift from production to consumption as the driving force in the city economy, a trend captured most poignantly in window-shopping as an allegory of urban experience and modern life in countless city texts from the period.[26]

The ascendancy of mass consumption affected all aspects of urban life. Before the war, department stores had supplied the nouveaux riches of the *Gründerzeit* with everything necessary for running a well-appointed household in the luxurious city palaces of the Tiergarten district. Now reaching out to a broader middle-class clientele, department stores promised a democratization of luxury while still providing customers with an experience of social distinction. Moreover, by offering a wide range of goods and services in one large unified space, department stores subtly redirected the stream of people within the metropolitan area: from the open and public spaces of the street to a semipublic environment controlled by private corporations; from the residential neighborhoods with their small retail stores to the commercial center with its large chain stores, luxury restaurants, and first-run movie theaters; and from the city's historic center in the east to the upper-middle-class residential areas in the *Neue Westen* (New West). This process, which signaled the arrival of the white-collar workers as the vanguard of Weimar consumer culture, contributed to the rise of Kurfürstendamm as the premier shopping boulevard after the opening on Tauentzienstraße of the Kaufhaus des Westens, the famous KaDeWe completed by Emil Schaudt in 1907. A novelty at the time, its closed floor plan served as the norm in department store design until the introduction of the postmodern shopping mall.[27]

Berlin's astounding growth during the Wilhelmine Empire had been fueled by the belated industrialization of Germany and the influx of large numbers of people from the impoverished eastern provinces. Responding to industry's ferocious appetite for workers, the city developed in an inconsistent fashion, subject to local politics, real estate interests, population movements, zoning laws, and other factors. Before World War I, the metropolitan area had been defined by the *Ringbahn* (circular line); outside lay low-density residential neighborhoods, upper-class suburbs with single-family residences, and semirural settlements and small villages. Already then, the historic center, or *City*, to use the term used by businessmen and entrepreneurs, had begun to lose apartment renters to the large banks, corporate offices, law firms, and department and retail stores that controlled the distribution and circulation of wealth in the metropolis. Around the turn of the century, Berlin architects and urban planners began to look for solutions to the many problems caused by urban sprawl, real estate speculation, housing shortages, and the commercialization of the historic center. Among other things, they studied models of urban planning that took account of the uniquely modern dynamics of change by acknowledging the street as the driving force behind all urban growth. In shifting their attention from solid bodies to hollow spaces and by focusing on the dynamic qualities of the space between buildings, their new proposals announced a momentous change in the very definition of the metropolis: from the concentration of urban functions in a small geographical area to a clear separation of urban functions according to rational principles and functionalist ideas.

The ensuing process of decentralization followed two trajectories, the shift of commercial areas from the eastern to the western part of the city described previously and the shift of residential areas from the center to the periphery that became the hallmark of modern city planning. Convinced of its social and economic benefits, city officials already before the war had actively promoted the separation of urban functions, with industries restricted to the periphery and with the center reserved for commerce, administration, and entertainment. While often promoted with reference to scientific studies about the benefits to public health, these new planning initiatives also responded to persistent fears, fueled by mass demonstrations, antiwar rallies, and the Russian Revolution, that the problems of the tenement could, literally and figuratively, spill into the streets and bring the city economy to a standstill. Consequently, the city government pushed for a rapid expansion of the mass transit system, including the *Ringbahn* that connected the long-distance Friedrichstraße, Anhalter, Lehrter, and Potsdamer stations and reached far into the outlying suburbs; an elevated train, the *S-Bahn* (*Stadtbahn* or city train) that connected the eastern and western parts of the city; and, after 1902, a new subway line that made commuting less time-consuming and more convenient for all residents. Factories and workshops built in the late nineteenth century were usually located in working-class neighborhoods, with AEG starting out in Wedding and Borsig in Moabit. Now more and more companies left these old mixed-use neighborhoods for outlying districts, with the Borsig locomotive factory eventually moving to Tegel and with the wartime armament production facilities in Staaken designed to include workers' housing from the beginning. This process culminated during the late 1920s in the building along the Lower Spree of the enormous Siemensstadt complex whose mixture of production facilities, office buildings, and residential areas for workers and employees announced a radically new way of organizing urban life in accordance with the changing class dynamics of white-collar society.

Many of the developments outlined thus far occurred under Ludwig Hoffmann, head of city planning (*Stadtbaurat*) from 1896 to 1924 and characterized by art critic Paul Westheim as the architect of the *juste milieu*, the happy medium between modern and traditional influences.[28] The numerous projects completed during his administration included schools, museums, hospitals, office buildings, courthouses, and public baths. Designing buildings based on their public function, Hoffmann chose an unassuming German brick architecture for the Märkische Museum (1896–1908), while he built the Stadthaus (1902–11) in the more imposing Palladio style. He was actively involved in the restoration (completed in 1930) of the Pergamon Museum on the Museum Island, a project originally started by Adolf Messel, and he turned the Auguste-Viktoria-Platz (now Breitscheidplatz) into a showcase of urban renewal. Under the influence of the life reform movement and the garden city movement, Hoffmann promoted the creation of public parks as an important contribution to social hygiene and public health. Applying ideas first formulated by Leberecht Mügge and Daniel Schreber, Hoffmann was responsible for the Schillerpark in the north and the Volkspark Friedrichshain in the east. According to Posener,

Hoffmann's contribution to the making of the modern Berlin reflected the contradictory nature of the Wilhelmine Empire, beginning with the historical compromise among the reactionary culture of empire, the drive toward modernization in business and industry, and the various social and cultural reform movements.[29]

Hoffmann's close attention to the infrastructure of what by 1910 had become the fastest growing city in Europe produced several general building plans. The unification of a vast urban conglomerate within one administrative structure and the implementation of a comprehensive plan that coordinated the restructuring of the center with the demands of decentralization had started with the founding in 1911 of the Association (*Zweckverband*) of Greater Berlin by the various independent municipalities. Yet because of their complicated administrative structure, the approach to city planning before World War I remained limited to basic necessities, such as the need for a municipal sewage system, and never produced a unified urbanistic vision or plan. In the existing system of streets and squares, new construction was permitted either inside the large perimeter blocks or alongside the main traffic arteries with their uniform fronts and distant vanishing points. The Hobrecht plan of 1858–62 had proposed to accommodate urban growth through the construction of main thoroughfares laid out in a radial pattern. For the 1910 Greater Berlin competition, Hermann Jansen once again had focused on the addition of thoroughfares, but this time to create pleasing cityscapes in the way proposed by Camillo Sitte in his writings on the city beautiful.[30] The fact that city governments before 1920 had influence only over the basic street layout severely limited all attempts to implement general building codes and made it extremely difficult to coordinate the infrastructure of the larger metropolitan area. After 1920, the concentric circles that had defined the traditional city limits and provided a basic structure to the Hobrecht plan were overlaid with a radial model that emphasized continuous expansion, movement, and change as the new principles of development. In a belated adaptation of Sitte's pronouncements about the art of building cities according to artistic principles, new building codes now also regulated the maximum building height, with the so-called Berlin *Traufhöhe* (eaves height) of twenty-two meters a clear expression of the new communal spirit of civic responsibility and urban identity.

Bringing together the major positions of the prewar debates, Martin Mächler's Greater Berlin Building Plan of 1917 was the first to distinguish clearly among commercial, industrial, and residential districts and to declare the *City*, the center of banking and commerce, the driving force behind all further development (fig. 1.4). Actively involved in the *City-Ausschuß*, a group of businessmen and entrepreneurs, and strongly influenced by the political economist Friedrich List, Mächler saw the modern metropolis, its culture and society, as an integral part of the world economy. Negotiating the complex relationship between urban planning and economic policy, the city planner of the future according to Mächler had to be "both a state builder and world builder."[31] Promoting economic growth as the solution to social problems, he called for a modernization of Berlin's historic center and an expansion of its mass transit system. He was one of the first to propose the construction of a north-south axis and a central train station. In his writings, Mächler identified five urban functions for the historic center: commerce, housing, administration, culture, and entertainment. Even in his architectural work, which included submissions to the competitions for Platz der Republik and Alexanderplatz, he was guided by two fundamental beliefs: that the separation of urban functions, including the building of so-called satellite cities on the periphery, was both inevitable and desirable, and that the difference between the small-town, family-oriented atmosphere in the suburbs and the cosmopolitan atmosphere in the center would lead to a renewed appreciation of urban life. Thus redefined in dynamic or relational terms, the modern metropolis, in Mächler's words, could finally realize its full potential as an agent of technological, economic, and social progress, which also meant as a symbol of capitalism in its most developed stage. In mapping this new relationship between the local and the global, Mächler became one of the first to make use of the conceptual framework that, according to Fredric Jameson, distinguished all Central European urbanistic projects of the 1920s. After all, "if the outer limit of the individual building is the material city itself, with its opacity, complexity, and resistance, then the outer limit of some expanded conception of the architectural vocation as including urbanism and city planning is the economic itself, or capitalism in the most overt and naked expression of its implacable power."[32]

II. Martin Wagner and the New Berlin

It was as part of these larger developments in the organization of the urban masses that the creation of Greater Berlin on 1 October 1920 marked both an end and a new beginning. With four million inhabitants, this vast

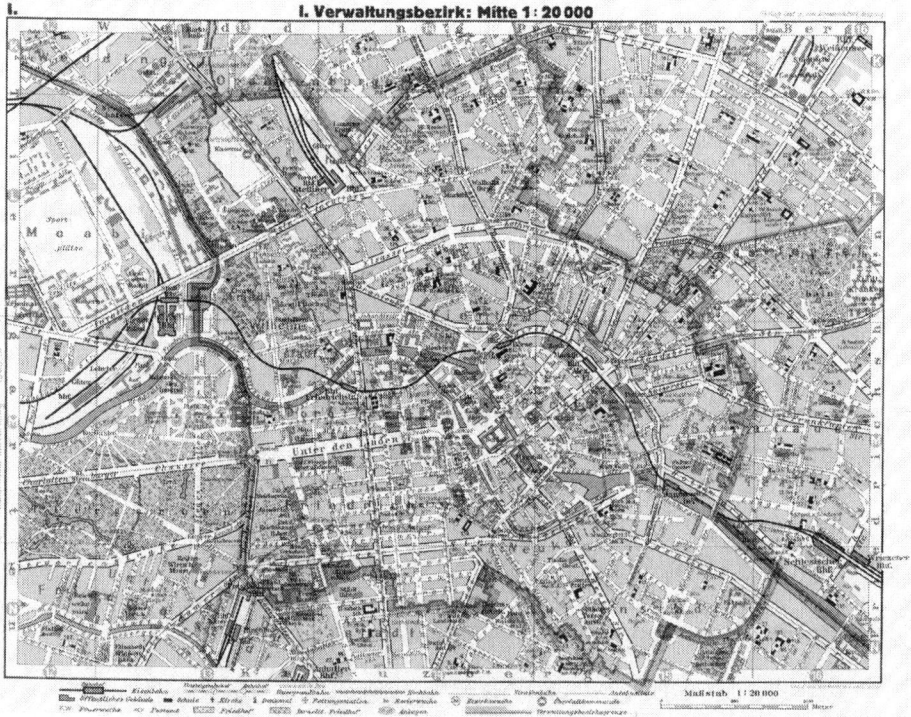

Fig. 1.4. Center of Berlin, Verwaltungsbezirk Mitte, ca. 1927 (1:20,000). Courtesy of Bildarchiv Preußischer Kulturbesitz Berlin.

conglomerate of eight independent cities, fifty-nine counties, and twenty-seven domains became the third most populous city in the world after London and New York. Moreover, covering an area of 883 square kilometers, the German capital stood out as the most spacious city in the world; Paris covered only one-tenth of the same area. The creation of a new administrative structure for the entire metropolitan area put an end to years of unprecedented, and often unregulated, growth. Nonetheless the geographical location of Berlin in the wide expanses of the Brandenburg Marches and its decentralized administrative structure contributed to the kind of urban sprawl that, now legitimated by repeated calls for decentralization, continued throughout the 1920s.

One of the new goals was the separation of urban functions into industrial, commercial, and residential areas and the revitalization of the historic center through extensive investment in the infrastructure (e.g., mass transportation, public parks and services). "Extreme decentralization of the parts, but greatest concentration of the whole"[33] is how Erwin Gutkind described the proposed creation of designated areas for industry, business, housing, and commerce. Meanwhile, the revitalization of the historic center through decentralization was meant to contribute to a much more elusive goal: the emergence of an image, or fantasy, of metropolitan life that could serve as a model for new perceptions and experiences and, even more important, new definitions of society beyond the existing divisions of class.

The move toward greater administrative unity corresponded with the self-representation of the Weimar Republic as a modern democracy, but it also reflected the need to deal with a number of pressing issues, beginning with the chaos and violence during the revolutionary upheavals of 1918 and 1919. Because of the continuing economic and political uncertainty during the hyperinflationary period, architects and city planners had to wait until 1925, the first year after the currency reform, before general building regulations for Greater Berlin could be passed. These further clarified the existing zoning laws and established new rules for site density, the permissible height of structures, and the maximum occupancy for buildings in residential, commercial, and industrial areas. A general building plan that established long-range planning goals was not introduced until 1929. Unfortunately, by that point, the Social Democratic Party (SPD)-led city government lacked the financial resources and political support to complete any large-scale building projects, including those already under construction. Whereas planning for many public housing estates had begun around 1924, the more ambitious projects in the center were initiated only in the late 1920s. They were either in the construction phase (Alexanderplatz) or the planning phase (Potsdamer Platz) when the world economic depression brought building to a complete stop in 1931 for all public works.

Compared to Frankfurt am Main, with Ernst May as the architect of the New Frankfurt, or Hamburg under the aegis of Ernst Schumacher, Berlin cannot really be described as a center of New Building, the architectural movement often conflated with what later became known as the International Style. Nonetheless, as the nation's capital and its largest metropolis, Berlin provided a laboratory for several guiding principles, including an acute awareness of the impact of rationalization on the organization of labor and leisure, close attention to the problems of working-class housing and industrial production, and a firm belief in architecture as an agent of social reform and political change. As noted earlier, few new buildings were added to the downtown areas, even fewer modernization projects were completed, and, with the exception of the large public housing estates, the Weimar capital never acquired a strong reputation as a center of modern architecture. While some architects developed their functionalist and rationalist ideas within the transnational framework established by the historical avant-gardes, others relied on traditionally German materials, forms, and styles to promote a compromise version of modern architecture, sometimes referred to as *gemäßigte Moderne* (moderate modernism).[34] In both cases, the modern spirit in architecture brought fundamental changes in the very definition of the metropolis, changes that dovetailed in significant ways with the transformations of class society initiated under the heading of the New Berlin.

As Weimar Berlin became a testing ground for competing theories of mass society, it also allowed for the spatial articulation of new class identities. The power of the metropolis as built environment and public sphere and the unique status of the capital as a metaphor/metonymy of nation found powerful confirmation in the world-historical events unfolding on the city's streets: from the abdication of the emperor to the declaration of the republic, from revolutionary uprisings to right-wing putsches, from mass strikes to political assassinations, from hyperinflation to the world economic crisis, and from the communist rallies to the Nazi takeover of power in 1933. The heightened expectations placed on modern architecture to articulate these moments of crisis through the spatial organization of modern society and to channel its destructive energies into more productive but also more durable forms were particularly evident in heated debates on the high-rise and the public housing estate; but they also influenced critical writings on the changing role of mass transit, mass consumption, and mass entertainment in the city economy. Confirming this mutual instrumentalization of architecture and ideology, the New Berlin has played a key role in the materialist historiography of the modern movement initiated by Manfredo Tafuri in his writings on New Building and social democracy and continued in the work of the Venice School: Francesco Dal Co, Massimo Cacciari, and, of special relevance for this chapter, Ludovica Scarpa on Martin Wagner.[35]

Wagner, the man most closely identified with the New Berlin, started his work in 1920 as head of city planning for Schöneberg, then still an independent municipality. He became Hoffmann's successor as head of city planning for Greater Berlin in 1926 and served in that capacity until 1933. Known for his socialist politics and active support of building cooperatives and building associations, his collaboration with the architect Bruno Taut on public housing estates, and his countless lectures and articles on modern city planning, Wagner elicited strong reactions beyond the small circle of architects and politicians. Hugo Häring alluded to his reputation as an indomitable force in the double project of urban reform and social reform when he replaced the official title of *Baurat* (building councilor) with his description of Wagner as a *Bauherr* (lord of building).[36] Contemporaries sometimes described Wagner's approach to urban problems through military metaphors that likened the city planner to a fearless soldier on the front of economic progress, technical innovation, and social change. As the embodiment of the modern technocrat, Wagner subsequently became closely associated with two equally important trends: the management of social conflict and the internationalization of urban development.

To begin with, Wagner saw modern city planning as part of the larger political project of influencing social practices through spatial interventions, an idea first articulated in his 1915 dissertation on public parks.[37] In the public housing estates, he argued, the old dream of community and the new spirit of objectivity could finally be reconciled. By channeling the city's disorganized multitudes into calculable quantities, he hoped to achieve socialization through rationalization, with the original dream of socialism now translated into reformist strategies and administrative solutions. In his thinking, Wagner broke with established approaches to city building that, in the spirit of Sitte, wanted to bring out the beauty of the big city and provide its inhabitants with a sense of home and belonging. He also differed from contemporaries like Otto Wagner in Vienna whose radical reconceptualization of districts as modules still adhered to an organic concept of growth. More of a social engineer than a traditional city builder, Wagner was heavily influenced by the ideas of Taylorism and Fordism, which he studied during an exploratory visit to the United States in 1929. The same reasoning that made him support the use of prefabricated elements in construction also informed his ambitious plans for a fully rationalized metropolis. While devoting much of his energies to the question of dwelling, Wagner believed strongly in the primacy of dynamic over static relations and focused his critical attention on traffic—that is, on the laws of circulation—as the driving force behind all urban development.

The growing power of the city administration in organizing modern urban life is evident in Wagner's public housing initiatives and his close collaboration with labor unions and building cooperatives. Wagner was one of the first to recognize that the Fordist system of mass production, distribution, and consumption required what Stephen Graham and Simon Marvin call "the integrated energy, transport, water and communications grids so central to the modern planning ideals of the time."[38] To establish these grids, the city government had to make a major investment in the city's infrastructure. At the same time, his acute awareness of the globalization of capital and its effect on the city economy can be seen in how he gained financing for some of the more ambitious projects, for instance, from the Chapman investment group for the modernization of Alexanderplatz and through an initial involvement of the French Galleries Lafayette for the Columbushaus project. With Wagner as their point man, the Social Democrats in power aimed at a workable compromise between economic and social factors, guided by the belief that technological progress could bring social peace and economic prosperity. As an integral part of what has elsewhere been described in the alternatively exuberant and foreboding terms of postwar Americanization, this compromise included the implementation of new principles founded "on the virtuous linkage of mass production techniques, mass consumption and advertising based on the nuclear family household, Taylorist work organization, collective wage bargaining, the hegemony of the large corporation, Keynesian demand management, the welfare state and the mass production of standardized housing."[39]

Weimar Berlin provided Wagner with the perfect laboratory for new approaches to public housing and big city traffic and inspired daring proposals for the future of the German capital. All initiatives were informed by the basic principles of what Tafuri describes as Weimar social policy: socialization of the construction industry and mass housing, technical and bureaucratic solutions to social problems, state management of conflicts within the Fordist economy, and rationalization in the place of class struggle—in short, socialization instead of socialism.[40] Subsuming the aesthetic under the political and displacing social struggles into rational solutions were an integral part of Wagner's activities as a critic and editor, too. As early as the first issue of *Das Neue Berlin,* the journal coedited with architectural critic Adolf Behne, Wagner announced a dramatic transformation of the cityscape taking place over the next twenty years, a transformation that would erase all residues of local idiosyncrasies and all legacies of a nationalist past, and fully align Berlin with international developments and universal principles. However, this kind of homogenization and standardization required effective organization and close coordination. Fond of metaphors, Wagner repeatedly evoked the image of an orchestra when he declared that "city planning is the coming together of technical, artistic, and economic insights under one organizer and conductor (*Dirigent*)."[41] A firm believer in centralized planning, he insisted on the importance of "strong leadership, the kind of direction (*Regie*) that unites all forces in creating metropolitan visual effects."[42] Taking these filmic references even further, he once described himself as "the director of the metropolis Berlin" who, like a movie director, brought together disparate elements into one coherent image, an image based no longer upon durable physical structures but upon the kind of urban effects achieved through movement and dynamism.

During his tenure as city building councilor, Wagner enjoyed the full support of Berlin mayor Gustav Böß and benefited greatly from his collaboration with the Social Democrats in city government.[43] Wagner also worked closely with Ernst Reuter, the city councilor for traffic and transportation. In fact, his reconceptualization of the modern metropolis would not have been possible without the unification of mass transit, with the city taking over all bus and rail systems, except for the *S-Bahn,* in 1920. Reuter oversaw a dramatic expansion of Berlin's public transportation system by adding several new subway lines, for which Alfred Grenander built stations in highly functional, understated designs. The remodeling of the Nollendorfplatz and the expansion of the Alexanderplatz stations greatly increased the efficiency of these two major transit hubs. As part of the further centralization of city services in 1928, the various mass transit systems were integrated in the Berliner Verkehrsgesellschaft (BVG); at that point, a unified rate system was also introduced. These changes established the conditions necessary for the planned transformation of the metropolis according to functionalist principles. Not surprisingly, Reuter spoke repeatedly of the power of traffic both to "fertilize" the center with the help of mass transportation systems and to "air out the center" and thereby extend the city—which also meant, discharge its tensions—into the tranquil lifestyles of the country.[44]

Wagner's vision of the New Berlin was a direct product of the so-called stabilization period during the Weimar Republic, which began with the stabilization of the currency in 1924 and ended with the world economic crisis in 1929. In less obvious ways, his unyielding belief in the power of organization must be seen as an aftereffect of the republic's early revolutionary days. What Tafuri identifies as Weimar social policy's problematic "system of compromises,"[45] and what other Wagner scholars describe as a "rationalization of happiness,"[46] bears witness to the inevitable blind spots in an urban discourse that sought to compensate for thwarted political hopes and failed social experiments with the chilly vision of the metropolis as a fully rational and hence ideally rationalized space. A number of additional factors contributed to the ascendancy of planning models that conceived of radical change primarily in organizational and managerial terms. On the local level, a precarious compromise had to be maintained between the progressive forces put into power after 1919 and the conservative forces identified with the city's old political and entrepreneurial elites. All initiatives required at least some cooperation among local businessmen and real estate moguls, the dominant political parties in city government, and the professional organizations of architects, builders, and the construction industry. The viability of the program for the New Berlin also depended on the availability of investment capital for large-scale projects and was directly affected by economic trends that fueled the city economy from the consumer side (e.g., increases in discretionary income). Ludovica Scarpa, following the model of Tafuri, has used the failed negotiations of the city government with the Chapman group of investors to highlight the discrepancy between urban theory and practice and to confirm economic forces as the determining factor in all urban projects and debates.[47] Yet, somewhat unexpectedly, the same disconnect between a proliferation of urban utopias and ambitious designs and a scarcity of material and financial resources also created the opening in which architecture, whether built or unbuilt, could serve other less obvious purposes in the imaginary economy of the metropolis and become an instrument of critical reflection and artistic intervention.

The contribution of Wagner to the debates on the modern metropolis can be further clarified through a brief comparison with Martin Mächler, a lesser-known Berlin-based urban planner and theorist from the 1920s. Both men believed in defining and coordinating urban functions more efficiently and responded to the ubiquitous signs of social conflict with a model of organization—indeed, an ideology of organization—that translated irreconcilable antagonisms into manageable differences. Concerned with the management of the modern masses, both men proposed practical solutions to the ongoing negotiation, carried out with particular intensity in the capital, of democratic politics, liberal economics, and the competing ideologies associated with Americanization and Bolshevization. Wagner and Mächler had their differences, however. Mächler's insistence on economic interests as the foundation of urban life grew out of his extensive work for Berlin-based businesses and corporations. In contrast, Wagner's strong community involvement, beginning with the public housing estates, aligned him with the progressive forces in the Weimar Republic frequently categorized under the label "white socialism." Where Mächler advocated slow growth and balanced development, Wagner aggressively argued for the benefits of radical change. Yet where Mächler, the personification of urban boosterism, hailed the concentration of all elements in the center as the ultimate expression of big city life, Wagner, the cool technocrat, insisted on the advantages of decentralization and, in so doing, betrayed an intense dislike of the metropolis as the source of diversity and instability.

In his activities as the city building councilor for Berlin and in his extensive writings on urban planning, Wagner always returned to two basic points: the dissolution of the traditional city and its reinvention according to the rules of functionality. His journal *Das Neue Berlin* (1929), which was modeled on *Das Neue Frankfurt* (1926–33) but ceased publication after only one year, became the main forum for what could be described as the historical alliance between architectural modernism and modern anti-urbanism. In polemical contributions prompted by local problems but always directed toward general principles, Wagner and Behne outlined their vision of the modern metropolis as process, movement, and flow, a vision that fundamentally redefined the terms of architectural design, city planning, cultural criticism, and urban representation. The momentous shift in the city's constitutive elements—from the immobility and permanence of buildings, to the transitoriness of new transportation and communication systems—found symptomatic expression in the privileging of processes over structures and of functions over volumes. By expanding the definitions of time and place, Wagner and Behne dissolved the material foundations of urban culture and reconfigured its elements under the organizing principles of pure functionality and perpetual change. No longer weighed down by history and tradition, the metropolis could thus be reinvented as a site of constant self-transformation, which also meant a home for the new mass individual and a classless society.

The program of the New Berlin was founded on principles that offered spatial solutions to social conflicts. For that reason, the task of the modern city builder would by no means remain limited to construction; in fact, it required repeated acts of destruction. As the executor of the collective will, the modern planner had to carry out the difficult work of demolition and obliteration as an integral part of urban renewal and without regard for the attractions of the historically developed cityscape. Under the motto "A nation that doesn't build, doesn't live," Wagner emphatically rejected tradition as a value in itself and insisted on the pure functionality and, hence, inherent obsolescence of all urban structures: "A building, in the first place, must serve a purpose, and when this purpose is no longer there or can no longer be fulfilled, then this building suffers a spiritual and economic death. What remains is an empty shell, an open-air museum, a memory, a romance for romantics."[48] Consequently, Wagner insisted on tearing down old structures and altering existing street patterns to accommodate future needs, for instance, by removing traffic obstacles such as the Brandenburg Gate, to mention one particularly provocative idea. "One has often accused the city of Berlin of not providing enough openings for new streets (*Straßendurchbrüche*) à la Haussmann in Paris,"[49] he noted on that occasion but was quick to point to public works projects that would rectify this situation. Wagner's fantasies of destruction extended even to the most venerable symbol of the Weimar Republic, the Reichstag. Thus his 1927 and 1929 competition entries for the Platz der Republik included not only proposals for the addition of a modern high-rise structure but also plans for the demolition of the famous landmark and its replacement by an amphitheater-like structure that, in the view of some critics, expressed more adequately the democratic spirit of the young republic. While relishing the creative energies unleashed by such bold gestures, Wagner showed little regard for those living in the apartment buildings surrounding the Platz der Republik. Instead, his conclusion that "perhaps a square of the monarchy would have long ago found its builder"[50] suggests that, democratic convictions notwithstanding, an authoritarian system would perhaps be better qualified to create a unified urban space, especially a modern one.

The mobilization of the masses within the imaginary topography of the New Berlin yielded the most noticeable results in two areas: big city traffic and mass housing. The question of mass housing as an integral part of other reform movements was first introduced into architectural debates as part of the enthusiastic reception of the English garden city movement around the turn of the century by Hermann Muthesius, the builder of Haus Freudenberg in Zehlendorf. The search for alternative forms of dwelling continued with the incorporation of some of these ideas into an existing tradition of German antiurbanism, most notably in the work of Heinrich Tessenow. It produced the first solutions to the dreaded tenement in the form of larger perimeter blocks with public gardens in the center (e.g., Paul Mebes's work in Steglitz) and culminated in the programs of healthy living promoted by the advocates of New Building and realized in the famous public housing estates built in and around Berlin during the 1920s and early 1930s.

Assessing Wagner's contribution to the question of mass housing requires some consideration of his close collaboration with the expressionist architect Bruno Taut. In the public housing estates, Taut's careful attention to local particularities and small-scale solutions often compensated for Wagner's relentless pursuit of universal principles and general laws. Through his bold experiments with color, Taut added a sensual, and occasionally playful, quality to the asceticism of Wagner's technocratic vision. The cult of mobility behind Wagner's advocacy of traffic as the new urban paradigm found a much-needed counterpoint in Taut's attention to individual rituals of belonging and communal symbols of settledness. Even on the rhetorical level, Wagner and Taut complemented each other, with the former relying on metaphors of modern warfare to illustrate the challenges of city planning and the latter alluding to pacifist imagery when describing the comforts of mass housing. Thriving on these differences, Wagner and Taut approached their work together as an ongoing negotiation between two basic responses to the political upheavals of the late 1910s and the social and economic instability of the early 1920s: the desire for order and the desire for change.

Throughout his career, Taut possessed a remarkable talent for translating utopian ideas into pragmatic solutions and for achieving the reconciliation of art and life under everyday conditions. This quality first became apparent in his work as city building councilor in Magdeburg from 1921 to 1924. He started collaborating with Wagner on the Hufeisensiedlung (Horseshoe Estate) in Britz, which was built between 1925 and 1927 by the GEHAG (Gemeinnützige Heimstätten Spar- und Bau AG) and named after its horseshoe-shaped central structure (fig. 1.5). Providing more than one thousand units, from apartments in multistory complexes to single-family row houses, the Horseshoe Estate set an example for many similar projects both in established residential areas and on the city's northern and eastern outskirts. Between 1924 and 1930, more than 135,000 rental units for white-collar workers and skilled blue-collar workers were completed. These communities combined elements of small-town living with all the conveniences of a large metropolitan area. Financed by the building associations of the influential white-collar unions, these public

Fig. 1.5. Horseshoe Estate. Aerial view, 1931. Courtesy of Landesarchiv Berlin.

housing estates offered a valid solution to the housing crisis and the problems of the tenement.

Even more important to social activists like Wagner and Taut, these projects demonstrated the power of architecture as an instrument of social change, reason for the continued interest in the public housing estates as exemplars of progressive modernism and social policy.[51] Speaking about the collective spirit embodied by the Horseshoe Estate, Taut described its formal relationships as an expression of social relationships: "We conceive . . . the collective mass of similar members as a living being that does not automatically obey the language of power but that, in every single member, carries a collective consciousness."[52] A short documentary, *Sozialistisches Bauen—neuzeitliches Wohnen* (Socialist Architecture, Contemporary Living, 1929), which covered the Horseshoe Estate, expressed it even more succinctly: "Modern architecture means socialist architecture."[53] Not surprisingly, during the 1929 elections, the SPD used an aerial shot of the Horseshoe Estate to emphasize the close affinities between New Building and social democracy.

Although part of the modern movement, the public housing estates exhibited a wide range of architectural forms and styles. Typical modernist elements, such as flat roofs, smooth façades, white walls, and angular forms, appeared in many designs but could not always be connected to progressive political convictions, despite right-wing claims to the contrary. In the same way, the rejection of the modernist grid in favor of a more irregular street layout with circulars and dead ends did not always suggest reactionary tendencies. However, there were clear correspondences between the look of a particular housing estate and the socioeconomic status of its inhabitants. Accordingly, the slick functionalist designs of Weiße Stadt, the White City Estate in Reinickendorf, built between 1929 and 1931 with participation by Otto Rudolf Salvisberg, expressed the minimalist tastes of its educated leftist middle-class tenants, such as theater producer Erwin Piscator. Siemensstadt (1929–31), north of Charlottenburg, was planned as a typical company development and featured rather inconspicuous rationalist and functionalist designs by Hans Scharoun, Walter Gropius, Hugo Häring, and Siemens house architect Hans Hertlein, among others, with apartment buildings and production facilities conceived as logical extensions of each other (fig. 1.6). While Taut's use of strong primary colors for a small housing complex on Schönlanker Straße offered a welcome departure from the beiges and grays of this Prenzlauer Berg working-class neighborhood, his small apartment houses and single family dwellings in the idyllic Freie Scholle Estate in the northern suburb of Tegel reflected, above all, the conservative tastes of its petit bourgeois tenants.

Polemical attacks on the public housing estates often relied on a highly charged conceptual opposition between "society" and "community" that implicated Weimar modernism directly in the making of the modern masses. The Onkel Toms Hütte Siedlung (Uncle Tom's Cabin Estate) in Zehlendorf, then an upper-middle-class suburb, was built by the GEHAG between 1928 and 1932 in a large, wooded area and included, apart from contributions by Häring and Salvisberg, several colorful row houses and apartment buildings by Taut. Adjacent to the Uncle Tom's Cabin Estate, from 1928 to 1929 Heinrich Tessenow oversaw the construction of the Am Fischtal Estate, whose quaint small-town layout was presented as a direct challenge to the aesthetic principles and political beliefs of New Building.[54] The author of *Handwerk und Kleinstadt* (Crafts and Small Town, 1919), an influential treatise on the small town as the foundation of German national character in the tradition of Ferdinand Tönnies's *Gemeinschaft und Gesellschaft* (Community and Society, 1887), had inten-

Fig. 1.6. Siemens Wernerwerk and surroundings. Aerial view, 1925. Courtesy of Bildarchiv Preußischer Kulturbesitz Berlin.

tionally chosen pitched roofs to reintroduce a conservative perspective into the architectural culture of Weimar Berlin. The ensuing *Dächerkrieg* (literally, roof wars) in Zehlendorf pitted the conservative advocates of the (Germanic) pitched roof against the progressive advocates of the flat roof associated with the International Style, with the latter held responsible by right-wing polemicists for the decline of national traditions and the destruction of indigenous organic *Gemeinschaft* (community) by the formal conventions and rational order of *Gesellschaft* (society).

Wagner was actively involved in the construction of public housing estates on the periphery, but his reconceptualization of the metropolis found its clearest expression in his approach to big city traffic, the opposite of settledness, of home and belonging. For him, traffic represented the central metaphor of modern life: "What is the spirit of our times?" he asked. "It is not the spirit of peacefulness and romanticism, of ivy-covered walls and small-town market places. It is the spirit of the great line and the wide space, of the curve described by the airplane, the track followed by the car, the tight clear form displayed by the machine and revealed in the movements of the human body."[55] This kind of movement opened up architecture toward new definitions of beauty, the beauty of the technological age and of the urban collective. For movement, according to Wagner, lets "the great lines and the silhouettes . . . step into the foreground. Our ideal of beauty is no longer the distinctive individual house but the sum of houses, the street space, the square and city space."[56]

As early as 1914, Peter Behrens had praised movement and rhythm as the great leveler of modern life, giving rise to new images and requiring new ways of seeing. For him, too, traffic had come to dominate all urban relationships, with the result that the cityscape had to be increasingly defined by hollow (rather than solid) spaces, that is, by streets and squares. The acceleration of perception in modern life made the individual building part of a unified front that Behrens saw as the most fitting expression of modern mass society and its efficient organization of social and economic relations. In assessing the impact of this mobilization of forms, energies, and perceptions on architectural practices, he turned to the metaphor of driving: "When we race in a fast car through the streets of our big cities, we are unable to see the details on the buildings . . . . Such a way of seeing our external world . . . can only be accommodated by an architecture that offers as unified and smooth a surface as possible, that through its flatness provides no obstacles."[57] Aware of the leveling effect of modernization on established urban hierarchies, Behrens believed that these rhythmical conditions—which also described the conditions of late capitalism—gave rise both to a new architecture and to entirely different forms of urban life: "Not only the individual building will take on a typical gestalt but the districts and cities themselves."[58] Yet where Behrens before the war still recognized a gestalt, Wagner in the preceding quotation spoke only of quantifiable elements, sums that needed to be organized and arranged in the most efficient way.

III. Case Study: Potsdamer Platz

Wagner's almost fanatical belief in traffic as the new urban paradigm found privileged expression in his extensive writings on traffic squares. He repeatedly used the need for workable solutions to traffic congestion to advance more far-reaching ideas on traffic as the future model of mass mobilization and urban subjectivity. Several of his proposals ban pedestrians entirely from traffic squares or limit their activities to specially demarcated areas. Unlike the main square in the classical metropolis, which derives its significance from the vibrant street life unfolding on its edges, Wagner's

Weltstadtplatz (world city square) was designed to minimize such mixing and mingling and ensure the smooth flow of all vehicles and, by extension, goods. Hence his assertion "that the channeling of traffic through this 'clearing'-point is primary and essential, and the formal realization, the functional form, secondary."[59] Similarly, the all-important distinction between *Fliessverkehr* (traffic) and *Standverkehr* (stores, restaurants, theaters) acknowledges the existence of two opposing forces or, rather, currents: directed movement, with its emphasis on speed and efficiency, and aimless movement, with its affinity for coincidence and play. Both aspects of traffic, he was quick to admit, represented an integral part of the modern metropolis, one as the most visible manifestation of economic growth, the other as a precondition of social and cultural life.

Both Wagner and the previously mentioned Mächler practiced what Ilse Balg calls the "architecture of conviction"[60] and what Franziska Bollerey describes as a unique combination of realist and utopian thinking.[61] The concept of the *Weltstadtplatz* allowed these two urban ideologues to map the flows of goods linking the local to the global economy and to measure the implications of this process of total integration on the spatialized manifestations of class, in the case of Wagner, and of nation, in the case of Mächler. For the latter, the capitalist metropolis remained inseparable from the nation-state. His definition of the *Weltstadt* (world city) acknowledges the dependence of the big city on world politics and the world economy but, at the same time, relies heavily on physiological metaphors and vitalist imagery to affirm concentration as an important precondition for urban productivity and to elevate dynamism to an essential principle in the organization of the modern masses. Accordingly, the *Weltstadtplatz* in Mächler functions as the most visible expression of the intricate relationship between urbanism and capitalism. The polarities established by its static and dynamic elements and micro- and macro-processes organize the urban masses according to specific formal principles and general laws. For that reason, the main task of the modern city builder was to bring these disparate forces together into one organic and harmonious whole. Finding a balance between individual and national interests meant to realize "the *Einheitsgedanken* (the idea of unity) in politics."[62] This idea found foremost expression in his holistic concept of demodynamism (*Demodynamik*) and the trinity of "city-building, nation-building, and world-building,"[63] a concept that, most problematically, combined liberal capitalism and modern nationalism with the kind of corporatist rhetoric prevalent after 1933.

Why this preoccupation with traffic squares during the 1920s? The historic center of Berlin had always suffered from the lack of a central square, with Spittelmarkt and Hausvogteiplatz offering only smaller traffic junctions and with Gendarmenmarkt serving merely decorative purposes. The modernization of Potsdamer Platz and of Alexanderplatz played a crucial role in the transformation of the New Berlin and functioned as test cases for the public reception of New Building. As typical examples of a *Weltstadtplatz,* Potsdamer Platz and Alexanderplatz represented classic urbanity in pure form: a concentration of streets and buildings, including some landmarks; a steady stream of street and pedestrian traffic; and a wide assortment of stores, cafés, restaurants, and theaters on the periphery. Under Wagner's direction, both squares were designated to contribute to the planned separation of urban functions and, by implication, the reconceptualization of urban experience according to functionalist principles. However, each required a different approach, with the Alexanderplatz project (to be discussed in chapter 6) part of the ongoing gentrification of its surrounding working-class neighborhoods and the unrealized Potsdamer Platz project inseparable from the celebration (or denunciation) of white-collar culture in the feuilleton.

With its complicated spatial layout, rich history, and multiple uses, Potsdamer Platz brought out the dilemmas of urban planning in Weimar Berlin more clearly than any other place. This may be one of the reasons why it was so frequently depicted in aerial shots and long shots, including one from 1930 that shows Haus Vaterland, Hotel Fürstenhof, and Potsdamer Station in the foreground, and Europahaus and Anhalter Station in the background[64] (fig. 1.7). Its peculiar shape alone, an intersection of six streets adjacent to the octagon of Leipziger Platz, made this veritable nonplace the perfect metaphor for the difficult negotiation of competing forces and influences within the modern cityscape, the kind of urban palimpsest described with much theoretical speculation and poetic license by Alan Balfour as "a landscape of denial driven by the failure to create the illusion of liberty for all."[65] This maze of streets, streetcar tracks, pedestrian crossings, traffic islands, and a central traffic tower gave rise to the myth of Potsdamer Platz in the Weimar imagination. According to Michael Makropoulos, the square attracted symbolic readings because, through its negativity as urban space, it symbolized the shift from a substantial to a functional definition of urbanity.[66] As the "square without qualities," to use Makropoulous's Musil reference, Potsdamer Platz staged the immaterial forces that came together in Weimar's famous cult of surface phenomena.

Fig. 1.7. Potsdamer Platz, ca. 1930. Courtesy of Bildarchiv Preußischer Kulturbesitz Berlin.

Whereas the intersection of Potsdamer Platz organized big city traffic in accordance with the requirements of maximum velocity and efficiency, the adjacent Leipziger Platz, within its central green spaces and surrounding structures, allowed for the kind of slower, deliberate movements necessary for window-shopping and urban flaneries. Together Potsdamer Platz and Leipziger Platz not only linked the old center, the Friedrichstadt, to the New West but also functioned as a gateway to the country's southern and western provinces. Through their differences, both squares brought together a range of building types, architectural styles, and urban experiences in one central location. These included the Wertheim department store on Leipziger Straße, designed by Messel as a classicist variation on Wilhelmine monumentalism; the spectacular Mosse-Palais, the city residence of publishing tycoon Rudolf Mosse; the neorenaissance façade of the Potsdamer Train Station for long distance and regional trains; and the recently renovated Haus Vaterland entertainment complex, that much-written-about "monster establishment" in "monster Germany."[67] For the famous Café Josty, where writers and artists met to witness the ebb and flow of big city traffic, the Luckhardt brothers and Alfons Anker designed a striking cylindrical structure made almost entirely of glass. While the latter was never built, Mendelsohn's Columbushaus with its streamlined curves and window bands added a decidedly modernist touch to Potsdamer Platz after 1932.

During the prewar years, repeated attempts had been made to deal with the increased traffic volume at what had become the busiest traffic intersection in all of Europe. Subway lines, elevated city train lines, and several streetcar and bus lines converged on Potsdamer Platz; the proximity of two terminus stations, Potsdamer and Anhalter Station, only exacerbated the problem. The addition of a grassy center island and, in 1924, of an electric traffic light helped to regulate traffic flows along the east-west and north-south axes. After 1926, the city government briefly considered tearing down several structures, including the Josty and the Pschorr building, in an effort to widen the main traffic arteries and streamline the odd shape of the double square. The modernization of façades and the addition of several high-rises were proposed to create a more unified, contemporary look. While minor changes in the layout of streets improved the situation to some degree, more ambitious plans for a relocation of Potsdamer Station and an extension of the subway line remained unrealized. In the interim, crossing the square on foot became a punishable offense that, as an act of individual rebellion, found its way into numerous essays and films.

Literary and filmic representations of Potsdamer Platz invariably focused on traffic as a central trope of Weimar modernity. The cultural short *Im Strudel des Verkehrs* (In the Vortex of Traffic, 1925) presents the dangers of big city traffic in the form of an animated monster stomping through crowded streets, a clear indication of the film's antiurban sentiments. Joe May's *Asphalt* (1929), a famous city film shot in the New Objectivist style, introduces as its main protagonist a *Schupo* (cop) directing traffic on Potsdamer Platz, a testimony also to the romance of big city traffic. City novels such as Rudolph Stratz's *Karussell Berlin* (Carousel Berlin, 1931) and Eva Maria Bud's *Bravo Musch* (1931), too, celebrated the *Schupo* as a sole figure of authorial control and narrative continuity amid the chaos of urban life. The choreography of vehicles and pedestrians and the resulting dynamization of urban space were regularly enlisted in triumphant narratives of individual self-realization, but they also served as a compelling metaphor for the destructive influence of modern technology on the fabric of urban life. Speaking in defense of tradition, Roth described the construction site on Potsdamer Platz as "a big, miserable, open wound in the city. And day after day, night after night workers dig in this wound."[68] Hermann Kesser, on the other hand, urged his readers to return to this founding site of Weimar modernity "because it hammers in truths. And is event. One can face Potsdamer Platz when one doesn't have any personal baggage and has a firm foundation."[69]

Both Roth and Kesser were responding to the first construction phase following the 1929 architectural competition for the modernization of Potsdamer Platz. Several submissions had called for a merging of Potsdamer and Leipziger Platz into one enormous oval. Wagner's own entry no longer even tried to accommodate pedestrians and vehicles on the same street level. Taking the form of a carousel, his design featured three separate levels for subways, streetcars, and pedestrians and derived its formal strength from the small number of intersections (fig. 1.8). Calling for a purely functional solution, Bauhaus architect Marcel Breuer came up with an oval-shaped, two-tiered design where traffic flowed continuously with-

Fig. 1.8. Potsdamer Platz. Proposal by Martin Wagner. *Das Neue Berlin* 4 (1929): 87. Courtesy of Birkhäuser Verlag Basel.

out any intersections or traffic lights. Neither the intersection nor the circular, he explained, could adequately express the ascendancy of traffic in modern life. For Breuer, the square of the future was no longer a place for human interactions but the culmination of the street as such: "The dramatic element in a big city is the traffic and what for now is its main medium: the street. At the intersection of the major streets, this drama reaches its apotheosis; accordingly, the city squares are nothing but the intensified nodes of streets."[70] In this new order, even buildings, according to Breuer, provided little more than structure and rhythm "to the city's constantly changing, unexpected, and multifarious forms of color and light"; they were nothing but "the naked body which the changing time dresses in different contemporary fashions."[71]

In light of the mass mobilizations described on the previous pages, it should not be surprising that big city traffic developed into a veritable obsession in the Weimar feuilleton. "The Berlin press is in the process of drumming into the Berliners a new idée fixe: traffic," Kurt Tucholsky declared in his typical ironic tone, only to continue: "The police support them in the most splendid way. It is absolutely ridiculous what this city does at the moment to organize traffic, to measure it statistically, to describe, to regulate, divert, and merge. Is it in fact so intense? No."[72] The small number of registered private cars corroborated his mock outrage but also, in an indirect way, confirmed the ubiquity of traffic as a metaphor of modern life.

Defined through movement, speed, and that unique phenomenon known as *Berliner Tempo* (Berlin tempo), the discourse of traffic allowed Weimar critics to explore the hidden mechanisms of the modern metropolis. Big city traffic made visible the accelerated circulation of commodities and the growing mobility of the workforce considered so essential to the city economy. As a new paradigm for urban relationships, big city traffic shed light on the dissolution of spatial boundaries—between street and building, but also among classes, ethnicities, and nationalities—that took place during the transition to the postwar from the prewar years. From the Weimar craze for motor touring to the cult of flanerie, the spectacle of movement allowed writers, critics, and architects to register the effects of urbanization on modern consciousness and subjectivity.

Translated into perceptual terms, the sensation of movement also allowed them to restore the sense of unity that had been eroded by the crises of legitimation in the social and political structure. Participation in the systems of circulation promised coherence through perpetual motion and continuity through constant change. Not surprisingly, the dynamization of urban space and its liberating effect on public life was often portrayed as a direct consequence of the democratization of society. Defying rigid hierarchies and fixed boundaries, the cult of movement and speed gave expression to the new promises of social mobility and economic prosperity. Writing about the pleasures of racing in a car on the Kurfürstendamm or surveying the crowds on Unter den Linden from the top deck of a double-decker bus, journalists frequently used traffic as a substitute scenario where city dwellers could freely enjoy the rewards of mass mobilization.

In closing, it might be useful to relativize this obsession with traffic from the perspective of detached observation and, in so doing, acknowledge the uniqueness of Potsdamer Platz compared to the wide open spaces and monotonous cityscapes evoked at the beginning of this chapter. Responding to growing concerns about the increase in traffic volume, Richard Korherr offered the following snapshot of Potsdamer Platz in 1928:

On 28 July 1928, from 8 AM to 8 PM, 33,037 vehicles (including 18,678 cars) were counted . . . Berlin alone has 145 elevated city train stations and 70 subway stations. In 1928, the network of the elevated city trains, ring trains, and the local routes of the Reichsbahn transported 413 million people. Covering more than 55 km, the subway system transported 265 million people, the city train's 234 km of tracks 900 million people, that is altogether 2.5 million every day, and the busses with 620 vehicles and 242 km of streets 222 million passengers. In addition, Berlin at the end of 1928 had 83,134 registered vehicles, among them 39,291 cars and 14,476 trucks. It had 9,129 motor cabs but only 226 horse-drawn cabs . . . The statistics of 1928 list 41,214 air passengers: tempo is the motto—even for those who have time! The number of accidents corresponds with the increase in speed: 218 dead and 11,755 injured in 1928 alone. A civil war without hostility![73]

The mock obsession with statistics confirms that the celebration of traffic in the feuilleton revealed very little about the social relationships established through such accelerated systems of circulation. Technocratic solutions only made the divisions in the city's social topography less accessible to critical analysis; the equivalences established by rationalist and functionalist models and popular fascination with movement and tempo distracted from the embeddedness of experience in spatial settings and social situations. While many of the projects initiated under Wagner were never realized, his underlying ideas exerted a tremendous influence on the representational and interpretive strategies that sustained ideologies of the urban through subsequent decades. The city streets and squares were no longer the only places where the metropolis came into its own, and architecture was no longer the primary medium of urban representation. Rather, it was through their participation in the laws of circulation, including the circulation of images, that the city dwellers expressed their sense of belonging; it was through their willing submission to the new order of movement and change that they partook in the pleasures of modern subjectivity and contributed to the search for a classless society.

In the middle of these unsettling scenarios of dislocation and dispersal, August Endell in 1928 returned to Potsdamer Platz to revisit a scene first described in an almost identical passage from his important 1908 book on *Die Schönheit der großen Stadt* (The Beauty of the Big City). Its updated version deserves to be quoted at length because it captures, in its nostalgic tones and retrograde qualities, the fundamental rupture between the prewar and postwar years and their respective forms of urban representation:

It is nine o'clock at night. The days are warm and rainless. The evening sky is still bright at this time. Two huge electrical lights illuminate the square; the light spreads over the square like a big dome. The houses glow in soft colors, more colorful than in the white daylight. The western sky above Bellevuestraße and Café Josty is light green; the light advertisements, normally so repulsive with their forsaken garish light, now glimmer softly in this pastel green. The Potsdam Station recedes in the dark, with its illuminated clock face floating like a yellow ball in the dark blue sky. The main ledge shimmers in its gray and a more somber red glows below, about to be absorbed by the smoky fog that seems to envelop everything. Things blend smoothly into each other; one hardly feels the retreating of perspective. All outlines dissolve. Of course, we are able to see them in focus if we fixate on a line, but then we only see this line. If we let our eyes take in the entire picture, everything turns soft.[74]

The famous *Jugendstil* architect, best known for building the horse track in Berlin-Mariendorf, uses Potsdamer Platz to celebrate perception as an internal process free of all social and spatial determinants and unburdened by any considerations of gender or class. His references to the "veil of day" and the "veil of night" confirm that this reenchantment of urban space can only be achieved through the means of stylistic concealment, of mystification. Several elements are noteworthy in his subsequent veiling of the urban scene: the emphasis on distance as a prerequisite of aesthetic appreciation; the almost fetishistic fixation on light and its auratic effects; the attention to the smallest nuances of color and shade; and the affinity for synaesthesia, including the tactile qualities of visual phenomena. Movement is captured in the blurred outlines of buildings, and the confinement of space overcome through the impermanence of visual impressions. Ironically, it is this untimely image of Weimar Berlin as aestheticist apparition—and the provocation of the urban masses that remains hidden behind its phantasmagoric effects—that requires us now to turn our attention to the other element in the sociospatial dialectic, the modern city dwellers and the infamous urban masses themselves.

CHAPTER 2

Mapping Weimar Society: On Masses, Classes, and White-Collar Workers

A specter was haunting Weimar Berlin, the specter of the urban masses. Their appearance on the stages of history could be felt everywhere: in the crowds on the streets and squares, in the architecture of mass entertainment and mass housing, and in the rituals of mass consumption and mass transportation. Yet the provocation of the masses also resonated in literary and filmic representations of the metropolis, in photographic snapshots of urban life, and in critical debates on the shape of mass society and the future of class society. As the most visible manifestation of mass society, urban architecture played a key role in articulating the relationship between masses and classes, from organizing their movements in spatial terms, with the public-private divide an integral part of these movements, to providing collective experiences in public places and buildings, including those associated with a counterpublic sphere.

Above all, the intense preoccupation with massification in everything from conservative cultural criticism to rationalist city planning revealed a fundamental crisis in the very meaning of class, a crisis brought about by the simultaneous emergence of a revolutionary proletariat and a new white-collar class and reflected in intensified struggles over the spatial articulation of social relations in the context of decentralization and deurbanization.[1] At this high point and turning point in the history of class society and classical urbanity, Weimar architectural culture not only provided the means for envisioning new forms of mass organization and mobilization, it also articulated the conditions under which to enlist spatialized thought in the service of a more fluid spatial imagination and radical social critique.

Whether addressed directly in polemics for or against rationalization, or translated into the social utopias of architectural modernism, the question of class provided the underlying structure for Weimar's vibrant archi-tectural culture, a point that, since Tafuri's critical interventions of the 1970s, has been all but ignored in scholarly writings on the period. With the phenomenal increase in white-collar workers and the political demands of a left-wing working class, the question of class became inextricably linked to the discourse of massification and its complex ideological effects. For that reason I devote this chapter to one central category in the writings on Weimar Berlin: the much-evoked and rarely defined urban masses. Yet who or what were these masses? A mass psychological chimera or an identifiable social phenomenon? A discursive construction of cultural pes-simism or a unique manifestation of modernity? A product of bourgeois anxiety or a manifestation of working-class strength? In what ways were these real or imagined masses brought forth by the modern metropolis, constituted through its spaces and places, and defined through its spatial-temporal coordinates? How, to introduce the concept that will serve as a recurring motif throughout the book, did they figure within the city's so-ciospatial dialectic? What was their contribution to the discourse of massification and its resonances in architectural culture? And what did it mean to build for these modern masses?

In order to answer these questions, we must move beyond the auto-matic equation of modern subjectivity with bourgeois individualism—or bourgeois analyses of the crisis of subjectivity—and return to the core problematic animating Weimar architectural culture: the reconfiguration and rearticulation of class. Many of the literary studies on Weimar Berlin published over the last three decades rely on a notion of urban experience largely untouched by the most pressing problems of the 1920s and early 1930s—economic inequality, social discrimination, and political oppres-sion—and that in spite of the ritualistic inclusion of class in the "race, gender, and class" mantra of culturalist identity politics. Treating urban experience as either a quasi-ontological or a purely textual category, some of these studies read the city text/textual city primarily as test sites for poststructuralist theories and, in the process, reduce the seismic shifts in the organization of urban society to a level of abstraction that fails to grasp the historical relevance and continuous provocation of Weimar Berlin.[2]

In recognition of the remarkable productivity of architectural culture, we may want to begin this conceptual opening toward the spatial and so-cial structures of the metropolis with sociologist Louis Wirth's definition of urbanism as a characteristic mode of life

that may be approached empirically from three interrelated perspectives: (1) as a physical structure comprising a population base, a technology, and an ecological order; (2) as a system of social organization
involving a characteristic social structure, a series of social institutions, and a typical pattern of social relationships; and (3) as a set of
attitudes and ideas, and a constellation of personalities engaging in
typical forms of collective behavior and subject to characteristic
mechanisms of social control.[3]

While comprehensive, Wirth's definition does not take into account the
centrality of conflict and contradiction to urban life; his empirical approach also leaves no room for the imaginary spaces produced by architectural designs and urban utopias and the kind of mental maps created
through city images in literature, photography, and film. The provocation
of the urban masses and the prevalence of crisis discourse can only be understood through a closer look at the intricate relationship between the history of capitalism and the history of urbanization. Doing precisely that,
urban geographer David Harvey defines the urban as "one of several spatial scales at which the production of spatial configuration, social organization and political consciousness might be examined."[4] His definition will
subsequently allow us to move beyond the phenomenology of the crowd
and examine mass discourse as an integral part of what Harvey calls the
urbanization of consciousness. Harvey argues that "to dissect the urban
process in all of its fullness is to lay bare the roots of consciousness formation in the material realities of daily life."[5] This means not just to read the
modern metropolis as a product of capitalism, to interpret architectural
form as a manifestation of capital and to discern how urban consciousness
both forms, and is formed by, this complex historical connection. Above
all, in the context of this study, it means to trace the impact of post–World
War I social and economic developments on notions of modern subjectivity and class identity and to measure their resonance in urban mentalities
and artistic practices.

Whether guided by humanistic approaches that confirm the individual at the center of the urban experience or informed by structuralist approaches, including neo-Marxist ones, that read all urban structures and
processes as determined by capitalism as the dominant mode of production, most definitions share a couple of basic assumptions: that the metropolis is distinguished through the effects of concentration (i.e., of buildings and people) and the laws of accumulation (i.e., of capital and labor),

that its unique qualities are based on the dynamic relationship between social and spatial structures, and that its generative potential is intricately linked to specific cultural forms and mentalities. These qualities manifest themselves most clearly in relation to the urban masses who, whether as sociological category or discursive figure, stand at the center of a number of oppositions. They reveal in what ways urban spaces are both agents of oppression and sites of resistance. It is through the dual meaning of massification as a material phenomenon and social process that architecture reveals its powers as an instrument of liberation and control. The built environment may be a destination for investment capital, but it also provides the conditions for encounters with otherness and for experiences of agency. Similarly, every city takes a slightly different approach to the ongoing negotiation of order and disorder, proximity and distance, homogenization and differentiation, and anonymity and sociability that finds privileged expression in the discourse of the urban masses.

One of the key questions of urban geography, which it shares with cultural studies, concerns the tension between the leveling effects of modernization, in particular the rationalization of urban life, and the preservation of social demarcations and cultural distinctions, especially around issues of urban identity and subjectivity. Most studies on the culture of modernity agree that modern subjectivities and urban identities are profoundly affected by the acceleration of time, the fragmentation of space, the mechanization of work, the medialization of experience, the mobilization of perception, and the rationalization of living. However, the materialization of these changes in urban life is complicated not only by the historically developed layout of cities but also by the spatial organization of class and gender and the constructions of self and other in the name of nationalism, racism, and colonialism. To use concrete examples, the uniquely urban effects of modernization were experienced differently by the society lady taking lessons at the Wannsee tennis club and the proletarian mother trying to put together the next meal in a Friedrichshain tenement. Modern subjectivity meant something very different for the young engineer working and living in shiny new Siemensstadt and the middle-aged worker looking for a day job at an unemployment office in Kreuzberg. Finally, urban consciousness assumed very different forms for the poor tenant farmer family arriving from a village in Upper Silesia and the carefree, cosmopolitan bohemians from England and France spending their days and nights on the Kurfürstendamm.

To make the same distinctions for the various contributors to Weimar architectural culture, the approach to the modern metropolis was always mediated by the position from which they themselves conceptualized identity and space, very much like Kracauer in a pensive piece entitled "Looking out of My Window."[6] We need only to peruse the Berlin telephone books from the 1920s and early 1930s for the home addresses of the leading architects, critics, photographers, filmmakers, and writers to position them within the city's social topography of residential neighborhoods and fashionable districts. As is to be expected, the overwhelming majority lived on the west side of the city in typical middle-class and upper-middle-class neighborhoods such as Charlottenburg, Schöneberg, Westend, and Dahlem. Only Alfred Döblin and a few of the lesser-known Communist writers called the proletarian east their home. And as we locate their favorite working and meeting places, we can easily connect their daily routes to the mental maps that found privileged expression in the essays, photographs, novels, and films presented in the following chapters.

Like typical members of their class and gender (i.e., overwhelmingly male), most of them moved comfortably and effortlessly throughout the city. Even highly cultured flaneurs regularly ventured into working-class neighborhoods, a testimony to the greater possibilities in the early twentieth century for unexpected social encounters especially in semipublic spaces, such as motion-picture theaters and department stores. Of course, the workers experienced the increased mobility in the metropolis very differently, a point illustrated by the frantic bicycling of young men in search of employment in Slatan Dudow's *Kuhle Wampe, oder wem gehört die Welt?* (To Whom Does the World Belong? 1932) and the patterns of exclusion described by Klaus Neukrantz from the perspective of that "self-contained ghetto of poverty," the working-class district of Wedding: "The city—that was over there. The city began on the other side of Nettelbeckplatz, and it was the great Berlin with its cars, traffic lanes, department stores, policemen, and a few million people. The people living here rarely get to go there."[7]

Class, status, and profession thus profoundly influenced places of association, modes of communication, and means of transportation and found expression in often subtle ways in the choice of frantic activity, detached observation, or forced idleness as one's preferred mode of being in the city. As the simultaneously most obvious and most invisible principle in the organization of public and private space, social class structured prevailing perceptions, sensibilities, and attitudes toward modernization and shaped the form and meaning of urban symbols, metaphors, and allegories in the most fundamental ways. The question of class entered into the writing of the city text and the planning of the city space on a number of discursive levels: the projection of current problems into future developments; the displacement of social anxieties into spatial terms; the replacement of social by formal solutions; the presentation of social problems as individual choices; and the conflation of visual perception with urban experience. The overdetermined topographies thus identified with the modern masses allowed Weimar contemporaries to confront the more elusive processes of quantification, standardization, and rationalization and to gain important insights into the functioning of the capitalist metropolis at a key moment in its twentieth-century history.

We can only reclaim class as the defining category of Weimar architectural culture by starting from the ground up, that is, by assessing mass discourse in relation to the empirical data supplied by urban geographers and by relying on contemporary sociological studies on the *Angestellten,* a term variously translated into English as white-collar workers, office workers, employees, or salaried masses. Consequently, this chapter approaches the uniquely urban configuration of mass society and white-collar society from several very different, but complementary perspectives: those of urban geography, modern sociology, cultural criticism, and intellectual history.

Relying on demographic data and empirical studies, the first part establishes the foundation by mapping the sociospatial dialectic in the most basic terms possible: the social composition and spatial organization of the city's population (as documented by Ferdinand Leyden) and the contribution of the white-collar workers (as analyzed by Siegfried Kracauer) to the remapping of that very dialectic. In the second part, I assess thenongoing controversies over Berlin as a symbol of the Weimar Republic and passionate declarations for and against the modern metropolis within the larger configurations of German antiurbanism and antimodernism, with a special emphasis on the Berlin texts of Karl Scheffler. The third part delineates the contradictory meanings and functions of the modern masses by relating contemporaneous mass theories both to underlying concerns about the crisis of traditional class society and to the more affirmative models of mass society in theories of urban planning. Finally, in the fourth part, the reconceptualization by Helmut Lethen, Peter Sloterdijk, and others of white-collar culture as an integral part of *Neue Sachlichkeit* (New Objectivity) allows me to measure the specific impact of white-collar society on cultural practices and urban mentalities. Yet it will be the nonsyn-

chronous perspective on modern subjectivity and urban mentalities provided by turn-of-the-century critic Georg Simmel that (as in the earlier
case of August Endell) sheds new light on the unresolved contradictions
that made Weimar Berlin the founding site of German mass culture and
modernity and the most powerful expression of the underlying crisis of
class society.

I. The Rise of the White-Collar Workers

The only geographical monograph published on Weimar Berlin, Ferdinand Leyden's *Groß-Berlin: Geographie der Weltstadt* (Greater Berlin: The
Geography of the World City, 1933), leaves no doubt that, based on income
levels and types of employment, the German capital was a working-class
city. However, Leyden's data on the living conditions of its population according to social class, marital status, income level, religious denomina-
tion, political affiliation, ethnic background, and nationality also corrobo-
rate two other often repeated assumptions: that Weimar Berlin was a
multiethnic, multinational, and multicultural city, and that many of the
changes that occurred during the 1920s were spearheaded by, or otherwise
connected to, the emerging new class of white-collar workers. Based on extensive statistical data for the first three decades of the century, Leyden
carefully reconstructs patterns of population movement from the historic
center to the surrounding residential neighborhoods and confirms the
strong continuities, already identified in chapter 1, between the prewar initiatives of businessmen and industrialists and the postwar urban programs
of New Building. He shows how the city center, beginning in the early
1900s, was being transformed from an area of mixed usage to one almost
exclusively limited to government, banking, commerce, and entertainment.
Based on census data and other sources, Leyden also suggests that the
character and reputation of individual neighborhoods remained essentially the same, with the Wilhelmine spirit still dominating the spatial organization of class relations, despite the new public housing estates built in
the suburbs.

    With divisions between working-class and middle-class neighbor-
hoods left intact by war and revolution, the places of greatest population
density could still be found in the tenements of Wedding, Prenzlauer Berg,
Kreuzberg, and Neukölln. These were the city's traditional working-class
districts but, according to Leyden's data, increasingly also home to many

lower-level employees.[8] More than 154,000 unionized transportation workers and more than 145,000 metalworkers lived in Weimar Berlin. The number of unionized employees—less than 74,000—was significantly smaller, and the total of unionized film workers, to mention a typical new profession, amounted to no more than 5,400.[9] The majority of industrial workers worked in the electric and mechanical industries (AEG, Siemens, Borsig, Osram), mass publishing (Ullstein, Mosse, Scherl), food manufacture (Bolle dairy products, Sarotti chocolate), as well as in clothing manufacture, the so-called *Konfektion* concentrated around Hausvogteiplatz. In accordance with the nineteenth-century model of industrialization and urbanization, most of these industries were located near the tenements, with Schering in Wedding, AEG and Bolle in Moabit, and Ullstein and Sarotti in Tempelhof. A few of the newer manufacturing plants had been built on the periphery, including Bussing-NAG in Oberschöneweide, Siemens & Halske in Lichtenberg, and the new Borsig plant in Tegel, areas that soon had the highest concentration of industrial laborers. By contrast, many of the specialized mechanical, optical, and electric firms were concentrated in the southern district of Kreuzberg and contributed greatly to its heterogeneous social milieu, with the concentration of clothing manufacture in Mitte and Prenzlauer Berg having similar effects on the organization of everyday life. The manufacturing shops and specialized businesses owned by small entrepreneurs added a distinct petit bourgeois element to what in Wedding and, to a lesser degree, Friedrichshain remained a self-contained working-class city with its own social organizations and cultural institutions.[10]

Known as the center of Red Berlin, these neighborhoods were home to a large number of union members, Social Democrats, and so-called *Konfessionslose,* people without religious affiliations who had strong leftist leanings. The SPD (Social Democratic Party) exerted a powerful influence over all aspects of neighborhood life, from party meetings in local pubs and bicycle clubs to theater festivals and musical groups; the same was true of the KPD (German Communist Party) whose Berlin section, with over fifteen thousand members in 1927, was the largest section in Germany.[11] Linking the strong presence of the working class to the unique potential of Berlin as a revolutionary center, writer Benjamin von Brentano expressed the hopes of many comrades when he concluded: "More even than the cities of the Ruhr region, Berlin is a proletarian city. In this place without tradition, the masses that lack a tradition at least no longer have to destroy something in order to leave their mark."[12]

Meanwhile, the class divisions that made the north and east centers of working-class life and that turned the New West into the preferred area for middle- and upper-middle-class families were steadily eroded by the recurring waves of immigration and ensuing problems of integration that had made Wilhelmine Berlin the most ethnically diverse and self-consciously cosmopolitan city in the nation. The statistics included by Leyden confirm that most Berliners originally came from elsewhere, not surprising in light of the city's explosive growth in the late nineteenth century. More often than not, they were first- or second-generation immigrants from surrounding provinces such as Brandenburg, Saxony, and Pomerania, as well as from East and West Prussia. The concentration of Catholics around Görlitzer and Schlesischer stations, the main arrival stations for Polish workers, bears out the close connection between immigration patterns and choice of neighborhoods. Yet only 6 percent of the city's inhabitants were actually foreigners, primarily from Poland, the Soviet Union, and the former Austro-Hungarian Empire, a fact that did not stop exaggerated claims about *Überfremdung* (foreign infiltration) made in the conservative and right-wing press.

Given Berlin's reputation as a culturally and ethnically diverse metropolis, it should perhaps not surprise us that racist and nationalist ideologies found many followers among the disaffected, disenfranchised, and disempowered there. Expressing widespread anxieties about immigration, some critics explained the city's ugliness, its lack of distinct characteristics, with reference to its uncontrolled growth and the resultant sense of dislocation and social anomie. Frequent characterization of Berlin as an American-style melting pot included veiled references—not always favorable—to the influence of new immigrant communities on the city's rich cultural offerings, exciting culinary scene, and sensational nightlife. Closely identified with experiences of exile, Weimar Berlin provided a cultural mecca for artists and writers from the former Austro-Hungarian Empire, a haven for political radicals, homosexuals, and artists and intellectuals from across Europe and the United States, a temporary home for unconventional, free-spirited young people from all parts of Germany, and a refuge for many Russians fleeing the country after the October Revolution. In fact, the German capital during the 1920s housed the largest Russian community outside the Soviet Union and sustained a vibrant cultural scene of Russian-language bars, restaurants, grocery stores, and bookstores.

The Jewish community, which made up only 4 percent of the city's total population, was sharply divided between assimilated middle- and upper-middle-class German Jews living in the old *Geheimratsviertel* (privy councilors' quarter) near Lützowplatz, the affluent Bayerische Viertel in Schöneberg, the western neighborhoods of Wilmersdorf and Charlottenburg and the orthodox East European Jews crowding into the so-called *Scheunenviertel* (literally, quarter of sheds) around Bülowplatz (now Rosa-Luxemburg Platz), which was sometimes called Jewish Switzerland because of its insular nature.[13] With one-quarter of its population of the Jewish faith, the surrounding neighborhood of Prenzlauer Berg served as an important center of Jewish life in the German capital that, with increasing frequency in the late 1920s, saw violent antisemitic attacks on its stores and synagogues. Similar attacks occurred in the New West, which included many of the preferred neighborhoods for the assimilated Jewish middle class. Exploiting this fact, right-wing polemics frequently used the postal code "Berlin W" and the image of "Kurfürstendamm" as shorthand for racial degeneracy and foreign infiltration.

Into these highly contested social and ethnic topographies, the new class of white-collar workers entered both as an extension of the established middle and lower middle class and as an entirely new social and cultural formation.[14] Its appearance announced the rise of a modern service economy, a process that subsequently required the Weberian analysis of modern bureaucracies to supplement the traditional Marxist equation of the metropolis with industrialization. Constituting almost 11 percent of the working population, white-collar workers by the mid-1920s became the fastest growing segment of the labor force, up from only 6 percent before the war.[15] Given the wide range of professions and skill levels, from saleswomen and typists to filing clerks and administrative supervisors, they can hardly be described as a unified group with shared interests and concerns. Their most influential members could be found in the modern state bureaucracies and corporate managerial elites. By the end of the 1920s almost one-third of all white-collar workers were women, with the overwhelming majority employed in typing pools and retail stores. The massive increase in female employment this represented in contrast to the Wilhelmine period was a major reason for the polemical equation of feared proletarization with feminization. Working in bank offices, insurance companies, corporate headquarters, and government agencies, the better-paid "knowledge" workers often rejected the traditional values of the bourgeoisie and loathed the provincialism and moral hypocrisy of the petite bourgeoisie. While closer to the former in educational background and social ambition, they shared with the latter a precarious economic situation that, especially during the world economic crisis, meant low wages, unemployment, and impending poverty. Afraid of downward mobility, the majority of employees believed in modern (and decidedly American) values such as self-reliance, self-determination, and self-fashioning, which made them resistant to the collective experiences forged in labor struggles and class solidarity. Young, educated, liberal, and cosmopolitan, they embraced Weimar mass culture and consumer culture with a vengeance and responded to the consequences of modernization with a mixture of enthusiasm, pragmatism, and quiet resignation. Passionate believers in the dreams of social mobility and economic prosperity, they were frequently regarded as both the ideal-typical inhabitants of the New Berlin and the personification of the spirit of New Objectivity.

With implications reaching far beyond the spatial dynamics of Weimar Berlin, white-collar workers forced sociologists, critics, architects, and city planners to redefine the meaning of social class and revisit the terms of contemporary class analysis. Were the white-collar workers an addition to the middle class, with the class antagonisms between capitalists and proletariat left firmly in place? Or did their arrival announce a fundamental transformation not only of existing social classes but also of class relations under late capitalism and its Fordist and Taylorist ideologies? Were Weimar's workers and employees to be described as social classes (*Klasse*) or social strata (*Schicht*)? To rephrase these questions in the proper German terminology, did white-collar workers belong to a *Mittelklasse, Mittelschicht,* or, to introduce yet another possibility, the *Mittelstand* (estate), three terms that in English can all be translated as middle class?[16] In some contemporary studies, white-collar workers were regarded as an extension of the middle classes and clear proof of a continued process of social differentiation. Others focused on the shared economic conditions of wage laborers and salaried employees to describe white-collar workers as part of the working class, separated from their comrades only through their false consciousness. As "value parasites," in the words of Weimar sociologist Hans Speier, they adopted their belief systems from other social groups, including civil servants, the educated bourgeoisie, and the old middle classes or *Mittelstand,* and relied heavily on symbolic markers of status, honor, respect, and prestige that aligned social distinctions increasingly with consumerist practices.[17]

Architects, writers, filmmakers, and critics made this new social group the main focus of their creative ambitions, aesthetic visions, and critical inquiries. Against the double provocation of a radicalized urban proletariat and a multicultural urban society, the white-collar workers promised the beginning of a homogeneous middle-class society presumably unburdened by social conflicts and divisions. The more laborers, immigrants, and foreigners were described as a disruptive and potentially dangerous force in the conservative Weimar press, the more white-collar workers, especially through their symbolic association with modern architecture and design, came to be identified in the progressive Weimar press with the opposite, namely, order, structure, clarity, and unity. Completing this cycle of projections, the dream of a white-collar society based on rational principles and functional laws made actual social conflicts in Weimar Berlin appear all the more unmanageable and turned the metropolis into an easy target for political ideologies that promised a radical solution to the crisis of traditional class society. Leyden briefly alludes to this danger when he notes that Berlin offered "a most unfavorable environment"[18] for the typical problems confronted by every world city: economic inequality, social discrimination, and political confrontation. Some of his doubts about the city's ability to overcome these problems were confirmed in 1933, the year his monograph was published and he was forced to leave Germany for England.

The white-collar workers depended fundamentally on urban culture for their consumerist habits, mass-produced diversions, and carefully managed public personae, a fact not lost on the Weimar sociologists who studied them, often with larger social and political questions in mind. In three influential empirical studies from the late 1920s, Erich Fromm, Theodor Geiger, and Siegfried Kracauer each set out to examine the ongoing reconfiguration and rearticulation of class by looking specifically at white-collar workers. For them, understanding the powerful forces unleashed by modernization meant acknowledging the specifically urban manifestations of capitalist development and social change. Berliners by choice (and, later, émigrés by necessity), Fromm, Geiger, and Kracauer approached the metropolis with a sense of openness, curiosity, and appreciation, attitudes that distinguished them from the cultural pessimism, political conservatism, and barely hidden xenophobia displayed by most established German academics writing on the subject. Relying on the methods of empirical sociology and critical theory, Fromm, Geiger, and Kracauer repeatedly ventured into city streets, department stores, and office buildings to record the day-to-day manifestations of white-collar culture, and they used their rich findings to formulate viable alternatives to the economic determinism of orthodox (Marxist) theories of class. Yet their focus on social behaviors, psychological dispositions, and cultural preferences did much more than confirm modern mass culture as a new locus of identity formation and social experience; above all, it drew attention to the spatial articulation of modern subjectivity, with Weimar Berlin providing a particularly fertile field of study.

Writing as sociologists, Fromm and Geiger were primarily concerned with expanding traditional class analysis to accommodate the formative influence of modern mass culture on urban life, the first through theories of social differentiation, and the second through psychoanalytic categories. In 1929, Fromm, a member of the Frankfurt School for Social Research, conducted a sociopsychological study on workers and employees, published in 1983 under the title *Arbeiter und Angestellte am Vorabend des Dritten Reiches* (translated as *The Working Class in Weimar Germany*). Interviewing workers and employees about their educational background, work environment, family life, social habits, political views, and cultural tastes (including their views on public housing estates), Fromm used psychoanalytic categories to gain insight into the unconscious psychological structures of workers and employees and particularly to uncover troubling correspondences between authoritarian personality types and conservative or reactionary ideologies.[19] In *Die Schichtung des deutschen Volkes* (The Structure of German Society, 1932), Geiger ended up confirming production (rather than consumption) as the central category of class identity but incorporated the challenge of white-collar workers to Marxist definitions of class by presenting a more nuanced model of social stratification based on profession, income, education, and lifestyle.[20]

Whereas Fromm and Geiger collected their data in a number of cities, Kracauer in *Die Angestellten* (The White-Collar Workers, 1930) limited his sociological excursions to Berlin, the "city of a pronounced white-collar culture; that is: a culture made by white-collar workers for white-collar workers and considered to be culture by the majority of white-collar workers."[21] Writing for the liberal *Frankfurter Zeitung,* where his excursions were published as a series of articles in 1929 and 1930, Kracauer approached the larger project as an anthropological expedition into the heart of the metropolis: the center of modern industries and bureaucracies, and a laboratory for the most advanced methods in mechanization, standardization, and rationalization. Critical of the false claims to objectivity shared by journalistic reportage and academic scholarship, he developed a unique mixture of social observation and spatial analysis that prompted Walter Benjamin to compare him to "a rag picker, in the dawn of the day of revolution."[22] Asserting that "reality is a construction,"[23] Kracauer observed white-collar workers in job consultation centers, training facilities, accounting departments, works-council sessions, union meetings, labor courts, and unemployment offices. After hours, he followed them to the popular rides at the Lunapark, the smoky interiors of the Romanische Café, the famous Haus Vaterland complex on Potsdamer Platz, and even a widows' ball in the typical Berlin *Milljöh* (Berlin dialect for milieu) of variety theaters and dance halls on Elsaesser Straße (today, Torstraße) near Rosenthaler Platz. Through the rationalization of labor and leisure observable in these places, Kracauer concluded, white-collar society took on an increasingly homogeneous form. This "dialectical turn from quality into quantity"[24] established quantity as a social, cultural, and aesthetic value in itself, with the fixation on surface effects most noticeable in the affinities between white-collar culture and the spirit of New Objectivity.

The *Angestellten* study, with its prognosis of increasing economic and political problems, also forced Kracauer to reevaluate earlier, more positive views on modern mass culture. Confirming what can be called a materialist turn in his thinking, his position now appears unambiguous:

The majority of white-collar workers differ from the worker proletariat in that they are spiritually homeless. For the time being, they cannot find their way to these comrades, and the house of bourgeois ideas and feelings in which they used to live has collapsed, its foundation eliminated by economic developments. At present, they are living without a doctrine to look up to, or a goal to pursue.[25]

Consequently, Kracauer concludes, it was left to the culture industry to produce surrogate fantasies and identities that glossed over the discrepancies between the proletarization of white-collar workers and their continued adherence to (bourgeois) notions of individual autonomy.

This diagnosis of entertainment as indoctrination, of mass culture as false consciousness, and of recreation as an instrument of depoliticization stands in sharp contrast to Kracauer's earlier reflections, presented most forcefully in his 1926 essay "Cult of Distraction," on the emancipatory potential of white-collar culture and its subversive urban manifestations: "It cannot be overlooked that there are *four million people* in Berlin. The sheer necessity of their circulation transforms the life of the street into the ineluctable street of life, giving rise to configurations that invade even domestic space."[26] Constituted through and transformed by such configurations, Weimar Berlin has become "home of the masses—who so easily allow themselves to be stupefied only because they are so close to the truth."[27] Here Kracauer not only describes their consumerist choices as necessary and legitimate but also defends their identification with modern mass culture and its cult of surface phenomena as the logical point of departure for a very different understanding of culture and society. After all, the fundamental transformation of the public and private spheres through modern mass media, he explains, can only be grasped through those surface phenomena that "aim radically toward a kind of distraction that exposes disintegration instead of masking it."[28] Understanding why this radical potential by the late 1920s had been co-opted or defused requires a brief digression on the conservative politics of Weimar antiurbanism, which provided the counterpoint to the progressive agenda of New Building in the New Berlin.

II. Weimar Berlin, the Quintessential Modern Metropolis

Moving from the empirical studies of Leyden, Kracauer, and others to the discursive constellations that linked contemporaneous attitudes toward Weimar Berlin to the ideologically charged theories about the modern masses means entering a highly contested ideological terrain. It means confronting the discursive slippages between the particular qualities of Berlin and the general characteristics of the modern metropolis that have informed German urban discourse since the late nineteenth century and implicated the capital of the Weimar Republic in larger social and political debates. Setting the terms of the debate, in an influential treatise entitled *Die Stadt* (The City, 1921), sociologist Max Weber conceptualized the modern metropolis through its difference from the community of the preindustrial and precapitalist city. In place of family ties and religious affiliations, social classes now determined social relations and interactions. Instead of political or military strength, it was economic factors—usually a combination of industry, trade, and consumption—that gave the metropolis its power. Rationality, autonomy, and anonymity emerged as the organizing principles of public culture and civic life, with administrative structures constantly mediating between the dual nature of the metropolis as abstract entity and lived community, with the latter referring either to the administrative sense of *Gemeinde* or the more experiential sense of *Gemeinschaft*.

Confirming the dependence of urban discourse on the kind of spatialized categories that served to distract from their social realities, the polemical opposition between city and country in these debates was often organized around topographical or geographical features that infused cultural interpretations of nature, including of certain landscapes (e.g., mountains, rivers) and forms of settlement (e.g., villages, small towns), with idealized notions of Germanness and that uniquely German concept of *Heimat,* to be translated as home or homeland.[29] In the ongoing struggle for cultural hegemony between conservatives and progressives, the big city was regularly blamed for the excesses of a mass-produced culture of diversion, including by those critics who depended on urban culture for their livelihoods. As a consequence, *Großstadtkritik* (critique of the city) always functioned as an essential part of the larger project of *Kulturkritik* (cultural criticism) and the impassioned defense of traditional German *Kultur* (culture) against the kind of (foreign) *Zivilisation* (civilization) promoted by urban lifestyles.

From Friedrich Nietzsche and his bitter pronouncements on the anonymous masses of the big cities, to Walther Rathenau's comments about the negative impact of mechanization on traditional communities, the debates on the modern metropolis always revolved around a double crisis: the loosening of the social bonds that had defined the place of the individual in traditional class society and the erosion of the humanistic values that had turned members of the German middle classes into culturally educated individuals (*Bürger*), rather than politically active citizens, a distinction recognized in the opposition of *bourgeois,* with its social foundation in urban life, and *citoyen,* with its origins in more abstract Enlightenment notions of the public sphere. From Max Weber, who emphasized the role of the big city in the process of social differentiation and the emergence of the entrepreneurial middle class, to Werner Sombart, who linked the dramatic changes in consumption patterns to the progressive objectification of human relations, the metropolis was frequently identified with "foreign" influences, including Jewish culture (e.g., in the work of Sombart). From Ferdinand Tönnies's distinction between the authentic folk culture of *Gemeinschaft* (community) and the formalized social conventions of *Gesellschaft* (society), to Julius Langbehn's indictment of rationalism as the main reason for the crisis in German spirituality and Oswald Spengler's rambling speculations on the contribution of the metropolis to the decline of the West, the discourse of urbanization was invariably equated with disassociation, disintegration, and degeneracy. Even Georg Lukács, in his famous description of transcendental homelessness as a modern condition, and Georg Simmel, in his passing references to organic rural societies, relied heavily on the romantic opposition between rootlessness and belonging that informed antiurban sentiments across the entire political spectrum, and that despite personal choices and preferences.[30]

As Berlin was regularly evoked to illustrate general tendencies, the resultant projections and symbolizations became an integral part of the city's hold on the urban imagination. Representing one side of this line of argumentation, Rathenau's claim that "in structure and mechanics, all larger cities . . . are identical" may be accurate as far as traffic networks, building types, and systems of circulation are concerned.[31] And Kracauer's observation that "all the cosmopolitan centers . . . are becoming more and more alike"[32] may have been true as regards the leveling effects of a homogeneous mass and consumer culture. Because of the historical circumstances outlined in chapter 1, however, Berlin stood out among other German—indeed, European—cities as the place where the reconfiguration and rearticulation of class society brought together especially extreme positions and took particularly violent forms.

In order to understand the surfeit of images produced by Weimar Berlin as the *locus amoenus* and *locus horribilis* of German modernity, we need to look at its unique function within heated debates on mass society since the late nineteenth century and consider their origins in widespread anxieties about the problem of class. Many contributions to these debates shared in a familiar critical lament about the city's lack of identity—that is, its aesthetic shortcomings in terms of natural setting and built environment and its underdeveloped urban culture and civil society. In Karl Scheffler's famous words of 1910, Berlin was damned "to always become and never be" or, to quote his much less assertive statement of 1931, "to become and never really be."[33] Of course, such pronouncements fail to acknowledge the insurmountable difference between the enthusiasm of the prewar years, captured in Heinrich Mann's declaration that "Germany's future is lived out in anticipation by Berlin,"[34] and the sense of postwar disorientation conveyed by Richard Hülsenbeck's observation that "Berlin is a movement without a center."[35] Wilhelm Hausenstein elaborated on this latter point: "One feels no ground—and precisely this would be the position of the city. . . . In Berlin the unstable as such, gliding as such, movement as such, the formal aspects of circulation seem to constitute the substance of being, and the people believe in this fiction of a substance."[36] Diagnosing a pervasive sense of disorientation, Benjamin von Brentano noted that in Berlin "everything is present. The past is mute. . . . And the present has not yet found its own expression."[37] Even more pessimistically, Joseph Roth declared that "Berlin is a young, unhappy, and future city. Its tradition has a fragmentary character."[38] Intent on introducing a comparative and, hence, more optimistic perspective, Lion Feuchtwanger asserted that "Paris is yesterday's, New York tomorrow's, and Berlin today's."[39] Interested in mediating between the different positions, Alfred Kantorowicz explained that "Berlin as a concept and as a problem has long been on the defensive. People . . . attack Berlin, because it is in Berlin where every new, coming development, the good as well as the bad, manifests itself clearly *for the first time.*"[40] Meanwhile, conservative critics such as Wilhelm von Schramm denounced all of this discursive hyperactivity as a troubling sign of social and cultural decline, with Berlin providing nothing but "a spiritual (*geistig*) battlefield"[41] in the confrontation of left-wing and right-wing ideologies.

Above all, the capital of the Weimar Republic functioned as a screen for the projection of various scenarios of urban decline, cultural degeneration, foreign infiltration, and social crisis. These arguments appeared as part of larger debates about the meaning of place and space in postwar definitions of national identity and urban culture. The prevailing sentiment among conservative philosophers and academics was fear of the big city and opposition to urban culture, whereas arguments in praise of the metropolis were usually correlated with the progressive politics pursued by Wagner, Behne, Taut, and their associates. Indicative of the highly symptomatic function of Berlin discourse, most contributions referenced streets and places (e.g., Kurfürstendamm, Alexanderplatz, *Scheunenviertel*) that were already well known through their status as examples of broader cultural phenomena, thus adding to the cycle of projections, symbolizations, and allegorical readings. Many conservatives openly questioned Berlin's qualifications as the capital because of its alleged lack of history and its remote location on the outer edge of Western Europe. Still harboring imperialist ambitions, some right-wing polemicists went so far as to describe Berlin as a frontier town, in relation both to the disputed German-Polish border and to the enemy within, which was alternately identified as American-style capitalism and what polemicists called "Jewish-Bolshevik world conspiracy." Perceiving irreconcilable differences between the nation and the capital, Wilhelm Stapel defiantly announced: "The spirit of the German people rises up against the spirit of Berlin. The call of the day is: revolt of the country (*Landschaft*) against Berlin."[42] With almost triumphant pessimism, others explained how this quintessential modern metropolis was rapidly destroying the country, weakening the nation, and perverting the German soul. Throughout, qualifiers such as *international* or *cosmopolitan* served as shorthand for xenophobic and antisemitic attitudes. Conjuring up images of biblical proportions, Hermann Korherr first described Berlin as "international—a world city on a grand scale, consisting of masses of men, masses of art, masses of intellect,"[43] only to conclude that "even for Berlin the day will come when the 'mene mene tekel upharsin' of the old Babel comes true."[44]

Not surprisingly, left-liberal intellectuals such as Kurt Tucholsky and others felt compelled to defend Berlin against such vitriolic attacks and proclaim that "filled with hatred, everyone imitates this city,"[45] a reference also to the degree to which even the city's most outspoken critics took advantage of the many opportunities for political agitation and mass mobilization. Especially in the last years before the Nazi takeover, political antagonisms dominated all other forms of controversy and found telling expression in the frequently evoked image of a city under siege. Promising victory, communist writer Edwin Hoernle thus announced in verse form that "We hold the steely front / Of the Red armies / And we will conquer the street. / Conquer, comrades!"[46] (fig. 2.1). Similarly, Nazi author Hermann Ullmann compared urban life to modern warfare and declared Berlin "one of its most important sections of the front,"[47] with the decisive victory for the Nazis occurring on 30 January 1933 when Hitler assumed control of the streets of Berlin (fig. 2.2).

Antiurbanism in general belonged to the standard repertoire of antimodernism and often joined forces with other discourses of resentment, such as antifeminism and antisemitism. Since the 1890s, various avantgarde movements and reform movements (expressionists, nudists, vegetarians, and *Wandervogel* youth groups) had fled the stifling atmosphere of the bourgeois metropolis. This youthful rejection of big city life for rural or communal utopias encompassed a diverse group of conservatives, reactionaries, socialists, and anarchists. After World War I, the question of urban culture became closely linked to the survival of Weimar democracy, with antiurban attitudes an integral part of new and old nationalist and *völkisch* ideologies and the promotion of a uniquely German nationalism and conservatism under the heading of the conservative revolution.[48] Confronted with the radicalized urban proletariat, on the one hand, and a streamlined consumer culture, on the other, many representatives of the traditional bourgeoisie held the modern metropolis responsible for every-

Fig. 2.1. Political demonstration on Kaiser-Wilhelm-Straße. View from Marienkirche toward Lustgarten, 1927. Courtesy of Bildarchiv Preußischer Kulturbesitz Berlin.

Fig. 2.2. Hitler leaving the Reichspräsidentenpalais on 30 January 1933. Courtesy of Bildarchiv Preußischer Kulturbesitz Berlin.

thing from the crisis of German identity to the end of Western civilization. While instrumental in the building of civil society during the Wilhelmine Empire, the educated middle class and the old middle classes of merchants and craftsmen felt increasingly marginalized within the social and cultural order of the New Berlin. The antiurban sentiments prevalent among academics, critics, and philosophers of all stripes typically found expression in statements like the following by sociologist Alfred Weber: "Centuries from now, even our city maps will give the cultural historian insights into the spiritual inferiority of modern urban culture."[49] Held together by their nationalist convictions and conservative values, these old middle and upper middle classes had started losing influence already during the prewar years, first to the bohemian counterculture of intellectuals, artists, and musicians that gathered in coffeehouses and cabarets, then to the democratic mass culture that formed in department stores, amusement parks, and movie theaters. The arrival of the new managerial and professional classes, including the young architects, planners, and technocrats associated with New Building, only heightened the bourgeoisie's sense of spatial dislocation and metaphysical homelessness and made them ideal recipients of the seemingly endless stream of urban writings in Weimar politics and intellectual life.[50]

Adding to the highly politicized nature of German debates on the metropolis, participants frequently relied on ideal-typical city models and symbolically charged geopolitical terms to make their points. A limited set of conceptual binaries informed most contributions, with the positive first term always associated with an idealized notion of Germanness: *Land* (country) versus *Stadt* (city), *Kleinstadt* (small town) versus *Großstadt* (big city), *Großstadt* versus *Metropole* (metropolis), and *Hauptstadt* (capital) versus *Weltstadt* (world city). Behind the regionalist focus and nationalist rhetoric of conservatives, these oppositions conveyed very class-specific attitudes toward urban culture, from the resistance to foreign influences and the hatred of emancipated women, to the kind of ethnic, religious, and political resentments that linked the rise of the modern masses to the disappearance of all boundaries and distinctions. As a defensive reaction to massification and what it represented, these attitudes had first appeared in response to Germany's belated industrialization and urbanization during the 1870s and 1880s and gained renewed relevance under the influence of intensified class struggles after World War I.

Berlin's location at the center of several spatial oppositions that juxtaposed Prussia and Germany, Germany and Europe, Eastern Europe and Western Europe, and Europe and America further complicated these imaginary topographies and discursive constellations. The competing models of urban culture that organized these oppositions all acknowledged the big city as the driving force behind economic and technological growth and the source of important social and political reforms during the first two decades of the Wilhelmine Empire.[51] After 1871, the idea of nation (and, to a lesser degree, of empire) often served as an integrative principle in reconciling these contradictory views as it implicated the urban imaginary in more expansive imperialist geographies. In contrast, the idea of the city during the Weimar years was to a large degree predicated on the diagnosis of the internal weakness of the new republic and inextricably linked to the presumed threat posed by the competing ideologies of Americanism and Bolshevism.

It is as part of this politically overdetermined mapping of urban modernity within Germany, Europe, and the world that we must pay special attention to the contributions made by architects, city planners, and cultural critics associated with the conservative revolution and with nationalist or *völkisch* styles in architecture. Antiurbanists such as Heinrich Tessenow, Paul Schultze-Naumburg, and Theodor Fischer openly exploited the widely expressed sense of estrangement for their vicious attacks on the modern metropolis as the agent of social and cultural decline. While not directly involved in the controversies about the New Berlin, all three contributed to the debate by promoting backward-looking alternatives: the small town in the case of Tessenow, the organic city in the case of Fischer, and a racialized view of society in the case of Schultze-Naumburg.[52]

In a treatise on modern city planning, Fischer, the teacher of Bruno Taut, Erich Mendelsohn, and Hugo Häring, asserted that "no part of architecture is as much an expression and result of the essence of a time as the urban form (*Stadtgebilde*)."[53] In the twentieth century, such a coherent urban form could no longer be attained; the modern metropolis had to remain a fragment because of the fragmentation of modern society. To make his point, Fischer pointed to the sense of bewilderment that overcomes the stranger who no longer enters the city on foot or by coach. Arriving by train, he lands right in its center without a clear point of view to assist his spatial orientation and without a unified cityscape to guide his movements. Rejecting existing architectural styles as an expression of "the egotism created by democracy, of the struggle of all against all,"[54] Fischer therefore called upon future city planners to develop organic models of the city and to forge a new community out of the estranged, disoriented masses.

The primary social entity for the new communities envisioned by Tessenow, Fischer, and Schultze-Naumburg was the *Volk* (folk, people, nation, populace), that elusive political body evoked equally by right-wing ideologues and mainstream commentators, and that romantic ideal always alluded to by those vilifying the modern masses. As untranslatable as *Heimat* and an essential part of German national identity, the notion of *Volk* was imbued with many different ethnic, social, political, and historical connotations that established the constantly shifting ground against which the masses could subsequently be denounced for their dangerous, threatening, destructive, and emasculating qualities. Suggesting an organic community, preindustrial society, and indigenous folk culture, the dream of *Volk* privileged regionalism over nationalism, nationalism over internationalism, and historicism (or revivalism) over the various modernisms promoted as part of the transnational forces of urbanization and modernization. Associated with the traditional values celebrated by Tessenow in *Handwerk und Kleinstadt* (Crafts and Small Town, 1919), an influential treatise on the small town as the ideal model for urban development and social and economic life, the notion of *Volk* organized a number of highly contradictory meanings. All revealed their origins in conditions of lack and experiences of crisis—the failure of community and solidarity during periods of need, the collapse of class identity and civil society under conditions of struggle, and the dissolution of all stable categories of explanation in the historical encounter with modernity. Providing the missing link between an idyllic past and a heroic future, *Volk* conjured up visions of unity, harmony, beauty, and justice: reason enough for architects from Taut to Tessenow to make it a key category in their otherwise very different urban utopias. The rhetoric of *Volk* continued to haunt the discourse of the masses throughout the Weimar period, returning in fantasies of the modern metropolis as organism and machine and aligning the iconography of the New Man with the aesthetics of progressive and reactionary modernism.[55]

Confirming the prevalence of social romanticism even among the proponents of progressive mass culture, Kracauer, in his suggestive reading of the mass ornament as a cipher of social change, joined in such nostalgic evocations of *Volk*. "The bearer of the ornaments," he declares, "is the mass not the people [*Volk*], for whenever the people form figures, the latter do not hover in midair but arise out of community. A current of organic life surges from these communal groups."[56] Contrary to standard accounts of modernism that emphasize cosmopolitan and international positions, the idea of *Volk* remained an important reference point for the advocates of New Building. In fact, Erwin Gutkind, one of the most prolific Berlin architects of the period, proposed to "modernize" the notion of *Volk* in a much-read 1922 treatise on city planning that envisioned Berlin as both *Weltstadt* (world city) and *Volksstadt* (folk city). First Gutkind extolled the ideal-typical citizen of Berlin as "the new nomad, the big city dweller, the *Tatsachenmensch* (man of facts) without tradition, assuming form only in formless fluctuating masses," but then he concluded: "The world city Berlin must become the first true folk city. . . . It must create the conditions that allow the nomad-like big city dweller again to reflect on himself and to become a subject where until now he has only been an object."[57]

The trajectory of Berlin discourse from the prewar to the postwar years and its contribution to a spatialized imaginary of class can be traced exemplarily in the writings of Karl Scheffler. Returning repeatedly to the subject over the course of two decades, the influential art critic articulated many of the contradictions that characterized the debates on Berlin and the modern metropolis, that found privileged expression in the context of architectural culture, and that all referred back to the experience of massification and the problem of class. In his Berlin texts, we encounter aestheticization as a defensive strategy of bourgeois individualism as well as identification with the destructive impulses of architectural modernism. We find both optimism about the liberating force of modernity and pessimism about the destruction of urban space.

His first book on the topic, *Berlin: Ein Stadtschicksal* (Berlin: The Fate of a City, 1910), had a tremendous influence on contemporaries and was very controversial, not least because of the author's detailed enumeration of the many shortcomings of this "capital of all modern ugliness."[58] Scheffler, after all, gave voice to the henceforth much-repeated complaint about Berlin as a city without identity, a city in which crass materialism ruled paramount and whose inhabitants distinguished themselves above all through their ignorance, vulgarity, and bad taste. When approaching that same city through the lens of *Lebensphilosophie* (life philosophy or vitalism), the philosophical movement that had made "life" an important category of critical inquiry, he had no problem seeing its uniformity as the expression of a new kind of modern beauty and praising its crudeness as a manifestation of raw energy and élan vital. This magical transfiguration, which shows contemporaneous urban ideologies at work, was achieved through the aestheticist strategies that cast a discursive veil over the entire urban scene. Sounding very much like August Endell, who had earlier asserted that "despite the ugly buildings, despite the noise, despite everything that one might find fault with, the big city is a miracle of beauty and poetry,"[59] Scheffler ends up raving about the "the way in which [in the big city] objects are illuminated and colored by the light . . . [and] how the magic veil of the atmosphere envelops everything profane."[60]

This sensualist celebration of beauty betrays Scheffler's underlying desire to initiate a permanent change in the cityscape and to reproduce the kind of harmony and unity found until then only in aesthetic experiences. Attesting to the impossibility of that desire, his proposal "to tear down half of Berlin and most of the suburbs and, under strict supervision . . . rebuild the ugly new city as a beautiful new city"[61] cleverly combines the conservative vision of a beautiful cityscape promoted by Fischer, Sitte, and others with the modernist calls for destruction, for tabula rasa, issued by Wagner and his associates. Similarly, in a 1913 essay on big city architecture, Scheffler first evokes the street as a powerful symbol of mass mobilization and describes the making of the modern collective in the most enthusiastic terms: "The front of houses facing the street will become a single coherent façade, entire urban districts will stand in architectural harmony, and this noble uniformity will eventually give rise to a monumental style that deserves to be called truly modern."[62] Yet in a 1926 essay on the future of the metropolis, he asserts that "the country, the entire country is becoming a city, a big city; it forces the city to expand its boundaries and allows the provinces to absorb the urban mentality,"[63] and concludes in the most ominous tones that "this street ideal has destroyed the city ideal. The street has defeated the city."[64]

By the late 1920s, these inconsistencies in Scheffler's urban writings could no longer contain the real conflicts that made the German capital such a contested terrain in the making of modern mass society. Thus in *Berlin: Wandlungen einer Stadt* (Berlin: Transformations of a City, 1931), he comes out once and for all in favor of aestheticization when, after driving aimlessly through the city, he arrives at the illuminated Kaiser Wilhelm Memorial Church to give one final demonstration of his considerable skills at ideological veiling. Ignoring the physical and spatial qualities of the location, his gaze remains focused on the as-yet-unrealized promise of big city life as an experience of plenitude, a plenitude that comes not from social action or community but from the cultivation of greatest individuality. Yet even here, in the rhetorical figures that turn spatial phenomena into sensory effects, the masses remain a disquieting presence, an energy that cannot be controlled:

> There the masses triumph as quantity. But the light spiritualizes and transfigures everything material: it creates a festivity for the eye . . . , a festivity of life which flares up anew every evening and whose inner shallowness is compensated for by the enormous amount of energies contained by it. This is the nightly apotheosis of the big city; this is the triumphant song that the New Berlin time and again sings to itself.[65]

III. Mass Discourse and White-Collar Culture

The traumatic experience of mass riots in front of the burning Palace of Justice in Vienna in 1927 prompted Elias Canetti to write his monumental essay *Masse und Macht* (Crowds and Power, 1960). Similarly, under the influence of the revolutionary November Days in Berlin, Theodor Geiger developed an urban phenomenology of the masses, *Die Masse und ihre Ak-*

tion (The Masses in Action, 1926), which examines the masses' dependence on the big city as the main stage for political action. Tracing the reverberations of the revolution through the postwar years, Geiger follows the organization of the masses from their violent eruptions in demonstrations, riots, and strikes to the more ordinary situations that facilitate the absorption of the individual city dweller into larger social and spatial entities, that blur the boundaries between urban subject and architectural object, and that give rise to new experiences of collectivity and community. Fully aware of the dependence of mass formations on the big city, he goes to great lengths to differentiate among coincidental and spontaneous forms of association that constitute street life, from small homogeneous groups and planned assemblies, to the crowds, swarms, and multitudes that occasionally erupt in public spectacles, mass panic, mob rule, and, especially important for his analysis, revolts and revolutions. Yet all of these distinctions ultimately fail to explain the radical negativity that turns revolutionary masses into historical agents, the moment when, in the words of Geiger, the "hatred of the dispossessed leaves behind the sphere of individual-subjective emotionality and enters into collective intentionality."[66]

Clearly, the growing awareness of the shifting ground of modern class politics and its urban manifestations cannot be separated from the highly

Fig. 2.3. Crowds in front of the Reichsbank during the hyperinflation of 1923. Courtesy of Bildarchiv Preußischer Kulturbesitz Berlin.

ambivalent discourse of the masses that, in the aftermath of war and revolution, resonated throughout Weimar culture, driven by the demands of the radicalized proletariat and fueled by the concerns of mostly middleclass observers about the disappearance of bourgeois privilege and the end of high art. Politically charged and sociologically imprecise, the discourse of the masses had allowed critics as early as the 1870s to express widespread concerns over the consequences of massification in all areas of urban life, a process personified by the industrial working class as its historical subject and object. During the Weimar Republic, massification became closely identified with the ongoing crises of modernity, from the mass deaths on the battlefields of World War I to the devaluation of money in the hyperinflation and the agonies of a disposable workforce in the world economic depression (figs. 2.3, 2.4). As *crisis* and *modernity* became almost synonymous terms, the masses assumed new discursive functions in mediating among the three main aspects of massification to be discussed in the next section: the encounter with the masses in the public sphere; the process of democratization through mass consumption; and the spatial articulation of mass society in urban architecture.

Fig. 2.4. Unemployment office on Sonnenallee in Neukölln. Photograph by Willy Römer, 1931. Courtesy of Agentur für Bilder zur Zeitgeschichte Berlin.

Many of these discursive functions are inextricably linked to the semantic field and ideological function of the German word *Masse* in Weimar cultural criticism and political rhetoric.[67] To begin with the choice of the singular or plural, *die Masse* (singular) in the texts under discussion is usually evoked to stand in opposition to the private individual and the bourgeois order and, as their other, it suggests a formless, passive, and malleable entity. For that reason, the term most often appears in the context of cultural pessimism and conservative thought. In the plural form, *die Massen,* too, are excluded from the existing power structures, but the conditions of their subordination are more precarious, unsustainable, and subject to change; hence their frequent equation with the proletarian or revolutionary masses in left-wing political treatises. The tension between the empowered collective and the compliant plebs subsequently marked the discursive field in which the masses and their presence in the metropolis were recorded, represented, and analyzed.

The term's negative connotation (in both the singular and plural form) remained predicated on the opposition, deeply rooted in Western philosophy, between the individual as the locus of reason, consciousness, and critical judgment and the masses as an agent of unconscious drives and instinctive behaviors; the rare positive attributions that imbued the masses with creative agency were primarily found in socialist and communist writings. Notwithstanding the masculine persona of these revolutionary masses, the experience of massification was for the most part portrayed as feminizing, and the masses endowed with stereotypical female qualities such as adaptability, irrationality, and emotionality. Aided by these highly gendered terms, mass discourse during the Weimar period compulsively reenacted this basic subject-object dynamic, with the individual as the embodiment of *Geist* (spirit) and the masses as the manifestation of *Materie* (matter), and projected these distinctions onto the sociospatial dialectic of the modern metropolis. There the opposition of masses and individuals found foremost expression in the spectacle of the urban crowd and the range of experiences made possible through observation of, and immersion in, that crowd. To what degree conflict and struggle were a constitutive part of this discourse can be seen in the observation of Friedrich Engels and Karl Marx that "this antithesis [of individual and mass] is expressed in history, in the human world itself, in such a way that a few chosen individuals as the active spirit stand opposed to the rest of mankind, as the spiritless mass, as matter."[68]

The elusiveness of the modern masses as a critical category is confirmed by scholarly disciplines that, from mass psychology and urban sociology to political theory and cultural anthropology, have repeatedly tried to explain their unique power and secret appeal. Many of the contributions reflect typical bourgeois anxieties, from the horror of being swallowed up by mass events and contempt for the base instincts of the crowd, to the fear of becoming as susceptible and manipulable as the reviled mass individual. Following the classic expression of mass psychology, Gustav Le Bon's *La Psychologie des foules* (The Crowd: A Study of the Popular Mind, 1895), during the 1920s writers and theorists used the trauma of massification in war and revolution both to identify the destructive potential of new mass formations and to analyze the relationship between social homogenization and cultural leveling. Throughout, the attitude toward the masses remained deeply ambivalent.

Some expressionists, such as Georg Kaiser, Ernst Toller, Hermann Finsterlin, and Bruno Taut, hailed the quasi-religious ecstasy of mass experiences as an antidote to modern alienation and a conduit to the future community, sometimes under the guidance of a charismatic leader. Sigmund Freud's 1921 essay "Massenpsychologie und Ich-Analyse" (Mass Psychology and Ego Analysis) examined the libidinal forces that allowed individuals to come together in some kind of mass body, often uniting against a powerful father figure. Paul Tillich in his 1922 study *Masse und Geist* (The Mass and the Spirit) offered a typology that distinguished among mechanical, mythical, and dynamic masses, with the latter referring to a transitional state articulated most clearly in Erich Mendelsohn's concept of dynamism in modern architecture. In *Die geistige Situation der Zeit* (Man in the Modern Age, 1931), Karl Jaspers linked massification both to the double threat of Bolshevism and fascism and to the domination of the individual by modern technology. During the same time period, proponents of Fordism and Taylorism painted a much more positive picture, emphasizing the benefits of social leveling in relation to the workplace, the housing question, and the city economy. Kracauer, in his 1927 essay "The Mass Ornament," utilized the term's allegorical potential to contemplate different aspects of massification as democratization and uncover the dialectics of rationality and irrationality that would eventually allow the masses to move toward a more enlightened state.

The characteristics attributed to the urban masses and the process of massification can be read on four levels, with contamination among these levels an inherent feature of much mass discourse. In phenomenological terms, the masses suggest a spontaneous, temporary, and often anonymous assembly of individuals in a public space, with their structured or unstructured appearances ranging from friendly crowd to violent mob. In psychological terms, the masses refer to the absorption of the individual into a collective body, a process accompanied by experiences of regression, incorporation, and ecstatic surrender. In sociological terms, the masses describe a heterogeneous mixture of social classes that, from proletarians to salaried employees, are brought together through the leveling effects of modern mass media and consumer culture. Finally, in economic terms, the masses are usually described as a product of late capitalism and its most advanced methods of rationalization, standardization, and quantification, with Americanization, Fordism, and Taylorism as primary reference points.

As we will see in the chapters that follow, Weimar urban discourse and architectural culture engaged all four levels to produce a complex and contradictory iconography of the modern masses. This iconography came into being through the spectacle of the crowd on the streets, in the factories, and in the tenements, but it also extended to the choreography of big city traffic, the rituals of mass consumption, and the organization of leisure time. Moreover, responses to modern mass society included the literary and filmic technique of montage, the defensive habitus of flanerie, and the constitutive tension between chaos and order, dynamism and structure, and movement and stasis established by mass discourse and projected onto the urban landscape by the representatives of New Building. While the desire to build for a mass audience found privileged expression in the mass theaters (e.g., Poelzig's Schauspielhaus) analyzed by Kathleen James-Chakraborty as a viable attempt to mobilize visions of preindustrial community in the making of democratic mass society, the mass subject imagined by these modern architects and urban planners typically necessitated much larger interventions into the organizational structure of urban society.[69] All of these eventually had to confront the challenge of white-collar workers to traditional notions of class and established forms of mass discourse, reason enough to consider the ways in which both required a radical reconceptualization of bourgeois individualism and modern subjectivity, though in very different ways. Returning to the main protagonists of this chapter, the white-collar workers, I will consequently use the last part to further clarify their central position as both a symptom of Weimar mass discourse and a possible solution to the problem of class, a solution closely linked to New Objectivity—and, by extension, New Building—as a historically specific compromise formation.

IV. White-Collar Culture and the New Objectivity

After identifying the working class as the largest social group in Weimar Berlin, after introducing the white-collar workers as the driving force behind the rearticulation of class, and after tracing the powerful resonance of these two social groups in contemporaneous debates about the metropolis and the masses, it must seem strange to introduce New Objectivity through a discussion of urban mentality in the sociological writings of Georg Simmel. After all, Simmel takes us back to the turn of the century, the high point of a metropolitan culture dominated by bourgeois society, organized around a liberal public sphere, and made available to aesthetic appreciation through the critical categories of *Lebensphilosophie*.[70] With Simmel, the quintessential urban intellectual, we return to prewar Berlin, where he grew up near Leipziger and Friedrichstraße and taught sociology at the University of Berlin. And with Simmel proceeding like a "sociological flaneur,"[71] we confront once again the nostalgic approaches to classical urbanity that place the crisis of bourgeois subjectivity at the center of all explorations of urban life. Evoking Simmel nonetheless means acknowledging the immense debt of Weimar's critics and artists to his method of reading surface phenomena and translating social configurations into spatial forms. Simmel, in sum, remains important for the discourse on Weimar Berlin for his use of spatial constellations and distinctly urban tropes in mapping the rise of what he calls objective culture, the objectification of human endeavors in commodities, technologies, and institutions, and for his focus on the money economy and its abstract laws of exchange as the unifying force behind the social and ethnic diversity and cultural heterogeneity of the modern metropolis.[72]

An assessment of Simmel's influence on Weimar urban criticism must, of course, begin with his famous 1903 essay "Die Großstädte und das Geistesleben" ("The Metropolis and Mental Life"). Its diagnosis of nervousness as the quintessential modern disease represents the first attempt to connect modern sensibilities and mentalities to the particular conditions of urban life. Given the equation of bourgeois culture with subjective culture, defined by Simmel as the ability to create, influence, and control the material, objective world, his essay must also be regarded as one of the first mappings of the affinities between the crisis of bourgeois subjectivity and the rise of the modern masses. Nervousness, according to Simmel, results from the failure to process external impressions in a continuous fashion and develop the kind of protective shield theorized by Freud in his writings on repression and the unconscious. To protect against the rapid onslaught of sensory stimuli, the metropolitan type in Simmel "creates a protective organ for itself against the profound disruption with which the fluctuations and discontinuities of the external milieu threaten it. Instead of reacting emotionally, the metropolitan type reacts primarily in a rational manner."[73] But who exactly is this metropolitan type? References to a pervasive intellectualism, to forms of reserve verging on aversion, and to a disposition vacillating between indifference and hypersensitivity suggest that Simmel models the *Nervenleben* (nervous life) of modernity on bourgeois life around the turn of the century. His emphasis on individuation not only leaves little room for the social processes that define the metropolis as a public space but also excludes all experiences that produce mass formations or promote collective agency. The rise of objective culture, which acknowledges the masses only in the most abstract terms, remains a problem of the individual; it can only be compensated for through subjective strategies. Here Simmel's description of the blasé attitude of the city dweller and of urban personality traits such as detachment and arrogance casts a revealing light on the close affinities between urban culture and the money economy.

Referring to the spatial dimension of capital, the critic Karl Joël once said about *Die Philosophie des Geldes* (The Philosophy of Money, 1900), Simmel's magnum opus, that it projects "the soul of the modern Berlin on a universal horizon."[74] Laying the foundation for his 1903 essay on the metropolis, the book was part of an extended effort, shared by Weber and Sombart, to reconstruct the urban genealogy of modern capitalism, with Weber famously identifying the Protestant work ethic as the driving force behind capitalist development and Sombart, more problematically, highlighting the contribution of Jewish entrepreneurs to the rise of the metropolis as a center of business and commerce. Simmel and Sombart believed in the importance of consumer culture to the making of modern identities, an aspect developed furthest in the latter's *Liebe, Luxus und Kapitalismus* (Love, Luxury, and Capitalism, 1902) about the centrality of luxury consumption to metropolitan life. The growing attention to commodity culture brought an acute awareness of capitalism's tendency toward abstraction, with the modern mass individual embodying the underlying tension between commodification and abstraction. To the degree that recurring crises were a by-product of the capitalist economy, alienation had to be considered an integral part of the urban experience as well, with Sombart concluding that in the big city, "the inhabitants are alienated from one another."[75]

Arguing along similar lines, Simmel uses the nervous life of modernity to uncover the growing dependency of the metropolis on the systems of circulation established by the money economy. Capitalism forces everything into its sphere of circulation, creating a system of universal equivalencies that extends from consumer goods to sensory perceptions. Under these conditions, exchange emerges as the main principle according to which city dwellers consume products, experiences, perceptions, and emotions with the same sense of calculation and detachment. It is Simmel's enormous contribution and great failing to present this process only through the lens of individual experience, an approach criticized by Harvey as a mere diagnosis of "alienated individualism."[76]

This problematic connection between bourgeois individualism and urban discourse is central to the emergence of spatialized thought in Simmel's work. Locating the capitalist economy in the quotidian manifestations of metropolitan life, he was one of the first to analyze modern culture through spatial phenomena and characterize urban experiences through architectural metaphors. Defining space in perceptual rather than topographical terms, he maintains that "space in general is only an activity of the soul (*Seele*), only the human way of linking originally unconnected sensual affects with unified concepts."[77] Spatial phenomena allowed him to make the all-important but ultimately incomplete move from individual to social forms—and, more generally, from subjective to objective culture—and focus on what urban sociologist David Frisby has called spatial projections of social forms.[78]

As in the case of Kracauer and Hessel, biographical factors contributed to Simmel's heightened sensibility to the spatial divisions in society and the experiences of discrimination that, among other things, found expression in moving reflections on the figure of the stranger. His outsider status, as a Jew in the conservative German university and as a sociologist without a clear scientific methodology, predisposed this passionate cosmopolitan to approach urban phenomena through the perambulatory style of the essay and the spatial phenomena—the boundary, the door, the dynamics of closeness and distance—that functioned as his favorite critical tropes. By the time Simmel was conceptualizing estrangement, however, the stranger in the city had already become the dominant mode of urban experience. Once stranger and native could no longer be distinguished, strangeness represented nothing but the very condition of modernity.

The importance of the phenomenological underpinnings of *Lebensphilosophie* to urban discourse and, as we shall see shortly, to New Objectivity lay in its conceptual ability to provide a model of unity and integration, even if only belatedly and in the form of a nostalgic return to some better past or a cynical adaptation to the status quo. The vitalist emphasis on individual experience helped to integrate the heterogeneous elements and contradictory forces of modern life into a meaningful whole, that is, a phenomenological reclamation of bourgeois subjectivity. Used as a metaphysical and existential category, *Leben* (life) promised to overcome the crisis of meaning through its dynamic, holistic, all-encompassing force. Yet in the context of early-twentieth-century German culture, such vitalist arguments not only promised an effective method of emotional crisis management, they also provided strategies of imaginary reconciliation that proved particularly important in the confrontation with the social, economic, and political problems of the Weimar years.

Under these conditions, *Leben* retained its appeal as an integrative category presumably unmarked by class divisions and ideological differences, untouched by the conceptual binaries that haunted the debates on the modern metropolis, and untainted by the political struggles taking place on the streets of Weimar Berlin. According to Martin Lindner, vitalist concepts allowed critics after World War I to absorb the oppositions of rationalism and irrationalism, subjectivism and objectivism, mysticism and realism, and individualism and collectivism into more fluid, dynamic configurations.[79] More specifically, the ideology of *Leben* facilitated the reconciliation of progressive social utopias with the kind of transhistorical myths shared by expressionists as well as traditionalists. It incorporated the diagnosis of alienation and fragmentation into the optimism of new beginnings, replaced the cultural pessimism of the middle classes with the pragmatic optimism of white-collar workers, and overcame the fears of urban decline through the new designs for living developed in the context of New Building. As such a transformative force, Lindner concludes, the "ideology of *Leben*" served both modern and antimodern movements, with the displacement of real conflicts to imaginary solutions as its primary ideological effect.

The postwar reverberations of *Lebensphilosophie* are most apparent in the aesthetic sensibilities of New Objectivity, an art movement, modern mentality, and lifestyle choice that continues to play a key role in our historical assessment of urban culture and white-collar society. Suggesting objectivity, sobriety, and matter-of-factness, New Objectivity initially referred to an art movement distinguished by its realist aesthetic, antipsychological stance, and deindividualized perspective, and known for its affirmative views of the industrialized, modern urban life world. Gustav Hartlaub, who coined the term in conjunction with the 1925 art exhibition at the Kunsthalle in Mannheim, spoke of "the widespread feelings in Germany today of resignation and cynicism after a period of exuberant hopes (which had found an outlet in expressionism). Cynicism and resignation are the negative side of New Objectivity; the positive side expresses itself in enthusiasm for unmediated reality, out of the desire to approach things objectively based on their material qualities without immediately investing them with meanings."[80]

By turning psychic defenses into aesthetic forms, the art and literature of New Objectivity display all the characteristics of a reaction formation, a defense against the traumas of modernity and an overidentification with its hopes and promises. Its affirmative but detached attitude toward social reality and the material world is most pronounced in visual media such as painting, photography, and film, with Christian Schad, Albert Renger-Patzsch, and G. W. Pabst usually mentioned as its main representatives. In literature, the term is closely identified with the *Zeitromane* (topical novels) and *Zeitstücke* (topical plays) of Erich Kästner, Ödön von Horváth, Irmgard Keun, and Marieluise Fleisser, all of whom thematized (often in highly gendered terms) the objectification, rationalization, and alienation that accompanied the rise of white-collar society. Most relevant for this study, New Objectivity functioned as an important reference point in contemporaneous debates on functionalism in modern architecture and design. Recent scholarship on the cult of tempo and the machine, the phenomenon of Americanism, and the myth of the New Man and the New Woman has shown that the conceptual oppositions used to define New Objectivity as an artistic movement—sobriety versus sentimentality, authenticity versus conventionality, reality versus fantasy, and masculinity versus femininity—do not always hold up to further scrutiny, and fail to account for the more complicated and ambiguous admixtures (e.g., the pathos of objectivity) that sustained its utopian pragmatism and collectivist rationalism especially in the context of Weimar architectural culture.

Of course, the same could be said about the political commitments of New Objectivity, as evidenced by its historical appeal to the proponents of both progressive and reactionary modernism and its remarkable compatibility with highly politicized as well as fully commodified cultural practices. A movement that achieved "the discovery of the object after the crisis of subjectivity"[81] was bound to enrage leftist critics such as Georg Lukács and Béla Balázs, who denounced New Objectivity as the product of late capitalism, Taylorism, and Americanism and condemned its art and literature as the expression of reification, alienation, and "the aesthetics of the conveyer belt."[82] Continuing in this line of argumentation, in the 1970s Helmut Lethen explicitly linked New Objectivity to the political program of *weißer Sozialismus* (white socialism)—the overcoming of class conflict through technological innovation, increased productivity, and the rationalization of labor and leisure. He argues that the novels and artworks are to be described as attempts at "making class society unrecognizable"[83] and interpreted as a "class-specific substitute for socialism."[84] Against standard descriptions of New Objectivity as the dominant style of the stabilization period, Jost Hermand likewise insists on its class-specific features, defining the movement as "the ideological and aesthetic means of expression of a relatively small group from the bourgeois liberal or middling bourgeois sectors between 1923 and 1929 who, partly consciously and partly unconsciously, let themselves be captivated by the deceptive illusion of a new stabilisation of social conditions, basing itself on technology and a higher standard of living."[85]

Given the term's resistance to formal definitions and its association with certain social groups, New Objectivity may be described most accurately as a mentality, a set of attitudes, beliefs, and behaviors embodied in almost ideal-typical form by white-collar workers and, more specifically, the proverbial New Man and New Woman found on the streets of Weimar Berlin. Speaking for this young generation in terms that are particularly relevant for understanding the continuities with Simmel's objective culture, the writer Frank Matzke declared:

> Objectivity is a feature of our forms, not of our contents. It does not mean to be an object, but to act objectively—to keep to the point. . . . We are objective because we perceive the reality of things and we find this more valuable than man's thinking about it. . . . Thus, we are objective because we are willing to communicate human experiences only through the language of objects, not directly from heart to heart.[86]

In such enthusiastic declarations, New Objectivity stood for full identification with the project of modernity, direct engagement in its offerings, and a pragmatic approach to social problems. In its more pessimistic versions, New Objectivity articulated the kind of modern unhappiness explored by Peter Sloterdijk in highly evocative reflections on cynicism as the central disposition of Weimar culture and a defensive reaction to both the

ecstatic utopianism of the immediate war years and the political and economic crises of the late 1920s.[87] In the end, it was precisely this productive
ambiguity and the underlying reversal of polarities that, captured in a later
study by Helmut Lethen in the suggestive term "cool conduct," accounts
for the remarkable ability of New Objectivity to mediate between the external world of objects and the internal world of sensibilities, dispositions,
and mentalities.[88]

   In the next five chapters, we will trace this elusive mentality of New
Objectivity in the context of New Building and white-collar culture, mea-
suring how it functioned as a defense against, and a confirmation of, modern mass society, and examining how it evoked the crisis of traditional
class society to anticipate other forms of urban subjectivity and collectivity. We will see how white-collar culture privileged coldness over warmth,
construction over growth, mobility over rootedness, distraction over concentration, and the type over the individual, to evoke some of the binaries
analyzed by Lethen. On the one side, we will find advocates of "cool conduct," men such as Martin Wagner, Adolf Behne, Ludwig Hilberseimer,
and Walter Ruttmann, who affirmed white-collar workers as the main protagonists of modern urban life and who proposed to forge the urban
masses into quantifiable categories. On the other side are Siegfried Kracauer and Ernst Bloch, two outspoken critics of New Objectivity, the
façade architecture of New Building, and the cult of surfaces in Weimar
mass culture, for whom white-collar culture (at least by the late 1920s) had
betrayed the promises of modernity and become synonymous with political affirmation and cultural commodification. Occupying a middle position, Bruno Taut and Erich Mendelsohn drew on both positions and made
them an integral part of their conception of modern mass society in
Weimar Berlin, a highly productive approach to be discussed in greater detail in the next chapter on the social utopias developed under the heading
of New Building.

CHAPTER 3

Organizing the Modern Masses: New Building in Weimar Berlin

Railing against the scourge of intellectualism that allegedly had taken hold of architectural culture, Heinrich de Vries in 1920 declared that

> it has only been a few weeks since the most radical group among you decided to distribute fifty thousand fliers on Potsdamer Platz, advertisements for a new journal intended to convey your ideas to the working population and to gain their support for your work. I assume that the thousandth part of those fliers brought fifty workers to you who now urgently wish to see a little piece of the promised paradise. . . . What would you have to offer these people? Where is the design, the model . . . tailored to the specific psychological condition of the proletariat? . . . "Nowhere" is my answer.[1]

The intentionally provocative remark by de Vries, who would soon become editor of the professional journal *Der Städtebau,* suggests two things about the young generation of architects rising to prominence after the war: that they saw the masses as the subject and object of modern architecture, and that they developed formal solutions to the decline of traditional class society and the rise of white-collar society.

Building on the spatial reorganization of the Wilhelmine metropolis described in chapter 1 and the social transformation mapped in chapter 2, this chapter focuses on the contribution of New Building to the mass discourses and urban utopias that dominated all aspects of Weimar architectural culture. Based on the discursive patterns outlined in the previous chapter, especially in conservative mass discourse, I discuss the formal solutions offered under the heading of New Berlin as a historically specific left-wing response to the crises of Weimar class society. The modernist fixation on structures, forms, and plans will be read as a concerted effort to control emerging new social groups and formations perceived as chaotic, disruptive, defiant—in short, as other. Likewise, the elevation of the modernist aesthetic to a secular religion will be interpreted as a defense against the heterogeneity of urban life, its association with multitude, diversity, and transitoriness. Against the frequent equation of modernism with modernity, my reading emphasizes the uneasy relationship of modern architects to a modernity defined simultaneously through uniformity and fragmentation, homogenization and differentiation. Similarly, against the facile characterization of modern architects as urbanites, this chapter emphasizes their deep ambivalence toward urban culture, with their desire for change reflected in their firm belief in destruction as a valid tool of urban planning and their need for order measurable by the sterility of their architectural utopias and designs.

My discussion of these complex issues begins with a brief overview of New Building in Berlin, with a special focus on Bruno Taut as one of its main representatives. The writings of Adolf Behne (in the second part) and Ernst Bloch (in the third part) will allow me to reconstruct the discursive field in which New Building assumed a key role in the left-wing reconfiguration and rearticulation of class. In the third and fourth parts of this chapter, I introduce the two architectural ideologies primarily concerned with organizing the urban masses, functionalism and rationalism, and trace their formal articulation in the built and unbuilt architecture of Erich Mendelsohn and Ludwig Hilberseimer. Functionalism and rationalism, I argue, represented two reactions to the crisis of modern subjectivity and the threat of social leveling. Consequently, they allow us to further clarify the role of architectural culture in articulating some of the underlying contradictions in the reconceptualization of class. Just as the unique qualities of New Building in relation to architectural modernism can only be understood in the larger context of Weimar social and political debates, the difficulty of distinguishing functionalism and rationalism in each instance must be considered an integral part of the intertwined ideological functions of these two strands of thought within contemporary architectural culture and its preoccupation with the organization of the masses.

The imagined audience addressed by de Vries could have consisted of the many young architects who, energized by the modern movement, approached the act of building at once as artistic self-expression, secular religion, and revolutionary act. As "a magician, a director of all human experience,"[2] the self-described modern architect set out to support the goals of democratization and modernization, to give formal expression to the processes of mechanization and rationalization, and to abandon the false dichotomy between individualism and collectivism in the traditional visual arts for the untapped potential of architecture as *Gesamtkunstwerk*. Promoting such a lofty view of his profession, Mies van der Rohe described the act of building as "the expression of man's ability to assert himself and dominate his surroundings,"[3] and he spoke passionately about architecture as "the spatially apprehended will of the epoch."[4] In typical expressionist prose, Bruno Taut conjured up "the concentration of all national forces in the metaphor of building and the cosmic character of architecture."[5] Adolf Rading described cities as "sedimentations of life processes"[6] and demanded that "the visible form must change as soon as the invisible processes are changing."[7] And Hugo Häring asserted that "in city planning, the real gestalt of society, and its ideological, economic, and sociopolitical structure in particular, is brought to light more clearly and more truthfully than in any other cultural practice."[8]

For many architects, Berlin after World War I offered rich opportunities for envisioning cities and buildings that would express the values and goals of an egalitarian, democratic, and self-confidently modern society. In taking up this challenge, modern architects responded to a strong utopian strain present in German architecture since the turn of the century, with the ensuing search for spatial interventions an attempt to both harness the energies of the masses and contain their destructive potential. Influenced by the German Werkbund and the international avant-gardes (futurism, constructivism), shaped by the *Lebensreformbewegung* (life reform movement) in its various manifestations, and conversant with the ideologies of socialism, communism, and anarchosyndicalism, this radicalized new generation made extensive use of the political investments that had transformed urban architecture into the most visible expression of modern mass society and the coming socialist collective. Their frank acknowledgment of the close connection between modern architecture and mass society was one of the main reasons for the broad resistance to New Building in the architectural establishment, the virulent attacks on its social and artistic vision by conservative critics, and the popular perception of modern architecture, in its national and international variants, as both elitist and communist in large parts of the educated middle class.

Translating modern visions of community into architectural forms, Weimar architectural culture generated an abundance of urban utopias, from Taut's expressionist fantasy of communalism in *Die Stadtkrone* (The City Crown, 1919) to Hilberseimer's stark vision in the late 1920s of a fully rationalized urban society. The unacknowledged reference point for all contributions was the revolutionary days of 1918 and 1919 when, for a brief moment, aesthetics and politics joined forces in the service of the revolutionary masses. Making this connection, Arthur Holitscher, in a review of Taut's book, asserted that utopia meant "a new world, the building and creation of a new, extraordinarily beautiful world, that cannot develop out of the old in an evolutionary process but has as its precondition the destruction of all existing conditions."[9] Whether mourned as a lost opportunity, described as an ongoing process, or projected into a distant future, the trope of revolution continued to dominate architectural debates and haunt the urban imagination throughout the 1920s. The revolutionary impulse survived in the destructive energies of modern architecture but also informed the self-image of Weimar culture as radically different, as marked by rupture and crisis. In both instances, the Latin root of *radical* (*radix, meaning root*) grants us access to the ambiguous nature of the resultant series of projections, with *radical* referring at once to the traumatic and liberating effect of uprootedness as a condition of urban modernity.

Translated into the formal language of architecture, this battle call for radical change continues to resonate in the long afterlife of modernism throughout the twentieth century and influence its scholarly assessment in architectural history. From the canonization of Bauhaus architects such as Gropius and Mies in the context of International Style, to the denunciation of the excesses of modern urban planning in Cold War Berlin (e.g., Märkisches Viertel, Marzahn), New Building has functioned as an important touchstone in the self-representation of Berlin at every stage in its turbulent political history. The underlying processes of rejection, integration, and modification began with the official denunciation of Weimar modernism by the National Socialists and the appropriation of key modernist principles in Nazi functionalist architecture. They continued in the competing postwar modernisms represented by capitalist and socialist city planning, including in the 1957 Interbau, and the postmodern revisions of the modernist paradigm in the 1987 International Building Exhibition. Since unification, the moderate modernism of New Building has remained a ubiquitous reference point in the rebuilding of Berlin's commercial center, with some iconic buildings renovated or rebuilt (Mossehaus, Shellhaus), with others proposed to be built for the first time (e.g., Mies's Friedrichstraße high-rise design), and with yet others (e.g., Hans Kollhoff's Daimler office tower on Potsdamer Platz) designed in direct dialogue with the Weimar past.

In most architectural histories of Weimar Berlin, New Building is seen

as an integral part of the political struggles of Weimar democracy, the social programs of the stabilization period, the aesthetics of functionalism,
and the mentality of New Objectivity.[10] By contrast, standard histories of
modern architecture, of what later became canonized as the International
Style, tend to limit their discussion of the German contribution to famous
architects like Gropius, Mies, and Mendelsohn, and foreground their international achievements at the expense of their collaborative efforts and
local initiatives. Both approaches downplay the stylistic range of New
Building and its formal affinities with moderate modernism, ignore its
overlaps with an emerging protofascist style, defined by Frank-Bertold
Raith as "heroic realism,"[11] and deny the continuities between the radical
modernism of the Bauhaus and the functional modernism of the Third
Reich. In revising these canonical accounts of Weimar architecture, architectural historians have drawn attention to the considerable influence of regional styles, historicist sensibilities, and national traditions on even the
most distinguished representatives of architectural modernism. Moreover,
instead of celebrating the modernist building as a solitary work of art, recent studies emphasize the embeddedness of architecture in Weimar culture and retrace its creative exchanges with everything from film, advertising, and consumer culture to product design, interior design, and set
design. Fritz Neumeyer, Kathleen James-Chakraborty, and Dietrich Neumann in particular have revisited the real and imaginary architectures of
Weimar Berlin in the context of modern mass culture and the historical
avant-gardes and reassessed the utopian potential of New Building within
the larger cultural and political debates marked by the competing forces of
innovation, tradition, and reform.

　　Functioning both as the producer and the product of such heterogeneous practices, modernism, defined rather conventionally by Hilde Heynen as "the body of artistic and intellectual ideas and movements that deal
with the process of modernization and with the experience of modernity,"[12] represents much more than a particular style, movement, or program. As evidenced by its most radical designs and utopian fantasies, the
modernist imagination functioned as a channeling of, or defense against,
those aspects of modernity associated with the irrational multitudes and
considered a threat to the dialectics of reason and rationality. Modernism
established a conceptual framework for aligning the modernization of the
city's physical infrastructure, mass transit systems, communication networks, large bureaucracies, and established industries with the more elusive
phenomena identified with modernity, including the explosion of the

space-time continuum, the disappearance of metaphysical certainty, the loss of totalizing perspectives, and the acceptance, to paraphrase Baudelaire, of the transitory, the fugitive, and the contingent as key characteristics of modern life. Into that historical configuration, modernism introduced a language, a mentality, an attitude, and, not to forget, a political program through which to deal with the public concerns and secret preoccupations of Weimar architectural culture: the intensification of class conflict through the rise of a radicalized proletariat and the erosion of traditional class society through the arrival of white-collar workers. Closely tied to the political fate of this new social class, New Building represented an attempt to complete the transition from an antagonistic class model that prevailed in the classical metropolis of the nineteenth century to more egalitarian formations and democratic structures associated with the new technocratic and administrative elites of the Weimar years. Describing the concomitant shift from architecture as representation of political power to architecture as instrument of social control, *Reichskunstwart* (Reich Art Commissioner) Edwin Redslob asserted triumphantly that, in the New Berlin, "the impersonal forces prevail."[13] Another name for these impersonal forces is the modern masses and their double manifestation in the working class (as their origins) and the white-collar class (as their presumed destiny).

The radical rhetoric of Weimar architectural criticism, however, cannot hide to what degree working-class culture was written out of the various scenarios of rationalization, functionalization, and modernization. It also fails to distract from the complicity of New Building in the leveling of social and gender differences and the propagation of an illusion of sameness and equality. In reconstructing these processes of erasure, we receive little guidance from the advocates of proletarian culture and the proponents of socialist building; they either remained silent on the question of modernism or, in the case of communist critics, took dogmatically antimodernist positions. Instead we must reclaim the underlying discourse on difference from the urbanistic concepts and architectural designs by the formally most innovative representatives of New Building. Notwithstanding the considerable differences between functionalists and rationalists described in many historical accounts, both groups sought to overcome two equally formidable oppositions: the opposition between the bourgeoisie and the working class, which would presumably be resolved through the empowerment of the white-collar class, and the opposition between the old city economy of commerce and industry and the new patterns of mass consumption, communication, and entertainment, which would be lessened through a spatial reorganization of urban functions. Exhibiting typical bourgeois (male) anxieties about massification that found expression in a minimalist aesthetics with ascetic overtones, some responded to the crisis of modern subjectivity with an almost masochistic embrace of serialization, standardization, and functionalization. In their architectural response to social problems, others asserted their unyielding belief in the formative power of art and the redemptive quality of the aesthetic. Yet in the end, most of the architects associated with New Building remained true to their class and profession and practiced, in the bitter words of Manfredo Tafuri, "architecture rather than revolution."[14]

I. Constructing the New Berlin

Many among the new generation of architects working in Weimar Berlin took on the challenges of modernism as part of larger political and artistic commitments. In the final stages of World War I, in 1918, Taut, Gropius, Behne, and other revolutionary artists and intellectuals founded the *Arbeitsrat für Kunst* (Workers' Council for Art), which aimed at the democratization of the fine arts and called for their productive alliance with architecture as the most public and collective form of artistic expression. During the same period Mendelsohn became involved in the *Novembergruppe* (November Group), a group largely made up of expressionists who sought a closer collaboration with revolutionary workers but also defended freedom of expression as an essential part of art's political mission. Both the Workers' Council for Art and the November Group were deeply committed to a utopian socialism that combined the visionary styles and ecstatic tones of early expressionism with the communal models found in anarchosyndicalism and the alternative movements associated with *Lebensreform* (life reform).

After the currency stabilization in 1924, the revolutionary fervor of the immediate post–World War I years quickly gave way to pragmatic reform initiatives, and fantastic visions were soon superseded by modest designs and a differentiated approach to public architecture. More than the end of social utopianism, however, this inevitable reorientation meant the translation of its guiding principles into concrete projects and actual commissions. According to Tafuri, many of the dilemmas of architectural modernism can be traced to this difficult historical juncture: "Architectural, artistic, and urban ideology was left with the *utopia of form* as a way of recovering the human totality through an ideal synthesis, as a way of embracing disorder through order."[15] No matter what the causes and consequences of such compromises, the main proponents of New Building continued to integrate their political convictions into their functionalist and rationalist designs for the remainder of the decade and thereby established the conditions for the historical alliance of modern architecture with radical left-wing politics and a progressive mass culture. That this ideologization of architecture was not welcomed by everyone is confirmed by a caricature of the "triumphant dream of the modern architect" (identified here as "Probius") published in 1930 in the conservative professional journal *Deutsche Bauhütte* (fig. 3.1).

In *Das Buch vom Bauen* (The Book about Building, 1930), Marxist critic Alexander Schwab (under the pseudonym Albert Sigrist) became the first to address openly the underlying political issues and controversies.

Fig. 3.1. "Triumphtraum des modernen Architekten." *Deutsche Bauhütte* 34, no. 1 (1930): 19.

Speaking of the Janus-faced nature of New Building, he described the different functions of architecture in the lives of the proletariat and the haute bourgeoisie and drew attention to the antagonistic class structure hidden behind the spatial organization of the capitalist metropolis. Schwab was fully convinced of the democratizing effect of modern architecture and design and hailed the post–World War I metropolis as an expression both of late capitalism and coming socialism.[16] He was also painfully aware of the fact that the modern vision in art and architecture had found its purest expression in the sphere of upper-class wealth and privilege, that is, under the conditions of individual patronage. For instance, the aesthetics of austerity in some of the lesser-known public housing estates reflected an acute lack of resources (e.g., acknowledged in the notion of *Existenzminimum*), while it served very different functions in the private residences of Zehlendorf and Dahlem, where minimalist aesthetics and a voluntary asceticism ruled supreme. Populated by the upper middle class and wealthy upper class, the western suburbs of Berlin, with their piney forests and spectacular lake views, indeed offered many opportunities for emerging architects. Aside from the prewar projects in Potsdam-Babelsberg that jump-started Mies van der Rohe's career, such commissions included the constructivist row houses by Hans and Wassili Luckhardt and Alfons Anker on Schorlemer Allee, completed in 1925 and at one point counting a newly separated Fritz Lang among their tenants; Walter Gropius's 1929 cubist minimalist design for the Villa Lewin in Fischerhüttenstraße; and Erich Mendelsohn's 1929 private home on Am Rupenhorn, a white stucco house overlooking the Havel river.

Attracting much public attention during the "roof wars" in Zehlendorf and similar controversies, New Building contributed to the discourse of the masses primarily through its large-scale public housing estates. A key element in the process of urban decentralization and integral to initiatives in public health and social reform, these large settlements on the outskirts of Berlin confirmed the importance of better housing to the social vision of New Building and advertised its salutary effects in emphatic calls for more light and fresh air and lots of public green. Yet even in established urban neighborhoods, rows of parallel slabs were promoted as a solution to the crowded tenement and its social inequities. The simple materiality of glass, iron, and concrete announced the leveling of social and national differences, while flat roofs, unadorned façades, and horizontal window bands captured the dynamism of the times in this clearest manifestation of the new mass body.

Participating in the spatial reorganization of private life, the housing estates represented one side of the planned transformation of class society, with the other side—the side privileged in this book—concerned primarily with the spatial reorganization of public life and of urban identity. The latter found symbolic expression not in the places usually associated with projections of identity—government buildings, public institutions, and national monuments—but in corporate office buildings that were alternately glorified and vilified as icons of Weimar modernity. As the two founding sites of white-collar society, the office building and the public housing estate subsequently came to stand in for the difficult balancing act between capitalism's dependence on the rational organization of labor and capital and Weimar democracy's promise of social equality and economic prosperity. The office building announced the rise of white-collar society and its modern bureaucracies; it marked the profound shift from industrial labor and production, to information and communication technologies as the driving forces in the new city economy; and it celebrated the triumph of rationality and functionality over the constraints of regionalism and nationalism. If the tenement and the factory were the structures most closely linked to Germany's belated industrialization during the 1870s and 1880s, and the department store the building type most spectacularly identified with the rise of consumer culture around the turn of the century, it was the public housing estate on the periphery and the office building in the center that most clearly symbolized Weimar modernity and its divided allegiances: to the egalitarian principles of social democracy as well as to the maximizing of resources under capitalism, and to the interests of the people as well as to the power of the organization. The rationalization of living and the socialization of labor deeply implicated both building types in the sociospatial dialectic of Weimar modernity and its hidden discourse on class.[17]

The office building may have been regarded by some as the clearest manifestation of corporate might, but in the larger context of prewar utopian thought, its towerlike shape and central location in the city also made it a compelling symbol of urban community, economic recovery, and national strength. Many of these symbolic investments came together in heated debates on the so-called *Turmhaus* (literally, tower house), the preferred German term for the high-rise or skyscraper during the 1920s.[18] Made possible by new construction methods, including steel frames and curtain walls, office high-rises were usually freestanding structures separated from the existing cityscape and sometimes surrounded by parks. In the United States, the high cost of real estate in metropolitan centers like New York and Chicago demanded vertical solutions that resulted in the well-known clusters of skyscrapers and famous skylines. By contrast, the German *Turmhaus*—especially the many unrealized designs submitted to the two Friedrichstraße competitions—responded to a widespread desire for symbols of community first articulated in the social utopias of early expressionism and finally realized through the precarious alliance of municipal agencies, real estate speculators, and large corporations.

In Berlin, the utopian impulse behind New Building was nowhere more in evidence than in the 1921–22 competition for a high-rise on a triangular piece of land near the Friedrichstraße Station. Many designs submitted were modeled on famous historical tower structures, from the Assyrian step pyramid (ziggurat) to the great medieval cathedral. The more minimalist submissions, including Mies's famous triangular glass structure, proved too revolutionary for the times and were immediately rejected by the selection committee; a second and equally unsuccessful competition in 1929 produced similar results.

Already during the Wilhelmine years, Walther Rathenau had pointed to the need for building up the center, the so-called *City,* and for "putting a second Berlin on top of the first."[19] After World War I, the productive tension between the communalism of the crystal cathedral and the supremacy of the modern corporation continued to complicate the public perception of the skyscraper as the most visible symbol of homogenization and Americanization. In its most utopian form, the *Turmhaus* embodied the promise of social transparency and critical illumination evoked by the authors of the Crystal Chain Letters and expressed in architectural form by Taut in his famous vision of the *Stadtkrone* as a central tower for communal celebrations.[20] Yet, in its most dystopian version, the *Turmhaus* symbolized the confusion of languages associated with the Tower of Babel and its more contemporary reincarnation in the vertical city designed by Erich Kettelhut for Fritz Lang's *Metropolis* (1927), Weimar's most famous commentary on the centrality of class struggle to the project of modernity and the need (to quote the closing intertitle) for "a mediator between the hand and the brain."

Concerns about a loss of social distinctions and national characteristics contributed to widespread opposition to the high-rise, including by Wagner predecessor Hoffmann himself, and resulted in protracted debates about the maximum building height in Berlin. It was not until the late 1920s that modernist styles appeared in the city's center. Heinrich

Straumer's expressionist eight-story Lenzhaus (1929) displayed construc
tion principles similar to his famous Radio Tower, built for the Broadcasting Exhibition in 1924. Bruno Paul's square twelve-story Kathreinerhaus
near Kleistpark (completed 1929) and Richard Bielenberg's Europahaus
complex with the large Odol and Allianz neon advertisements on Askan-
ischer Platz (1931) distinguished themselves through their unadorned
façades, cubic forms, and functional use of building materials. On Potsdamer Platz, Mendelsohn's nine-story Columbushaus (1932) with the characteristic window bands stood as a testament to the feats of modern engineering and the elegance of *streamline moderne* (fig. 3.2). A similar
attention to the dynamism of architectural form distinguished Emil
Fahrenkamp's travertine-clad Shellhaus on the Landwehr Canal (1931).
Planned as part of a larger horseshoe design, Peter Behrens's Alexanderhaus and Berolinahaus (1929–32) achieved a perfect compromise between
the autonomy of the buildings and the functionality of a major city square.
Despite growing acceptance of modernist styles, many corporations re-

Fig. 3.2. Erich Mendelsohn, Columbushaus, on 9 April 1932, the day before the
second round of the elections for Reich President. Courtesy of Bildarchiv
Preußischer Kulturbesitz Berlin.

mained beholden to the mixture of historicism and monumentalism perfected by Eugen Schmohl in the expressionist Borsigturm in Tegel (1924) and Ullsteinturm in Tempelhof (1926), as well as by Philipp Schäfer in his neoclassicist designs for the Karstadt department store on Hermannplatz (1929) and its corporate headquarters near Alexanderplatz (1931) (figs. 3.3 and 3.4).

The architect who best personified the ideological tension within New Building between revolution and reform was the prolific Bruno Taut. Usually identified with expressionist architecture, Taut shared with Hans Poelzig and Otto Bartning a preference for organic forms, earthen tones, and modest proportions. Yet the utopianism of his early architectural sketches and writings also reveals more radical social ambitions. From the architectural fantasies in *Alpine Architektur* (Alpine Architecture, 1919) to his program of deurbanization in *Die Auflösung der Städte* (The Dissolution of the Cities, 1920) to his apotheosis of the building crafts in *Der Weltbaumeister* (The Master World Builder, 1920), Taut consistently approached the project of architecture through what he perceived as a universal human need for symbols of community. Inspired by Paul Scheerbart, the author of the architectural fantasy *Glasarchitektur* (Glass Archi-

Fig. 3.3. Eugen Schmohl, Ullsteinturm, 1928. Courtesy of Landesarchiv Berlin.

Fig. 3.4. Karstadt department store, Hermannplatz, 1929. Courtesy of Bildarchiv Preußischer Kulturbesitz Berlin.

tecture, 1914), Taut and contemporaries Hermann Finsterlin and Wassili Luckhardt found in the natural form of the crystal—and, by extension, the cathedral and modern high-rise—the perfect symbol of spirituality and transparency, a quality first explored by Taut in his famous Glass House built for the 1914 Werkbund Exhibition in Cologne and developed further in the horizontal window bands of his later office and apartment buildings. Visualizing the need for renewal, the crystal (i.e., glass) stood for enlightenment as well as mysticism and served as a medium of intellectualization as well as spiritualization.

In ways that must be considered typical of the times, Taut's left-wing politics, according to Iain Boyd Whyte, brought together seemingly incompatible positions, ranging from Wilhelm Worringer's reevaluation of spirituality in the arts, to the romantic socialism of Pjotr Kropotkin and Gustav Landauer.[21] This uniquely German mixture of romantic anticapitalism, communitarianism, and Eastern spirituality found foremost expression in Taut's use of colorful façades as a form of modern ornamentation, as well as in his borrowings from medieval forms of settlement in the layout of his Berlin housing estates. In addition to the famous Horseshoe Estate in Britz (1925–27) and Uncle Tom's Cabin in Zehlendorf (1926–32), Taut designed numerous residential complexes in working-class districts, including the Carl Legien Estate in Prenzlauer Berg (1930). Working between 1924 and 1931 as the chief architect for GEHAG, one of the larger cooperative housing associations, Taut and his team built more than ten thousand new apartments. His preference for brick architecture and his bold experiments with color distinguished his apartment buildings from the at times uncompromising austerity of a Gropius or Mies. Yet Taut was not just seeking a workable middle ground between tradition and avant-garde. An outspoken Social Democrat and active union supporter, he remained firmly committed to creating the mass utopias of early expressionism within the actual challenges of city planning in Weimar Berlin.

II. The Project of New Building

Understanding the pivotal role of individual architects in the making of Weimar architectural culture means, above all, to understand modern architecture as a social and artistic practice and an integral part of the urban imaginary. Referring to this historical constellation, Adorno once described modern architecture (and its post–World War II legacy of functionalism) as

> the ability to articulate space purposefully. It permits purposes to become space. It constructs forms according to purposes. Conversely, space and the sense of space can become more than impoverished purpose only when imagination impregnates them with purposefulness. Imagination breaks out of the immanent connections of purpose, to which it owes its very existence.[22]

Accordingly, the representatives of New Building translated the modernist ethos of honesty, clarity, purity, openness, and truthfulness into the simple structures, cubic volumes, geometric forms, smooth surfaces, flat roofs, and white walls that would soon become codified as the modernist aesthetic throughout the first half of the twentieth century. In doing so, Weimar architects took part in a fundamental struggle over questions of modern subjectivity and class identity. The act of building allowed these middle-class professionals to redefine their relationship to the modern masses while at the same time reaffirming their authority as both the personification of the bourgeois artist and the leader of the new building collective. Searching for solutions to modern alienation, fragmentation, and dislocation, they experimented with new formal registers and spatial regimes in order to restore the sense of authenticity, though one that acknowledged the experience of fragmentation and dislocation, and to regain control over the physical reality of modern life, in part through the irreducible qualities of simple materials such as glass, steel, and ferroconcrete. Yet in their preoccupation with structure and order, they often betrayed a masculinist bias against urban culture and its presumably feminizing effects, reason enough to think of modernism as not only a transposition of social conflicts into architectural terms but also a highly gendered response to the threat of social leveling.

The modernist imagination presented itself as an extension of the modern mass body hardened in World War I's baths of steel, streamlined by Taylorist and Fordist production methods, and liberated from the divisions and antagonisms of class and nation. It thus engaged the urban imaginary on all levels of public discourse, whether as revolutionary manifesto, social reform initiative, spatial intervention, or artistic statement. Against the dark, overstuffed Wilhelmine interior, the new buildings conjured up the regenerative power of sunshine and fresh air, the transcendental beauty of glass and steel, and the metaphysical clarity of smooth, shiny surfaces and simple geometrical forms. Against the derivative styles identified with eclecticism and historicism, modern design presented its austere and sober styles as the expression of an uncompromising integrity and honesty that fully accepted homogenization as a condition of modern life. Against the prewar infatuation with monuments to nation and empire, postwar architects and city planners promoted their ambitious projects as an essential part of the progressive dissolution of social, ethnic, and national differences initiated in the artistic realm by the historical avant-gardes. And in the apotheosis of the New Man, architects argued for a direct connection between the body of modernity and the modern body politic, again with all the problematic gendered inflections. Their ultimate goal was to transform the amorphous urban masses into a unified machine for modern living, and to overcome the antagonistic class struggles of the November Revolution of 1918–19 through the rational organization of economic and social processes according to universal principles.

The heterogeneous and often contradictory meanings of New Build-

ing and the contribution of functionalism and rationalism to the reconceptualization of modern mass society are best examined via the writings
of the prolific Adolf Behne. Through his extensive activities as critic, editor, teacher, and lecturer, Behne emerged as one of the most influential
figures on Berlin's architectural scene during the 1920s. After completing
his studies at the Technische Hochschule and the Friedrich-Wilhelm University (with Simmel, among others), he became actively involved in adult
education, was an outspoken member of the Workers' Council for Art, and
wrote numerous articles on modern art, architecture, and film for such diverse publications as *Die Weltbühne, Das Tagebuch,* and *Sozialistische
Monatshefte.* Behne's critical writings attest to his passionate commitment
to socialist politics as well as his firm opposition to the instrumentalization
of art as a political weapon, with the inevitable contradictions an integral
part of his larger critical project. His articles on architectural developments in the Soviet Union, France, and the Netherlands helped integrate
New Building into the international modernist movement, while highlighting its unique role as a mediator between East and West, that is, between
the revolutionary constructivism of Tatlin and Proletkult and the rational
elegance of Le Corbusier's *esprit moderne.* At the same time, his extensive
involvement with questions of urban planning, including as the coeditor
with Wagner of *Das Neue Berlin* (1929), placed him in an uneasy position
between the radical program of the international avant-gardes and the
day-to-day challenge of urban reform in the New Berlin.

As the modern *Gesamtkunstwerk,* architecture for Behne proved ideally suited to bring together social(ist) and cosmological utopias and reinstate art as the foremost expression of *Volk* (people) as well as *Gemeinschaft* (community). Under the influence of vitalist and expressionist
thought, he turned to architecture to overcome the dualism of spirit and
matter, subject and object, and, most important for our purposes, the opposition between art and life considered key to the continuing disempowerment of the urban masses. Like many of his contemporaries, he relied
heavily on essentializing concepts such as Life, Art, and Man, both to
mask the contradictions between the dream of the precapitalist community and the reality of the modern metropolis, and to justify his dependence on holistic and biologistic models in the conceptualization of social
classes and political change.[23] Architecture, in this context, provided him
with a master discourse through which these disparate influences and contradictory positions could be reconciled. Acknowledging this integrative
quality, Behne described the ultimate goal of New Building as "the com-

plete accommodation of the life world"[24] to the general trend toward objectivity, or matter-of-factness, in all areas of modern life, from fashion and design to sports and sexuality.

As one of the first to recognize the phenomenon of massification as a central concern of architectural culture, Behne repeatedly wrote about the relationship between modern architecture and collective trauma. Implicating decoration in the need for concealment and fortification, he declared somewhat mysteriously that "decoration is inextricably linked to warfare."[25] By rejecting the ornament, architects according to Behne were able to move beyond the double trauma of the lost war and the failed revolution, and embrace *Sachlichkeit* (objectivity, matter-of-factness, or sobriety) as an aesthetic and political principle in the name of pacifism, egalitarianism, and internationalism. In works such as *Der moderne Zweckbau* (The Modern Functional Building, 1926) and *Neues Wohnen—Neues Bauen* (New Living—New Building, 1927), Behne further clarified the proposed synthesis of form and function in the all-important concept of *Zweck* (aim, purpose) and its precarious balancing act between Reason and Ratio. Like *Sachlichkeit,* the notion of *Zweck* brought together a wide field of connotations, beginning with purpose and necessity, and intention and practicality. It represented a rejection of transcendence but also, in less obvious ways, its reclamation through the elevation of purposefulness to an almost spiritual experience—reason enough to make *Zweck* a key concept in the ideological project of New Building.

In promoting objectivity and purposefulness rather than any particular form or style, New Building for Behne aimed at a radically new social reality that was still unstructured and in the process of becoming: "The organization and construction of our life, of life in its totality—this, ultimately, describes a new architecture that no longer works only with forms, but with all aspects of reality, and that no longer enhances the life of individuals alone but completes the life of everyone."[26] The ultimate goal in both cases was to end the denunciation of the masses in the dismissive terms of *en gros* or *en masse* (Behne's terms) and to support the emergence of a collective consciousness until "the masses are no longer treated as an object."[27] The precise meaning of such statements remains closely tied to his problematic distinction between the social and the human, however, as the one still acknowledges class difference as a historical reality, while the other absorbs all differences into the utopian dream of a peaceful humanity. On one hand, Behne asserts that "to build *sachlich* means to build socially,"[28] while, on the other hand, he maintains that, "humanness is predicated on *Sachlichkeit.*"[29] In reconciling these two positions, his contributions not only enlist both humanist and socialist thought in the project of New Building but also establish an ideological matrix for what, during the 1920s, offered an alternative to (red) communism in the form of *weißer Sozialismus* (white socialism), the overcoming of social conflicts through technological progress and a democratic mass culture.

Behne's commitment to New Building was inextricably linked to his strong belief in architecture as an instrument of democratization and a symbol of massification. Its collectivist orientation required a radical shift from the traditional focus on the individual building toward the heterogeneous artistic, social, and economic practices brought together by architectural culture as a whole. As in the case of constructivism, the underlying principles of New Building thus reached full articulation not in the rarefied world of art but in applied arts such as fashion, advertisement, and design. It was in everyday life, rather than the sphere of high culture, that the new spirit exerted its most profound influence on contemporary tastes, sensibilities, and attitudes. Consequently, the big city street, according to Behne, had to be regarded as the quintessential work of modern art. With its myriad forms and structures, its vivid color scheme and stylized typography, and its visual, acoustic, and kinetic effects, only the street was able to give rise to "a powerful collective: the new human type."[30] It was only in urban culture and, more specifically, in shopwindow design, light architecture, and product advertising that the avant-garde project, the breaking down of the boundaries separating art and life, could be fully realized.

Exhibitions such as the 1924 Broadcasting Exhibition, the 1928 *Berlin im Licht* (Illuminated Berlin) festival organized by the electric companies, the 1929 World Advertising Congress, and, most important, the 1931 German Building Exhibition, hailed by Hegemann as "the world's most important cultural exhibition,"[31] displayed in concentrated form what the typical modern metropolis, according to Behne, was achieving on an everyday basis: spatially reorganizing modern subjectivity and urban collectivity. There was widespread agreement in the Weimar press that Berlin offered an ideal location for such urban exhibitions, but Behne went one step further and declared the entire city an exhibition space: "The most beautiful art exhibition of Berlin is also the least expensive one. It is open free of charge—day and night: the shopwindows and façades in the big shopping streets."[32] In more problematic ways, however, the celebration of the shopping boulevard as an art exhibition also revealed the limits of the avant-garde dream of reconciling art and life: namely, in confrontation with the rituals of consumer culture and the laws of commodity fetishism. Anticipating Horkheimer and Adorno's critique of the culture industry, Behne captured this dialectics of modernity in a suggestive description of the street, as it creates "a powerful collective, the new type of man. . . . Here people receive their mental and emotional costume from a gigantic fashion conglomerate (*Riesenkonfektionstrust*)."[33]

III. Erich Mendelsohn and the Functionalist Aesthetic

The ambivalence toward the modern masses inscribed in New Building found privileged expression in a number of distinctions that aligned specific architects with specific attitudes toward functionalization and rationalization. Referred to as functionalists and rationalists in most architectural histories, during the 1920s these two groups appeared under a number of labels, beginning with the tripartite distinction among functionalists, utilitarianists, and rationalists introduced by Behne. According to his criteria, functionalists, such as Hans Scharoun, Adolf Rading, Hugo Häring, and, above all, Erich Mendelsohn, could be regarded as individualists. Utilitarianists, with Mies van der Rohe as their main representative, rejected the functionalist cult of interiority but still believed in the power of the creative individual. Finally, rationalists, such as Le Corbusier, were universalists who embraced standardization and typization as the most effective solutions to the social and economic problems in Europe after World War I. Distinguishing among functionalists, utilitarianists, and rationalists allowed Behne to clarify his own concerns about the goals of functionalism and what he saw as an individualistic retreat from generally accepted principles of organizing society. In his view, rationalist models were better suited to deal with urban growth in a systematic fashion than functional models that exhausted themselves in a sensory cult of movement, impermanence, and surface effects. Unlike the streamlined "advertising architecture"[34] that aestheticized the rule of the commodity, the homogeneous urban structures proposed by rationalists had the advantage of revealing the underlying principles of domination and exploitation.

In this context, the distinction between functionalists and rationalists allows us to reconstruct lines of argumentation that speak directly to the crisis of traditional class society and the emergence of new forms of subjectivity, sociability, and collectivity associated with white-collar culture. Both functionalism and rationalism responded to the mobilization of the masses with an ambitious program aimed at minimizing conflict, establishing order, and achieving efficiency. Both dealt with the problem of social conflict by rhetorically enlisting the opposition of body and machine in their radical reconceptualization of urban life and juxtaposing form and function in their competing views of the modern metropolis. In that regard, rationalist and functionalist positions cannot be separated from the three crisis moments in Weimar culture mentioned earlier: the trauma of the lost war, the threat of revolution, and the shock of hyperinflation. Their totalizing visions promised to overcome this historical constellation through the discourse of order and the aesthetics of the grid, in the case of the rationalists, and the discourse of movement and the aesthetics of the curve, in the case of the functionalists. In both cases, the rise of white-collar workers reactivated familiar patterns of displacement, with the redemptive powers attributed to the New Man as the symbol of a new collectivity preserved in the cult of pure functionality and rationality. The desire for stability and continuity after years of chaos gave the aesthetics of rationality and functionality additional compensatory powers as well, with the streamlining of the building and the structuring of the city achieving what Weimar society had presumably failed to offer: a sense of order and purpose.

The rationalists, who counted Walter Gropius, Hannes Meyer, and Ludwig Hilberseimer among them, were primarily concerned with the basic needs of the urban collective and the effective organization of the public sphere, an approach to be illustrated later by an unrealized Hilberseimer project. Gropius captured the basic premise of the rationalist approach—that is, the belief in quantification as an expression of social equality—when he declared that "the necessities of life are the same for the majority of people."[35] Translating these principles into formal terms, the rationalist architect thus sought "simplicity in multitude, limitation to typical basic forms and their serialization and repetition, and the structuring of all constructive elements in accordance with the function of buildings, streets, and means of transportation."[36] Rationalism was to bring liberation from the confines of time and place and the distinctions of class, gender, ethnicity, and nationality; it meant overcoming the differences between city and country and achieving what Gropius described as "a loosening (*Auflockerung*) rather than dissolution (*Auflösung*) of the cities."[37]

By minimizing or eliminating difference, the rationalists used the anticipatory force of architectural form to create new structures and experiences based on the assumption of social and economic equality. A firm believer in the transformative effect of architecture and urban planning, Meyer hailed the radical expansion of space by new transportation, communication, and media technologies as the beginning of a new internationalism: "Pure construction is the trait of the new world of forms. The constructive form knows no fatherland."[38] The rationalists' preference for straight lines, perpendicular angles, and the structure of the grid best reflected their unyielding belief in the power of enlightened rationality and systematic planning. Similarly, their reliance on standardization and serialization as design principles attested to their deep conviction that form and structure could be enlisted in breaking down the class divisions that haunted the capitalist metropolis, a conviction that, in 1930, prompted Meyer to leave the Bauhaus and Berlin for Moscow and begin his work with the "Left Column."

Committed to Enlightenment principles, the rationalists relied on general principles and laws to develop their basic models for architectural and urban design, while the functionalists proceeded from the individual to the universal to establish formal principles in accordance with their vitalist celebration of life. Erich Mendelsohn, Hugo Häring, Hans Scharoun, and Adolf Rading set out to transform urban space by "turning aesthetic space into life space (*Lebensraum*)."[39] In their preference for organic forms, they validated the human being as the ultimate reference point in the reorganization of modern life, and in their attention to dynamism as an architectural principle, they reinstated the individual as the final measure of modern urbanity. Confirming Behne's earlier point about the anthropocentrism of functionalist architecture, Häring described the act of building as a process driven by fundamental human needs and responsive only to the requirements of daily use; for him, even machines were merely an extension of the human organism. Resisting the trend toward typization and serialization, Häring likewise insisted on the importance of geographical and historical specificity and defended the primacy of a human—and, by extension, humanistic—perspective against the leveling effects of general laws. "Cities," he declared, "are individualities; the city as such does not exist."[40]

It would be simplistic to denounce the rationalists as cold ideologues and extol functionalism as modernism with a human face. Both approaches offered architectural solutions to social conflicts and contradictions, with the functionalists and rationalists each seeking a formal compromise between the two historical models of modernization and mass mobilization available at the time: capitalism and communism. Simone for instance, has shown that by embracing individual and machine, the functionalist notion of dynamism sought to mediate between the (American) program of mechanization and rationalization and the (East European) tradition of utopian thought associated with both messianism and Bolshevism.[41]

These ideological underpinnings of functionalism are most pronounced in the work of Erich Mendelsohn, whose most famous Berlin project, the 1923 addition to Mossehaus, is the subject of the third case study (chap. 5). For Mendelsohn the horizontal line represented the perfect expression of modern rhythm and movement and the principle of dynamization. His streamlined forms, cylindrical shapes, elongated lines, curved corners, and horizontal window and brickwork bands articulated the mobilization of the masses in architectural form, but they also gave spatial expression to dynamism as the most effective technique for individual survival in the modern metropolis. Coming to prominence through his work for the Schocken department store chain, Mendelsohn played a key role in developing the uniquely urban architecture of department stores, motion-picture theaters, and office buildings, as well as in perfecting the formal language of openness, flexibility, and accommodation that perhaps expressed best the spirit of the stabilization period. His 1924 glass façade renovation for Herpich furriers in Leipziger Straße, though controversial at the time, was soon praised for its effective use of light architecture (*Lichtarchitektur*) and inspired many similar commercial modernization projects in the city's center. Mendelsohn's exploration of movement and form continued in the 1928 WOGA apartment complex on Kurfürstendamm, which included the famous Universum Theater, and found its final expression in the 1932 Columbushaus on Potsdamer Platz.[42] Originally built for the French department store chain Galleries Lafayette and later used as an office building with retail stores on the ground floor, Columbushaus combined the modernist principles of construction with the equally innovative practice of mixed use and variable functions. Contrary to claims made by Alan Balfour in his palimpsestic reading of Potsdamer Platz, this late example of Weimar modernism was never an SS holding cell; Columbiahaus in Tempelhof was.[43] Consequently, it makes little sense to use the Mendelsohn building for speculations about the continuities between modernism and fascism; instead we must focus on the momentous shifts in the terms of urban experience announced in Columbushaus's elegantly curved front and façade.

The functionalist aesthetic initiated a momentous shift from the building to the street as the formative principle of modern architecture and facilitated its radical rearticulation of time-space and subject-object relationships. In the words of Otto Rudolf Salvisberg, "the force of space erodes the consistency of matter and endows it with a vital function of expression. Matter dissolves into space."[44] Taking this process of dematerialization even further, Adolf Rading described the changing roles of built and unbuilt space, and of vehicles and pedestrians, in the following way: "We will no longer have streets—that is, some ordered space, and something unordered behind it—but a complete structuring (*Durchbildung*) of the whole."[45] Just as the façade provided the surface on which modern architects projected their radical ideas about pure forms and suitable materials, the street became the stage on which a new generation of urban planners envisioned the metropolis from the perspective of continuous change and perpetual movement.

In a 1919 lecture to the Workers' Council for Art, Mendelsohn succinctly described architecture "as the most revealing expression of a time's will to form"[46] and defined its formal requirements and social functions entirely in the overdetermined language of massification, from the movement of the masses (*Massenbewegung*), to the tension between rule by the masses (*Massenherrschaft*) and domination of the masses (*Massenbeherrschung*). His conclusions about the composition of the collective of the future were entirely unambiguous: "Social classes in the traditional sense will not bring about this future,"[47] he wrote, at the same time implying: But the modern masses will. In an important 1923 lecture, "Dynamics and Function," Mendelsohn translates these political prognoses into constructive principles, beginning with his exaltation of the horizontal as the perfect symbol of the emergent culture of tempo, movement, and equality. Moreover, he uses the notion of dynamics, defined here as "the logical animated expression of the forces inherent in the material,"[48] to distinguish his interactive understanding of architecture from approaches that reduce the meaning of dynamics to mechanical movements or a particular sensation, emotion, or mentality. For Mendelsohn, dynamics in architecture remained inseparable from the democratic process; yet to what degree his functionalist architecture embodied the principle of compromise and accommodation remained a subject of heated debate already among Weimar critics.

One of them, Ernst Bloch, took on the ideology of functionalism in several highly suggestive essays and critical aphorisms on Weimar Berlin and the mentality of New Objectivity. For this close associate of Adorno,

Benjamin, and Kracauer, expressionism remained the most appropriate response to fragmentation and discontinuity; only expressionism preserved the utopian potential inherent in all art, namely, as a pre-appearance that anticipates the realization of social utopias. Consequently, the various manifestations of functionalism in modern architecture and design allowed Bloch to delineate what he saw as a problematic connection between the cult of objectivity and the spirit of capitalism. Uninterested in (or not even aware of) the distinctions between functionalism and rationalism, he used spatial tropes and architectural metaphors to map the ideological function of functionalism in the larger context of Weimar culture. In "Berlin: Functions in Hollow Space," which is part of *Erbschaft dieser Zeit* (Heritage of Our Times, 1935), Bloch begins his attack on New Objectivity and, by extension, functionalism by describing the German capital as "extraordinarily 'contemporaneous' (*gleichzeitig*), a constantly new city."[49] A key category in Bloch's conceptualization of modernity, noncontemporaneity or nonsynchronicity (*Ungleichzeitigkeit*) refers to the simultaneous existence of historically distinct ideologies within a shared but nonidentical present. The term seeks to make sense of the coexistence of progressive and reactionary modernists and connect the urban and antiurban factions among the intelligentsia to the larger ideological constellations—of nationalism, provincialism, authoritarianism, and antisemitism—complicating the German path to modernity. On one hand, Bloch's diagnosis of social and aesthetic leveling and its fateful alliance with the capitalist principle of abstraction resembles conservative arguments against New Objectivity. To what degree the functionalist city remains an inhospitable place for Bloch can be seen in his reference to the *Heim* (home) that is no longer a *Heimat* (homeland) in the true sense of the word; the only thing that survives under such conditions according to Bloch is "architecture as surface." On the other hand, the modern metropolis functions as a privileged site for the manifestations of utopian thinking, which inspires his more hopeful conclusion: "Other cities are often mere ghosts of a better past; the hollow Berlin is possibly—there is no other choice—the ghost of a better future."[50]

The critical force of "Berlin: Functions in Hollow Space" as negative utopia is confirmed by Bloch's highly allegorical reading of the ornament as both the ultimate other and the hidden principle of the modernist aesthetic. A central but ambiguous trope in then-contemporary analyses of modernity, the notion of the ornament references both the stylistic excess attacked by Adolf Loos in his influential 1908 pamphlet "Ornament and

Crime" and the process of rationalization denounced by Kracauer in his evocative analysis in "The Mass Ornament" (1927). Far from being just an embellishment, the ornament functions as a site of ongoing negotiation; in its forms, the encounter between the aesthetic and the social takes place. Combining tactile, visual, and conceptual aspects, the ornament in Bloch and Kracauer organizes the tension between nature and history and articulates the problem of authenticity within the modern cult of surface phenomena. Transforming the ornament into a conceptual device, Bloch cuts through the fashionable rhetoric of progress and efficiency and, in a truly dialectical fashion, reveals the machine aesthetic as a mere substitute for the ornament and, hence, an aesthetic and conceptual disguise for the increasingly abstract relationships prevalent in late capitalism. In his words, "such Objectivity makes an ornament out of having none. . . . Its mechanical model has long since become an end in itself, serves as an ornament substitute and once again for no other purpose than that of strengthening the façade. It is finally served by the *last* motive of Objectivity, namely, *rationality* taken to extremes and yet disjointed, i.e., remaining *abstract;* at the same time this corresponds, in its abstractness, to the big business style of thinking."[51]

As a result, functionalism for Bloch fails on two fronts: the aesthetic and the political. In eliminating the ornament on a formal level, it perpetuates its ideological functions on a discursive level. Initially introduced as a necessary first step toward socialization, rationalization ends up only aligning the project of modernity more closely with the logic of late capitalism. The ambitious building projects in Berlin reveal this deeply compromised nature of functionalism on several levels. They give spatial form and material expression to a cult of light without enlightenment and a myth of transparency devoid of content. They emphatically reject stylistic and cultural diversity for a rational order based on repetition and sameness. They celebrate traffic as the model of an economic system unhindered by boundaries and disruptions; and they confirm rationalization as the foundation of modern experience and the guarantor of continuous progress. However, by uncovering the ideological project of New Building, Bloch also outlines the possibility of a more critical position, taken by many of the architects mentioned here, that hinges on its ability to externalize the effects of alienation and fragmentation. Thus what in the context of modernist architecture could be described as an aesthetic of rootlessness becomes, in the heterogeneous spaces of the modern metropolis, an invitation not to settle, but to stay mobile; not to claim certain places as one's own, but to benefit from their provisional nature. Inspired perhaps by Mendelsohn's ocean liner–shaped apartment buildings, Bloch alludes to such a possibility when he notes that "in many places [today], houses look as if they are ready to travel. Although they are unadorned, or precisely because of that, they express their farewell."[52]

IV. Ludwig Hilberseimer and the High-Rise City

If Kracauer is right to describe spatial images (*Raumbilder*) as the dreams of society, in what ways can we use Ludwig Hilberseimer's unrealized Berlin projects to uncover some of the contradictions within the urbanistic vision of New Building? Initially, the choice of Hilberseimer seems counterintuitive—but only if we focus on actual buildings rather than the social imaginary that find privileged expression in urban utopias and dystopias. In fact, his avant-garde credentials—if avant-garde is to mean both modernism's logical extension and its radical other—give access to a subversive position of negation, if not of radical negativity, that is rarely translated into architectural practice.[53] Known today primarily for his critical writings and avant-garde designs, Hilberseimer remained an outsider to the visions of the New Berlin promoted by Wagner and his closest collaborator, Taut. Involved with leftist and socialist causes, Hilberseimer was an early member of the November Group and the association of progressive architects known as *Ringgruppe* (ring group); he participated in the 1928 founding of CIAM in La Sarraz, Switzerland. While living and working in Berlin, he submitted proposals to the 1927 competition for a central train station (now Lehrter Station) and the 1929 competition for the remodeling of Alexanderplatz. Total commitment to architecture as a profession for him also meant writing for an avant-garde journal like *G*, published since 1923 by Hans Richter as a forum for avant-garde art, architecture, design, and film, as well as teaching, like Mies, at the Bauhaus during its final years (1929–33). In the architectural debates of the 1920s, he sided with the rationalists against that loosely defined group known as functionalists, organicists or, to use his term, elementarists.[54] While highly respected by fellow avant-gardists in France, Switzerland, and the Netherlands, his German colleagues often dismissed his designs as inhuman, with Häring at one point remarking that "to the degree that human beings are still human, they had better live somewhere else"[55] than in a Hilberseimer house. In the context of this study, it is precisely this radical negativity that makes

Hilberseimer so essential to a better understanding of the rationalist fixation on structure and order and what it seeks to control or deny: the mutability, changeability, and sheer energy of the modern masses.

Hilberseimer's response to the problem of modern mass society is most apparent in two famous (or infamous) proposals, his 1928 proposal for an office complex and his 1924 proposal for a high-rise city. In their formal radicalism, these two unrealized projects reveal modular design and serialization as key principles of rationalization not only in large-scale construction, but also as primary functions of social engineering and control. Conceived without a commission, the 1928 proposal for an office and business complex in the Friedrichstadt section of Berlin allowed Hilberseimer to work out some basic ideas about urban planning in relation to an actual site. The proposal features parallel rows of eight-story slabs oriented north-south that, in the surviving photo collage, are inserted in the existing urban environment through the principle of cut and paste. The layout confirms Hilberseimer's commitment to the *Zeilenbau* system, the ribbon development or straight row system, as a useful alternative to the dreaded block system of the tenement and a perfect embodiment of

Fig. 3.5. Ludwig Hilberseimer, office complex in the Friedrichstadt, ca. 1928. Courtesy of The Art Institute of Chicago. Photography copyright The Art Institute of Chicago.

the modernist credo of light and air. Shown from a bird's-eye perspective, the rows of buildings impose their geometrical order on the existing street layout and assert their abstract construction principles against the historically developed site. The proximity to Gendarmenmarkt, that famous monument to the Prussian Enlightenment, and to the center of government on Wilhelmstraße underscores the violent gesture of erasure, but it also suggests a hidden affinity between historical and modernist topographies of power (fig. 3.5).

One way of understanding the proposal's significance as an avant-garde manifesto is to compare it to a more famous architectural intervention into urban space: Mies van der Rohe's proposal for a high-rise on Friedrichstraße[56] (fig. 3.6). Like Hilberseimer, Mies uses a photo collage to make visible the provocation of modern architecture; but unlike his colleague, he uses a pedestrian point of view to show in what ways, to quote K. Michael Hays, "aesthetic continuities can mediate the discontinuities of

Fig. 3.6. Mies van der Rohe design "Wabe" for the 1921–22 competition for a high-rise near Friedrichstraße Station. Courtesy of Mies van der Rohe Archive, Museum of Modern Art. Copyright 2007 Artists Rights Society (ARS), New York / VG Bild-Kunst, Bonn.

experience."[57] In both proposals, architecture is used to draw attention to the chaos and disorganization of modern urban life. Both architects keep the multitudes at bay by relying on an almost Nietzschean definition of style, modulated by Rieglian *Kunstwollen,* to contain the heterogeneous forces within one unifying principle. Yet by presenting the modernist structure from the city dweller's point of view, Mies at least acknowledges the contingencies and discontinuities of modern urban life. In so doing, he also affirms the power of architecture to articulate the underlying sense of shock and disorientation; the transcendent beauty of his design arises precisely from this complex aesthetic negotiation. In contrast, Hilberseimer refuses any form of engagement with urban reality and instead offers a perfect demonstration of the traumatic effect of massification, its translation into modernism as a defensive reaction, and what Benjamin, to whom we will return later, diagnoses as the "poverty of experience."

Within the larger constellations of modernism and mass culture, Hilberseimer's proposal for an office complex in Friedrichstadt can be read as either a case study of the death (or death wish) of the avant-garde or a radical response to the crisis of bourgeois subjectivity. In both cases, its notions of space and place organize key binaries such as interior versus exterior, public versus private, and individual versus collective. According to the first reading, Hilberseimer's solution to the most pressing urban problems of his times could be described as compulsive in its belief in quantification, neurotic in its cult of order, megalomaniac in its totalitarian ambition, paranoid in its fear of diversity, and masochistic in its denial of sensory pleasure. From a feminist perspective, Hilberseimer's conception of apartment houses as bachelor machines betrays the masculinist ultrarationalism that also surfaces in the Weimar writings of Gropius and others. And the clear distaste for nature, a trait shared with De Stijl, suggests an almost pathological hatred of the life world. For all of these reasons, we would agree with Richard Pommer's observation that "hating the city, Hilberseimer also hated modernity."[58] We might even conclude with Pommer that this antiurban impulse originated in a Nietzschean hatred of the masses that, channeled through the elitism of the avant-garde, facilitated the fateful transition "from a social and technical definition of the city to a purely formal vision."[59]

On the other hand, we might take K. Michael Hays's position and interpret the Friedrichstadt proposal as an articulation of the formal principle of negativity that must be considered central to all modernist impulses, and the avant-garde aesthetic in particular. According to such a reading, the principle of serialization allows for a radical rearticulation of the dominant forces of late capitalism. Likewise, the emphasis on rationalization brings into relief the ascendancy of new bureaucracies and ideologies of management. Questioning the false alternatives of humanism and inhumanity, Hays introduces the notion of the posthumanist subject in order to praise Hilberseimer's antireformist stance as a critical, if not subversive force. Of course, the disappearance of the autonomous, self-conscious subject and the disintegration of bourgeois humanist thought after World War I were thematized by many artists and architects, whether through the functionalist or rationalist theories of urban space or through the stylistic registers of expressionism and New Objectivity. Yet when Hays describes modern architecture as "a conscious response, whether with applause or with regret, to the dissolution of psychological autonomy and individualism brought by technological modernization," a process, in short, with far-reaching implications for the "humanist concept of subjectivity and its presumptions about originality, universality, and authority,"[60] he obviously believes that this reaction formation found almost programmatic expression in Hilberseimer and, with different implications, in Meyer.

The opposition of antihumanist versus posthumanist in the critical assessment of Hilberseimer's work leaves out one important category of urban identity and modern subjectivity: that of class. Both Pommer and Hays link modernism to the crises of modern subjectivity, but it remains a subjectivity undifferentiated in terms of class and, to evoke an equally important category, of gender. Yet the appearance of this anti- or posthumanist discourse within New Building cannot be explained through general references to modernization, urbanization, and rationalization alone. Instead, it must be linked to the particular challenges to traditional class society posed after World War I by the radicalized working class and the emerging white-collar class. In this context, the crisis in the humanist concept of subjectivity was only heightened by the decline of the traditional alliance between urban culture and bourgeois culture, and the appearance of a homogeneous mass culture. All modern urban utopias inscribed specifically bourgeois theories of social conflict and change in the reorganization of the metropolis, from the separation of urban functions of industry, commerce, and housing, to the less obvious mechanisms of inclusion and exclusion achieved through zoning laws, gentrification, and so forth. For these reasons, the project of the architectural avant-garde can and must be read as a projection of specific bourgeois anxieties about the feared tyranny of the masses.

Throughout the 1920s and early 1930s, Hilberseimer was actively involved in organizing these modern masses: through his interest in quintessential urban building types, such as the office and the apartment building, and through his promotion of serialization as a formal, structural, and organizational principle. As the most outspoken proponent of rationalist city planning, he advocated approaches that anticipated the disappearance of social and economic differences in their formal languages and registers. Striving toward greater efficiency, Hilberseimer aimed to "develop the fundamental principles of urban design out of contemporary needs" and to formulate "general rules that make possible the solution of specific concrete tasks."[61] Among other things, these rules allowed the urban planner to extend the principles of serialization from the module to the modular. The problem of form remained inseparable from the notion of the Type and its origins in industrial production, but found its boldest application in the vision of a postindustrial, presumably classless society. Hilberseimer's assertion that "what the room is on a small scale, the layout of the city is on a large scale: the comprehensive organization of reciprocal needs and relationships"[62] takes the utopian potential of this aesthetic to an extreme and ultimately ends up reproducing the principle of negation in the dystopian rule of means-ends rationality. Hilberseimer not only ignores the problem of scale and size entirely, he also glosses over the political processes necessary to achieve compatibility and adaptability among the various urban functions. Such a leveling of urban phenomena reenacts the traumatic experience of massification and ultimately aims at the annihilation of the creative potential of chaos, coincidence, and diversity embodied by the modern metropolis.

Hilberseimer's programmatic writings shed further light on his contradictory views on urbanism and capitalism and their shared origins in Weimar discourses of the masses, including the strange mixture of constructivist, corporatist, technocratic, and vitalist ideas. In *Großstadtarchitektur* (Big City Architecture, 1927), a treatise on the principles of modern city planning, Hilberseimer describes the metropolis as "a creation of all-powerful big capital, as an expression of its anonymity, as an urban type with specific economic-social and collective-psychic foundations, allowing at once for the greatest isolation and closest association of its inhabitants."[63] His heavy reliance on terms such as "centers of energy," "force fields," and "total organism" suggests that his is a capitalism without classes, free of the conflicts and confrontations of the Weimar period that nonetheless interfere with his analyses through his reliance on its prevailing urban metaphors. On a few occasions, he elaborates on the role of the modern metropolis in the imperialist stage, a period of increasingly violent confrontations over contested territories both globally and locally. Yet in order to protect his urban theory from the incursions of social reality, he then deprives his proposals (e.g., on the building of satellite cities) of all geographic or historical specificity and reduces possible solutions to the structural relationships between the elementary cell and the organism as a whole.

Where the critics of the Weimar feuilleton found the most redeeming feature of urban culture, namely, in the spectacle of the street, Hilberseimer encountered nothing but a deplorable state of disorganization that had to be overcome through a comprehensive building plan. Concretely, this meant building new residential neighborhoods on the periphery and limiting the center to commercial and governmental uses. Only big cities designed according to a rational plan, he believed, would be able to respond adequately to the problems of modernization (and, of course, the movements of global capital); for this reason, he openly condoned the leveling of historic structures and neighborhoods. Questions of style should be considered only insofar as "the general case, the law, will be honored and emphasized, the exception in contrast will be put aside, the nuances eradicated—the rule becomes master, and chaos is forced to become form: logical, unambiguous, arithmetic, law."[64] In the process, everything irregular, inefficient, and obsolete was to be eliminated. Thus aligned with rational processes, architecture could become the "expression of a new mentality that is not of a subjective-individual but objective-collective nature."[65] Another name for this mentality would be the ideology of corporate capitalism.

The underlying class politics of avant-garde architecture are even more apparent in Hilberseimer's schematic model of a high-rise city first published in *Die Form* in 1924 (fig. 3.7). This much discussed proposal for a city of about one million inhabitants includes a north-south and an east-west bird's-eye view of identical parallel slabs, fourteen stories high and designed in typical minimalist style. For Hilberseimer, the high-rise city offered a solution to the most pressing urban problems (e.g., traffic congestion, unsanitary housing) by reducing all points of contact and, hence, of conflict to a minimum and by reorganizing urban relations along

Fig. 3.7. Ludwig Hilberseimer, proposal for a high-rise city. *Die Form* (1924). Courtesy of The Art Institute of Chicago. Photography copyright The Art Institute of Chicago.

a vertical, rather than horizontal, axis. Reminiscent of the medieval city, the vertical structures serve integrative functions, with commerce located on the street level, with housing "above the store" as it were, and with mass transit hidden underground. Industrial production and mass entertainment remain strangely absent from this uncanny city of the future, however. Acknowledging the bleakness of such an urban vision, but making no reference to the historical conditions under which it was conceived, Hilberseimer in exile would later describe his 1924 high-rise city as "more a necropolis than a metropolis, a sterile landscape of asphalt and concrete, inhuman in every respect."[66]

In ways that are highly relevant to our discussion of functionalism, rationalism, and the kind of architectural dystopias envisioned by Hilberseimer and others, toward the end of the Weimar period Benjamin, too, considered the double-edged character of architectural modernity in provocative reflections on a new barbarism arising in the aftermath of World War I. Instead of following the proponents of New Objectivity in celebrating the triumphant merging of man and machine, he approached the modernist project through a concept that, at first glance, seems utterly misplaced in a critical evaluation of Hilberseimer: the concept of experience. In a highly speculative essay published in 1933, Benjamin's question "What does poverty of experience do for the barbarian?" thus provokes the following answer: "It forces him to start from scratch; to make a new start; to make a little go a long way; to begin with a little and build up further, looking neither left nor right."[67] Resisting the cult of immediacy that, in the prewar tradition of Endell and others, sustained the defenders of traditional urban culture, Benjamin introduces the distinction between the continuities of time and place and the layers of tradition established through *Erfahrung* (experience) and the repetitive, shocklike moments identified with *Erlebnis* (often translated as "lived experience"). This conceptualizing of modernity from the perspective of shock, in turn, allows him to uphold the critical power of lack as a condition of tentative openness and possible change: "Poverty of experience. This should not be understood to mean that people are yearning for new experience. No, they long to free themselves from experience; they long for a world in which they can make such pure and decided use of their poverty—their outer poverty, and ultimately also their inner poverty—that it will lead to something respectable."[68]

Under such conditions, the experience of lack can have a profoundly liberating effect, promoting critical awareness and creating the conditions for social change. The wide, open spaces and clear lines and smooth surfaces of New Building actualize these layered meanings of poverty according to many of its practitioners. However, Benjamin (and with him Bloch) does not follow the advocates of modern architecture and city planning in their enthusiastic pronouncements on technological progress and rational planning. As his reflections on the destructive character suggest, the modernist infatuation with order and emptiness, which culminates in a ferocious desire for tabula rasa, only brings out the destructive underside of modernity: "The destructive character knows only one watchword: make room. And only one activity: clearing away."[69] The elimination of all traces of history and tradition and the leveling of social and cultural differences must consequently be interpreted as a spatial expression of the central problematic of modern experience, a defense against the threat of being absorbed into the amorphous body of the modern masses. In the terms used by Benjamin, the urban utopias conjured up by Hilberseimer and others provide an *Erlebnis* of urbanity by eliminating the very conditions of *Erfahrung*. Positioned between the poverty of experience and the desire for destruction, New Building can therefore be described as both an activist and a reactive response to the process of modernization, and its emphatic rejection of the humanist tradition interpreted as an expression of revolt as well as despair. In recognition of these dialectical effects, the broader implications for the conceptualization of bourgeois subjectivity will be examined in the next chapter through the urban excursions of two influential critics, Franz Hessel and Siegfried Kracauer, and their fascination with the mechanisms of adaptation and appropriation that translated the high modernism of Mies, Mendelsohn, Gropius, and Hilberseimer into the vernacular modernism of the Kurfürstendamm and other centers of mass consumption and entertainment.

CHAPTER 4

Walking in the Metropolis:
The City Texts of Franz Hessel
and Siegfried Kracauer

While architects such as Gropius, Mendelsohn, and Hilberseimer were directly involved in organizing the modern masses, the representatives of the literary feuilleton turned to architecture for entirely different reasons: to examine the crisis of modern subjectivity and to respond to the threat of deindividualization through the literary forms and means available to them. In their critical engagement with architecture, they did not limit themselves to the signature buildings that have come to represent the New Berlin. Instead, in staging the drama of modern subjectivity, their city texts—or textual cities—engaged the entire range of architectural culture: the new commercial structures and façade renovations in the city center, the modernist styles in light advertising, shopwindow design, and cinema architecture, and the architectural tropes that, on the pages of the feuilleton, functioned as metaphors of mass culture and allegories of modernity. All three levels come together in the trope of walking, which will serve in this chapter to shed light on the role of the city text within Weimar discourse on modern architecture and mass society: first through a study on the Kurfürstendamm, the famous boulevard where modern architecture entered into a new alliance with commodity culture and mass entertainment, and then through the writings of Franz Hessel and Siegfried Kracauer, two quintessential Weimar strollers or, to use the richer critical term, *flaneurs.*

In "Walking in the City," Michel de Certeau describes moving inside the cityscape as a complex, creative activity. It is only through the presence of pedestrians that the heterogeneous spaces of the city are brought to life, through walkers "whose bodies follow the thicks and thins of an urban 'text' they write without being able to read it. . . . The networks of these moving, intersecting writings compose a manifold story that has neither

author nor spectator, shaped out of fragments of trajectories and alterna-
tions of spaces: in relation to representations, it remains daily and
indefinitely other."[1] These pedestrians, strollers, and flaneurs turn spaces
into places, endowing them with individual meaning and social purpose.
Experiencing the city at the ground level, one step at a time, the pedestrians actualize the hidden urban text that makes up the city in the popular
imagination, that resonates in literary and filmic representations of the metropolis, and that finds its clearest expression in the spatial interventions of
architects and city planners. Given their diversity and fluidity as a social
body and urban phenomenon, these pedestrians at first glance appear to
have little in common with the rational organization of urban space envisioned by Wagner, Gropius, and Hilberseimer, not to mention their postwar successors worldwide. However, even de Certeau's fantasy of walking
as a subversive act remains fundamentally dependent on the totalizing vision provided by architecture, as confirmed by his privileged view from the
World Trade Center in New York that, in this particular text, allows him to
imagine the pedestrians below as unconscious agents of a city text seemingly writing itself.

Walking or strolling in the city text indeed represents one of the most
immediate ways of exploring the urban environment and of negotiating
the place of the individual in the crowd. Yet writing as a flaneur not only
means articulating the problem of modern subjectivity within the imaginary spaces and architectural tropes of the city text, it also means staging
the sociospatial dialectic under certain historical conditions and in class-
specific and gendered terms. To continue lines of argumentation started in
chapter 1, the central problematic addressed through Weimar flanerie is the
relationship between architecture and class, a point downplayed in the extensive scholarship on the representation of Berlin in the Weimar feuilleton.[2] More specifically, it is the connection between New Building and
white-collar society that informs the urban excursions of Kracauer and
Hessel especially in their strategies of resistance and denial. Both respond
to the provocation of modern mass society as typical representatives of the
educated middle class and, more specifically, the literary intelligentsia.
Through walking, they demarcate a textual space within which to confront
their increasing marginalization as a social class and to develop new strategies for surviving in modern mass culture. As a literary trope and heuristic
device, walking thus allows them to uphold individual agency and sense
perception against the abstract principles of mass organization. Walking
validates coincidence and contingency over the predetermined order of the

plan, and walking preserves pleasure, fantasy, and play as important alternatives, or at least supplements, to the modernist preoccupation with efficiency and functionality. As a defensive habitus inextricably linked to the crisis of bourgeois identity (and male identity, for that matter), however, walking in the ways utilized in the Weimar feuilleton also highlights individual strategies of resistance that are key to our understanding of modern mass society. These include the withdrawal of the individual from the groups and structures that define urban life, the separation between individual desire and social or political engagement, and the retreat from the modernist master narratives to the traditional views and individual attitudes that sustain the hegemonic city text.

In the larger context of Weimar architectural culture, the city texts of Kracauer and Hessel are part of the same antimodernist formation that produced the conservative attacks on New Building. Both reintroduced individual agency into the organization of urban space and, through their passionate defense of the classical metropolis, directly challenged the modernist dream of perfect order and total control. Yet as we will see on the following pages, both authors articulated this opposition in very different terms. In fact, their writings reenact the two strategies available to the bourgeois subject in response to the fear of massification: projection and introjection. Whereas Kracauer projects the crisis of subjectivity onto the cityscape, seeking to regain some sense of certainty through critical reflection, Hessel incorporates the sensory stimuli in order to reconstruct the subject in crisis. Both critics also develop specifically spatial strategies of coping: Kracauer by deciphering the spatial image and Hessel by reading the city like a text. Whereas Kracauer uses architecture to confront the inherent violence of modernity and its destructive impact on the texture of urban life, Hessel's urban wanderings come with detailed instructions for retreating to a position of prewar aestheticism and sensualism. Accordingly, in Kracauer, writing the city text means acknowledging the tension within mass society as both an emancipatory force and a site of oppression; in the work of Hessel, the same problematic is resolved through a retreat to the narcissistic pleasures of flanerie. In the end, such individual strategies can never include a plan for social action; the dream of individual redemption remains impossible, for it excludes the urban collective and the experience of community. Pointing to a dilemma that applies equally to the city texts of Kracauer and Hessel, Michael Keith writes:

> Theoretically, city spaces cannot restore the lost certainties of identity, centre the decentred subject, precisely because they, themselves,

are produced in the multiple discourses of urban spatiality. Resonant with politically contested meaning, they are sites of struggle which themselves are decentred, rendering the sort of identity formation that they engender always contingent.[3]

I. Case Study: The Kurfürstendamm

If there was one place in Berlin where white-collar workers could take in modern architecture and design and find their own dreams and desires reflected in the cult of surface phenomena, it was on the Kurfürstendamm or Kudamm, as the boulevard was commonly known. And if there was one street where the threat to the artistic traditions and cultural distinctions of bourgeois culture became most apparent to literary critics, it also was on that major east-west traffic artery, favorite weekend promenade, and premier shopping boulevard in the New West, or Berlin-W, to give the postal code often used in the feuilleton. According to a travel guide written by Eugen Szatmari, Friedrichstraße may have been the center of entertainment for tourists but the Kurfürstendamm was "the center of entertainment for Berliners."[4]

Developed during the 1910s, the commercial and residential area roughly defined by the length of Tauentzienstraße/Kurfürstendamm from Wittenbergplatz to Olivaer Platz and the side streets up to the city train tracks in the north and Hohenzollerndamm in the south emerged as the foremost symbol of the stabilization period and its promises of social mobility and economic prosperity. With its dazzling lighting schemes and innovative neon signs, the Kurfürstendamm, especially in the short stretch between Kaiser Wilhelm Memorial Church and Uhlandstraße, functioned as a showcase not only for a dazzling array of consumer goods and popular diversions but also for the most advanced architectural styles and designs.[5] Referring to its relentless promotion of all things modern, Curt Morek called the boulevard "the display window of Berlin."[6]

There, variety shows, revue theaters, dinner clubs, wine restaurants, dance establishments, and hotel bars vied for the attention of the local population and a growing number of international tourists. In the Nelson-Revue, where Josephine Baker entranced mass audiences, in Rosa Valetti's Größenwahn cabaret, and in Max Reinhardt's Komödie, artistic innovation and popular appeal were no longer treated as mutually exclusive. By bringing the sensibilities of the street onto the proscenium stage, these popular establishments contributed to the democratization of the performing arts and created a new mass audience indifferent to the old divisions of high and low culture. Spectacular motion picture palaces, like the Marmorhaus, the Gloria-Palast am Zoo, the Capitol (designed by Hans Poelzig), and the Universum (designed by Erich Mendelsohn), showed the classics of expressionist cinema, the earliest sound films, and the newest foreign productions and provided the environments where glamour and luxury became available even to Kracauer's proverbial little shopgirls. In establishing the conditions under which ordinary citizens could mingle with the rich and famous, the Kurfürstendamm seemed to fulfill the dream of a democratic mass culture unified by the rituals of mass consumption and mass entertainment. This symbolic function prompted Weimar critic Christian Bouchholtz to refer to new cultural tastes, trends, and sensations through neologisms such as *Kurfürstendammgeschmack, Kurfürstendammangelegenheit,* and *Kurfürstendammsensation,* that is, the tastes, events, and sensations of modern life.[7]

Within the city's social geography and spatial imaginary, the westward move along this famous boulevard of theatrical, cinematic, and culinary attractions signaled a momentous shift from the old power elites based in the historic Friedrichstadt, to the new middle classes, educated elites, and nouveaux riches living in Charlottenburg, Wilmersdorf, and Dahlem. Rising rents and real estate prices on Kurfürstendamm and its frequent identification with inflation-made wealth and conspicuous consumption contributed to growing concerns about the divisive effects of such unchecked growth. In 1926, a group of businessmen formed the *City-Ausschuß* (city commission) to stop the departure of retail businesses from the old center and to improve traffic connections between the city's eastern and western parts. While the area around Friedrichstraße remained the center of banking and government, Kurfürstendamm quickly emerged as what some contemporaries called a *City-Filiale,* an offshoot of the old center, with several traditional Berlin-based businesses, including the Kempinski wine restaurant, the famous Café Kranzler, and the venerable Grünfeld textile store opening branches on the modern shopping boulevard.[8] Small, exclusive retail stores selling furs, shoes, lingerie, chocolate, teas, perfumes, watches, and books satisfied the discerning tastes of the fashionable men and women of the New West (fig. 4.1). Countless cafés, tearooms, wine bars, specialty restaurants, dance clubs, variety shows, dinner theaters, and even one self-serve restaurant catered to the needs of an upwardly mobile, self-fashioned, and pleasure-seeking clientele intent on taking full advantage of the offerings of an Americanized mass culture. The displays of

Fig. 4.1. Kurfürstendamm, Trumpf chocolate store, ca. 1930.

wealth and the rituals of privilege were recognizable by, and accessible to, everyone, with foreigners and natives alike promenading on the boulevard and sitting in bars, restaurants, and cafés and all playing their parts in this uniquely urban mise-en-scène of modern architecture, urban modernity, and what Miriam Hansen and others have called vernacular modernism.[9]

The inevitable tension between the surface appearance of democratic mass culture and the underlying mechanisms of social differentiation profoundly affected the ways in which modern architecture made its spectacular entrance on the Kurfürstendamm. Decried by Kracauer as a telling expression of the commodification of urban life, the new *Fassadenarchitektur* (façade architecture) gave the prevailing fantasies of social mobility and individual freedom a necessary spatial framework and aesthetic expression. Soon the first floors of many apartment buildings were converted for commercial use and the ornate Wilhelmine stucco façades removed to make room for streamlined modern designs; the fact that the upper floors were usually left untouched confirms the highly superficial approach to modern styles as mere embellishment. The architecture of glass and light, which in the expressionist utopias allowed for the apotheosis of the crystal as a symbol of community and spirituality, now gave rise to the profane

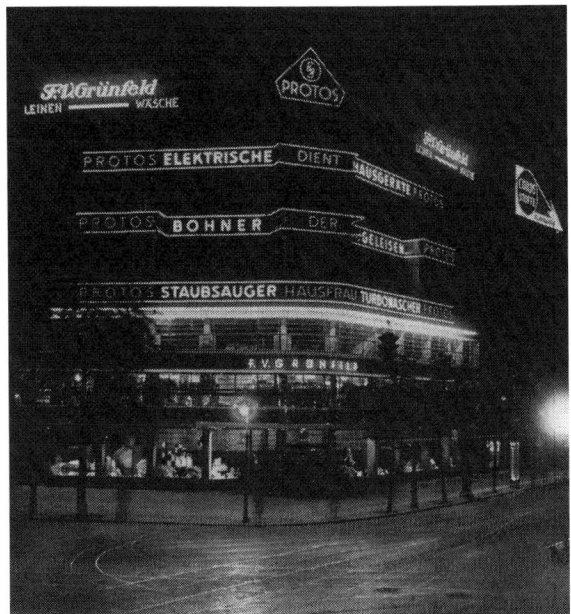

Fig. 4.2. Kurfürstendamm, Leinenhaus Grünfeld, façade renovation, during the "Berlin im Licht" festival, 1928. Courtesy of Berlinische Galerie, Photographische Sammlung.

rituals of commodity culture. In 1928, the Grünfeld textile store on the corner of Joachimsthaler Straße added a spectacular glass façade and elevator (designed by Otto Firle) that, like Mendelsohn's earlier design for Herpich furriers on Friedrichstraße (1924), prompted hostile reactions by defenders of traditional architecture (fig. 4.2). In 1929, the stucco façade of the Café Uhlandeck (at the corner of Uhlandstraße) was replaced by a smooth, minimalist front with an attractive lighting scheme (fig. 4.3). The most famous new construction completed during the period, Mendelsohn's 1928 WOGA complex, not only aestheticized the acceleration of urban experience in its streamlined forms but, through its combination of apartment house and entertainment complex, also signaled the full integration of modern living with the cinematic diversions offered by the Universum Theater (fig. 4.4).

Moreover, through the technical and artistic possibilities of electric light, the Kurfürstendamm during the 1920s was transformed into a showcase for innovative advertising schemes and contemporary window and store designs. The historical role of electrification in the making of the

Fig. 4.3. Kurfürstendamm, Uhlandeck, façade renovation, ca. 1930. Courtesy of Bildarchiv Preußischer Kulturbesitz Berlin.

Fig. 4.4. Erich Mendelsohn, WOGA complex with Universum Theater, 1928.
Courtesy of Bildarchiv Preußischer Kulturbesitz Berlin.

modern metropolis had started with the liberation of the city night from its
exclusive association with crime and vice and continued with the introduction of new instruments of mass observation and social control. Now light
played a key role in establishing commodity culture as the organizing principle of urban society. Through electrification, the boulevard acquired a
double identity, with the architectural solids and structured spaces of the
daytime dissolved by the nightly spectacle of street lighting and neon advertising. Promising profane illumination, artificial light turned the city
night into a stage set, complete with floodlights, spot lighting, and
chiaroscuro effects and often modeled on the visual regimes of film. Not
surprisingly, the illuminated big city night served highly contradictory purposes in the feuilleton. As a symbol of transparency, immateriality, and
transitoriness, electric light for many critics embodied the Weimar spirit of
openness, progress, and democracy. For others, such as Heinz Pollack, the
rhythmic on-off-on-off of the neon lights failed to distract from the pressing economic problems and signaled nothing but "the last desperate con-
vulsions of someone doomed to die."[10]

As has been shown by Janet Ward in her highly original 2001 study of
Weimar surfaces, light architecture (*Lichtarchitektur*) played a central role

in transforming modern architecture into an object of mass consumption.[11] While large, animated neon advertisements featured whimsical slogans and famous corporate logos, modern shopwindow design relied heavily on indirect lighting, dramatic highlights, theatrical framing, and frosted or colored glass to lure potential buyers into the fetishistic scenarios of commodity consumption. Hailed by architects as the most important new building materials in commercial architecture, light and glass radically redefined the relationship between interior and exterior, volume and structure, matter and space, and, by extension, commercial life and public sphere. Through its ability to highlight, accentuate, animate, and illuminate, artificial light facilitated the transition from the solidity of architectural structures to the techniques of make-believe shared by window design and film. The derealization of urban space by light architecture and neon advertising completed the process of dematerialization that implicated the Kurfürstendamm—indeed, the entire commercial center—in specifically filmic sensations and kinetic effects. The illuminated letters that appeared on theater marquees and in shopwindows, the animated images that moved across roofs and firewalls, and the elaborate set designs and live scenes staged in many department store windows took full advantage of this growing interdependency of urban space and urban imaginary. Consequently, the city night had to be regarded as the true test of the modernist aesthetic, with darkness bringing out its unique qualities. The proliferation of light as a building material in its own right and its contribution to new forms of stimulation and simulation caused Wilhelm Hausenstein to praise electric light as "the texture and the substance of the street."[12] Similarly, the changed dynamics between the material and immaterial elements constituting urban space prompted Wilhelm Schnarrenberger to conclude that "advertisement creates the architecture that it needs."[13]

As an essential part of commercial architecture, the modern façade played an equally important role in the convergence of modern subjectivity with the urban rituals of consumerism. While conceptualized in terms of its functionality, the modern façade was often perceived as an extension of the goods, services, and experiences available inside, in the motion picture theaters, gourmet restaurants, and specialty stores. Yet as a signifier of the modern spirit, the new façade architecture on the Kurfürstendamm remained contradictory and ambivalent. With the rhetoric of simplicity, honesty, and truth undercut by the calculated superficiality of the remodeling process, the double meaning of *Schein* as both illusion and illumination precisely expresses this ambivalence. To cultural conservatives, the façade culture of Weimar modernity attested to the compromised relation-ship between modern art and consumer culture and the cooptation of art by the laws of the commodity. Thus for Ernst Reinhardt, whose attack on New Building combined antimodernist and anticapitalist arguments, the reviled ornament returned in contemporary culture in the form of the cor-porate logo.[14] Similarly, Joseph Roth, an ardent defender of old-fashioned urbanity, made his pointed attack on surface culture part of a larger cri-tique of New Objectivity. For him, the Kurfürstendamm represented the modern infatuation with innovation and change at its worst:

> Its frightful ability to renew itself constantly—in short: to "reno-vate"—contradicts all natural laws of being young and growing old. I have been trying for a long time to uncover the secret that enables it, despite every unexpected change in its physiognomy, to still remain recognizable, yes even to increasingly become Kurfürstendamm. Its changeability is unchangeable. Its impatience is indefatigable. Its in-consistency is unrelenting.

By dissolving all oppositions and by reversing all values, the Kurfürsten-damm for Roth deprived urban culture of all authenticity; that is why the new restaurants and theaters fail even as successful imitations and repre-sented nothing but "unsuccessful originals."[15]

Yet to many others, the simple, smooth surfaces announced architec-ture's long overdue liberation from the tyranny of the ornament and, with it, from history and tradition. For Walter Riezler, the editor of *Die Form,* the organ of the *Deutsche Werkbund,* this development ultimately aimed at the reconceptualization of the façade as separate from the building. Once the individual building was absorbed into the perimeter block, he argued, the façade could become an essential part of the unified cityscape and gain new meaning "as a boundary of the street itself."[16] Describing the dissolu-tion of spatial boundaries through light architecture as liberating, Riezler spoke out against all attempts to regulate light advertising through city or-dinances and emphasized instead the productive relationship between art and industry captured in its spectacular effects. Dazzling and awe-inspir-ing, but also chaotic and confusing, the illuminated Friedrichstraße (or Kurfürstendamm) at night had to be seen as an emblem of the free market principle of competition and thus a founding site of Weimar modernity.[17]

The observation by Hermann Sinsheimer that "whatever the city does, becomes visible on Kurfürstendamm"[18] explains the symptomatic readings that allowed cultural critics to explore the hidden affinities among modern architecture, mass consumption, and white-collar society. As a symptom and a symbol, the boulevard brought together three separate but interconnected developments: the proliferation of American-style mass culture and consumer culture, the popularization of modern architecture and design, and the changing role of writers and intellectuals in the marketing of urban culture. Reflections on the Kurfürstendamm as a laboratory for new mentalities and sensibilities could be found throughout Weimar culture, with the boulevard functioning, in the words of Erhard Schütz, like a "site of convertibility for all individual phenomena within the invisible whole of the big city Berlin."[19] Beginning with an early Richard Oswald feature film, programmatically titled *Kurfürstendamm* (1920), the center of the New West regularly appeared in feature films

Fig. 4.5. Kurfürstendamm. Photograph by Hans G. Casparius, 1931. Courtesy of Bildarchiv Preußischer Kulturbesitz Berlin.

where filmmakers and protagonists explored its cinematic qualities on their obligatory strolls and motorized excursions. Contemporary novels, such as Gabriele Tergit's *Käsebier erobert den Kurfürstendamm* (Käsebier Conquers the Kurfürstendamm, 1931), depicted the milieu of war profiteers, business speculators, and nouveaux riches with a mixture of detached curiosity, moral disapproval, and lurid fascination. From countless feuilleton pieces, to nostalgic memoirs in the style of Paul Erich Marcus's *Heimweh nach dem Kurfürstendamm* (Homesick for the Kurfürstendamm, 1952), writers, artists, and critics time and again returned to Café Kranzler, Café Wien, Café des Westens, and above all, Romanisches Café, to write, chat, drink, gossip, and observe the society ladies, stock market profiteers, aging dandies, influential lawyers, famous actresses, and fashionable young boys and girls promenading on the sidewalks in front of them (fig. 4.5).

Urban enthusiasts, who felt reminded of the grand boulevards of Paris, praised the Kurfürstendamm for its sophistication, tolerance, and cosmopolitanism. Detractors railed against the material and sensual excesses, the atmosphere of social and sexual permissiveness, and the feverish pursuit of new pleasures and diversions. Conservatives enlisted its offerings in their moralistic campaigns against big city life and used the ubiquitous signs of Americanization to diagnose the imminent decline of German *Kultur.* Denounced as a symbol of *Asphaltliteratur* (asphalt literature) and *Gossenkunst* (gutter art) and vilified for its "un-German" culture of corruption, speculation, prostitution, addiction, and degeneracy, the Kurfürstendamm played a particularly heinous part in the right-wing attacks on Weimar mass culture and democracy. Especially after 1933, the boulevard's unique mixture of art and commerce and its openness to diverse influences inspired countless antisemitic diatribes against foreign infiltration and racial degeneration in the style of Friedrich Hussong's *"Kurfürstendamm:" Zur Kulturgeschichte des Zwischenreichs* (On the Cultural History of the Transitional Period, 1934).[20]

The precarious position of urban intellectuals between the traditional bourgeoisie and the modern middle classes, between the cultural elites and the artistic avant-gardes, and between established literary culture and the new world of mass publishing made them particularly susceptible to the reconfiguration of class and hence uniquely qualified to register its broader implications in their urban writings and public personalities. Imitating the habitus of the old-fashioned flaneur, some critics strolled without apparent aim or purpose; others watched the spectacle of the crowds from inside a café; and yet others relied on busses and automobiles to take in the totality of a thus mobilized cityscape. In their encounters with what Simmel calls objective culture, they alternately assumed the personae of the detached observer, the involved participant, the old-fashioned poet, and the modern-day reporter, always prepared to respond to the threat of massification with various strategies of resistance and compliance. The quintessential sites of Weimar modernity—the shopping boulevard, the traffic square, the train station, the motion-picture theater, the hotel lobby, and the department store—provided them with the spatial coordinates through which to make the transformation of class society visible and accessible to critical reflection. In translating spatial phenomena into textual effects, they profited greatly from the remarkable textual productivity of the street itself: the advertisements, neon signs, and storefronts, the writing on busses, trams, kiosks, and advertising pillars, and last but not least, their secret doubles in the writing of the city text, the ubiquitous sandwich-board men.

Associated with names such as Siegfried Kracauer, Kurt Tucholsky, Joseph Roth, Alfred Polgar, Benjamin von Brentano, and Franz Hessel, Weimar culture has often been characterized as the golden age of the feuilleton. Ranging from detailed accounts and objective reportages to more speculative pieces and impressionistic vignettes, the city texts published in the daily newspapers and illustrated magazines were part of a concerted effort by middle-class intellectuals to come to terms with the leveling effects of modern mass culture. Writing for the feuilleton allowed writers to avoid the proletarization of many other *Geistesarbeiter* (mental workers) and to make the new conditions of writing in, and about, the city an integral part of their urban poetics; this meant accommodating the dramatic changes in mass publishing, literary production, and, most important, the reading habits of city dwellers, including the white-collar workers. In utilizing the long tradition of essayistic writing, including its unique combination of mundane observation and philosophical reflection, these urban critics resisted what Benjamin would later diagnose as the decline of experience in the age of mechanical reproduction, with his scathing remark that the role of the feuilleton was "to inject experience—as it were, intravenously—with the poison of sensation"[21] referring to precisely this strategy.

Functioning as an instrument of self-reflection, the many essays on the difficulties of walking in Berlin shed an important light on the difference between prewar and postwar years and present the modern flaneur as a figure of nonsimultaneity, if not tragic belatedness. Whereas Wilhelmine Berlin gave rise to various urban types, including the stroller (*Spazier-*

gänger), idler (*Bummler*), and loiterer (*Eckensteher*) depicted in numerous novels and novellas, Weimar Berlin tended to frustrate the aspiring flaneur. Many critics complained, at times with bitterness, about the city's tempo and efficiency. Berliners, they argued, either hurried from one place to the next or went on invigorating nature walks, but they hardly ever strolled in a leisurely fashion. According to Alfred Polgar, only the Kurfürstendamm was able to satisfy the needs of the old-fashioned flaneur: "It is one of the few streets in Berlin for promenading, a rarity in this town where no one leads an idle life (*müßiggehen*) or, for that reason, walks idly (*müßig gehen*)."[22] Others like Eugen Szatmari found evidence only of the infamous Berlin tempo: "On Unter den Linden, Tauentzienstraße, and the Kurfürstendamm, one does not see people who just want to stroll. Everyone hurries. Everybody walks with a purpose."[23] Walther Kiaulehn pointed out that even "the stroller, the most charming appearance among men, has a difficult time in Berlin. After all, to walk in Berlin and not despair requires a special technique."[24] Resigned Otto Flake concluded that "flanerie is no fun here [in Berlin]."[25] Explaining these shortcomings with reference to national peculiarities, Rudolf Binding remarked: "The Germans on the street, man as well as woman, are slightly out of practice, slow and timid. They walk like they live: a little uncertain."[26] And speaking for the many Paris lovers among his colleagues, Kracauer asked: "Can someone walk with Berlinish tempo in Paris, even when he is really pressed for time?"[27] only to answer with an emphatic "no." For him, too, Berliners were condemned to remain mere passersby, incapable of surrendering, like the Parisian flaneurs, to the attractions of the metropolis.

In a humorous experiment with modern alternatives to walking, the *Berliner Tageblatt* for their 1 January 1929 issue invited Alfred Polgar, Alfred Döblin, Arnold Zweig, and others to ride on a bus from Unter den Linden to Halensee, with each author describing a different segment of the journey.[28] Other critics used automobiles to reenact the dissolution of the cityscape in a rush of animated images and bodily sensations. Benjamin von Brentano, for instance, chose driving over walking with the argument that "when I walk on foot, I barely get ahead. In Berlin one cannot even walk from the Kurfürstendamm to Friedrichstraße. No one has so much time."[29] Arthur Eloesser remarked: "It is much more natural to drive through a street in Berlin, passing over or under it, than to wander along its sides with measured haste."[30] The last frontier in the writing of the city text was reached when critics discovered flying as the form most suited to give them a sense of personal control. It was with such intentions that Polgar referred to the view from above as "the ideal position for the observer,"[31] and that Alfons Paquet advocated aerial photography as a model for all future writing: "We become apprentices in reading the earth and experience the overwhelming victory of a new kind of seeing."[32]

As a social type, aesthetic disposition, and critical attitude, the flaneur brought together the main elements for articulating the crisis of bourgeois subjectivity. Excluded from the urban utopias promoted in the name of a future community or society, flanerie came to be identified with the unproductive (i.e., also largely female) bourgeois culture that had reached fullest articulation in the subjectivism and aestheticism of the turn of the century. After World War I, this anachronistic figure allowed writers to register their opposition to the process of quantification, standardization, and massification and to maintain a sense of individual agency and control, even if from a position of marginality or through the rituals of simulation.[33] Precisely these regressive strategies contributed to the rediscovery of the flaneur—and with it, of Hessel—as a figure of narcissistic self-realization in the New Subjectivity of the 1970s, and they explain its continued relevance as a model of postmodern subjectivity and contemporary urban life, for instance, in critical studies on the shopping mall or the worldwide web.

The elevation of flanerie to a theoretical concept has prevented a closer look at the historical conditions that accompanied its introduction into the specific configurations of German urbanism and modernity.[34] Despite calls for a more precise typology of "those who walk" by Hanns-Josef Ortheil, Michael Bienert, Joachim Schlör, and Jörg Plath, the Weimar flaneur continues to inspire sweeping claims by, among others, Anke Gleber about flanerie as "the central perspective of Weimar reality."[35] The appearance of the female flaneur, or *flaneuse,* in the writings of Irmgard Keun, Vicki Baum, Gabriele Tergit, and Charlotte Wolff undoubtedly signaled the greater freedom of movement claimed by a new generation of emancipated women. As has been shown by Gleber, this female flanerie is indeed inseparable from the assertion of female subjectivity in the public sphere. However, both male and female flaneurs continued to move within an urban environment divided and demarcated along class lines. As a consequence, the pleasures of flanerie cannot be separated from the assumptions of bourgeois privilege, especially when the flaneur crosses the lines of propriety, transgressing into forbidden sexualized territory, or explores the consequences of unemployment, poverty, and homelessness. More specifically, the equation of the flaneur with a perceptual mode, psychological disposition, or conceptual framework ends up bracketing the social dimensions of urban experience and transforming the external world into a projection screen for individual pleasures and anxieties. Based on such defensive strategies, the nostalgia for the flaneur since the 1980s has perpetuated what this retrograde figure promised to achieve already during the 1920s: to preserve or restore a position of subjectivity, even if that means reducing the cityscape to a mere extension of the fragmented, threatened self. As an integral part of Weimar architectural culture, the flaneur may indeed have been "a harmless figure,"[36] to use Bienert's characterization, but he also occupied a somewhat problematic position in the changing topographies of class, a point confirmed by the different modes of walking chosen by Kracauer and Hessel.

Aside from the lack of historical specificity in the allegorical readings of flanerie, it is the figure's innate resistance to social experiences that accounts for his extraterritorial status within the social upheavals and political confrontations of the period. In this sense, the difficulties of walking in Berlin reflect not only the accelerated speed of urban life, the changing composition of the urban crowd, and the worsening economic situation; these difficulties also refer to growing obstacles to the freedom of individual movement in the form of new racisms and nationalisms. In their desire to be free of the delusions of bourgeois individualism, a few urban intellectuals subsequently joined the revolutionary masses; others identified with the emancipatory effects of modern mass culture. Cognizant of the central role of the metropolis in the history of Jewish emancipation, German-Jewish intellectuals in particular used the affinities between the metropolis and the feuilleton to develop more contemporary forms of cultural critique out of the original meaning of *discursus,* that is, of walking or running around. Their experience of discrimination made them acutely aware of the modern metropolis as a hostile and dangerous place. After all, what in Paris, capital of the nineteenth century, could still be celebrated as a "botanizing on the asphalt" (to cite Benjamin) turned, during the lifetimes of Kracauer, Hessel, Tucholsky, Roth, Polgar, and Benjamin, into movements driven increasingly by lack of choice. Under these precarious circumstances, a generation of "intellectual nomads,"[37] to use Spengler's disparaging term, made the streets and cafés near Kurfürstendamm their provisional home, a testimony to the productive alliance of modern architecture and consumer culture that sustained Weimar Berlin and endowed its founding sites with rich allegorical meaning.

II. Hessel's Urban Flaneries

Among the critics walking and writing on the Kurfürstendamm, Franz Hessel indeed stands out because of his remarkable ability to enjoy its myriad attractions without experiencing any of the difficulties reported by his colleagues. While his friend Kracauer suffered intensely from spatial alienation, this quintessential Weimar flaneur maintained a perfect distance from the urban scene and produced highly impressionistic city texts more typical of the prewar world of Simmel and Endell than the hustle and bustle of the so-called Golden Twenties:

Since there are so many opportunities on the stretch from Wittenbergplatz to Halensee to shop, eat, drink, visit the theater, cinema or cabaret, one can risk promenading without a clear aim and focus only on the undreamed-of adventures of the eye. His [the flaneur's] endeavors are greatly helped by glass and artificial light, the latter especially with a bit of daylight or at dusk. Then everything becomes indeterminable, new proximities and distances appear, including the auspicious combination *où l'indécis au précis se joint.*[38]

Hessel's anachronistic stance is important for this study because it sheds further light on the defensive strategies available to Weimar intellectuals and their middle-class readers. Using the old-fashioned habitus of the flaneur as a protection against the threat of social leveling, he clearly defines the conditions under which the metropolis can be reduced to its sensory qualities and aesthetic effects. Whereas Kracauer's city texts uncover the violence inherent in the urbanization of consciousness, Hessel de facto reduces the cityscape to an extension of the narcissistic (male) subject and his contradictory desires for complete control over, and full absorption into, the cityscape. Where Kracauer uses architecture to measure the distance between subject and object, individual and collective, Hessel creates phantasmagoric spaces that promise a sense of harmony and wholeness but, in the end, only implicate him more closely in the laws of commodity culture.

The preceding quotation is taken from *Ein Spaziergänger in Berlin* (A Stroller in Berlin, 1929), the book that, since its reedition in 1984 as *Ein Flaneur in Berlin,* has made Hessel the most famous Weimar flaneur and a central figure in the Benjamin-inspired scholarship on Berlin urbanism, modernism, and flanerie. After spending several years in Paris, Hessel had returned to Berlin in 1927 to write for *Das Tagebuch* and *Die Literarische Welt* and to work as an editor for the Rowohlt publishing house. *A Stroller in Berlin* combines early writings on the flaneur, inspired by the crucial encounter with Paris, and later writings on Berlin, which began with various journalistic assignments. Much of the book is devoted to the kind of well-known facts and anecdotes easily available in popular city histories and tourist guides. Yet once he leaves the sightseeing tour that starts on Unter den Linden and covers most of the historical attractions, Hessel, or his literary persona, stops being a pedestrian (*Spaziergänger*) and becomes what his critics have described as a flaneur.

Like Benjamin's "art of straying" and his "obstinate and voluptuous hovering on the brink,"[39] Hessel's art of walking always requires an initial willingness to let the city determine his movements. Yet for this personal friend of Benjamin, the urban settings are less emblems of modernity than parts of an ever-changing rebus that, despite its enigmatic appearance, hides no secrets except its complete availability to free association. Consequently, the convergence of walking, reading, and writing in the city text generates little of the allegorical force found in Kracauer and Benjamin and functions above all as an instrument of solipsistic wandering or wondering. With the Kurfürstendamm and Tauentzienstraße as his teachers, Hessel proclaims: "*Flanerie* (*Spazierengehen*) is a kind of reading of the street in which people's faces, displays, shopwindows, outdoor cafés, trams, cars, trees turn into letters that together form words, sentences, and pages in a perpetually new book."[40] In writing the city text, this flaneur-critic receives inspiration from the fashionable neon signs, "the glowing letters that run along the roofs across billboards,"[41] and guidance from the ubiquitous advertising literature (*Reklameliteratur*) on advertising pillars, buildings, subways, and busses. By translating spatial relations into textual effects, Hessel turns the metropolis into a projection screen that changes with every new impression and mental processing of that impression. In artificial light he finds both a medium and a metaphor for his ambulatory method, with three-dimensional space transformed into two-dimensional images by "the fleeting band of neon signs that are about to conquer the façades of Berlin, flattening and leveling them in the process."[42] Artificial light superimposes a layer of dreams and promises on the solidity of brick and stone and conceals the social formations inscribed in the spatial layout of the metropolis. The resulting dematerialization of urban architecture and the incorporation of spatial phenomena into the dreamscape of modern subjectivity create an imaginary city space safe from the provocations of class (and gender, for that matter) and the incursions of mass culture and modernity; the pleasures of flanerie as a "waking dream"[43] are inextricably linked to such processes of exclusion.

Using the flaneur persona as a filter and a shield, Hessel approaches the city's diverse neighborhoods in the same appreciative but detached manner. Typically alone, but sometimes with a female companion, he moves on foot and by car, takes the bus or, for a long tour of the rivers and canals, even embarks on a boat trip. He pays equal attention to movie palaces and historical palaces, department stores and homeless shelters, the large flower market and the central slaughterhouse, and the zoological garden and the Sportpalast, a famous meeting hall. During the day, cafés and restaurants are his favorite places from which he turns urban experience into a form of free association. At night, hotel bars, popular revues, theater plays, sporting events, and amusement parks reveal to him the attractions of big city life. While Hessel takes advantage of public transportation when venturing into the outskirts of Berlin, walking remains his preferred form of moving in the historic center. The tempo and rhythm of walking establish the conditions under which the familiar sites are translated into textual effects; the shifting perspectives afforded by walking turn the surrounding objects and events into dreamlike images waiting to be deciphered. Describing his poetics of walking, Hessel recommends that "this somewhat old-fashioned form of advancing on two legs should be elevated to an especially pure, purposeless pleasure" because it makes possible "a letting-go of oneself (*Sichgehenlassen*)."[44] Such an approach to everyday phenomena is founded on a regressive desire to recover the freshness of perception through a clear separation between the city as signifier and as signified. Hessel confesses: "I want to linger on the First Look. I want to discover or recover the First Look at the city in which I live."[45] By walking without apparent aim and by practicing a slow-motion gaze, the flaneur transforms the metropolis into the mythical world of childhood where feelings of omnipotence are not yet compromised by the recognition of difference. In instructing his readers on how to reach this state of passive receptivity, Hessel advises them to "visit your own city," "take a vacation from everyday life," "get to know thresholds," and "become part of the crowd," but he also warns them not to "walk entirely without goal. . . . Plan to arrive somewhere."[46] In this context, his admonition to the modern flaneur— "read it [the street], but do not criticize it too much"[47]—must be understood as a tacit acceptance of the status quo or, even worse, as sensualist indulgence without any consideration of the social realities bracketed by these playful exercises.

Not surprisingly, from the perspective of the native as tourist, inarticulate wonderment is bound to be the standard response to New Building. "I want to begin with the future";[48] this is how Hessel, with an architect (probably Jean Krämer) as a guide, moves from Mendelsohn's celebrated Universum Theater on the Kurfürstendamm and the large exhibition grounds at the end of Kaiserdamm to the architect's own construction projects on Knobelsdorffstraße in Charlottenburg and Müllerstraße in Wedding (fig. 4.6). Faced with a city-in-progress, Hessel ruminates on the relationship between blueprint and building and its implications for the process of writing. His observation that "around us grows an entire city out of the architect's words" betrays his fascination with the power of language to create, like architecture, "a unified total character (*Gesamtcharakter*)."[49] In a typical moment of disengagement from the provocation of modern mass society, he then uses his experience of these construction sites to defend the limits of his critical imagination and assert that "I am still incapable of describing this new, coming Berlin. I can only praise it."[50]

Fig. 4.6. Jean Krämer, Müllerstraße residential district. Hajos and Zahn, *Berliner Architektur,* 73. Courtesy of Gebr. Mann Berlin.

The literary strategies that balance such a persistent infatuation with things in the state of becoming with an equally stubborn refusal of judgment or involvement are very apparent in Hessel's detailed description of a large department store, possibly the Wertheim flagship store on Leipziger Straße. Under his desiring gaze, the store's interior dissolves into a series of visual impressions that give rise to highly fetishistic investments. Hessel's appreciation of the skillful scenarios of seduction is aided by his passive response to the displayed splendor. Confronted with "clearly laid-out scenes of great organization that spoil the visitor through the high level of their comfort," he experiences complete self-abandon through the encounter with mundane objects such as "circulating brass stands," "shining parquet floors," "luminous atria and winter gardens," "decorative canopies of velvet and silk," and so forth.[51] A very similar celebration of objects irrespective of their function can be found in a piece on Behrens's AEG Turbine Hall on Hüttenstraße. Like the department store, the production site gives rise only to the spectacle of perpetual change and the pleasure of disengaged spectatorship. Through a series of associations that ignore the conditions of production, the factory hall is magically transformed into one of the city's famous "temples of the machine" and "churches of precision."[52] Remaining true to his aesthetics of disengagement, Hessel concludes once again that "it is not necessary to understand everything; one only needs to watch how things are constantly moving and changing."[53]

Whether visiting public housing estates in Britz, upscale residential areas in Dahlem, or working-class tenements in Kreuzberg, Hessel approaches all neighborhoods with the same peculiar mixture of amazement and indifference. Whether traversing famous squares like Potsdamer Platz or visiting their cinematic doubles in the Tempelhof film studios, he always resorts to the same rituals of reading the city as text—that is, of using the external stimuli as a prosthetic device in achieving internal closure and, in the process, denying the power of the metropolis as public sphere. On his expeditions into poorer neighborhoods he is confronted with many signs of urban squalor and decay, but his descriptions highlight only their picturesque qualities. All external distinctions—between old and new, and rich and poor—are integrated into a larger system of identifications and incorporations. Social and economic relationships in the modern metropolis become relevant only insofar as they present to the flaneur a spectacle of ongoing transformation. Needless to say, such subjectivism blinds Hessel entirely to the political confrontations taking place on the streets of Weimar Berlin. Thus one of the first events organized by the Nazi Party at the Sportpalast on Potsdamer Straße prompts the observation that "without their insignia, the brazen Berlin boys from both political camps [the Nazis and the Communists] would be indistinguishable. . . . Both are a manifestation of the same joie de vivre."[54]

Such politically naive statements bring into relief the interpretative strategies through which the Weimar flaneur protects his bourgeois sensibilities from the conflicts and struggles of postwar urban society. A similar lack of awareness informs Hessel's defensive explanation that his kind of walking, far from being "a bourgeois-capitalist pleasure,"[55] is also a luxury and privilege of the poor, presumably those looking for jobs or lining up for food rations. Under the sway of turn-of-the-century aestheticism but no longer able to rely on its ideological support structure, the modern flaneur can only turn the metropolis into an extension of his threatened sense of self, which is one of the reasons why Weimar flanerie remains so closely tied to the crisis of masculinity and takes on very different meanings when practiced by the few female flaneurs. Bernd Witte comments on this dilemma when he defends Hessel against accusations of escapism by arguing, "In accordance with his deepest intention, he seeks to remove his own life, and that of his friends, from the power structures of society and transform it into a text—the only way of realizing the hoped-for freedom from power and the renunciation of possession."[56] In the process, the entire question of referentiality—and by extension, of empathy, solidarity, and commitment—is bracketed in favor of the endless possibilities of combining objects, forms, materials, textures, images, and events in the individual's field of vision. This regressive, self-protective function is most apparent in the equation of aimless walking with the act of reading, which confirms the flaneur as the creator of his own experiences. In his review of Hessel's *A Stroller in Berlin,* Benjamin, who just before had completed *Einbahnstraße* (One-way Street, 1928), his modernist montage version of Weimar flanerie, acknowledges the connection by describing Hessel's metropolis as a bourgeois interior: "For the masses as well as the flaneur, glossy enamel corporate nameplates are as good a wall-decoration, as an oil painting is for the homebody sitting in his living room, or even better; the firewalls are their desks, the newspaper kiosk their library, letterboxes their bronze statuettes, benches their boudoir, and the café terrace the bay window from which they can look down on their property."[57]

When Benjamin refers to *A Stroller in Berlin* as "a process of memorizing while strolling around" and portrays Hessel as "this great philosopher of thresholds,"[58] he really speaks about his own critical investment in walking as a mnemonic device. In Benjamin's reading of Hessel, the pre-history of modernity in nineteenth-century Paris finds a logical continua-tion in Weimar Berlin as the full realization of modernity. In calling Hessel the "priest of the genius loci,"[59] Benjamin projects his own theoretization of history and memory on his friend's literary excursions and claims the latter's sensualist approach for the very different problems of the modern allegorist. This is reason enough for Gudrun Klatt to interpret Benjamin's reading of Hessel as a way of dealing with his own "Berlin syndrome."[60] The degree to which both Hessel and Benjamin in fact remained outsiders to the larger debates raging throughout Weimar architectural culture can been seen in the way they responded to Werner Hegemann's highly critical history of urban development offered in *Das steinere Berlin* (Berlin Built in Stone). Detecting beauty even in the infamous tenements, Hessel dismisses Hegemann's bleak diagnosis and expresses the hope "that we should be able to build an honest city out of the muddle of the horrible and the valu-able, the solid and the fake—today as well as tomorrow."[61] Responding to what he calls Hegemann's fanatical negativism, Benjamin, too, evokes the presence of beauty in the midst of deprivation, but at least he does so from the perspective of those living in dilapidated houses and run-down areas. "Even the unplanned rawness of this neighborhood," he rightly insists, "has its beauty, not only for the snobbish flaneur from Berlin West but also for the Berliner, the Zille Berliner himself, a beauty that is deeply related to his language and his customs."[62]

III. Kracauer's Urban Hieroglyphics

Assessing the defensive strategies available within the Weimar feuilleton means continuing with the figure of the flaneur, but this time less as a so-cial type than a reaction formation that combines perceptual, conceptual, as well as affective positions. Like Hessel and Benjamin, Kracauer will-ingly submitted to the "street intoxication (*Straßenrausch*)"[63] that took hold of him in Berlin (and, above all, in Paris), and he refers to it throughout his work, including in his later philosophy of history. Since the harmless "pleasure of flanerie" can at any given point turn into the more dangerous "intoxication of flanerie," the urban critic must master a difficult balancing act between detachment and surrender and perfect his skills in the "pro-fession of the flaneur."[64] For Kracauer this means restoring the link be-tween urban experience and social practice; hence Eckhardt Köhn's conclusion that "Kracauer's metaphysical flaneur interprets the big city by living it."[65] Defining its implications in aesthetic terms, David Frisby describes Kracauer's work as a deconstruction of urban experience that moves historical debates on the metropolis beyond the sensualism of flanerie and the modernist paradigm of shock.[66] Frisby's reading of Kracauer suggests that the productive tension between the textual and the spatial, and between the allegorical and the social, allows for both possibilities: a recovering of the visible without fetishizing perception and a deciphering of the modern without denying its material basis. However, neither Köhn nor Frisby moves beyond the constellations of Weimar flanerie that acknowledge the crisis of subjectivity as a constituent element of modern architectural culture and metropolitan life but hesitate or fail to connect this typically bourgeois dilemma to the crisis of traditional class society.

To what degree Kracauer's flaneur perceives the streets as inhospitable can be seen in the description of an underpass near Charlottenburg Station that prompts the revealing remark, "It is probably the opposition between the closed, unshakable system of construction and the volatile human muddle that creates the horror."[67] Psychologically, this confrontation finds expression less in classic agoraphobia as a fear of open spaces than in what Freud calls *Angstlust,* that peculiar mixture of fear and pleasure, terror and excitement, which for Kracauer encapsulates the experience of modern urbanity.[68] The metropolis as *Angstraum* (space of fear) can be found everywhere in Kracauer's descriptions of Weimar Berlin. "Our architecture is terribly dynamic," he writes at one point. "It either surges up unexpectedly into the vertical or tries to get away in a horizontal fashion. And the streets—when I think of Kantstraße, I am immediately overcome by the irresistible desire to escape without further delay to its vanishing point, which must lie somewhere in infinity, near the radio station."[69] The same vacillation between flight and enticement propels the protagonists in Kracauer's fictional tours through Berlin. In *Ginster* (Broom, 1928), a young architectural student indulges in "long, lonely walks, topographical excursions that have nothing to do with ordinary walks,"[70] and that are as much an exorcism of personal anxieties as an instrument of critical reflection. Confirming this point, in the posthumously published *Georg,* which was written in 1929, a young journalist arrives on the Kurfürstendamm, attracted by the neon lights and pulled in by the masses as they "formed dense clusters that continued to disperse and, in the same moment, combine anew," thus giving form to the same spatial configurations that preoccupied the Berlin correspondent for the *Frankfurter Zeitung*.[71] Time and again, Kracauer uses the spatiality of social phenomena to address the dilemmas of modern subjectivity, applying a strategy that goes back to his "old desire to live extraterritorially"[72] and that reflects his deep discomfort with the conventions of bourgeois culture. Central to this process of textual spatialization is the confrontation of the bourgeois subject with the power of the modern masses and their ubiquitous presence in the principles of quantification, standardization, and massification.

The underlying tension between the defensive strategy of a bourgeois subjectivity in crisis and the tentative opening toward the urban collective can be studied exemplarily in Kracauer's writings about the Kurfürstendamm. To him this "modern victory boulevard"[73] represented an important test site in the making of the textual city: as the setting that gave rise to his critique of façade architecture, that extended his notion of the mass ornament to urban phenomena, and that motivated his most suggestive comments on the importance of waiting and forgetting, formulated within a larger theory of modernity and philosophy of history. It was the wave of storefront renovations on Kurfürstendamm that inspired the notion of façade architecture in the first place and prompted him to analyze the condition of modernity through its surface phenomena. The systematic assault on tradition, he argued, has profound implications for the organization of urban life: "Elsewhere the past remains attached to the places which it inhabited during its lifetime; on Kurfürstendamm it exits without leaving traces. . . . The ornaments, which formed a kind of bridge to yesterday, have been knocked off from many buildings. Now the violated façades stand without any support in time—symbols of a change without history that takes place behind them."[74] In failing to provide the city dweller with a sense of continuity, Kracauer argues, the "street without memory" thus becomes "the embodiment of an empty flowing time in which nothing is able to last."[75]

At the same time, in its very superficiality and transitoriness, the Kurfürstendamm divulges to Kracauer the hidden mechanisms of modern mass society and displays the unredeemed possibilities of a progressive mass culture. The photos of celebrities in the display cases still attest to the underlying pursuit of happiness and desire for beauty, and the new motion-picture palaces still convey a sense of the medium's original power. "Here, in pure externality, the audience encounters itself," he observes. "Its own reality is revealed in the fragmented sequence of splendid sense impressions. Were this reality to remain hidden to the viewers, they could neither challenge nor change it; its disclosure in distraction is therefore of *moral* significance."[76] Even when complaining about the demolition of old buildings, Kracauer never tries to salvage the past at the expense of the present or to downplay the oppressive effects of tradition. His characterization of Berlin as a city without history remains surprisingly unsentimental: "Berlin is the place where forgetting is easy; indeed, it seems as if this city possessed a magic potion to erase all memories. It is presence and makes it its goal to be all presence. . . . I know no other city that is able to shake off the past so promptly."[77] Forgetting, to be sure, represents an important part of urban development and growth. Yet when all traces of the past are sacrificed to the modernist cult of innovation and change, the resulting lack of substance produces the kind of buildings that "assert themselves only through the laws of physics and end up staring like hollow cardboard buildings into the metropolitan sky."[78] Walking on the Kurfürstendamm, Kracauer experiences this tension as an intense feeling of spatial alienation and metaphysical homelessness:

> One strolls through the streets in the evening, filled by a nonfulfillment from which no fullness can arise. Over there illuminated words move across the roofs, and sooner than expected one is projected from one's own emptiness into these alien advertisements. The body grows roots in the asphalt, and the mind, which is no longer our mind, moves with the enlightening light revelations endlessly from the night into the night![79]

Kracauer's close attention to the physical characteristics of urban space is inextricably linked to his professional biography. After completing a 1915 dissertation on Prussian wrought iron and after briefly working as an architect, he joined the *Frankfurter Zeitung* in 1921 and, in 1931, became head of feuilleton in the newspaper's Berlin office, a position he held until his emigration in 1933. During that time, he published countless film reviews, cultural essays, political commentaries, and short articles on consumer culture, mass entertainment, and other phenomena of urban life. Whether writing about amusement parks, movie theaters, homeless shelters, building exhibitions, department stores, or hotel lobbies, Kracauer always tested the material consistencies, spatial dimensions, and underlying stresses and fissures of modern mass society. The famous sites of Weimar Berlin allowed him to assess the contribution of modern mass media to new modes of perception and to contemplate the power of modern architecture in organizing the urban masses. Plans to publish the city texts in a book called *Straßen in Berlin und anderswo* (Streets in Berlin and Elsewhere) never materialized, however.[80]

In Kracauer's urban writings, Berlin's neighborhoods, squares, streets, and buildings are transformed into a mise-en-scène of modernity, with allegorical reading and social critique maintaining a perfect balance. In revealing the principles of construction shared by architecture and the city text, he systematically uncovers the new divisions and fault lines in the production of social space. By foregrounding the primacy of vision in the writing of the textual city, he acknowledges the influence of the cinema on both his own writing and the making of urban experience. At the same time, he uses a uniquely urban typology of spaces and places to counterbalance the derealization of metropolitan space promoted by photography and film. He systematically seeks out locations that reveal the growing social inequities and the uneven distribution of wealth, from the unemployment offices, homeless shelters, and shady gambling halls around the Zoologischer Garten Station to the racetrack in Mariendorf and the luxury stores on the Kurfürstendamm. His deep sympathies with those excluded from the plans for the New Berlin are evident throughout, from the lower-class woman waiting in front of a movie theater in Münzstraße to the unemployed gathering in a warming hall on Ackerstraße.

Focusing on the spatial organization of social relations allows Kracauer to reclaim questions of class for a textual reconstruction of the metropolis that neither dissolves urban phenomena into purely textual effects nor falls back on a naive belief in the representability of social processes. Especially his analysis of white-collar culture and its challenge to traditional class distinctions makes productive use of writing as a reconstruction of urban reality. This close attention to the spatial dialectics of mass culture and modernity makes Kracauer's writings a model for urban criticism, which explains why his city texts are often discussed without much reference to the particular conditions in Weimar Berlin. Insisting on a purely textual analysis, Michael Schröter observes that Kracauer's city images cannot be read outside the literary conventions that turn images into texts.[81] Gerwin Zohlen notes that Kracauer's textual cities must be described in physiognomic rather than phenomenological terms.[82] Taking this line of argumentation even further, Anthony Vidler argues that in Kracauer the café, the hotel, and even the city itself are "purely textual spaces,"[83] constructed only for discursive purposes. However, given the many connections between his city texts and his studies on white-collar workers, given the almost obsessive naming of specific streets and locations, and given the profound changes in his conceptualization of modern mass culture during the last years of the Weimar Republic, it would be a serious misreading not to consider Kracauer's contribution to the ongoing reconfiguration and rearticulation of class as a central category of urban life.

In fact, Kracauer wrote most of his Berlin texts during a period in which he abandoned philosophical speculation for more empirically based categories and the sociological inquiries presented in chapter 2. This materialist turn has been read in the context of old intellectual debts and new political challenges, but it must also be placed within a long-standing fascination, first expressed in relation to architecture, with the materials and materiality of urban life.[84] While the hidden correspondences between spaces (e.g., in reflections on the hotel lobby) remained central to his more speculative reflections on mass culture and modernity, the stabilization period brought greater attention to the dialectics of reason and myth and their resonance both in Weimar architectural culture and in the mentality of New Objectivity. Focusing on the spatial articulation of modern subjectivity allowed him to utilize aspects of architectural theory, urban sociology, film criticism, and vitalist thought for the kind of materialist critique usually identified with Critical Theory, reason enough to consider what Martin Jay calls Kracauer's "materialist dialectics"[85] and its unique tension between disenchantment and reenchantment as a preconfiguration of Adorno's dialectics of enlightenment.

In the most basic terms, Kracauer's contribution to Weimar architectural culture departs from the proposition that "reality is a construction."[86] What better way to test this proposition than by looking at the actual constructions that made up urban space and considering their functions within his city texts? In light of his emphatic calls for a progressive mass culture, which are most pronounced in the writings on film, his intense hostility toward modern architecture seems initially counterintuitive, but only if we fail to take into account his deep attachment to the classical metropolis as the ideal model of civic society and the bourgeois public sphere. Gerwin Zohlen has shown to what degree Kracauer's tastes and preferences express traditional views of the art of building first articulated in his own work as an architect and strongly rooted in prewar conceptions of metropolitan life.[87] Given the modernist rhetoric of form and function, it should not surprise that his main objections to New Building, those "high-rises and office buildings that no longer maintain any connection to things human,"[88] come together in highly speculative reflections on the meaning of the modern façade. Organizing the move from architectural element to discursive device, the façade assumes distinctly allegorical functions whenever he addresses more fundamental questions about authenticity, functionality, and everyday life. Whether richly embellished or stripped of all adornment, façades in Kracauer are invariably equated with concealment, deception, and falsification—in short, with ideology. Especially prevalent in the centers of mass consumption and entertainment, façade architecture brings into relief the tension between the emancipatory potential of modern mass culture and its corruption by commodity aesthetics and the culture industry. Surprisingly, it is the renovated storefronts on the Kurfürstendamm rather than the products of Wilhelmine historicism that become the main targets of his ideology critique; it is in the modernist attack on the ornament rather than the traditional forms of ornamentation that he locates the crisis of urban culture. Less concerned with the formal aspects of architectural modernism than its strategic enlistment in the rationalization of labor and leisure, Kracauer assumes such an antimodernist position in the name of enlightened modernity.

His passionate defense of grown urban structures and of urban traditions created through regular use is part of a multifaceted and not unambiguous response to the leveling of difference and the erasure of history in the modern metropolis. Whether writing about the renovated Linden Arcade between Friedrichstraße and Unter den Linden, the rituals of consumption in the Karstadt department store on Hermannplatz, the reopened Lunapark with its New York skyline and roller-coaster ride or the false worlds created at the Ufa studios in Babelsberg, Kracauer time and again uses the façade as a conceptual surface on which to articulate the failures of the project of modernity and to delineate the fault lines in the sociospatial dialectic. That his allegorical readings of the façades of Weimar modernity come with their own set of contradictions, including a metaphysically charged opposition between surface and depth, can be seen in his revealing remarks on the remodeled lobby of the famous Haus Vaterland amusement center that proves to him that New Objectivity is only a "façade that hides nothing, that does not wrest itself away from some depth but merely feigns to do so"[89] (fig. 4.7).

While the modernized interiors and exteriors of these great temples of mass diversion attracted Kracauer's greatest attention, it was in the modern building exhibitions and architectural competitions that he found the clearest evidence of the tyranny of architectural modernism and its false ethos of simplicity and equality. Thus the 1931 Building Exhibition with its

Fig. 4.7. Haus Vaterland, lobby. Hajos and Zahn, *Berliner Architektur* (1928), 16. Courtesy of Gebr. Mann Berlin.

Fig. 4.8. Ludwig Mies van der Rohe and Lilly Reich, glass room in *Die Wohnung* exhibition, Stuttgart, 1927. Courtesy of Mies van der Rohe Archive, Museum of Modern Art. Copyright 2007 Artists Rights Society (ARS), New York / VG Bild-Kunst, Bonn.

chilling visions of modern living inspired ominous comparisons to a "steel bath."[90] And the 1932 Weekend Exhibition "Sun, Air, and House" left him with frightful "scenarios of a new world"[91] whose didactic displays on public health and physical fitness appear to offer nothing but an argument for more rationalization. A rare acknowledgment of the subversive power of all such negativity can be found in an article on the 1927 Exhibition of the German Werkbund in Stuttgart (fig. 4.8). Describing Mies van der Rohe's and Lilly Reich's model rooms, he is particularly intrigued by the tension between architecture's utopian promise and the austerity of its designs, surmising that

> these new houses are probably *residues,* that is, contemporary configurations of elements purged of bad excess. And certainly present-day society alone is to be held responsible for these enduring compositions. But it would be good if they expressed, even more than is the case today, their mourning over the renunciation that they have to practice—that odd mourning, which clings to those phenomena banished into the glass surface. For building skeletons are not means in themselves, but the necessary threshold to a plenitude that no longer needs to be reduced and that today can only be produced negatively through mourning.[92]

Clearly, the opposition to New Building by a cultural critic known for his left-liberal leanings has less to do with stylistic preferences than with the symbolic meaning of architectural form, that is, its embeddedness in the material conditions of urban life. The unity of aesthetic and social practice, Kracauer implies, is destroyed by the modernist belief in absolute form and pure functionality. In ignoring historical continuities, the new buildings prevent experience from becoming part of the organization of spatial relations. Rather than formulating his critique in aesthetic terms, Kracauer reads the excesses of modernism in symptomatic terms—which means in terms of crisis—and concludes, "We are denied almost all positive statements at the moment. We can neither bear them in the language of literature nor in the language of architecture. That modern churches look like grain silos or train stations is certainly no coincidence, and it is definitely fitting that, of all things, the purely functional buildings . . . are the only true monuments of our times."[93]

What in Benjamin is alluded to in provocative reflections on the destructive character and what in Bloch inspires suggestive comments on the utopian potential of negativity finds its foremost expression in Kracauer's theorizing of surface phenomena as a similarly subversive trope of resistance and expectancy. His carefully phrased suggestion that New Building embodies progressive tendencies that elsewhere have not yet broken through to the surface introduces precisely such a possibility. Translated into political terms, this tentative opening toward the ethos of sobriety in New Building is most apparent in his recommendation in conjunction with the 1931 architectural competition for the remodeling of Schinkel's *Neue Wache* (New Guardshouse); for he advises that the chosen design "refrain from all false monumentality, that it be as sober as we should be and that it stand for nothing more than we deserve."[94] The winning design by Heinrich Tessenow possessed precisely this aura of modesty.

At their core, Kracauer's writings on urban architecture represent highly mediated reflections on the spatial organization of social difference. Formulating an urban hermeneutic that, in its imagery, recalls Benjamin's *Denkbild* (thought image), but without the latter's archaeology of modernity, remains primarily concerned with contemporary problems, Kracauer asserts at one point:

> Every social class has its space attributed to it. . . . Every typical space is produced through typical social conditions . . . [and] everything that is purposely overlooked participates in its construction. The spatial images (*Raumbilder*) are the dreams of society. Wherever the hieroglyphics of any spatial image are deciphered, there the basis of social reality presents itself.[95]

The reference to dreams is central to understanding the privileged position of architecture as a discourse of forced integration as well as hopeful anticipation. Kracauer's spatial images demarcate the conceptual and textual space where exterior and interior city are continuously negotiated and where individual perceptions connect to collective experiences. Just as films are "the daydreams of society,"[96] spatial practices are inextricably linked to the production of fantasies and illusions. Deciphering these *T/Raumbilder* (dream/spatial images) requires reading strategies that make explicit use of the Freudian distinction between manifest dream form and latent dream content. In the words of Kracauer: "the knowledge of cities is tied to the deciphering of their images as if spoken in a dream."[97] Reading the city text requires above all a willingness to abandon traditional modes of urban representation for the unstable grounds and the fragmented perspectives found in the essayistic tradition and the allegorical method; it also means accepting the indecipherability of the cityscape and its openness to ongoing revisions. Looking out of a window, he pensively alludes to the unavoidable blind spots and misreadings: "Wherever masses of stones and lines of streets come together, with their elements originating in vastly divergent interests, a cityscape materializes that . . . is as unstructured as nature and resembles a landscape in that it asserts itself unconsciously."[98]

Yet how are these spatial images, these dreamlike constellations, to be deciphered? According to Kracauer, reading the city texts requires specific strategies of defamiliarization until the streets resemble "the maze of lines on a pattern chart."[99] A model for such strategies can be found in the architectural plans studied by the young architect in *Ginster,* Kracauer's anonymously published semiautobiographical novel: "If he looked at them independently of the meaning they took on in combination with the front elevation, they appeared like black-and-white compositions of lines, letters, and empty planes whose beauty derived from their purposeless being."[100] Ignoring the purpose of these plans frees the spatial imagination from the confines of habit and convention and makes the most utilitarian objects available for aesthetic pleasure and the utopian promise inherent in all art. His detailed knowledge of the formal language of architecture functions like a solvent or catalyst in this process. "The architectural scraps are ciphered communications which only the initiated can decipher," observes Kracauer's fictional stand-in, only to add later that "as little as the writer can still rely on his sense of self, as little does the world provide the necessary props to hold him up, for both are mutually dependent."[101] From the plans' geometric patterns, a direct line leads to the notion of the mass ornament and the underlying belief that "the position that an epoch occupies in the historical process can be determined more strikingly from an analysis of its inconspicuous surface-level expressions than from the epoch's judgments about itself."[102]

The notion of the mass ornament has been used by Henrik Reeh to describe Kracauer's unique way of conceptualizing urban culture and assessing the tension between what he calls the desire for resubjectification and the desire for community and sociability. In the same way that the mass ornament for Reeh is a meeting place for Reason and Ratio—rationalized, but not rationalized enough to realize the progressive potential of mass culture—the spatial image mediates between subject and society, or, to be more precise, it makes problematic this very opposition. Placing Kracauer in the tradition of Simmel, Reeh writes: "Like Simmel, Kracauer attempts to revive the subjective factor to its former dominant position. But whereas Simmel saw the work of 'resubjectivizing' the so-called objective spirit as a predominantly individual project, Kracauer gives it—even in its individual aspects—a *social perspective.*[103] For Reeh, this process has three stages: the critique of the notion of the autonomous individual and the disintegration and expansion of the subject into the city space; the gradual recognition of social reality but still from an individual perspective; and, finally, the manifestation of social subjectivity in the material culture of the metropolis. As a "unifying optics," the mass ornament shows both the potential and the limits of this process of resubjectivization in its tentative opening toward the urban collective. It links the concreteness of embellishment to the abstractness of allegory and, in so doing, functions as what he calls "an abstracted expression of reality."[104] The same might be said about the spatial image, with the tension between conception and desire, self-affirmation and self-abandonment an integral part of its semiotic instability and discursive elusiveness.

In closing, we might want to use Kracauer's extensive remarks on the remodeling of Alexanderplatz to consider the dialectical force of the spatial image in relation to the utopian vision of the New Berlin. Functioning as a social space, an architectural form, and a spatial metaphor, the famous square allows him to theorize modernity in the dialectical terms of destruction and preservation, but it also enables him to affirm a thus diagnosed subjectivity in crisis as the only position from which to comprehend this constitutive tension. Thus the ubiquitous signs of devastation in these "torn-up landscapes of stone" occasion the observation that "the discomfort emanating from them is better than the false peace of palaces."[105] Confessing to spatial anxieties in terms that, beginning with references to the wind rushing across the open terrain, bear a close similarity to *Berlin Alexanderplatz,* Kracauer is particularly unsettled by the lack of clear perspectives and boundaries. The frantic building activities prompt his ironic praise for the new Alexanderplatz as "a model of organization" and an image of "artificial perfection,"[106] two phrases that could have been taken from a textbook on modern city planning. At the same time, his reference to the functionalist credo "make room (*Platz*) for the square (*Platz*)" and his use of military terms such as "no man's land" expose the violence behind the project of urban renewal, as does his description of the fortresslike new corporate headquarters of a department store chain on the square's outer edges—a reference to Philipp Schäfer's 1931 building for the Karstadt corporation. In what ways Kracauer's highly suggestive observations on Alexanderplatz as a battlefield of modernity were shared by others will become apparent in the next chapter when the spatial images return as actual photographs. Moreover, in what ways the crisis of subjectivity remained closely linked to the rearticulation of class will become very obvious in *Berlin Alexanderplatz*'s Franz Biberkopf, Kracauer's uncanny double from the lumpenproletariat.

CHAPTER 5

Picturing the New Berlin:
Photography, Architecture, and Modern Mass Society

Bertolt Brecht once famously remarked that "the 'simple reproduction of reality' says less than ever about that reality. A photograph of the Krupp works or of the AEG yields almost nothing about these institutions. Reality as such has slipped into the domain of the functional."[1] Similarly, in a critical review of New Vision photography, Walter Benjamin asserted that photography "can no longer record a tenement block or a refuse heap without transfiguring it. Needless to say, photography is unable to convey anything about a power station or a cable factory other than, 'What a beautiful world!'"[2]

Determined to challenge the false claims on the real made in the name of modern photography, Brecht and Benjamin probably would have said the same about the many photographs of Mossehaus (1921–23), the headquarters of the Mosse publishing company and one of Erich Mendelsohn's signature buildings in Berlin. They would have come to similar conclusions about Weimar photographers' repeated efforts to capture the new Alexanderplatz in its spatial and social dimensions. Furthermore, they would have been right in detecting a close connection between the two developments explored in this chapter: on the one side, the growing influence of visual culture in creating new urban identities and subjectivities, a process to which the Mosse corporation contributed in significant ways, and, on the other side, the becoming-invisible of the power structures in the modern metropolis, a process with particular implications for Alexanderplatz as the most contested site in the Berlin of the Weimar Republic. Moving beyond Brecht's and Benjamin's exclusive focus on the individual photograph and paying greater attention to the image-text relationship, this chapter uses images of Mossehaus and Alexanderplatz to reconstruct the contribution of architectural photography to the discourse of massification and examine the rarely discussed role of urban photography within the spatial politics of class.

In the photographic archives of Weimar Berlin, specific images of famous buildings, streets, and squares have come to serve as conduits to a historical cityscape romanticized in the myth of "the golden twenties," theorized in reflections on urban subjectivity and Weimar flanerie, and scrutinized in scholarly works on German mass culture and modernity. Confronted with yet another image of this street or that square, we sometimes cannot help but fall into certain patterns of misrecognition.[3] The traffic tower on Potsdamer Platz, the new storefronts on the Kurfürstendamm, the construction site on Alexanderplatz: we have seen it all before. In coffee-table books, exhibition catalogues, scholarly monographs, and tourist brochures, as well as in official publications by the new city council and federal government, Weimar Berlin has taken on a ghostly afterlife in the medium of photography. From the nostalgia postcards with their brown tints to the Berlin-related Web sites with their virtual tours, the snapshots from the 1920s now appear so self-explanatory that we no longer recognize to what degree they themselves once participated in the profound transformation of urban space through new visual media and practices.[4]

In fact, the nostalgic investment in these Berlin photographs perpetuates patterns of excluding, bracketing, and forgetting that were already fully in place during the period under investigation. Speaking about the hidden meanings of photographs, Allan Sekula maintains that "a photograph communicates by means of its association with some hidden, or implicit text; it is this text, or system of hidden linguistic propositions, that carries the photography into the domain of readability."[5] Accordingly, what is missing entirely in the photographic representation of Mossehaus and what is barely acknowledged in the countless images of Alexanderplatz are the city dwellers themselves, who depend on visual representations for acquiring urban identities and developing mental maps. Likewise, what is written out of most photographic histories of Weimar Berlin are the conflicts, struggles, and antagonisms produced by the transition from the traditional class society of the prewar years to the kind of functional differentiation envisioned in the program of the New Berlin. In recognition of this dynamics of presence and absence, our discussion of architectural photography and urban photography approaches the visualization of modern mass society through one of its central tropes, architecture, and reconstructs the complex mechanisms of displacement that define the relationship between architecture and class.

Urban photography in the Weimar period participated in two interrelated projects, the production of an iconography of the modern city dweller, as personified by the white-collar worker, and the containment of the spectacle of the urban masses, as embodied by the revolutionary proletariat. Even a cursory look at Weimar era publications confirms that the masses, as a photographic subject, could not simply be ignored; they were ubiquitous, perspicuous, but also unpredictable and elusive. The snapshots from demonstrations, rallies, strikes, and street battles on the front pages of Berlin's leading newspapers attest to the power of the radicalized working class—and, in similar ways, of the nationalist and *völkisch* right—to disrupt the smooth functioning of the city economy and to influence the direction of local and national politics. At the same time, the vignettes of daily life on shopping boulevards and in outdoor cafés, department stores, and movie palaces conjure up a cosmopolitan society fully aware of social, economic, and ethnic differences, but united in the dream of mass mobility and individual self-realization. Photographers participated actively in the transformation of these multitudes into a discursive and aesthetic phenomenon and established a framework, quite literally, through which to define the modern city dweller in visual and spatial terms. Through innovative page layout, typography, and image-text relationships, the illustrated newspapers and magazines trained new modes of perception and cultural sensibilities and thus invited their readers to participate in new forms of sociability, community, and collectivity.

The close alliance between New Building and New Vision photography established the conditions under which architectural photography acquired important new functions within the changing sociospatial dialectic and confirmed the increasing significance of "architecture as mass media."[6] Translating spatial elements into visual terms, Weimar photographers completed the cycle of imaging/imagining on which New Building so greatly depended, not least because many of its projects remained unrealized. Their photographs of buildings, streets, and squares contributed to the ongoing remapping of public and private space, interior and exterior space, and built and unbuilt space. They participated in the spatial organization of housing, commerce, industry, transportation, entertainment, and recreation. They profoundly influenced prevailing definitions of urban culture, civic life, and the public sphere. Last but not least, these carefully composed and purposefully framed images of the modern metropolis participated in the transformation of urban space into perceptual space and made possible the superimposition of an ideal, or imaginary, city onto the contested topographies of Weimar urbanism. This pervasive medialization of urban life played a key part in aligning modern architecture and city planning with the urban imaginary of the Weimar Republic as the first German experiment in democracy. In that context, making sense of the metropolis as the home of the modern masses meant seeing architectural interventions as the preconfiguration, in formal terms, of very different and yet to be realized social configurations. It is as part of these complicated processes that we must assess the contribution of architectural photography to the sociospatial dialectic of modern mass society.

I. Architecture and Photography in Weimar Culture

No photograph exists in isolation; it is always part of an extended dialogue—carried out across different art forms, media technologies, and interpretive registers—about that which remains inaccessible to the camera; in this particular case, the reconfiguration and rearticulation of class society. Because of the overriding concern with representability, most of the photographers discussed in this chapter adhered to a realist aesthetic despite growing awareness of its aesthetic limitations and epistemological pitfalls. Photographic realism offered the (illusory) promise of immediacy and transparency in a predominantly literary culture haunted by the crisis of language and the decline of literature as a master discourse. Yet harnessing the critical powers of photography invariably meant compensating for the indeterminacy of the image by adding captions or texts and supplementing its singular perspective through the multiperspectivism of photomontage or the photo essay.

Consequently, we must approach the visualization of Weimar mass society through three artistic practices—photo reportage, architectural photography, and art photography—that greatly influenced its forms and functions throughout the 1920s. Likewise we must read these images through the publishing practices—of the illustrated press, the architectural profession, and the art establishment—that defined their systems of distribution and modes of consumption. To begin with, the illustrated magazines favored image-text relations that anchored photographic meaning in the larger narratives of Weimar mass culture and modernity. The architectural publications added critical readings that turned modernist architecture into an object of aesthetic appreciation and an agent of social change; and the art books introduced formal techniques that transformed the metropolis into a laboratory of new sensations, experiences, and identities.

Thinking about the relationship between modern architecture and photography means, first of all, acknowledging the ubiquity of city images in Weimar culture. Photographs of Berlin could be found everywhere: in daily newspapers and their illustrated supplements, in photobooks and travel guides, and in cultural magazines and architectural trade journals. Their proliferation was largely due to a veritable explosion of mass publishing during the Weimar Republic and a progressive medialization of metropolitan culture that, in turn, made the discourses of the urban increasingly dependent on media practices and mediated experiences. In the feuilleton, Berlin was regularly hailed as a laboratory for new ways of seeing, with film and photography at the forefront of a mechanization of perception often diagnosed through phrases such as "the shock of the new" and "the snapshot quality of things." Yet Berlin was not just the center of the publishing industry, with the *Zeitungsviertel* (newspaper district) home to the conservative Scherl, the liberal Ullstein, and the progressive Mosse publishing houses. The German capital also had one of the most diverse newspaper scenes in the world. In 1932, thirty-nine daily newspapers appeared in Berlin alone, from mass publications such as Ullstein's *Berliner Morgenpost* (with an edition of almost 600,000) and Scherl's *Berliner Lokal Anzeiger* to highly specialized newspapers with a circulation of no more than one or two hundred copies. As names such as *B.Z. am Mittag* or *Nachtausgabe* suggest, many newspapers were published several times a day, making the reading of newspapers an integral part of everyday life in the big city.[7]

Through its influential *Bilderdienst* (photo agency), Ullstein, which published the popular *Berliner Morgenpost,* played a key role in the production and distribution of photographic images and contributed to what some contemporaries denounced as an Ullsteinization of the visual imagination. Yet in terms of numbers, it was the ultraconservative Hugenberg concern that truly dominated the contemporary media landscape. Combining the Scherl publishing house, the Telegraphen-Union news agency, and various advertising firms in the largest German media conglomerate, Alfred Hugenberg's influence increased even more after he acquired the Universum Film-AG (Ufa). In the mid-1920s, the communist media mogul Willi Münzenberg used the organizational structure of the Internationale Arbeiterhilfe (IAH) to build a powerful media empire that almost rivaled the Hugenberg concern in scope and influence. Offering a viable alternative to the bourgeois media, he took over Neue Deutsche Verlag in 1924 to publish *Berlin am Morgen, Welt am Abend,* and most famously, *Arbeiter-Illustrierte Zeitung (AIZ),* all of which relied heavily on photography in their reporting of daily news from Berlin and the world.

Illustrated magazines could be found everywhere in Weimar Berlin, but especially at the ubiquitous kiosks and in bars and cafés, with the available choices ranging from Scherl's conservative *Die Woche,* Mosse's more progressive *Weltspiegel,* and *Zeitbilder* of the liberal *Vossische Zeitung* to party publications such as the Social Democratic *Volk and Zeit,* the illustrated supplement of *Vorwärts,* and the *Roter Stern,* the illustrated supplement of the Communist Party's *Rote Fahne.*[8] The most influential was *Berliner Illustrirte Zeitung (BIZ)*, published by Ullstein as part of a diverse assortment of daily newspapers, illustrated magazines, and literary journals that all profited from the convergence of visual media, urban culture, and white-collar society. *BIZ* started publication in 1890 and reached a circulation of two million in 1930, the highest among all illustrated magazines in Europe. Kurt Korff, its influential editor-in-chief, responded to the acceleration of modern life and the growing need for image-based information by making photographs a central part of the magazine's graphic design and editorial profile. Highly critical of such trends, Kracauer linked the entire illustrated press to the conformist culture of illusionism and concluded: "In the illustrated magazines, people see the very world that the illustrated magazines prevent them from perceiving. . . . Never before has a period known so little about itself."[9]

Photojournalists played a key role both in establishing a corpus of city images for easy consumption and in making mass publishing an integral part of urban culture. Equipped with light-sensitive film stock and smaller cameras, including the legendary Leica and Ermanox, they were able to enter many public spaces unnoticed, documenting, like Erich Salomon, "famous contemporaries in unguarded moments" or recording, like Felix H. Man, the daily and nightly rituals of Berlin street life in a famous 1929 reportage on the Kurfürstendamm at night.[10] In illustrated magazines, Friedrich Seidenstücker, Hans Casparius, Andreas Feininger, Alfred Eisenstaedt, Marianne Breslauer, and countless lesser-known photographers chronicled the rituals of urban life and trained their lenses on the newest social group to appear on the city's boulevards, the white-collar workers. In hotel lobbies and fancy restaurants, at art openings and sports events, and during official celebrations and diplomatic summits, photographers—often working for Simon Guttmann's Berlin-based Dephot picture agency—perfected the possibilities of candid camera to capture the rich and powerful of German politics and Berlin high society. Throughout the period, an army of anonymous press photographers depicted the big city as a place of danger, chaos, and violence as well as of play, amusement, distraction, and self-discovery. With troubling frequency, they also presented a less easily consumable image of the metropolis, one involving demonstrations, strikes, riots, putsches, political assassinations, and violent confrontations with the police. Often unexpected and always unsettling, the specter of the masses remained a constant challenge and a provocation, reason enough for architectural photography to step into the arena and banish the threat of massification into the stable order of glass and stone.[11]

The majority of illustrated magazines aimed to educate their readers in the appropriate ways of living in the modern metropolis. This meant showing them how to make their way through subway stations and big city traffic, how to be simultaneously a member of the crowd and an outside observer, and how to enjoy the various attractions without being overwhelmed by any of them. Photographing Berlin, in this context, meant showcasing famous buildings, as well as typical settings and identifying familiar social types and everyday situations. In more elaborate photo essays, this meant emulating narrative genres in the form of "An April Morning on Unter den Linden," "A Day on Wilhelmstraße," or "The City before Dawn between 4 and 6 AM,"[12] and offering occasional humorous pieces on survival in the big city in the vein of "About the Art of Falling."[13] With surprising regularity, photographing Berlin also meant reflecting on the medialization of urban consciousness as an inescapable fact of modern life. Accordingly, a short piece about tourists taking pictures of famous landmarks such as the Brandenburg Gate commented on the close affinities between mass tourism and urban culture.[14] An eyewitness report about the appearance of two cinematographers on Potsdamer Platz used the curious reactions of bystanders to reflect on the difficulties of capturing the hustle and bustle of the street, a difficulty also encountered by Walter Ruttmann and Karl Freund when they shot street scenes for their 1927 city symphony.[15]

If *Berliner Illustrirte Zeitung* was the leading *Boulevardzeitschrift* (literally, magazine of the boulevard), Friedrich Seidenstücker was its most famous chronicler of urban life. Seidenstücker devoted much of his Weimar career to capturing the physiognomy of white-collar society in the same way that Heinrich Zille had documented Berlin underclass life before World War I.[16] Seidenstücker began working for Ullstein in 1927 and publishing in *Berliner Illustrirte Zeitung, Die Dame,* and *Der Querschnitt.* Referring to himself as a *Knipser* (snapshot photographer), he photographed ordinary city dwellers at train stations and farmers' markets, in elegant cafés and public parks, on shopping boulevards and traffic squares. His

Fig. 5.1. Puddle jumpers near Zoological Garden Station. Photograph by Friedrich Seidenstücker, ca. 1930. Courtesy of Bildarchiv Preußischer Kulturbesitz Berlin.

fascination with the Alexanderplatz area is evident in his portraits of orthodox Jews in the *Scheunenviertel* and the small stores and businesses located on the square's northern and eastern edges. If social critique was part of his physiognomic project, it functioned that way only through his privileging of social and ethnic diversity over any normative categories of identity. This "flaneur with the camera"[17] photographed old women looking out of windows and unemployed men standing on street corners. He captured the foot soldiers of the city economy—the garbage men, coal carriers, construction workers, locksmiths, and meat packers—and, time and again, turned his gaze on the New Man and the New Woman. In fact, his 1925 series of fashionable young women jumping over puddles after a sudden rainfall can be read as a humorous comment on the white-collar ethos of social mobility and pragmatism that we will encounter again in the pretty shopgirls and typists rushing to work in Ruttmann's *Berlin* film (fig. 5.1).

Determined to provide an alternative to the uncritical celebration of diversity by Seidenstücker and other photographers of the mainstream illustrated press, the photographers of the left-wing *AIZ* approached the same locations and situations with, to quote chief ideologue Edwin Hoernle, "the eyes of our class."[18] In the late 1920s, the *AIZ*, with a print run of half a million copies, became the second largest illustrated magazine in Germany, not least because of its provocative photomontage covers designed, as of 1930, by John Heartfield.[19] Started in 1921 by Münzenberg and published under this name from 1924 on, *AIZ* proved extremely important to the building of a proletarian public sphere during the Weimar Republic. Anticapitalist and internationalist in orientation, the journal sought to build the revolutionary spirit in a metropolis enthralled by the consumerist fantasies of white-collar culture but also shaken by the increasingly violent political confrontations in the early 1930s between left-wing and right-wing groups. Against this backdrop, city photography was to function as "an indispensable and superior means of propaganda in the revolutionary class struggle."[20]

Offering an alternative to the naive realism prevalent in the mainstream illustrated press, the *AIZ* and similar publications set out to turn photography into a political weapon. The media activists on the left experimented with textual practices that affirmed the working class as the foundation of urban society and the driving force in the struggle for political change. Developing a class-conscious photography meant rejecting individual perspectives as an expression of petit bourgeois consciousness and advancing the collective point of view exemplified by the worker photographers and worker correspondents. The economic inequalities and social conflicts that were presented in the *BIZ* and similar publications as an unavoidable side effect of modernization stood at the center of the photographic project of the weekly *AIZ* and the monthly *Der Arbeiter-Fotograf,* founded in 1926 as the main organ of the worker photographers. Working-class photography made visible the material conditions of working-class life, from the many places of misery and destitution (e.g., the welfare agencies, unemployment offices, crowded tenements), to the first glimpses of an alternative proletarian public sphere (e.g., at workers' sports competitions, theater festivals, and political demonstrations). Turning photography into a weapon also meant documenting the KPD rallies in the Lustgarten, the annual May Day demonstrations, including the Bloody May Day of 1929, and the commemorative events held as of 1926 at Mies's Monument to the Victims of the November Revolution in Friedrichshain.[21]

How exactly would the communist photographers achieve what Franz Höllering called the "conquest of the observing machines"?[22] And how could the combination of images and texts give rise to the "correct" photographic *Gesinnung* (ideology) as defined by Walter Nettelbeck and others?[23] Through an effective combination of images and texts the left-wing press sought to uncover the class divisions in Weimar society and identify the lines of demarcation, areas of contestation, and sites of struggle in the capitalist metropolis. Rejecting traditions of aestheticization that, in architectural photography, separated artistic interventions from social struggles, the photographers of *AIZ* and *Arbeiter-Fotograf* relied primarily on montage techniques to achieve the politicization of architecture and urban space. The most famous practitioner of photo reportage at *AIZ* was Egon Erwin Kisch, also known as the *rasende Reporter* (roving or roaming reporter). In a 1929 piece entitled "Big City Berlin," Kisch uses architectural elements to juxtapose two perspectives on the German capital, that of a worker for whom Berlin means tenements and that of a tourist who sees only the famous historical monuments.[24] Addressing the question of labor, his 1927 reportage "Berlin at Work" shows the hard physical work necessary to keep the city running smoothly, with the subway construction on Alexanderplatz a recurring motif.[25] Finally, in "Arrival in Berlin" from 1930, Kisch draws attention to a very different form of flanerie when he follows a new arrival in his futile attempts to find a job.[26] The considerable influence of the *AIZ,* and Kisch in particular, on the Weimar illustrated press can be seen in the increasing use of montage techniques in mainstream publications such as *Weltspiegel,* which in 1932 published an influential photo essay on social and economic inequality by Alfred Eisenstaedt under the suggestive title "Janus-Faced Berlin"[27] (fig. 5.2).

Rejecting the conventions of the picturesque that romanticized the life of the urban poor, *AIZ* photographers repeatedly returned to the problem of workers' housing to expose architecture as an instrument of oppression and to attack the reformist rhetoric that dominated official discussions about public health and the tenement. Several reportages on the infamous Meyers Hof tenement on Ackerstraße and the appropriately named *Wanzenburg* (bedbug castle), a tenement in the former city bailiwick on Molkenmarkt, offered alternative spatial narratives: from exploitation to resistance, from subordination to pride, and from individual isolation to collective strength.[28] Confirming the *AIZ*'s considerable influence, the spatialized representation of working-class life in "A Cross Section of Berlin Tenements" (1926) inspired a very similar 1932 piece by Felix H. Man in the

Fig. 5.2. Alfred Eisenstaedt, "Janus-Faced Berlin." Cover of *Weltspiegel* 34 (1932).

conservative *BIZ*. The *AIZ* reportage may have served as a model for Döblin's literary cross section of a tenement in *Berlin Alexanderplatz,* whereas the *BIZ* piece, with its reflections on the metropolis as the place where "the individual lives with the masses" visualized insights first narrativized in that famous city novel.[29] Given this ubiquitous presence of the tenement in Weimar photo journalism, the formal conventions of architectural photography must have appeared rather strange to contemporary readers, reason enough to look at the photographic representation of the most famous buildings of the New Berlin and consider its contribution to Weimar's topographies of class.

II. Case Study: Mossehaus

During the 1920s, the streamlined façade of Mossehaus emerged as one of the most recognizable icons of New Building, a symbol of the new spirit of mobility, functionality, and adaptability and hence a key site in the visual imaginary of an emerging white-collar society. Depicted in daily newspapers and the illustrated press, photographed for tourist guides and photo albums, discussed in architectural surveys and cultural magazines, and adapted as a trademark by the company's advertising division, Mossehaus in 1927 was one of the few new buildings to be included in Ruttmann's *Berlin* film. Two years later, Mossehaus also became the only building chosen to represent the New Berlin in three influential photobooks about Weimar Berlin: Mario von Bucovich's *Berlin* (1928), Sasha Stone's *Berlin in Bildern* (Berlin in Pictures, 1929), and Laszlo Willinger's *100 x Berlin* (Berlin Times One Hundred, 1929).[30]

What accounts for this iconic status of Mossehaus? A first clue can be found in the historical events that made the façade renovation necessary in the first place. Located on the corner of Jerusalemer Straße and Schützenstraße in the famous newspaper district, Mossehaus was the headquarters of the eponymous Berlin-based publishing company. The newspaper district had seen heavy street fighting during the revolutionary uprisings in the first half of January 1919, an indication of the central role of media conglomerates in sustaining the precarious balance between democratizing tendencies and imperial power structures during the Wilhelmine Empire. Spartacists had taken over the editorial offices of the *Berliner Tageblatt,* the influential daily newspaper founded by Rudolf Mosse in 1871. In response, government troops had surrounded the armed revolutionaries and, using considerable firepower, regained control of this important site in the continuing battle over images. The price of this victory of law and order was a heavily damaged building that required major repairs to the ornate neorenaissance sandstone façade, completed in 1903 by Cremer und Wolfenstein.[31]

Confirming Tafuri's damning remark that Germans in 1918–19 chose "architecture rather than revolution,"[32] the Weimar Republic was founded on a precarious compromise between the newly empowered Social Democrats and the old political and military elites. Soon after order was restored in the capital, Hans Lachmann-Mosse, son-in-law of the company's founder, approached Erich Mendelsohn to come up with a design that would express Mosse's identity as a liberal, progressive publishing house more adequately than the old historicist façade did. Lachmann-Mosse, a patron of modern art, chose the young Mendelsohn after seeing a photograph of the Einstein Tower in *Berliner Tageblatt*. For Mendelsohn, the Mosse commission marked the beginning of a remarkable career that, as we saw in chapter 3, made him one of the most sought-after young architects working in the Berlin of the 1920s. Mendelsohn and Lachmann-Mosse, who both belonged to the city's German-Jewish liberal bourgeoisie, continued to collaborate on other projects until the world economic crisis and the rise of antisemitism and National Socialism put an end to their various endeavors.[33]

Replacing Mossehaus's damaged historicist front with a modernist exterior was a symbolic act that required specific strategies of mediation and integration. Mendelsohn, together with his assistant, Richard Neutra, came up with a highly original solution. He used a protruding entrance canopy and a three-story entrance bay of curving window bands to create the distinct curved corner that soon became a distinguishing mark of his department stores and office buildings. Three additional floors ended in a roofline reminiscent of an ocean liner, another characteristic feature of Mendelsohn's contribution to the functionalist style. Contemporaries hailed the aerodynamic design as a perfect expression of the modern cult of movement, speed, and functionality. The black ceramic tiles of the cornice and the shiny window bands only heightened this effect, as did the clear simple lines that projected the acceleration of urban life, as symbolized by the shift from pedestrians to motorists as its main protagonists, into the building's rhythmic order of horizontals and verticals.

The transformation of Mossehaus into an icon of Weimar modernity must be read as an expression of two closely related developments: the erasure of the memories of war and revolution through the cult of surface phenomena, and the promotion of white-collar diversions and mentalities by the powerful culture industry. During the first days of the uprisings in January 1919, images of revolution appeared on the cover pages of most daily newspapers and illustrated supplements. For obvious reasons, the street fighting in the newspaper district and the destruction of Mosse's editorial offices attracted particular attention. In all cases, selecting the right image required choosing the right perspective. Thus on the cover of *Weltspiegel,* the illustrated supplement of *Berliner Tageblatt,* the confrontation was depicted from the point of view of the government troops, with the heading "Berlin under the Sign of Terror," establishing the soldiers as the legitimate protectors of a terrified population (fig. 5.3). By contrast, the

Fig. 5.3. "Berlin under the Rule of Terror." Cover of *Weltspiegel* 2–3 (1919).

few independent photographers who, like Willy Römer, spent those fateful January days on the side of the Spartacists documented the events from inside Mossehaus, a choice that attests to their solidarity with the insurgents[34] (fig. 5.4). On the tenth anniversary of the occupation of the newspaper district, several illustrated magazines reprinted these dramatic images, presumably to highlight the difference between the chaos of the immediate postwar years and the political and economic stability achieved during the mid-1920s.[35] However, the juxtaposition of past failures and present achievements also brought back the specter of revolution, this time through images of a class-conscious urban proletariat and radicalized Communist party marching in the streets of Berlin in 1929. Not surprisingly, in the same year, *Der rote Stern* reprinted the previously mentioned

Fig. 5.4. Inside Mossehaus, January 1919. Photograph by Willy Römer. Courtesy of Agentur für Bilder zur Zeitgeschichte Berlin.

Römer photograph of armed revolutionaries seeking cover behind rolls of newsprint—a clear indication that the political conflicts of the prewar period had not been resolved.[36]

Between these two pivotal moments in the photographic history of Weimar Berlin, the Mendelsohn building emerged as an easily recognizable symbol for the Mosse concern and the liberal, cosmopolitan spirit of its signature publications. Lengthy features on modern architecture and city planning gave readers the opportunity to become active participants in the convergence of urban consciousness and white-collar mentality. The *Weltspiegel* regularly published photo reportages that, along the lines of "On the Roofs of Berlin" or "Witnesses of the Night," celebrated diversity, novelty, mobility, and flexibility as the guiding principles of a modern consumer society no longer held back by the old divisions of class.[37] Entertaining features on the pleasures of window-shopping, bar-hopping, and people-gazing coexisted with more critical ones on the infamous tenements on Ackerstraße and other typical working-class settings.[38] Extensive reportages on the annual Radio Exhibition (after 1924), the World Advertis-

Fig. 5.5. Advertisement for Mosse advertising business. *Weltspiegel* 28 (1928): 13.

ing Congress of 1928, and the World Trade Week in 1932 took full advantage of the close affinities between the city as tourist attraction and exhibition space, on one hand, and the illustrated magazine as a training ground for distinctly urban sensibilities, on the other. Unlike the more conservative illustrated supplements, *Weltspiegel* regularly published photo essays on New Building in Berlin, from the public housing estates in Zehlendorf and the planned modernization of Potsdamer Platz and Alexanderplatz to the Karstadt department store on Hermannplatz and the Wernerwerk in the Siemensstadt. Throughout, the work of Mosse's house architect was displayed prominently, for instance, in a piece on Herpich Furriers on Friedrichstraße that defended the design against its conservative critics.

The Mosse publishing house showed a remarkable understanding of the functioning of the culture industry when it chose the Mendelsohn façade to present itself as a modern corporation and cultural institution. From 1928 on, a minimalist graphic rendition of the corner design served as a trademark for the company's profitable advertising business (fig. 5.5). The synergies between mass publishing and modern architecture extended even to the marketing of Mendelsohn as house architect as well as author of the house (*Hausautor*), as it were. Mosse published two Mendelsohn books and produced the first survey of his career, *Das Gesamtschaffen des Architekten* (Erich Mendelsohn: The Architect's Complete Works, 1930); all of these books were advertised in *Weltspiegel*. Promoting the architect's vision of modernity thus became synonymous with selling modern lifestyles to typical Mosse readers: the technical and managerial elites and the diverse group of white-collar workers.

The importance of photography in increasing public awareness of architecture as a collective art form is openly acknowledged in Mendelsohn's own sojourns into architectural criticism and photography. The architect published *Amerika: Bilderbuch eines Architekten* (America: Picture Book of an Architect, 1926), a travelogue of his 1924 visit to the United States that featured his photographs, as well as the uncredited work of others, including traveling companion Fritz Lang.[39] Working with light instead of glass, the architect-as-photographer relied on symmetrical frame composition and graphic chiaroscuro effects to celebrate the modernist monumentality of New York skyscrapers and reveal the functionalist beauty of grain elevators in the Midwest. Mendelsohn again turned to photography when putting together an international survey of modern architecture, programmatically titled *Russland–Europa–Amerika* (Russia–Europe–America, 1929), that placed contemporary European culture between the political alternatives of Americanization and Bolshevization. His juxtaposition of "Russia and America, the collective and the individual . . . and America and Russia, the material and the spiritual"[40] revolved around architecture as the only artistic practice capable of articulating and mediating the competing demands of individuality and collectivity. Under these conditions, the uniquely German equalities of New Building for Mendelsohn opened up a viable third way between capitalism and communism, an argument supported in the book through the effective combination of images and texts and put into practice in the various architectural projects he completed during the Weimar period.

"No more reading! Looking!"[41] declared a New Objectivity pamphlet, asserting the inherent superiority of the image as an instrument for under-

GEBÄUDE DES
BERLINER
TAGEBLATT
BERLIN, JERU-
SALEMERSTR.

1921 — 1923

Fig. 5.6. Mossehaus. Erich Mendelsohn. *Das Gesamtschaffen des Architekten: Skizzen Entwürfe Bauten* (1930): 28.

standing and mastering modern urban life. New Building would never have attracted such public interest or acquired such symbolic capital without its photographic reproduction on the pages of cultural journals, illustrated supplements, and, of course, trade publications. Familiarity with the newest architectural styles became an essential part of urban consciousness and a distinguishing trait of the educated city dweller. However, the iconic status of particular buildings cannot be separated from the growing significance of language in situating New Building within contemporary debates on modernity, urbanism, and mass society.

Literalization, the anchoring of photographic meaning through short captions or longer texts, was considered the most effective way of controlling visual indeterminacy and ambiguity. As if following Benjamin's call for "the literalization of the conditions of life,"[42] Mendelsohn, too, relied on short texts in fixing the meaning of his buildings. In *Das Gesamtschaffen des Architekten,* he included Mossehaus twice, first in a filmstriplike design alongside what many consider his most important essay on dynamics and function in architecture, and later in a narrow frame that showcased the distinctive corner design in profile (fig. 5.6). In the second example, the accompanying text unequivocally links the building's balancing of verticals and horizontals to the interplay of movement and standstill in the choreography of big city life:

> Just as the overall expression visibly echoes the rapid tempo of the street, the movement intensifying to an extreme toward the corner, at the same time, through the balance of its powers, it tames the nervousness of the street and the passersby. . . . By dividing and channeling traffic, the building stands, despite its tendency toward movement, as an immovable pole in the agitation of the street.[43]

Presenting Mossehaus as a work of art necessitated its clear separation from the historical cityscape through framing, cropping, and masking. More important still, such decontextualization made possible its recontextualization in accordance with the program of the New Berlin. The visual presentation of Mossehaus in the two most important contemporary books on New Building in Berlin, Elisabeth M. Hajos and Leopold Zahn's *Berliner Architektur der Nachkriegszeit* (Berlin Architecture of the Postwar Period, 1928) and Heinz Johannes's *Neues Bauen in Berlin* (New Building in Berlin, 1931), attests to these underlying dilemmas and, once again, brings back the hidden connections to the revolutionary days of January 1919. In *New Building in Berlin,* whose Bauhaus-inspired cover design and

Fig. 5.7. Mossehaus. Heinz Johannes. *Neues Bauen in Berlin* (1931), 16.

sans serif typography suggest uncompromising commitment to modernism as a way of life, the Mendelsohn building is shown from the opposite street corner, with the streamlined entrance canopy in the center axis and the two symmetrical sight lines highlighted as its most significant features (fig. 5.7). The one-point perspective and the converging diagonals integrate the building into the perimeter block and, in this manner, create a powerful symbol of massification. It is left to the accompanying text to describe how the building nonetheless rises above the forces of leveling and asserts its artistic originality: "Expansion of the old publishing house and modernization of the corner, built during the revolutionary triumphs of the early postwar years." This is how Johannes describes Mossehaus: "A new spirit (*Gesinnung*) is searching for expression. Forcefully the streaming masses of the new addition envelop the ossified façade of an exhausted eclecticism."[44]

Adding further proof to the pervasive need for literalization, Hajos and Zahn in *Berliner Architektur* use the same photograph of Mossehaus as Johannes but offer a slightly different reading:

The protruding ceramic ledge, which separates the old building from the new, sharply moves toward the corner, falls down and lands in the energetic four-meter-wide canopy over the entrance. The building is no longer a passive observer of the cars driving by, of the ebb and flow of traffic; it has become a receiving, participating element of movement.[45]

Where agency was once the prerogative of social classes, Hajos and Zahn suggest, the modernist building now assumes their place as the instrument of a more democratic, egalitarian society. Where revolutionary masses once fought the forces of reaction, Johannes implies in his more utopian view of New Building, Mossehaus remains the vessel that preserves their subversive energy in the formal registers of functionalism.

Confirming the identification of New Building with the disembodied gaze of the urban masses, most architectural publications do not include the names of photographers; the credits given to Sasha Stone, Laszlo Moholy-Nagy, or Lucia Moholy-Nagy in Wagner's *Das Neue Berlin* are truly an exception. In most cases, photographs appear next to elevations, cross sections, and floor plans, all of which treat buildings as self-contained, independent entities. This decontextualized view of architecture was achieved through a preference for photographs that are devoid of any signs of urban life (e.g., pedestrians, traffic) or are altered (e.g., through retouching or cropping) to minimize the presence of other urban structures or objects. Separating the building from the cityscape created architectural icons that were instantly available to the kind of allegorical readings that, as demonstrated by Johannes and by Hajos and Zahn, conceptualize the process of urbanization in purely aesthetic terms. In so doing, the authors end up contributing to the dominant view of architecture, articulated by Edwin Redslob in the introduction to *Berliner Architektur,* as an expression of the "artistic will (*Kunstwille*) of our present time" through its unique qualities "as a *Raumkunst* (spatial art),"[46] a revealing application of the impersonal *Kunstwollen* (will to art) and its foundation in a more general worldview as described by art historian Alois Riegl to an architectural movement presumably committed to realizing the political will of the people.

The images of Mossehaus in von Bucovich's *Berlin,* Stone's *Berlin in Pictures,* and Willinger's *100 x Berlin* shed further light on the contribution of New Building to the imaginary topographies of Weimar Berlin. Throughout the 1920s, photobooks were promoted as a novel hybrid form

Fig. 5.8. Mossehaus.
Mario von Bucovich.
Berlin (1928), 55.
Courtesy of Nicolaische
Verlag Berlin.

Fig. 5.9. Mossehaus. Sasha Stone.
Berlin in Bildern (1929), no. 57. Courtesy
of Serge Stone, Amsterdam.

Fig. 5.10. Mossehaus. Laszlo Willinger.
100 x Berlin (1929), 3. Courtesy of
Gebr. Mann Berlin.

that benefited from the visualization of urban culture and the proliferation of photographic consciousness while still referencing bourgeois modes of art appreciation.[47] Published in 1928 and 1929, the high point and turning point in Wagner's ambitious programs for the New Berlin, the books by von Bucovich, Stone, and Willinger all participated in the aestheticization that transformed Mossehaus into a corporate icon and a symbol of architectural modernity, but they did so through very different photographic styles. To begin with the more traditional approaches, von Bucovich and Stone both present Mossehaus as an integral part of the perimeter block and its combination of old and new buildings. Von Bucovich achieves this integrationist approach by capturing the streamlined façade from the perspective of Schützenstraße (fig. 5.8). Like von Bucovich, Stone avoids the high drama of the corner diagonal by assuming a position on the other side of Jerusalemer Straße (fig. 5.9). Whereas von Bucovich demonstrates the successful integration of old and new by acknowledging Mossehaus's position next to an eighteenth-century building, Stone places greater emphasis on the harmonious relationship between building and street traffic, that is, the participation of the modernist icon in the ebb and flow of urban life. The reduction of architecture and photography to their essential elements is most pronounced in the approach taken by the young Willinger. His narrow frame and skewed angles, so typical of Bauhaus photography, turn the curved window bands into an almost abstract reflection on surfaces and structures (fig. 5.10).

Photobooks about cities represented an important part of Weimar visual culture. With its 254 plates, beautifully reproduced and presented in a square format, von Bucovich's *Berlin* was advertised by the Berlin-based Albertus-Verlag as the first volume in a proposed series called "The Face of Cities"; the only other volume, a portrait of Paris, appeared in the same year. Aiming at a cultured, middle-class readership, the book included a preface by Alfred Döblin, who himself had just confronted the difficulties of narrating the modern metropolis in *Berlin Alexanderplatz* (see chap. 6). Similarly, the well-known Vienna-based art book publisher Epstein published Stone's *Berlin in Pictures* as part of a series, titled *Urbis Urbium: Schöne Städte in schönen Bildern* (Beautiful Cities in Beautiful Pictures), that produced other volumes on Vienna, Venice, Budapest, Prague, and Dresden. Here it was Adolf Behne who used Stone's book to situate the program of the New Berlin within the continuities of the city's rich architectural history. Inexpensively produced by the Berlin-based Verlag der Reihe, Willinger's *100 x Berlin* (like von Bucovich's *Berlin*) appeared as part of a series of city portraits that only saw the 1929 publication of a second book, *100 x Paris,* this time with photographs by Germaine Krull. The accompanying texts in German, French, and English and the preface by Karl Vetter addressed a cosmopolitan readership fully conversant with modernist styles.

The sequential arrangement of plates in these three photobooks deliberately imitates the act of walking in the city and, in so doing, suggests both a narrative of progress, or progression, and an experience of individual agency akin to photographic flanerie. In light of the fact that von Bucovich, Stone, and Willinger were not only foreign-born but also forced to leave Germany after 1933, we might even detect hidden affinities between the figure of the stranger and the condition of exile—as if individual agency were only possible within the terms of otherness. Von Bucovich, an Austrian baron who from 1926 to 1930 owned a photo studio on Budapesterstraße, made his living by photographing Berlin nightlife and cultural events before his exile routes took him to Ibiza and Mexico, as well as to Washington, DC, and New York, the latter the subjects of two other photobooks published in the late 1930s. The Russian-born Stone regularly worked for Ullstein publications such as *Berliner Illustrirte Zeitung, Der Querschnitt,* and *Die Dame.* His studio (1924–27 on Kurfürstenstraße, 1927–30 on Kaiserin-Augusta-Straße) produced commercially successful and artistically innovative work until his departure for Brussels in 1932. In 1940, still hoping to cross the Spanish border and reach the United States, Stone died in Perpignan. Finally, in contrast to the more established Bucovich and Stone, the Hungarian-born Willinger was only twenty years old at the time of his book's publication and had just started working for the *Berliner Illustrirte Zeitung,* Stefan Lorant's famous *Münchener Illustrierte Zeitung,* as well as several international press agencies; in American exile, he became famous for his glamorous portraits of MGM stars.

All photobooks situate Mossehaus within a narrative trajectory that claims the totality of Weimar Berlin for individual perspectives and affirmative readings. Yet how did the three photographers manage to "enter into the heart of the city," as Hessel described the work of Stone, and "make visible an entire Berlin,"[48] as he wrote in a review of von Bucovich? Presenting the individual plates in the form of a typical journey through Weimar Berlin, von Bucovich, Stone, and Willinger start out in the historic center around Unter den Linden and proceed along landmarks and monuments such as the Reichstag, Brandenburg Gate, Old Museum, Opera House, Berlin Dome, and Imperial Palace. The absence of people and vehicles suggests the buildings' status as timeless works of art, far removed from the pressures of contemporary life. From the center, their journeys advance in two directions, toward the remnants of the Old Berlin (e.g., Krögel, *Scheunenviertel*) and toward the landmarks of the New West, with Wittenbergplatz, Kaiser Wilhelm Memorial Church, and the Kurfürstendamm as the main stopping points. The photographic excursions invariably end on the city's periphery where the public housing estates in Zehlendorf and Britz and the famous monuments to Prussian architecture in Potsdam once again confirm the compatibility of tradition and innovation in the self-presentation of Weimar Berlin. In all three photobooks, this spatial reenactment of the cityscape is overlaid by a functional view of the modern metropolis, with commerce, transportation, and recreation identified with the city's centers of entertainment (Friedrichstraße) and consumption (Leipziger Straße), the pedestrian and automotive traffic on its major squares (Potsdamer Platz, Alexanderplatz), and the outdoor activities in its popular parks and lake areas (Tiergarten, Wannsee). Throughout, the presence of the modern masses is acknowledged through the quintessential urban architecture of train stations (Wittenbergplatz, Nollendorfplatz), department stores (Tietz, Wertheim, Karstadt), and entertainment complexes (Wintergarten, Aschinger) that, like the modernist office buildings and traffic squares, organize these masses according to the principles of standardization, homogenization, and functionalization.

Nonetheless, there are notable artistic differences among the three volumes. Resisting the provocation of modernity in his formal choices, von Bucovich, in *Berlin,* appropriates Mossehaus to an impressionist tradition of city photography more suited to leisurely turn-of-the-century Vienna than the fast-paced capital of the Weimar Republic. His preference for soft focus, subtle gray tones, and dramatic backlighting endows the city with a romantic aura intended to compensate for the harsh realities of modern life. The ninety-six photographs chosen by Stone for *Berlin in Pictures* clearly privilege the Berlin of the Prussian Enlightenment and the Wilhelmine Empire. Subsequently, the aesthetics of monumentalism allows him to link the classicist buildings by Schinkel and Messel to the modern structures completed since the end of the war, from Mendelsohn's Mossehaus and the enormous Klingenberg power plant to well-known Wagner projects such as the Zehlendorf public housing estate and the Wannsee public baths. Last but not least, Willinger's selection for *100 x Berlin* emphasizes the collectivist spirit of the new times, as evidenced by the awe-inspiring architecture of modern media conglomerates (e.g., Ullstein Tower,

Mossehaus) and what they stand for—namely, acute awareness and full acceptance of massification as the dominant principle in the organizing of urban life.

Partaking in contemporary debates on text-image relationships, all three photobooks address the complex dynamics of the social, spatial, and visual directly in their prefaces. Introducing *Berlin,* Döblin reflects on the shift from the visible regimes of social class to the invisible order of functional differentiation and remarks that "Berlin is for the most part invisible. A strange phenomenon. . . . Only the whole has a face and a meaning: that of a strong and sober modern metropolis, of a productive mass settlement . . . the great serious mass being Berlin."[49] Less interested in the crisis of urban representation than in showcasing the accomplishments of the New Berlin, Behne in his preface to *Berlin in Pictures* elaborates on how "the task of the modern city builder is not to place monumental buildings in favored locations. He is no longer a tactician but a strategist of building in the city."[50] Finally, in an openly political reading that reflects its author's left-wing sympathies, Vetter in his contribution to Willinger's *100 x Berlin* takes up Döblin's diagnosis of a crisis of the visible to describe Berlin as a city without tradition and, for that reason, the perfect setting for radical changes that advance "the tendency toward the collective spirit and the common will."[51]

Architectural photography, as my discussion of Mossehaus has shown so far, served two principal purposes during the Weimar years: to determine the place of individual buildings within the cityscape and to promote New Building as an artistically important, socially significant, and politically relevant practice.[52] A third set of functions, the transformation of architectural structures and urban spaces into allegories of collective agency, was frequently diagnosed but rarely analyzed. Questions of visualization and discursivization (e.g., the literalization proposed by Benjamin) played a key role in the elevation of New Building to a symbol of modern mass society and proved instrumental in promoting modernization projects as an effective solution to social problems. In engaging the dynamics of individual building and perimeter block, architectural photography restaged the complex relationships between city dwellers and their built environment in visual terms. Especially the textual anchoring of the images allowed for the reconciliation of two opposing tendencies in Weimar architectural culture: the cult of the modern architect as social visionary and the affirmation of the urban masses as the true agents of history. The replacement of collective resistance by individual achievement and the displacement of social activism onto the dynamism of architectural form once again seem to confirm Tafuri's earlier diagnosis of "architecture instead of revolution." By articulating the tension between building and cityscape, architectural photography established a representational model for the changing dynamics of the social and the spatial that continued to haunt Weimar Berlin, a point that will become even more apparent in the chapter's third and last part, on Alexanderplatz.

III. Images of Alexanderplatz

Photographs played a key role in turning Mossehaus into a modernist icon and in promoting large-scale urban projects on Alexanderplatz. Yet if the iconic status of Mossehaus hinged on the historical compromise between modernism and corporate culture, what would be the equivalent function of the countless photographs of Alexanderplatz published in the daily press? If Mossehaus represented the quintessential white-collar workplace and was the perfect advertisement for the smooth, integrated look of modern mass society, how would we define the connotative field marked by Alexanderplatz in the city's evolving post–World War I identity? Finally, if the Mossehaus trademark was controlled by the Mosse concern, what determined the emblematic function of Alexanderplatz? In trying to answer these questions, we must begin by recognizing one important difference: Whereas the Mendelsohn building, through its clearly defined volumes, forms, and materials, remained accessible to aestheticization, the heterogeneous city square resisted similar efforts to assess its contribution to the New Berlin, a point confirmed by the difficulties of photographers trying to capture that which often escapes representation: the question of class.

Documented by Römer from the side of the insurgents, the occupation of Mossehaus in January 1919 marked the beginning of a large body of photographic work produced in the context of Weimar left-wing culture. The history of violent confrontations and its photographic documentation reserved a special place for Alexanderplatz, first photographed by Römer during the general strike in March 1919, with the police headquarters looming in the background and an armored vehicle keeping the crowds under control (fig. 5.11). Alexanderplatz not only presided over the most socially diverse area in Berlin, it also was the site of the only large-scale urban modernization project initiated and partially completed during the Weimar years. Located to the east of the city center, the square had al-

Fig. 5.11. Willy Römer. Alexanderplatz during the general strike in March 1919. Courtesy of Agentur für Bilder zur Zeitgeschichte Berlin.

ways been characterized by the vast open spaces in its middle rather than by the undistinguished buildings on its periphery. With the removal of the bronze Berolina statue in 1927, the square lost the one monument that had given it the kind of instant recognizability achieved by Potsdamer Platz after the installation in 1924 of its famous *Verkehrsturm,* a traffic tower with built-in clock. Alexanderplatz remained a construction site for almost two decades, first during the subway construction in 1913 and the long overdue replacement of a chaotic intersection by a modern traffic circle and then, from 1929 to 1932, as part of Wagner's planned modernization of the entire square, to be discussed in greater length in the next chapter, on *Berlin Alexanderplatz.*

The square's changing appearances, from chaotic traffic intersection and small public green with newspaper kiosk during the 1910s to a much larger traffic circle by the early 1930s, was documented by urban photographers as a series of incursions and erasures. Construction functioned as a central trope in most contributions, standing in for the dream of a modern society defined by mobility, adaptability, and uniformity and a modern metropolis ruled by efficiency, functionality, and rationality: Willy Pragher's

Fig. 5.12. Berolinahaus in 1930. Willy Pragher. Courtesy of Staatsarchiv Freiburg.

1930 photograph of Behrens's Berolinahaus perfectly illustrates this approach[53] (fig. 5.12). As an architectural metaphor replete with meaning,
construction allowed photographers to depict the New Berlin at its most
visionary and most destructive, with the ongoing gentrification of the surrounding neighborhoods an unavoidable reference point. The fascination
with Alexanderplatz as *the* construction site in the New Berlin gradually
displaced an older iconography of the square as a center of working-class
life and a major arrival point for immigrants from Eastern Europe, including the orthodox Jews of the *Scheunenviertel*. Identified with abject
poverty, urban squalor, petty crime, cheap diversions, illicit pleasures, ethnic diversity, proletarian culture, and left-wing radicalism, Alexanderplatz
in this other sense stood for the underside of the modernization project, a
locus of resistance and an emblem of alterity. It was this threatening otherness that always hovered around the edges of the square, sometimes
making an appearance but more often than not subsumed by the modernist discourse of construction and its various strategies of destruction
and erasure.

The difficulties in photographing Alexanderplatz—and the difficulties

Fig. 5.13. Alexanderplatz. Mario von Bucovich. *Berlin* (1928), 55. Courtesy of Nicolaische Verlag Berlin.

in writing about these images—are clearly evident in von Bucovich's *Berlin,* Stone's *Berlin in Pictures,* and Willinger's *100 x Berlin.* All three photographers acknowledge the impossibility of capturing the spatial totality of the square and recording the many signs of change. Each one chooses a different strategy, to compensate for, respond to, or defend against the speed and scale of urbanization. Keeping his distance, von Bucovich presents Alexanderplatz as an unmarked and undistinguished open space defined primarily by the buildings on its periphery and shrouded in the soft grey tones typical of his impressionist style (fig. 5.13). His photographic plate is accompanied by a brief history of the square that conveys a deep sense of loss: "The northern part of Alexanderplatz, with Tietz department store that opened in 1905. In front of it, parts of the gigantic excavation site for the subterranean tower station for four subway lines. Next to the Palm kiosk, from 1895 to 1927, stood the popular bronze statue of Berolina before it had to yield to the subway construction."[54] Willinger's take on Alexanderplatz foregrounds the construction site and the intersection of streets while reducing the surrounding buildings to a spatial border and pictorial frame (fig. 5.14). Capturing the modernist sense of urgency and heroic accomplishment, his sloganlike caption reads in the English version: "Alexanderplatz being rebuilt. Point of departure to the eastern parts of the City. Important traffic centre. Underground station of many storeys being built."[55] Viewing Alexanderplatz from inside a pub or restaurant, Stone uses the silhouettes of a fellow guest, a horse and cart, and several passersby to guide the view toward the monumental block of the Wertheim store on Königstraße and the *Rote Rathaus,* the famous City Hall built of red brick (fig. 5.15). The interior point of view makes the vast square appear almost manageable, with its buildings reduced to familiar outlines in the distance. This surprisingly intimate mise-en-scène reenacts the peculiar tension between agoraphobia and claustrophobia that, by the late 1920s, had become a recurring theme in literary representations of Alexanderplatz, though rarely with the sense of caution and detachment here exhibited by a photographer otherwise known for his avant-garde credentials. Not surprisingly, film critic Rudolf Arnheim dismissed Stone's photographic portrait of Berlin as "a very tradition-laden, un-Berlinish Berlin."[56]

Indeed, Stone's take on Alexanderplatz is particularly puzzling in light of his other Berlin photographs from the late 1920s, his outspoken commitment to "photography as document,"[57] and his strong belief in "the photographer and cinematographer as chroniclers of our times."[58] In conjunction with the 1927 advertising campaign for Ruttmann's *Berlin, Symphony of the Big City,* Stone actually created several photomontages that captured the spirit of the times through filmic means. His interest in modern architecture culminated in a 1928 photo series that included Mendelsohn's Einstein Tower in Potsdam, the Klingenberg power plant in Rummelsburg, and Breuer's interior design for Piscator's apartment in the White City Estate in Reinickendorf.[59] That same year, he designed the book covers both for *Alfred Döblin: Im Buch—Zu Haus—Auf der Straße* (Alfred Döblin: In Print, at Home, on the Street, 1928) on the occasion of the author's fiftieth birthday and for Walter Benjamin's *Einbahnstraße* (One-Way Street, 1928), with its maze of traffic signs a fitting introduction to the text fragments and urban snapshots found inside the book.[60] Stone's awareness of fragmentation as a condition of modern life is also evident in two photomontages of Alexanderplatz completed (as part of a series of

Fig. 5.14. Alexanderplatz. Laszlo Willinger. *100 x Berlin* (1929), 15. Courtesy of Gebr. Mann Berlin.

Fig. 5.15. Alexanderplatz. Sasha Stone. *Berlin in Bildern* (1929), no. 5. Courtesy of Serge Stone, Amsterdam.

montages) around the same time, the second in collaboration with Otto Umbehr. Under the motto "What If Berlin Were Innsbruck," Stone in the first example defamiliarizes the square through the insertion of an Alpine panorama, with the humorous juxtaposition of the center of Berlin working-class life and a main setting of Austrian winter sports alluding to the irreconcilable differences in the metropolis (fig. 5.16). Referencing cubism and constructivism, the multiperspective montage—of wooden boards from the construction site on Alexanderplatz—published in *Das Neue Berlin* allows him in the second example to reflect on the invasive nature of the modernization process and the shaky foundations being laid for the city of the future (fig. 5.17).

These images of Alexanderplatz mark a clear departure from the pictorialism of city photography established during the nineteenth century, partly under the influence of Eduard Gaertner's famous Berlin panoramas from the 1830s. The fundamental shift from a traditional to a modern view of this famous "world city square" (in Wagner's terminology) becomes apparent once we compare the photographs by von Bucovich, Willinger, and Stone to those by an older generation of Berlin photographers, including F. Albert Schwartz, Georg Bartels, Lucien Levy, Hermann Rückwardt,

Fig. 5.16. "If Berlin Were Innsbruck . . ." Sasha Stone. Courtesy of Serge Stone, Amsterdam.

Fig. 5.17. Alexanderplatz. Photo montage by Sasha Stone and Otto Umbehr. *Das Neue Berlin* 1 (1929): 2. Courtesy of Serge Stone, Amsterdam.

Waldemar Titzenthaler, and, most famously, Max Missmann. Specializing in technical and architectural photography, Missmann owned a photo atelier on Gneisenauer Straße in the working-class district of Kreuzberg and regularly published his work in trade journals and tourist guides. Combining a firm belief in the camera as an almost scientific instrument with an equally strong belief in the metropolis as a highly structured, organized space, Missmann throughout the 1910s and 1920s used his large-format camera to document the process of urbanization in a very systematic fashion by photographing streets, squares, bridges, and train stations in the same detached fashion and by repeatedly returning to famous Berlin buildings and locations over the course of three decades.[61]

Taking the panorama as an aesthetic and conceptual model, Missmann's photographs stand out for their strong central perspectives and vanishing points as well as their balanced composition and depth of field. Their anachronistic quality, especially in the later Alexanderplatz photographs, derives from the tension between the old-fashioned technology and technique (i.e., large-format cameras, photographic plates, and long exposure times) and the modern subject matter captured more appropriately by fragmentary perspectives and dynamic compositions. In repeated returns to Alexanderplatz, Missmann reaffirmed his unshakable belief in an almost geometrical order against the many signs of destruction and disarray. Thus an early photograph from 1911 shows the shafts, ditches, casings, and construction equipment that preceded the 1913 opening of the first subway line from Alexanderplatz to Schönhauser Allee (fig. 5.18). To compensate for the chaotic appearance of the square, Missmann assumes a panoramic perspective that brings out the underlying order of parallels, diagonals, and crescents. In 1925, Missmann returned to the scene to produce yet another wide-angle, panoramic shot of the square, with the Tietz department store and Berolina statue in the background and the empty green of the roundabout in the foreground (fig. 5.19). Again the image reveals nothing of the social conflicts and urban developments in which Alexanderplatz played such a pivotal role, a fact that may have contributed to the enthusiastic rediscovery of Missmann in recent years.

In the nineteenth century, panoramas had provided one of the useful technologies for the emerging metropolis to represent itself (e.g., in stereoscopic images), but this function had slowly been taken over by illustrated magazines and city films, and subsequently been redefined within the aesthetics of fragmentation and shock. Yet these developments did not prevent some Weimar photographers from holding on to the conventions of

Fig. 5.18. Alexanderplatz in 1911. Max Missmann. Courtesy of Stiftung Stadt-museum Berlin.

Fig. 5.19. Alexanderplatz in 1925. Max Missmann. Courtesy of Stiftung Stadt-museum Berlin.

the panorama and its simulation of spectatorial control. In August Fuhrmann's Welt-Panorama (formerly Kaiser-Panorama), located in the famous Linden Arcade between Behrensstraße and Friedrichstraße and sought out by urban archaeologists such as Kracauer and Benjamin for its obsolete treasures, the new and old paradigms of representation briefly achieved a bizarre compromise when a hand-colored image of Behrens's Berolinahaus was added to the stereoscopic displays, creating effects as outdated as Missmann's photographic panoramas.[62] In a rare departure from his usual street scenes, even Seidenstücker climbed to the roof of the Georgenkirche to survey the final stages of the subway construction some-time during the early 1930s[63] (fig. 5.20). In the same way that the Welt-Panorama provided the nineteenth-century visitor with an illusion of mas-tery, Seidenstücker's high-angle shot allowed the Weimar city dweller to partake in the monumentalism of Wagner's vision, but only from an aerial perspective that separated the observer from the events on the ground. In the background, Berolinahaus and Alexanderhaus stand like a bulwark separating the historical center, with the solid brick structure of City Hall as its outer wall, from the working-class neighborhoods surrounding the empty space in the center. The frame composition leaves open the question whether the spatial layout of Alexanderplatz protects the historical center against the incursions of modernity or whether it prevents the disruptive energies of the east from spilling out into other parts of the city.

To conclude, between the masses of stone and the masses on the street, Weimar Berlin emerged as a photographic corpus constituted through and sustained by the underlying discourse of class. This photo-graphic history began with the revolutionary uprisings of January 1919 and its unforgettable scenes of civil war: street fighting between revolutionaries and government troops, armored vehicles patrolling the streets, and shelled apartment buildings and torn-up sidewalks in a city that had remained un-touched by the devastation of World War I.[64] That same history in 1933 ended with the coming of a very different order: not the dream of a ho-mogeneous middle-class society celebrated in the Weimar illustrated press, not the vision of a socialist society inscribed in Wagner's program of the New Berlin, and not the functionalist and rationalist designs for living pro-moted by the architects of the New Building.

If the photographic apparatus allowed Weimar contemporaries to un-cover what Benjamin calls an "optical unconscious,"[65] can the historical photographs from the period help us today to work through the myths of Weimar Berlin and reclaim what might be called its historical unconscious?

Fig. 5.20. Alexanderplatz. Friedrich Seidenstücker, ca. 1932. Courtesy of Bildarchiv Preußischer Kulturbesitz Berlin.

If photography allows us, to once again quote Benjamin, to "find the inconspicuous spot where in the immediacy of that long-forgotten moment
the future subsists so eloquently,"[66] can we use the productive alliance of
architecture and photography to shed light on the contested and sup-
pressed mass imaginary of Weimar modernity? If history is essentially
imagistic, what are we to make of the problem of un/decipherability that

seems to haunt Weimar Berlin more than other founding sites in the making of modern mass society? And in what ways is this struggle over representation linked to the crisis of class society, between the threat of a socialist revolution in 1919 and the arrival of the racialized community in 1933?

"The true picture of the past flits by. The past can be seized only as an image which flashes up at the instant of its recognizability, and it is never seen again,"[67] writes Benjamin in his famous thesis on the philosophy of history. For him, the fascination of historical photographs resides in their ability to preserve the material foundations of history, to remind us of that which remained unredeemed, and to uncover the signatures of the future in the past. It is in this spirit that I have used the photographic representation of Mossehaus and Alexanderplatz to retrace the changing topographies of class in Weimar society. In the same spirit, the last two chapters will examine the making visible of modern mass society in two canonical texts of Weimar Berlin, *Berlin Alexanderplatz* and *Berlin, Symphony of the Big City.*

CHAPTER 6

Deconstructing Modern Subjectivity: On *Berlin Alexanderplatz*

True to its sensationalist style, in 1932 the *Berliner Illustrirte Zeitung* described Alexanderplatz as "the setting for many tragedies in real life and in fiction. Here Berliners feel the heartbeat of their hometown most strongly."[1] Confirming this point, Eugen Szatmari, in an alternative travel guide to Berlin, declared that tourists would not learn anything about the city's four million inhabitants by limiting their excursions to Unter den Linden and the Kurfürstendamm and advised his readers to venture into the residential neighborhoods to the north and east.[2] Alfred Döblin's *Berlin Alexanderplatz: Die Geschichte vom Franz Biberkopf* (*Berlin Alexanderplatz: The Story of Franz Biberkopf*, 1929), the most famous German city novel and a celebrated example of literary modernism, simultaneously confirms and complicates such widespread views about Alexanderplatz as the center of working-class Berlin. At first glance, the story of Franz Biberkopf, a former cement and transport worker just released from prison, seems to bear out the area's reputation as a hotbed of crime, vice, and illegality. Yet the centrality of Alexanderplatz to Wagner's plans for the New Berlin also allows Döblin to explode the very terms that have defined urban identity and space until that point and to rewrite the city text in accordance with the spatial manifestations of modern mass society. Doubly marked as other, extraterritorial within the class divisions of Weimar Berlin and anachronistic within the classless society envisioned for the New Berlin, Alexanderplatz functions as an instrument of construction as well as deconstruction—qualities that make the Döblin novel a particularly instructive text for an analysis of architecture, identity, and what I have been calling (following Soja) the sociospatial dialectic.

The architectural principle of construction is central to the functioning of the novel on several levels. The intricate layers of realist description, objective reportage, modernist montage, stream of consciousness, and mythological references present the modern metropolis as a construction site and make these principles of construction an integral part of urban representation and identity. At the same time, the metaphor of construction establishes a direct connection between the writing of the modern city novel and the making of modern subjectivity. As indicated by the full title, the novel has two protagonists: the square and the man who sets out to conquer it. When Biberkopf returns to the city's eastern center after having spent four years in Tegel prison for the murder of his prostitute girlfriend, he gets off the streetcar at Rosenthaler Platz and slowly makes his way back to his old haunts: "The punishment begins"[3] (fig. 6.1). His plan? To start a new life and become respectable; in other words, to assert himself as an autonomous subject. As he soon learns, however, the existential struggle of "Biberkopf or Berlin"[4] can no longer be resolved through categories of subject and object, self and other, that guarantee the autonomy of the bourgeois subject and guide his interactions with the world. In the almost deadly encounter with what Döblin calls fate, Biberkopf is subsequently beaten three times, a victim of his weakness, ignorance, arrogance, and hubris. At the end of the novel, we find him working as an assistant watchman in a small factory, having finally recognized that "a man cannot exist without many other men" and "that much unhappiness comes from walking alone" (*BA*, 632–33). His thus becomes an example to all those "who, like Franz Biberkopf, live in the human skin, and, like this Franz Biberkopf, ask more of life than a piece of bread and butter" (2).

The return of this ordinary man of the lumpenproletariat to one of the most contested and embattled sites in the New Berlin allows me to utilize the many functions of construction—as a literary motif, narrative technique, representational mode, and discursive strategy—for a critical perspective surprisingly absent from the extensive scholarship on *Berlin Alexanderplatz:* the novel's contribution to Weimar discourses of class.[5] As my discussion in the previous chapters has shown, the double crisis of modern subjectivity and urban space cannot be analyzed apart from its multilayered, multiperspectival, and multivoiced manifestations in textual practices. Döblin addresses this problem without succumbing to the universalism of bourgeois humanism or the determinism of proletarian literature. Instead he assumes the decentered perspective of the lumpenproletariat to imagine alternative models of modern urbanity and collectivity. Retracing the footsteps of his urban discourse, we will therefore reconstruct the tectonics and textures of the modern metropolis through three

Fig. 6.1. Max Missmann. Rosenthaler Platz, ca. 1904. Courtesy of Stiftung Stadt-museum Berlin.

interrelated spatial trajectories: through construction as a central metaphor in the making of the modern square and the modern city novel; through walking as a key device in registering the effect of mass culture on the city dweller and the cityscape; and through the competing iconography of the city as body and as machine, and the underlying assumptions about space, class, and mass society that sustain both tropes.

The city text or textual city of *Berlin Alexanderplatz* partakes in a con-tinuing process of exclusions, incorporations, invasions, and erasures. Within these parameters, the streets that converge on Alexanderplatz—Landsberger Straße, Turmstraße, Klosterstraße, Brunnenstraße, and Frankfurter Allee—demarcate an urban milieu dominated by the indus-trial working class and an unusually diverse social underclass. These streets also belong to the neighborhood where the vision of the New Berlin was to be fully realized and where Biberkopf experiences, through his mere being in the city, the extreme violence unleashed by the process of moderniza-tion. Committed to the notion of literature as a form of consciousness and empowerment, Döblin extends his modernist sensibilities to a group usu-ally associated with naturalist aesthetics and the rhetoric of social reform.

He uses the underworld of thieves, pimps, thugs, murderers, and prostitutes to move beyond the surface splendor of metropolitan life and to uncover the social and spatial divisions that sustained the project of Weimar modernity. In the process, he fundamentally redefines the basic coordinates of the city novel and the modern epic. By placing Biberkopf within a complex network of psychological, sociological, physiological, theological, meteorological, economic, literary, historical, and mythological references, Döblin abandons the deterministic categories of social class and urban milieu and recasts the problem of modern subjectivity in full awareness of its highly mediated and discursively constructed nature. Because of their diminished resources and destructive choices, including their ill-fated strategies of individual survival, the characters from the underclass only magnify this crisis of subjectivity and identity and draw attention to its material foundations. From the perspective of social outcasts, who have no recourse to compensatory myths of self-realization, the vision of the New Berlin erected on Alexanderplatz is thus revealed as an integral part of the sociospatial dialectic of Weimar modernity and its underlying politics of class.

I. Case Study: Alexanderplatz

"What is Alexanderplatz in Berlin?" Walter Benjamin asks in an enthusiastic review of the Döblin novel. "It is the site where for the last two years the most violent transformations have been taking place, where excavators and jackhammers have been continuously at work, where the ground trembles under the impact of their blows and under the columns of omnibuses and subway trains; where the innards of the metropolis . . . have been laid bare to a greater depth than anywhere else."[6] As a major traffic hub for the railroad, subway, and city train lines and a commercial center for the eastern districts, Alexanderplatz, in the words of real estate developer Heinrich Mendelsohn, represented the "heart and soul of the east."[7] Known for his boosterist pronouncements, Mendelsohn was not the only one who felt that Wagner's general building plan for Alexanderplatz would determine the face of the city for the next hundred years. "East" in Mendelsohn's description meant the working-class neighborhoods of Friedrichshain and Prenzlauer Berg and the East European Jews of the infamous *Scheunenviertel*. "East" meant the thieves, pimps, con men, and prostitutes who gathered in the cheap dives on Münzstraße; it meant the workers, servants, and small employees who called the tenements around Rosenthaler Platz their home; it meant the foreigners, transients, bohemians, and dropouts looking for a cheap meal at the famous Aschinger restaurant; and it meant the working-class men and women who shopped at the Tietz department store and other Berlin institutions located on the square's periphery.

During the 1920s, references to Alexanderplatz functioned as short-hand for social tensions, economic problems, ethnic differences, and political confrontations, with the square's surrounding streets regularly described as a source of crime, vice, and threats to public health. Thus identified with otherness, Alexanderplatz evoked a metropolis in transition: heterogeneous, multifaceted, contradictory, provisional, and impervious to established modes of urban representation. *Conflict* and *crisis* were the terms most frequently used to describe its contribution to the making of the New Berlin. In the popular imagination, two buildings in particular symbolized the dangers emanating from the larger area: the enormous police headquarter, called "Alex," located on its southern edge, a feared destination among many area residents, and the KPD party headquarters in the Karl-Liebknecht House near Bülowplatz (today, Rosa-Luxemburg-Platz), the site of many political rallies and violent clashes between Communists and Nazis.

Yet the association of Alexanderplatz with otherness extended far beyond the sensationalist accounts about a criminal underworld and culture of political radicalism. The *Scheunenviertel,* the densely populated area bordered by Grenadierstraße, Dragonerstraße, and Linienstraße, had always been a center of immigration for the Polish and Russian Jews portrayed so sympathetically by photographers Friedrich Seidenstücker and Roman Vishniac, described with great attention to detail in Sammy Gronemann's *Tohuwabohu* (1920) and Martin Beradt's *Die Straße der kleinen Ewigkeit* (The Street of Small Eternity, 1933) and acknowledged by Döblin himself through the figure of the red-bearded Zinnowitz in the opening chapter of *Berlin Alexanderplatz.*[8] Repeated attempts at de-slumification since the turn of the century resulted in the razing of entire city blocks, but they failed to disperse the *Scheunenviertel's* inhabitants. With their surrounding wooden fences, these vast empty lots became a recurring motif in the photographs of Heinrich Zille and the drawings of Hans Baluschek where they served as a reminder of erasure as an essential part of urban change. During the late 1920s and early 1930s a different kind of violence manifested itself in vicious attacks on everyone personifying difference or resisting assimilation. In right-wing antisemitic treatises, Jews from the

Scheunenviertel were singled out as the embodiment of racial degeneracy and cultural backwardness. Döblin in his novel acknowledges these troubling developments in repeated references to the Nazi slogans and pamphlets circulating in the pubs and streets around Alexanderplatz.

Since the late nineteenth century, concerted efforts had been made to stop the westward movement of businesses and turn the square into an attractive center for commerce and entertainment. Two department stores had opened around 1910: Tietz, with its ostentatious storefront (complete with Atlas figure), designed by Cremer & Wolffenstein, and Wertheim, whose monumental structure dominated the adjacent Königstraße. Even before the addition of two new subway lines in the late 1920s, Alexanderplatz functioned as a major transit station in the city, bringing together the regional train and the city train lines, with the first subway line opening in 1913. Yet by the mid-1920s the square could no longer accommodate the increased vehicle and pedestrian traffic. Members of the city planning office, the business community, and the architectural establishment agreed that only a fundamental redesign of the entire square would solve these problems. Especially the second and third phases of subway construction were regarded as key elements in the gentrification of the surrounding neighborhoods and therefore carried out with a sense of great political urgency. An indication of widespread resistance to these planned changes, the temporary removal of the Berolina figure in front of the Tietz department store prompted loud protests among dyed-in-the-wool Berliners and members of the nationalist right. These protests only increased after rumors about the bronze being melted down and recast in a more contemporary rendition of the popular figure.

By 1928, the year Biberkopf returns to Alexanderplatz, the subway construction was already fully under way. Four years earlier, the city government had begun to buy adjacent lots and tear down buildings. Striving for a unified look, Wagner's general plan for Alexanderplatz called for a horseshoe-shaped, medium-rise structure with underpasses that made the square a clearing point for the converging streets. In an article announcing the 1929 competition for the new Alexanderplatz, he asked participating architects to submit designs that incorporated big city traffic patterns and took into account the projected increase of traffic volume over the next twenty-five years. With reference to his vision of a *Weltstadtplatz* (world city square), he specifically called for designs that differentiated among cars, trams, and pedestrians, that accommodated different speeds on different levels, that took into account the square's changing appearance dur-

Fig. 6.2. Martin Wagner. 1928 Alexanderplatz competition. *Das Neue Berlin* 2 (1929), 34. Courtesy of Birkhäuser Verlag Basel.

ing day and night, and that gave formal expression to its double nature as a gathering place and transit point (fig. 6.2).

In addition to Wagner himself, Mies, Behrens, and the Luckhardt brothers submitted much-discussed proposals. In a typical gesture of defiance, Mies ignored Wagner's guidelines entirely. Instead of subordinating the form of the buildings to the existing layout of the streets, he insisted on the aesthetic autonomy of architecture. His design for the new Alexanderplatz—freestanding buildings asymmetrically arranged in seven rectangular blocks—foregrounded the contrast between the traffic circle and the angular form of the monolithic blocks and derived its formal strength from the powerful tension between structure and movement. In a spirited defense of Mies's design, Hilberseimer declared: "It used to be that architecture did violence to traffic. Today the opposite seems to be the case."[9]

In the end, the Luckhardt brothers won first prize with a circular design that, shown from the perspective of Königstraße, featured seemingly weightless, streamlined buildings made of glass and steel (fig. 6.3). Unfortunately, due to budget constraints, their apotheosis of traffic as the foundation of urban life remained unrealized. Instead, it was the much more modest design by Peter Behrens, featuring several office buildings arranged in a semicircle, that found the shared support of city officials and financial backers[10] (fig. 6.4). Only the end points of the planned horseshoe structure were built, and those only after a much-needed infusion of capital by an American investor, the so-called Chapman Group. Construction of the Berolinahaus started in 1929, and of Alexanderhaus in 1930; both were completed in 1932. Because of the world economic crisis, even Hans Poelzig's large-scale design for the Bülowplatz area, an integral part of the Wagner plan, only produced the apartment complex that still houses the famous Babylon-Theater (1927–29).

In an early sketch for *Berlin Alexanderplatz,* Döblin uses the architectural term *Durchbruch,* "with architects drawing a straight line through an entire block of houses from Frankfurter Straße to Alexanderplatz," to connect Wagner's ambitious project of urban renewal to his own reconceptualization of the city novel. "This is going to be a colossal *Durchbruch,*"[11] he concludes, with the term, which means clearing but also, more generally, breakthrough, referring at once to the provocation of modern city planning and the modern city novel. Since its publication in 1929, initially in serialized form in the *Frankfurter Zeitung* and in two short excerpts in Wagner's *Das Neue Berlin, Berlin Alexanderplatz* has been hailed as a radical challenge to the traditional city narrative and the conventions of urban representation. The novel, the standard argument goes, cites the elements of the nineteenth-century city novel to demonstrate their inevitable failure under the conditions of Weimar modernity. It is in full awareness of the disintegration of the urban master narrative that the relationship established by the title engages for one last time the elements of classical realism and bourgeois individualism, but only in order to facilitate the dialectics of construction and destruction and initiate the mobilization of the masses in the literal and figurative sense.

In that sense, the subtitle *The Story of Franz Biberkopf,* suggested by the publisher to make the novel more marketable, imposes a narrative order on the spatial coordinates of *Berlin Alexanderplatz* and reorganizes the

Fig. 6.3. Luckhardt brothers. 1928 Alexanderplatz competition, model.

Fig. 6.4. Alexanderplatz, ca. 1928–29. Postcard. R.-J. Kern-Luftbild, Berlin.

multiplicity of urban effects according to the oppositional structure of the traditional epic. The almost deadly struggle between city and protagonist, presented in nine books, or chapters, provides the connecting points between the narrative events, the stream-of-consciousness passages, the extended montage sequences, and the recurring mythological themes and motifs. No longer held in check through the techniques of narrative integration and psychological internalization, the modern metropolis asserts its formative powers through its physical and sensory assaults on the main protagonist. The reverberations of the pile driver on Alexanderplatz in what might be called the archi-textures of the city novel bring out the violence of the modernization process, a process that can be traced from Biberkopf's terrifying episodes of agoraphobia and paranoia to the radical expansion of urban discourse in the montage sequences. It is at the *Central-Viehhof,* the central slaughterhouse near Landsberger Allee and Storkower Straße, that the full meaning of Alexanderplatz is revealed in all of its allegorical force. With the rhythm of the pile driver repeated by the hammer that kills the livestock, the central slaughterhouse enacts the violence of modernization and translates its meaning into the most existential, creaturely terms. A city within the city, with its own guided tours, but also a mirror image of the city that it feeds, the slaughterhouse defines the terms and conditions under which Biberkopf, like the young bull, will have to face death in order to be reborn as part of the modern masses and the city's anonymous system of production and consumption.[12]

In the same way that the program of New Building is predicated on rationalized construction as a formal principle, the modernism of *Berlin Alexanderplatz* is tied to montage as a narrative and discursive device. Surprisingly, the author never referred to montage in conjunction with the novel. The term was first introduced by Benjamin who, in discussing Döblin's modern epic in the larger context of urban culture, noted strong similarities to Dada collages and silent film. In his review, Benjamin asserted that "the stylistic principle governing this book is montage . . . The montage explodes the framework of the novel, bursts its limits both stylistically and structurally and clears the way for new epic possibilities."[13] Whereas the cross-section principle in Ruttmann's *Berlin* film (to be discussed in chapter 7) closes off the possibility for alternative readings, montage in Döblin facilitates reflection on the very conditions of meaning production. While cross section celebrates the surface quality of things, montage acknowledges fragmentation and dislocation as an integral part of modern life; the ultimate goal of montage is destruction through construction. Instead of relying on psychological interiority and narrative agency, Döblin emulates the rational principles of construction, promoted by modern architects also for financial reasons, and selects and combines his prefabricated text elements in similarly economic ways. By drawing on diverse textual sources, such as newspaper articles, medical treatises, legal documents, product advertisements, weather forecasts, stock market results, political analyses, local news, public health statistics, police reports, administrative decrees, personal letters, and telephone books, he draws attention to the dependency of all urban practices on both textual production and discursive construction. These found texts integrate fiction and reality, past and future, and subjectivity and collectivity into the architextures of the modern city novel. The ubiquitous popular songs, political slogans, public lectures, local idioms, and urban sounds, with the pile driver a constant presence, add an important aural dimension to the novel and confirm the power of metropolis as a multivoiced body.[14] Similarly, the psychotic episodes, mythological figures, and biblical references open up this hallucinatory cityscape to the vacillation between modernity and myth that plays such a key role in the conceptualization of mass society throughout Döblin's entire work.

More specifically, the montage sequences expand the coordinates of time and space and confirm fragmentation, simultaneity, and nonsynchronicity as distinguishing features of the modernist aesthetic. No matter whether these sequences rely on serialization or parallelism, or whether they privilege an analytical or a synthetic approach, they are always testing the limits of urban representation and thereby achieve the kind of discursive breakthroughs described here. With Berlin providing the raw material and Döblin writing like a monteur, Biberkopf functions like a test site for the novel's construction principles and montage effects. Montage eliminates the boundaries between public and private life, for instance, by revealing the inner thoughts of a stranger in the crowd, by introducing the diary entries of a young woman, and by commenting on the main protagonist's temporary impotence in great medical detail. Occasionally, these sequences extend the conditions of urban life into the past and future, as in the case of several passengers on a bus, including fourteen-year-old Max Rüst, whose entire life is being foreshadowed (*BA*, 55–57). Similar effects occur in the cross section of an apartment building on Linienstraße that offers brief biographies of all inhabitants (156–61) and in a summary overview of the legal cases heard in the Labor Court on Zimmerstraße on that particular day (412–24). Montage organizes the relationship between a city text that seems to write itself and a narrator/author who intervenes at key points to offer explanations, commentaries, and digressions. Last but not least, montage facilitates the mutual articulation of narrative space and narrated space that, through the compulsive listing of street names and tram stations, acquire an almost architectural, topographical quality. The pub on Rosenthaler Platz and the movie theater on Münzstraße, Biberkopf's walks on Invalidenstraße and his meetings with the Pums gang on Alte Schönhauser Straße, the public baths at Wannsee, and the deadly pine forest in Freienwalde—all of these names do not merely denote specific locations and social milieus. As part of very different mental maps and affective spaces, these sociospatial markers also establish coordinates for the evocation of that other city, the urban discourse of quantification, classification, and massification.

II. On the Streets with Franz Biberkopf

Franz Biberkopf, the former cement and transport worker, occasional street peddler, and small-time thief and pimp, is a man from the lumpen-proletariat (sometimes translated as rabble proletariat) or, to cite the curi-ous term coined by one contemporary reviewer, the "upper lumpenprole-tariat."[15] Biberkopf's precarious position in the city economy resists easy categorization and is therefore ideally suited to problematizing the crisis of traditional class society. In Marxist terms, the lumpenproletariat usually refers to those members of the working class who are not proletarians, that is, those who live outside the wage-labor system. Found primarily in in-dustrial centers, they include small-time criminals, prostitutes, beggars, swindlers, hoodlums, homeless people, and the permanently unemployed. Like the term *proletariat, lumpenproletariat* is a historically specific term and must be understood within the larger history of class struggle.

According to Marx, its members are distinguished from the prole-tariat through their lack of class consciousness and must be regarded as a counterrevolutionary force. *The Communist Manifesto* describes this social class as follows: "The 'dangerous class' (*Lumpenproletariat*), the social scum, that passively rotting mass thrown off by the lowest layers of the old society, may, here and there, be swept into the movement by a proletarian revolution; its conditions of life, however, prepare it far more for the part of a bribed tool of reactionary intrigue."[16] Made up of downwardly mo-bile elements from the lower classes, the lumpenproletariat in the Weimar

Republic proved to be highly susceptible to political demagogy; this connection is alluded to in Biberkopf's brief and inconclusive flirtation with National Socialism. Yet in *Berlin Alexanderplatz,* the rejects and castoffs of the capitalist economy also destabilize the fantasies of white-collar prosperity and the dogmas of Marxist class analysis, as well as call into question the overriding emphasis on technological progress and economic productivity. As the embodiment of nonproductivity and nonintegratability, a type like Biberkopf challenges the centrality of industrial labor and of labor struggles in the politically polarized atmosphere of the late 1920s. At the same time, by profiting from the city economy through his criminal activities, he draws attention to the dark underside of the capitalist system of exploitation.

Assessing the connection between this class problematic and modern urbanity means following Biberkopf on his long walks through Berlin and analyzing the construction of narrative space with regard to its main architectural tropes. The novel is structured around two recurring motifs, the falling roofs and the pile driver, which come to signify the problem of modern subjectivity within the imaginary city body and the audiovisual cityscape. Their invasive movements dissolve the boundaries between the real and imagined (external and internal) cityscape and produce the phantasmagoric space of modern mass society that finds foremost expression in the experience of spatial estrangement. Functioning as tropes, the falling roofs and the pile driver translate architectural discourse into anthropomorphic terms, with the individual house conceived as a body and the city square as an organism. Each trope relies on a different sense to achieve these subversive effects—hearing in the case of the pile driver, vision in the case of the falling roofs. Throughout, the falling roofs function as an indicator of Biberkopf's struggle for physical survival and mental integrity, whereas the pile driver represents the heart of the modernist project, with its rhythmic pounding a constant reminder of irrational forces below the appearance of order and stability.

The falling roofs appear for the first time when Biberkopf, just released from prison, finds himself confronted with a changed cityscape: "And there were roofs on the houses, they soared atop the houses, his eyes wandered straight upward: if only the roofs don't slide off, but the houses stood upright" (*BA,* 7). From then on, his relationship to Berlin becomes an ongoing negotiation between identification with its physical structures and projection of his anxieties onto its spatial features. While the memory of past traumas forces the man's glance upward, the reassuring permanence found in building materials and architectural details provides only a temporary support structure for his free-floating anxieties and ultimately fails to prevent his descent into madness: "But then his glance slipped with a jerk up the house-fronts. . . . That might get the roofs started, carry them along with it; they are liable to start rocking. The roofs could slide down, obliquely like sand, like a hat falling down from a head" (165–66). It is only after his release from the insane asylum in Berlin-Buch that the spatial order of modern mass society can be restored: "The houses keep still, the roofs lie quiet, he can move securely below them, he need not creep into any dark courtyards. Yes, this man—let's call him Franz Karl Biberkopf, to make a difference between him and the former one . . . now walks slowly up Invalidenstraße past Ackerstraße" (624).

Yet in *Berlin Alexanderplatz* subject formation and modern urbanity are not merely posited as interrelated or interdependent; Döblin shows that they are constitutive of each other. The illusory opposition between character and milieu or, to phrase it in more conceptual terms, between biography and topography, can no longer be articulated through the familiar distinction, perfected in the classical city novel, between the spatiality of the subject and the subjectivity of space. The deadly struggle between city and protagonist, one of the central topics in the secondary literature, is invoked but never quite gains narrative dominance; instead, the oppositional structure is constantly destabilized by the more flexible, dynamic configurations brought about by the quantification of narrative elements and devices. Having asserted his autonomy in several violent encounters, including the rape of a women friend, Biberkopf appears ready at the beginning of the fourth book to confront Alexanderplatz directly and take on its masses of people and goods. The narrator describes the scene with full awareness of the anxieties lurking below such compulsive listing and naming:

> On the Alexanderplatz they are tearing up the road-bed for the subway. People walk on planks. The street-cars pass over the square up Alexanderstraße through Münzstraße to the Rosenthaler Tor. To the right and left are streets. House follows house along the streets. They are full of men and women from cellar to garret. On the ground floor are shops. Liquor shops, restaurants, fruit and vegetable stores, groceries and delicatessen, moving businesses, painting and decorating, manufacture of ladies' wear, flour and mill materials, automobile garage, extinguisher company. (*BA,* 154)

In articulating the relationship between urban space and perceptual space, the pile driver from the construction site reveals the textual city as the site of a perpetual invasion, unearthing, and violation. Not surprisingly, Döblin's use of the pile driver as an urban motif and formal device prompted a contemporary reviewer to note, "Just as the pile driver rams into the ground on Alexanderplatz, transforming it in accordance with the demands of modern traffic, he—with the pile driver of description—rams facts into the ground on which we are accustomed to walk without difficulty."[17] Thus defined in its real and imaginary dimensions, the square gives rise to the novel's central allegory for the crisis of modern subjectivity. The destabilization of urban space through the mobilized gaze enters into the metaphorical circle of city as body as city until it turns into its exact opposite: the city as a powerful machine for producing perceptions and experiences. This momentous shift from perception to projection or, to use literary terms, from representation to simulation, is thematized in several extended explorations of Alexanderplatz as the founding site of the new mass individual.

Like the falling roofs, the pile driver functions as an extension of Biberkopf's urban consciousness and serves similarly destabilizing functions, but this time primarily on the level of auditory sensations. The movements of the pile driver facilitate the projection of physical sensations and unconscious drives onto a violated earth and, in the process, reenact what has been called inner urbanization.[18] Its hypnotic pounding is first heard during the second traversing of the city's central square: "Boom, boom, the steam pile driver thumps in front of Aschinger's on the Alex. It's one story high, and knocks the rails into the ground as if they were nothing at all . . . Boom, boom, the steam pile driver batters away on the Alex" (*BA*, 216). Its invasive rhythm destabilizes even the function of language, eroding grammatical conventions and undermining communicative patterns. The machine injects its violent beat into human relations as it occasions a conjugation: "I beat everything, you beat everything, he beats everything" (217–18). This senseless grammar exercise establishes the conditions for the more disturbing shift from the identification with destruction—"I beat everything to pieces, you beat everything to pieces, he beats everything to pieces" (218)—to the projection of these violent impulses back onto the imaginary center of the modern metropolis: "Rrr, rrr, the pile driver thumps down, I beat everything, another rail" (222).

In these hallucinatory episodes, the pile driver functions as a powerful symbol of life and death. It introduces the repetitive pattern that, like the beating of the heart, guarantees the survival of, and survival in, the metropolis. At the same time, the pile driver provides a rhythm for the process of urbanization that links Alexanderplatz to the other allegorical sites in the novel's destruction and (re)construction of modern subjectivity: the Tegel prison, the insane asylum in Buch, and, of course, the central slaughterhouse. When the pounding of the pile driver is temporarily overlaid by the fateful winds blowing over Alexanderplatz, sound turns into noise, and noise triumphs as the original language of human suffering. A later psychotic episode further expands on the close affinities between wind, breath, noise, and voice, beginning with the observation that "all the wind does is to expand the chest a bit" (*BA*, 491) and ending in mere stammering: "I am yourn, come now, we'll soon be there, I'm yourn. Boom, zoom . . ." (492). The winds of destruction return once more during Biberkopf's stay at the Buch asylum. Vestiges of speech surface briefly in the equation of wind and breath: "Boom, zoom, the wind stretches his chest, draws in his breath" (584). Soon attention shifts from the physical body to the auditory hallucinations that announce the appearance of the Whore Babylon and complete the protagonist's internal demontage: "Boom, crash, zoom, crash, boom, a battering ram, zoom, a hammering at the door. Bashing and crashing, crackling and smashing. Who is this lying fool, Franz Biberkopf?" (589). The hammering through which society asserts its claims on the subject confirms the ultimate triumph of the pile driver and, through the identification of man and machine, announces his successful integration into the urban masses. With the return of the new Biberkopf, these voices disappear, and the construction site on Alexanderplatz again becomes nothing more than a monument to urban progress. Just as the mass individual is reconstituted as a subject without voice, the modern metropolis is confirmed as a machine without subject.

My discussion so far has shown how *Berlin Alexanderplatz* narrativizes urban experience as a terrifying exposure and forceful submission to hallucinatory spaces and transitional states. Biberkopf's status as a member of the lumpenproletariat—that is, his marginality to both fantasies of social mobility and dreams of class revolt—plays a key role in the deconstruction of the modern metropolis and its prevailing myths. From his earliest manifestations of agoraphobia, to his more violent paranoid episodes, Biberkopf's spatial estrangement—his exclusion from the ongoing rearticulation and reconfiguration of class society—functions like a solvent on the traditional terms of urban representation. At the same time, his unwillingness, or inability, to comply with the new rational and functional order reveals the foundation of urban life as one of existential needs and desires. The result is a radical dismantling of bourgeois notions of subjectivity and their replacement by the archaic—and therefore shockingly modern—concept of man as a mere physical body and conglomeration of sensory organs.

Sustained by the primacy of vision in modernity, the dynamics of body and space establish the new parameters through which the metropolis can be theorized in terms of projections, hallucinations, incorporations, and lines of convergence and disintegration, rather than through the conceptual binary of society versus community that aims for stable relationships and clear distinctions within the sociospatial dialectic. Seen in this light, the disruptive power of spatial estrangement must be read in two ways: as a delimiting and scrambling of urban discourses that throws into relief the violence inherent in the process of modernization; and as a subversive energy in the urban text that resists traditional notions of subjectivity and spatiality. Moreover, in deconstructing the constituent elements of modern subjectivity, the paranoid main character introduces the possibility of a nonlinear, nonhierarchical discourse without authorial center: in other words, without (class) agency.

Organized around the experience of spatial estrangement, Döblin's multifaceted approach to urban representation combines seemingly contradictory moves: the displacement of urban experience into the modernist terms of fragmentation and its reconstruction through the simulation of myth and the myth of simulation. Both strategies participate in inscribing the conditions of urbanization on the cityscape and the mass body. As the most extreme form of estrangement, Biberkopf's paranoid episodes uncover the economy of means behind the "struggle" of city and protagonist. Its relationship is simultaneously constructed and deconstructed through the coupling and uncoupling of the constitutive elements of urban experience in a process of endless generativity. In facilitating such regimes, paranoia introduces the possibility of writing the city text outside the traditional oppositions of individual and collective, fantasy and reality, and interior and exterior space. The paranoid gaze draws attention to the myriad forces that partake in the making of urban experience, not in the form of a forward and backward motion, or as acceleration and retardation, but in the terms of simultaneity, contingency, multiplicity, and heterogeneity; not through the alternatives of destruction and preservation, but with the possibility of their productive coexistence; not just under the rule of terror, but also in an atmosphere of curiosity and exhilaration.

The lack of a spatial order capable of establishing clear hierarchies among urban elements compels the narrator to turn to serialization and classification as the only strategies left to preserve the city as a narrative agent. In Biberkopf's repeated crossings of the square, the almost ritualistic naming of streets (and, later, of streetcars) provides an illusory sense of stability, as does the introduction of various classificatory schemes. Even the businesses around Alexanderplatz are divided into those that have survived the onslaught of modernization, such as the Wertheim and Tietz department stores and the Schlossbräu and Aschinger restaurants, and those, such as the Loeser & Wolff tobacco store, the Jürgens stationery store, and the popular Berolina statue, that have been sacrificed to the project of urban renewal. Their demolition not only draws attention to the contested nature of public places, but also announces the return of myth in evocative references to the vanquished cities of antiquity. The accompanying shift from a critique of modern city planning to a mythological scenario of rise and decline is announced by the description of the vacant Friedrich Hahn department store as "emptied, evacuated, and eviscerated, with nothing but red tatters hanging over the show-windows. A dump heap lies before us. Dust thou art, to dust returnest . . . Thus Rome, Babylon, Nineveh, Hannibal, Caesar, all went to smash, oh, think of it!" (*BA*, 219–20).

While the buildings and streets establish the structure for sustained reflections on rationalized construction as a modernist principle, the crowds around Alexanderplatz allow Döblin at the same time to destabilize the scene of modernist construction. Throughout, city dwellers are engaged in typical urban activities such as standing, walking, and running, strolling on sidewalks, crossing intersections, entering and exiting stores, glancing into shop windows, and riding on busses or streetcars. Observed from afar, they represent the amorphous urban mass associated, in most contemporary Berlin novels, with the specter of deindividualization. Here, however, people are also identified by name and given a biography—with the result that the narrative perspective, too, shifts repeatedly from the public to the private sphere. While the sum of these descriptions suggests confusing multitudes, if not outright chaos, the multiperspectivism produced through this vacillation between individuals and masses in fact validates diversity as the underlying principle of a modern subjectivity beyond spatial and social hierarchies.

Biberkopf's third traversing of Alexanderplatz confirms the diagnosis of disintegration and dissociation, but, in foreshadowing his final transformation, the earlier experiences of spatial alienation quickly give way to an almost uncanny factuality. Instead of signs of overwhelming chaos, stereo-typical images of city life now predominate. The initial experience of shock is banished into an insurmountable feeling of detachment:

> On the Alexanderplatz they go on fussing and bustling around. On the Königstraße, at the corner of Neue Friedrichstraße, they want to pull down the house over the Salamander shoe store. They are already pulling down the one next to it. Traffic beneath the Alex arch of the municipal railway becomes enormously difficult: they are building new pillars for the railway bridge; here you can look down into a nicely walled shaft where the pillars put their feet. (*BA,* 416)

The accompanying shift in agency, acknowledged in the pronoun *they,* from the mechanical listing of commercial buildings in Biberkopf's first encounter with Alexanderplatz, to his belated recognition of the construction workers tearing them down, opens up the novel's ambiguous ending to a wide range of interpretations. In light of the protagonist's difficult "educational journey," this change could be interpreted as a sign of his gradual acceptance of the working collective; the sudden reference to a *you* supports such a claim, though not necessarily in the reductionist terms demanded by Döblin's contemporary left-wing critics.

In fact, Biberkopf's final return to Alexanderplatz clearly spells out the conditions of such social integration and political stabilization, which are predicated on the elimination of all categories of difference, including that of class. It is his full acceptance of social leveling that now keeps the architectural elements in check and prevents any single element from dominating, be it the pounding of the pile driver or the threat of spatial phobias. Yet in the moment that the visual and auditory hallucinations stop, Alexanderplatz loses its function as the battlefield of modern subjectivity. From then on, the square governs its surroundings through an almost uncanny presence-unto-itself. Seen in this light, the novel's ending may be read as reassuring because of its acceptance of the reality principle, but it remains also deeply disturbing in its dependence on a concept of normalcy that eliminates all possibilities of resistance—and spatial estrangement, after all, must be considered as a form of resistance—through the fiction of a stable relationship between subjectivity and spatiality. The new Biberkopf returns to the scene as part of the urban collective, but it is a collectivity that remains troublingly undefined especially in its social structures and political allegiances:

First the Alex. It's still there. There is nothing to be seen there. It was terribly cold all winter, so they did not work and left everything lying around, just as it was, the big steam shovel is now standing on the Georgenkirchplatz, they are dredging sand and dirt from Hahn's Department Store, they've put in a whole lot of rails there, maybe they are going to build a railway station. A lot of other things are happening on the Alex, but the main thing is: it's still there. (*BA*, 626)

III. The City Novel and Weimar Literary Culture

Why approach the problem of urban representation through a figure from the lumpenproletariat and not, as so many other Berlin-based *Zeitromane* (topical novels) of the period, from the perspective of young white-collar workers, struggling artists and intellectuals or the radicalized working class? As I have argued in the previous section, Biberkopf's marginality—the fact that he, in the words of one contemporary reviewer, "lives between the classes, without ties to the community"[19]—makes him an effective device in mapping the changing topographies of class as well as the changing parameters of urban representation. Confirming this point, Biberkopf's position outside the master narratives of Weimar modernity and the innovative nature of Döblin's modernist project can be examined through a brief comparison to then-prevalent approaches to social class and milieu in the literary representation of Weimar Berlin.

Leftist writers typically chose specific places or settings to expose the ubiquitous signs of oppression and exploitation to a traditional Marxist class analysis. Thus in their descriptions of Alexanderplatz, the spectacle of labor and technology leads to a very different mobilization of the masses that often culminates in violent confrontations such as the infamous Bloody May Day of 1929. Making precisely such a connection, Klaus Neukrantz in *Barrikaden am Wedding* (Barricades in Wedding, 1931) approaches the construction site on Alexanderplatz from the perspective of class struggle but also with a keen appreciation of the spectacle of labor. The communist writer, who earlier denounced *Berlin Alexanderplatz* as "a reactionary and counterrevolutionary attack on the program of organized class struggle,"[20] uses the movement of workers, machines, and materials in his novel to conjure up a thrilling scene of capitalist productivity:

On Alexanderplatz, the pile driver from the subway construction rumbled and hissed. Clattering and swaying, the busses drove over thick wooden boards under which the workers crawled around in tunnels and shafts. The elevated trains rattled over the railroad bridge, which was supported by mighty beams, and stopped in the train station with screeching brakes. The pedestrians pushed through narrow passageways between wooden fences. Alexanderplatz—day and night, a pulse beat of labor, surrounded by smoke, dirt, and noise, by hurrying and harried people . . . [21]

Making even more explicit references to Alexanderplatz as the source of, and stage for, a new class consciousness, Karl Schröder in *Klasse im Kampf* (Class Struggle, 1932) enlists the violence of modernization, including its traumatic culmination in World War I, in mapping the path to a better future. A friend of Alexander Schwab, the *Buch vom Bauen* author discussed in chapter 6, and an active member of various left-radical groups, Schröder leaves no doubt about the meaning of this very different scene of mass mobilization:

On the Alex they are building . . . A small theater of war. Rows of houses decimated, street layouts disrupted, sewage lines torn open, support columns, trusses, crossbars, huge piles of dirt. Peaceful trenches in a restlessly working city. Behind high wooden fences lie peaceful ammunition, peaceful weapons in the struggle of human beings sweating over spades and carts, not rifle butts and ammunition belts.[22]

Stunned by the sheer scale of Wagner's modernization project, Alexander Graf Stenbock-Fermor, known as the Red Count, came to Alexanderplatz during his travels through "Germany from below" and descended into its chaotic underworld with an engineer as his guide. Even in his seemingly objective account, the subterranean setting remains charged with allusions to social inequality and economic exploitation:

Below ground, all forces have been mobilized. Subterranean passages and stations, an underground construction of phantastical dimensions is growing 16 metres below street level. An unintelligible confusion of beams, girders, pillars and ladders, fills the gorge which is being formed from a concrete box sunk deeply into the ground. . . . More and more masses of concrete, iron, and wood are lowered into this gorge and transformed into stairs, platforms, rail tracks, pillars and roofs. The biggest underground station in Berlin is being built here.[23]

Döblin shares with Neukrantz, Schröder, and Stenbock-Fermor an intense fascination with the material spectacle of the Alexanderplatz construction site and a deep compassion for the exploited and the oppressed. Yet where the other authors situate their excursions within sympathetic accounts of working-class life, Döblin leaves behind the entire system of social determinations that guide the representation of the metropolis in the realist and naturalist traditions. In his radical reconceptualization of the city novel, he self-reflexively alludes to the two constitutive elements of the *Zeitroman,* social class and social milieu, but refuses to depend on either one of them for explanatory purposes or atmospheric effects. His antipsychological tendencies and mythological references put Döblin equally at odds with the prevailing narratives of urban culture and class society. He obviously has little motivation in showing Weimar Berlin from the perspective of disillusioned members of the middle class, as does Leonhard Frank in *Der Bürger* (The Bourgeois, 1924), or the materialistic nouveau riche, as does Kasimir Edschmid in *Feine Leute, oder Die Großen dieser Erde* (High-Class People, or The Great of This Earth, 1931). Opposed to any kind of stereotyping or proselytizing, Döblin is equally reluctant to thematize the problems of the unemployed, in the reductionist manner of Bruno Nelissen Haken's *Der Fall Bundhund* (The Bundhund Case, 1930), or to highlight the misery of working-class housing, in the social realist style of Günter Birkenfeld's *Dritter Hof links* (Third Courtyard on the Left, 1930). Not interested in telling yet another story of upward or downward mobility, he neither pays attention to the familial consequences of impoverishment, as done by Hans Fallada in *Kleiner Mann, was nun?* (Little Man, What Now? 1932), nor gives voice to the professional ambitions harbored by the office workers featured in Martin Kessel's *Herr Brechers Fiasko* (Mr. Brecher's Fiasco, 1932) or the young secretaries portrayed in Rudolf Braune's *Das Mädchen an der Orga Privat* (The Girl at the Orga Privat, 1930).

Döblin's transformation of social class into a heuristic device is crucially important to a critical assessment of his narrative voice and epic style. Breaking with well-established traditions, he approaches the urban underclass without the sentimentality and romanticism often captured in dismissive references to the Zille milieu found in Paul Gurk's nostalgic portrayal of a street peddler in *Berlin* (1927), the literary figure closest perhaps to Biberkopf in terms of social class. Equally indifferent to exploring the connection between class and political ideology, Döblin makes only cursory references to the right-wing extremism and antisemitism that assume center stage in two earlier Berlin novels, Joseph Roth's *Im Spinnennetz* (In the Spider's Web, 1923) and Arthur Landsberger's *Berlin ohne Juden* (Berlin without Jews, 1925). Instead of using the journalistic milieu to diagnose the progressive medialization and commodification of urban experience, a strategy employed by Heinrich Eduard Jacob in *Blut und Zelluloid* (Blood and Celluloid, 1930), Peter de Mendelssohn in *Fertig mit Berlin?* (Finished with Berlin? 1930), and Gabriele Tergit in *Käsebier erobert den Kurfürstendamm* (Käsebier Conquers Kurfürstendamm, 1931), the author of *Berlin Alexanderplatz* makes modern mass media an integral part of his narrative structure (e.g., when citing newspaper articles in the montage sequences). Uninterested in the erotic scenarios that inform the highly gendered flaneries of Erich Kästner's *Fabian* (1931) and Irmgard Keun's *Das kunstseidene Mädchen* (The Artificial Silk Girl, 1932), Döblin simply accepts the coupling of sexuality and violence as a constitutive element of the urban economy. And despite his graphic descriptions of rape and murder, he carefully avoids the sensationalizing of contemporary social and sexual mores—drug addiction, homosexuality, promiscuity, and other phenomena of "degeneracy"—abundantly found in Otto Zarek's *Begierde: Roman einer Großstadtjugend* (Lust: A Novel of Big City Youth, 1930) and Rudolph Stratz's *Karussell Berlin* (Carousel Berlin, 1931) and thereby dislodges sexual desire from its privileged position in the literary construction of modern subjectivity.[24]

Döblin's rejection of the notion of milieu and his unorthodox approach to the question of class made him an easy target within the divided class politics of Weimar culture. As an outspoken member of the left-liberal intelligentsia, he was denounced by conservative critics as radical, elitist, and decadent; but he actually found his harshest critics among Communist writers. Using the Döblin novel to fuel the rivalry between Social Democrats and Communists, the reviewer in the KPD organ *Rote Fahne* dismissed it as a sensationalist portrayal of proletarian Berlin written for the middle-class readers of the New West: "Berlin workers, is that your Alex? Without the party, without politics, without Zörgiebel [the controversial SPD chief of police]?"[25] Speaking for the Bund proletarisch-revolutionärer Schriftsteller (BPRS, League of Proletarian-Revolutionary Writers), Johannes R. Becher declared: "The transport worker in our novel will be a class subject, a transport worker and not an artificially created laboratory product like Döblin's transport worker."[26] And Otto Biha concluded: "*Berlin Alexanderplatz* is the confession of a cultural nihilist, of a weak, indecisive, and resigned bourgeois who has finally found an external form (his style) for his inner ambivalence."[27]

The majority of liberal and progressive critics writing for the feuil-

leton immediately recognized the enormous provocation and literary innovation of *Berlin Alexanderplatz*. The extensive reviews and inevitable par-
odies published in 1929 established the novel's status as both an instant
modernist classic and the quintessential Berlin novel.[28] Many critics wrote
of being moved or shaken to the core and described the act of reading as
an existential experience, an almost physical reenactment of the author's
diagnosis of a modern subjectivity in crisis. While differing in their evaluation of the novel's formal qualities and political message, most reviewers
agreed that *Berlin Alexanderplatz* had to be read within the tradition of the
great nineteenth-century city novel (Dickens, Balzac) and its early-twentieth-century reconceptualization in two other modernist city novels, James
Joyce's *Ulysses* (1922) and John Dos Passos's *Manhattan Transfer* (1925).
Joyce was repeatedly called an important source of inspiration for Döblin's
use of stream of consciousness, whereas Dos Passos invited comparisons
because of his extensive experiments with simultaneity.[29] Similarly, many
critics were keenly aware of the close affinities—on the level of formal
strategies and subject effects—between the novel and new mass media. Not
surprisingly, two ambitious adaptations under the same title soon followed
suit, first in the form of a radio play for the famous Berliner *Funkstunde* in
1930, based on a script by Döblin himself, and then as a sound film directed
by Piel Jutzi in 1931 and starring the character actor Heinrich George.[30]

Döblin's reconstruction of the sociospatial dialectic proved central to
most critical assessments that used terms such as simultaneity, synchro-
nism, parallelism, polyphony, intertextuality, and stream of consciousness.
Introducing the terms that would continue to dominate the novel's scholarly reception, several critics praised the work as the first city novel in
which Berlin appeared as both the narrator and the subject of narration.
Speaking for many, Julius Bab saw a great epic work in which "Berlin is
represented: represented, and not just described."[31] The remark by another
critic, that "Alexanderplatz is at once a landscape of stone and of the
soul," captures this double articulation of external and internal cityscape
with all its broader implications.[32] And Benjamin von Brentano's suggestion that Döblin's mode of writing be positioned "between the bourgeois
novel that can no longer exist and the kind of poetic practice that will give
rise to a different reality"[33] points to some of the political debates that
made modernist experimentation an integral part of wider realignments in
the sociospatial dialectic and that, in this chapter's final section, can only
be clarified through a closer look at Döblin's highly ambiguous conception
of the city as body and machine.

IV. Alfred Döblin and Berlin

In *Berlin Alexanderplatz,* the ultimate goal for protagonist and narrator alike is "the conquest of Berlin," in the case of Biberkopf as part of his social rehabilitation, and in the case of Döblin as part of his deconstruction of the metropolis as narrative and social space. Just as the novel's opening chapter relies on physical movement to register fundamental changes within the cityscape, Döblin during the early writing stage "initially only knew this much: the man wants to leave Tegel Prison and go to Berlin."[34] Both Döblin and Biberkopf use the inherent violence of the process of modernization and urbanization to register the collapse of existing models of bourgeois subjectivity and sociability. While frequently walking together, the omniscient narrator obviously has more powerful means at his disposal; he recites a list of city offices to assert his authorial control, gives biographies (present and future) of the tenants in an apartment building, and comments on specific situations and events in extensive scientific, historical, sociological, and mythological digressions. The act of walking establishes the rhythm and pace of his wanderings and organizes the dynamic of internalization and externalization that gives rise to the textual city. Yet walking, for Döblin, is not only a mode of literary production; the making of the textual city also extends to the reader as an active participant. Comparing the act of reading to the act of walking, he appeals to the reader's sense of critical judgment and common sense: "The reader, left alone, must walk through real streets, where he must find his way around and learn to cope."[35] Not surprisingly, Harald Jähner reads the trope of walking in *Berlin Alexanderplatz* as an ongoing mediation between the crisis of subjectivity and a powerful, devouring city.[36] Andreas Freisfeld similarly speaks of a reconstruction of the city text through walking.[37]

To describe Biberkopf and Döblin as flaneurs, however, would entirely miss the point. Biberkopf lacks the sense of self-confidence that keeps the typical Weimar flaneur in possession of himself, even as he indulges in narcissistic pleasure and regressive fantasy. Indicative of his inability to maintain a sense of distance, Biberkopf suffers debilitating episodes of agoraphobia, an indication of the spatial estrangement diagnosed earlier in Kracauer's city texts and analyzed as a defensive reaction to the process of inner urbanization. With the dissolution of boundaries between interior and exterior cityscape, Biberkopf's subsequent descent into madness proves the impossibility of remaining a subject in the old sense and confirms the need for a new conception of mass subjectivity and urban collectivity. Like his main protagonist, Döblin lacks the sensualism and hedonism available to the bourgeois flaneur in the tradition of Hessel and others. The author's ability to empathize with the suffering of the urban underclass and to speak out for those left out of the program of the New Berlin opens him up to a critical discourse that moves beyond the reductivism of communist approaches, without abandoning the categories of collectivity and solidarity.

Döblin's autobiographical writings and critical essays place *Berlin Alexanderplatz* at the center of an extensive and intensive involvement with the problems of the modern metropolis. He repeatedly portrays himself as the quintessential city dweller, relying on Berlin for inspiration and resonance. "There are things to see, to hear, to smell," he exclaims during a walk through Old Berlin, and describes his arrival in the city as being born for the second time.[38] His close familiarity with the eastern districts was a direct result of his personal and professional choices (fig. 6.5). A trained physician, whose internship in a psychiatric hospital inspired the Berlin-Buch episode, Döblin opened a general practice on Frankfurter Allee that served the working-class populations of Prenzlauer Berg and Friedrichshain; only after 1928 did he move to Kaiserdamm in the New West. In "East of Alexanderplatz," a first sketch for the novel published in 1923, Döblin writes of his identification with the impoverished, the displaced, and the disenfranchised—in other words, with those excluded from the benefits and rewards of modernity.[39] Mapping the social and spatial divisions of the city, he begins "An Excursion to the West" on the city train from Schlesischer Station via Alexanderplatz to Zoological Garden Station; it takes him to the Kurfürstendamm and then, via Tauentzienstraße, to Wittenbergplatz and Nollendorfplatz, the point at which he finally begins to feel at home again.[40]

Writing in and about Weimar Berlin allowed Döblin to both draw attention to the traumatic impact of modernization and confirm the vitality of the metropolis as an agent of transformation and regeneration. Responding to a 1922 newspaper questionnaire about the influence of the city on his writing, he states emphatically that "this excitement of the streets, stores, cars is the heat that I must absorb whenever I am working, which is really all the time."[41] Another newspaper questionnaire in 1928 prompts the confession, "I can write everywhere: at home, on the street, in the restaurant—but really only in Berlin. Without the city I feel distracted."[42] At times, writing the city text takes on the characteristics of a repetition compulsion, betraying his never-ending quest for the metropolis as his

Fig. 6.5. Subway construction on Frankfurter Allee at the corner of Warschauer Straße, 1929. Courtesy of Landesarchiv Berlin.

main source of creative imagination; hence Döblin's admission that "whether I spoke of China, India, or Greenland, I have always spoken of Berlin, of this great, strong, and sober Berlin."[43] As David Dollenmayer has pointed out, an earlier Berlin novel by Döblin, *Wadzeks Kampf mit der Dampfturbine* (Wadzek's Fight with the Steam Turbine, 1918), already contains a brief description of Friedrichstraße that uses some of the montage techniques perfected later in *Berlin Alexanderplatz*.[44] Short milieu studies, such as "Dialogue in the Münzstraße," foreshadow Biberkopf's visit to one of the street's sleazy movie houses after his release from prison; and on extended walks through "Old Berlin" and the region "East of Alexanderplatz," the author relies heavily on found texts—the language of advertising and commerce—to "explore the periphery of this powerful being."[45]

The impact of the modern metropolis on Döblin's writings does not remain limited to his choice of subject matter but extends to his reconceptualization of epic writing through a pronounced preference for architectural terminology, beginning with the central trope of construction. The notion of construction first appears in Döblin's 1913 "Berlin Program," with its provocative motto "There is no place for bad storytelling in the novel; one does not tell, one builds."[46] Construction also takes center stage in a lengthy essay entitled "The Structure of the Epic Work," which was published in 1929 as a commentary on *Berlin Alexanderplatz*. Describing writing as a dialogic process involving author and reader, Döblin asserts the "truly productive [author] has to do two things: he must get really close to reality, to its factuality, its blood, its smell; and then he has to pierce through the material: that is his specific task."[47] In the case of *Berlin Alexanderplatz*, the work of "piercing through" is performed by the pile driver on Alexanderplatz, the ultimate writing tool in the city novel.

Combining the rich symbolism of expressionist prose with the factual style of New Objectivist reportage and pushing the principle of intertextuality almost to the breaking point, *Berlin Alexanderplatz* vacillates between construction and destruction in the sense of previously dominant traditions, established rules, and literary styles as well. Polemically, Döblin declares that "the object of the novel is reality freed of the soul,"[48] and points to architecture and cinema as key elements in this new materialist aesthetics. He introduces the neologism *Kinoismus* (literally, cinema-ism), which he defines as grasping modern life in all of its intensity and diversity, to describe the resulting process of *Entäußerung* (externalization) and what he elsewhere describes as an imagination built on facts. As the most public of all art forms, architecture offers an important model for the kind of modern epic capable of reconciling individual and collective, and reuniting urban reality with the spatial imagination. Praising the materiality of architecture as the only valid alternative to the tired psychologism of bourgeois culture, he declares, "I am not I, but the street, the streetlights, this and that event, nothing more. That is what I call the style of stone,"[49]—words that resonate deeply with the archi-textures of *Berlin Alexanderplatz*.

Yet these architectural references do not automatically align the novel with a modernist aesthetics of construction and destruction, nor do they necessarily establish the foundation for a functionalist or rationalist model of the modern metropolis. Just as the tension between expressionist, realist, and New Objectivist elements remains ultimately unresolved, the opposition between modernity and myth fails to enter into a dialectical relationship; instead these elements become part of the heterogeneous spatial fantasies and social imaginaries that conceive of the modern metropolis as both a body and a machine. In "The Spirit of the Naturalist Age" (1924), Döblin acknowledges this constitutive tension between the organic and the

mechanical when he describes the metropolis as a driving force in the renewal of modern culture in the age of technology: "The new [naturalist]
spirit turns cities into its body and instrument."[50] In its ambivalence and
inconsistency, Döblin's conception of the metropolis exists squarely within
the sociospatial dialectic of his times: between an Enlightenment tradition
that celebrates the metropolis as an instrument of reason and progress, and
new forms of mythological thinking that implicate the big city in the rise
and fall of civilizations; between the functional structures favored by the
international avant-gardes, and the organic designs proposed by conservative regionalists; between the modern machine aesthetic promoted in the
context of Dada and New Objectivity, and the search for a new folk tradition and culture of the small town; and between the left-wing insistence on
a class-based analysis and the right-wing dreams of a national community.
Needless to say, all of these groups, movements, and ideologies saw
Weimar Berlin as the primary battleground over the future of the modern
masses.

The construction of the textual city in *Berlin Alexanderplatz* establishes a connection between two discourses, the city as machine and the
city as body or organism. As we have seen in previous chapters, the former
is usually associated with a modernist view of the city; it suggests functionality, rationality, and, most important, social equality and mobility. By
contrast, the latter tends to be identified with a traditionalist view that emphasizes innate differences and hierarchical structures. Throughout the
1920s, the iconography of the city as machine served to articulate the kind
of radical social changes envisioned during the revolutionary days of
1918–19. The idea of revolution survived in the modernist obsession with
planning, while the social utopias found a compromise solution in the rationalist or functionalist organization of quantifiable differences. Most often, the metaphoric use of the city body functioned as a vehicle for conservative, nationalist, and *völkisch* views of settlements as the founding cell of
the national community. Its underlying purpose was to promote a corporatist model of society that could hold in check the threat of class struggle
(and, in other contexts, of foreign infiltration and racial contamination).
Safeguarding the purity of these two models required placing them outside
history: the one in a yet-to-be-realized future, the other in an eternal past.
Applied to actual urban problems or spaces, these highly charged oppositions between community and society were invariably tempered, modified,
and reconfigured. Similarly, the filmmakers, writers, and critics—Döblin
among them—ended up combining the imagery of the city as body and

machine in much more fluid and ambiguous ways. In doing so, they not only undermined the totalizing impulse behind the two discourses, they also called into question their continued relevance as historically specific responses to the crisis of modern class society. Thus the urban imagination of Döblin offers a first glimpse of what a society beyond or outside the traditional class system might look like: heterogeneous, nonsynchronous, multibodied, multivoiced, and resistant to conventional readings and interpretations.

On one hand, allusions to the machine aesthetic reenact the violent but ultimately liberating effect of modernization on urban culture and society. Sounding very much like Wagner, Gropius, or Hilberseimer, Döblin repeatedly compares the modern metropolis to a gigantic machine that organizes the masses according to the principles of functionality and rationality. "The big cities are a remarkable and powerful apparatus," he observes, but not without acknowledging the difficulties of the city dwellers in adjusting to this new spatial order: "In their streets one can feel almost physically the impulses and tensions experienced by these people."[51] As a writer, Döblin is particularly interested in the close connection between urbanization and democratization. In facilitating an endless circulation of images and texts, the metropolis frees artistic production from its class-based distinctions and creates what he describes as the censorship-free zone of modern culture. Window displays become broadsides, poems, and manifestos, and the existing forms of aesthetic appreciation and cultural consumption are radically expanded and transformed under the ascendancy of new mass media and communication technologies. Like Behne in his tribute to Berlin as a gigantic exhibition space, Döblin welcomes this dissemination of art into everyday life: "The inconspicuous shopkeeper can decorate, illuminate, and suggestively display his wares. One glance reveals what goes on here: needs are being met and new needs created. Man is being worked on in a very practical way. The technical spirit walks through the streets, campaigning and creating."[52]

On the other hand, mythical figures such as the Whore of Babylon and rich allusions to biblical figures such as Job and Jeremiah can at any moment turn Weimar modernity into the ahistorical world of myth and rewrite the city's modernist future as its ancient prehistory. Based on the proposition that "nobody can speak about a part of Berlin or focus on one single building. Only the whole has a gestalt," Döblin translates quantities into qualities and integrates the individual parts into a unified whole, the "sober, modern city, the productive mass settlement."[53] Only such a gestalt, he asserts, gives rise to the collective as a unified body and realizes the inherent truth of society, for "truth only appears on a massive scale."[54] His holistic view of cities as enormous conglomerations finds expression in effusive references to "newly awakened sensory organs that have no boundaries."[55] Significantly, the author often relies on comparisons to biological or physiological processes, as in a reference to the metropolis as "the coral reef of man as a collective being."[56] His descriptions suggest an almost physiocratic view of society as a corpus or corporation in which different social groups perform their roles according to preexisting rules and a natural selection process. Extending these principles to the organization of urban functions, Döblin writes that "specialties are concentrated in certain districts, like lungs in the chest, the brain in the skull, the teeth in the jaws."[57] While these comparisons acknowledge the unique ability of cities to respond to change and integrate difference, given the specter of applied biology raised by such imagery, they also bring into relief the more problematic influence of Ernst Haeckel's monism and its right-wing applications.

In the end, it is the lack of individual or social agency—and in that, of class discourse—that makes the city body and the city machine such highly compatible and mutually dependent systems of urbanization. Döblin draws on his philosophy of nature to argue that the novel's modernist self-reflexive strategies and construction principles cannot be separated from the mythological figures and organicist metaphors. City body and city machine are merely two manifestations of the same social conglomerate, and they remain subject to the same processes of construction and destruction. Therefore every description of the "terrible muddle of organs" that makes up the human body is followed by an enthusiastic machine reference: "It is fantastic what this apparatus is made up of. It is an entire factory, a group of factories, an incubator, a machine, a series of machines, a corporation. In what kind of society have I landed?"[58] Relegating the corporeal to the realm of ancient mythology, or rejecting the organism as regressive or reactionary, would mean misreading the provocative quality of Döblin's critique of instrumental reason and social determinism. That is why the dynamics of modernity and myth find the most appropriate expression in the endless circulation of trams, people, materials, and goods, that is, the spectacle of quantification and commodification that extends even to figures from a mythological past. They all enter the city's "wide body," which, in accordance with mythological tradition, is marked as female but that, given the leveling of all differences, also renders such gendered categories ultimately meaningless and obsolete.[59]

In making possible this mutual contamination of urban discourses, construction—and its uncanny double, destruction—asserts itself once again as the central organizing principle of *Berlin Alexanderplatz*. Its powers extend from the actual construction site on Alexanderplatz to the three blows against Biberkopf that result in his stay at the Buch asylum and end with his rebirth as a well-adjusted mass individual. The tools and techniques of construction replace the narrative conventions that, in most other Berlin novels of the time, organize modern subjectivity and urban experience along class lines, whether of a disempowered middle class, a radicalized working class, or a rising white-collar class. Most important, construction connects the formal principles of montage to the self-reflexivity of urban discourses and creates a provocatively and disconcertingly heterogeneous cityscape that resists appropriation to the dominant discourses of the urban in Weimar Berlin.

Given the importance of construction—and, by implication, of montage—to the archi-textures of *Berlin Alexanderplatz*, it should not surprise us that comparisons to film have been an integral part of the novel's critical reception from the start. Döblin himself encouraged such readings when he declared that his novel "was destined to become a radio play or film,"[60] though perhaps not the kind of conventional melodrama created by Jutzi in his 1931 screen adaptation. Rejecting this film adaptation as too literary, Herbert Ihering insisted nonetheless that "in Döblin's novel, the film form is mapped out. It resembles a written film."[61] Since then, it has become a critical commonplace to describe the montage sequences as filmic, to compare the narrator's excursions to the roaming movements of a camera, and to liken the literary reconstruction of everyday life to the power of the cinematic apparatus in training new modes of perception and new sensibilities.[62]

However, the characterization of Döblin's narrative style as filmic distracts from the considerable differences between filmic and literary forms of montage. Continuity editing in classical narrative cinema seeks to establish relations among individual shots and provide spatiotemporal continuity; even the use of associative or analytical montage in nonnarrative genres creates continuity through unifying audiovisual effects. From the perspective of construction as a self-reflexive principle, there could hardly be a greater difference in the approach to urban representation than between Döblin's deconstruction and Ruttmann's reconstruction of Weimar Berlin. As we will see in the book's final chapter, Ruttmann's *Berlin, Symphony of the Big City* overcomes the crisis of modern subjectivity and the fragmentation of urban life through forms of spectatorship that, modeled on modern consumer culture, aim to reconfigure the sociospatial dialectic in accordance with the goals of white-collar society. As I have argued in this chapter, *Berlin Alexanderplatz* pursues the opposite strategy. Through the futile attempts of Franz Biberkopf to conquer Berlin, Döblin deconstructs not only the disparate elements that constitute the modern metropolis but also the urban discourses that promoted modern architecture as an instrument of social engineering. Through a figure from the lumpenproletariat, he cuts through the determinations of class without abandoning the all-important belief in solidarity and community; therein lies the continuing provocation of *Berlin Alexanderplatz.*

CHAPTER 7

Reconstructing Modern Subjectivity:
On *Berlin, Symphony of the Big City*

"Our bars and city streets, our offices and furnished rooms, our railroad stations and our factories seemed to close relentlessly around us. Then came film and exploded this prison-world with the dynamite of the split second."[1] This is how Benjamin in his famous Art Work Essay describes the impact of film on the urban imagination. Providing new technologies of vision, film, like photography, radically expanded the spatiotemporal coordinates of metropolitan life. Both re-created key elements of the urban experience in the formal language of montage, especially through experiments with contingency and discontinuity, and both realigned modern subjectivity and class identity with highly mediated regimes of looking and what Benjamin in the same essay calls the optical unconscious. Much has been written about the historical constellation of urbanism and cinema and the rearticulation of identity and space through new forms of mental mapping. By contrast, surprisingly little research has been devoted to the ways in which cinema contributed to the dissolution of rigid class divisions and participated in the production of a collective urban imaginary beyond social hierarchies and spatial boundaries. This latter connection between film and class was frequently acknowledged in early writings (and later scholarship) on film as a revolutionary mass medium and speculations about silent cinema as an alternative proletarian public sphere, categories that mark the point of departure for the following discussion of Walter (or Walther) Ruttmann's *Berlin, die Sinfonie der Großstadt* (Berlin, Symphony of the Big City, 1927) and its unique contribution to Weimar Berlin's topographies of class.

In chapter 5, we saw how architectural photography promoted the social program of New Building by emphasizing the emancipatory force of modernism and by aestheticizing the experience of mass society. Architectural publications and popular photobooks mediated the shock of the new by providing a narrative of spatial integration and historical continuity, most notably through highly suggestive captions and accompanying texts. We examined how the radicalized urban proletariat and the new class of white-collar workers used the ubiquitous city images in the illustrated press to claim their place in the new dynamics of urban life. The exploration of space, place, history, and identity through the lens of architectural culture found a logical continuation in the visual regimes of city photography and city film. In the preceding chapters, the contributions by Wagner, Behne, Fromm, Geiger, Hilberseimer, Mendelsohn, Kracauer, Hessel, and Döblin have been presented as part of a larger debate on the double crisis of the big city and class society, with the proposed solutions closely linked to the fate of bourgeois subjectivity. The responses of architects, sociologists, novelists, and essayists ranged from the enthusiastic embrace of a fully rationalized society to the retreat into old-fashioned flanerie as a gesture of individual opposition; from identification with the stranger as a discursive position mediating among social classes and local cultures to the radical demontage of traditional conceptions of identity and subjectivity through a figure from the lumpenproletariat; and from architecture as an expression of individual taste to its transformation into an instrument of mass mobilization and social control. References to film and photography could be found in almost all contributions, whether in the reliance on film as a model for urban writing and architectural design or the use of the photo-camera/photo-eye as a metaphor for the mechanization of perception and the medialization of experience.

Contributing to this process, Ruttmann's *Berlin* must be described as the first film that presented Berlin as "the home of the masses" (to evoke Kracauer's "Cult of Diversion" essay) and that thematized the transformation of the modern metropolis through explicitly filmic terms. The dynamization of time and space in the innovative genre of the city symphony radically expanded the terms of urban experience beyond the physicality of the built environment, and of the individual city dweller, while closely aligning the project of urban representation with the new technologies of visual perception and cultural consumption. Once again, it was the ideology of form that, as in the urban imaginaries of a Wagner or Hilberseimer, made possible the filmic simulation of a modern subjectivity beyond the divisions of class. Yet the constitutive tension between mimetic impulse and formal abstraction in the city symphony and its contribution to the making of the modern mass individual cannot be understood outside the discourses of quantification, rationalization, and functionalization that served as the hidden reference points for Ruttmann's formalistic urban excursions.

A compelling portrait of Weimar Berlin during the stabilization period, *Berlin* must be described through a series of contradictory terms: documentary and experimental film, film art and political program, an expression of creative filmmaking, and a by-product of the international film trade. Produced by Karl Freund for Fox Europe, a German subsidiary of the famous Hollywood studio, the Ruttmann film was a so-called quota quickie, an inexpensive production made to satisfy the contingency laws limiting foreign access to domestic markets. Hailed as an important contribution to the film avant-garde, *Berlin* premiered in the Tauentzienpalast on 23 September 1927, with a live orchestra playing an original Edmund Meisel score. The advertisements for the film highlighted both its urban themes and its architectural construction principles, with one poster featuring little but unadorned red façades with empty window squares and angular sans serif type fonts (fig. 7.1). Displayed in theater lobbies and published in *Illustrierte Filmkurier,* another series of photomontages (some attributed to Otto Umbehr) emphasized Weimar Berlin's debt to the American high-rise city and its culture of speed, noise, and mass consumption.[2]

Whether described as a documentary, avant-garde or abstract film, *Berlin* remains the most famous example of the productive encounter of cinema, urbanism, and modernism during the Weimar period and its broader implications for the end of traditional class society. The vacillation between affirmation and critique, first diagnosed by Kracauer's reference to the film's "ambiguous neutrality"[3] and much debated in critical scholarship ever since, bears witness to the changing constellations of reformist politics, utopian aesthetics, functionalist ideologies, and vitalist philosophies that characterized the German path to modernity and defined the post–World War I confrontation between German nationalism and conservatism, on the one hand, and an American-style egalitarianism and consumerism, on the other.[4] Under these conditions, the combination of documentary material and avant-garde technique, and the reliance on cross section (*Querschnitt*) as a formal and conceptual montage principle, prove ideally suited to gloss over the contradictions produced by economic growth, technological innovation, and social change and to celebrate the ascendancy of commodity culture and its laws of equivalences in the surface splendor of the city symphony.

Fig. 7.1. Film poster for *Berlin, die Sinfonie der Großstadt.* Courtesy of Deutsches Filminstitut DIF e.V., Deutsches Filmmuseum Frankfurt am Main and Deutsche Kinemathek Museum für Film und Fernsehen Berlin.

Visualizing the effects of quantification and standardization, Ruttmann's approach to rhythm and montage completes the historical transition from the class-based social distinctions of the nineteenth-century metropolis to the system of functional differentiation of Fordism, Taylorism, and white-collar culture. Even the differences between organicist and rationalist models of society, which played such a key role in the debates among architects and urban planners, are eliminated through the leveling force of associative editing and the integrative structure of a typical day in the big city. Similarly, Ruttmann compensates for the fragmentation in modernity through the totalizing perspective of cross section and its own system of prototypes and equivalences. He contains the shock of the new through the detached perspective offered by New Objectivity and its sobering assumptions about the factuality of modern life. In presenting what Derek Hillard calls an "allegory for a historical transition,"[5] the film reenacts a deep ambivalence about mass culture and modernity that, in terms not yet fully acknowledged in the existing scholarship, can only be overcome through its fantasy of a homogeneous mass society.

In close collaboration with cameraman Robert Baberske and producer Karl Freund, filmmaker Walter Ruttmann captured the vibrant atmosphere of late 1920s Berlin through an innovative cross section of typical urban buildings, locations, settings, rhythms, moods, and activities. The director responded to what Benjamin described as the legitimate need of the masses for self-representation when he shot and assembled short scenes that highlight the shared ability of urban and filmic space to provide collective experiences and create public spheres. Yet by organizing the images according to the paradigmatic and syntagmatic principles of cross section, Ruttmann transformed the urban masses into mere raw material for what one advertisement called "the film of six million actors and one hundred thousand buildings."[6] Thus the city dwellers function not only as representatives of different classes, genders, generations, and lifestyles, but also as agents of the very laws of quantification that, according to Antje Ehmann, confirm abstraction as the dominant mode of organization in the modern metropolis.[7] Abstraction, as analyzed by Simmel and other theorists of urban culture, represents the unifying principle of the money economy that gave rise to the classical metropolis of the nineteenth century and that, after World War I, aligned the mobilization of the masses ever more closely with the rituals of mass consumption. Furthermore, abstraction can be described as the one principle shared by rationalist and functionalist visions of a future metropolis, reason enough to examine how Ruttmann's "symphony of the big city" contributed to this trend toward abstraction in visually compelling and conceptually problematic ways.

In this chapter, I use the Ruttmann film to diagnose the disappearance of class difference as the central category of urban life and the emergence of white-collar culture as an agent of social and cultural leveling. *Berlin,* I argue, reenacts the making of the modern masses through its use of acceleration and quantification, its reliance on equivalencies and homologies, and its emphasis on spectacle and visuality. By aestheticizing modern mass society, the film not only compels city dwellers and movie audiences to accept their lack of agency and control but also to embrace the techniques of derealization developed by the urban cultural industry. As in the case of *Berlin Alexanderplatz,* I reconstruct this elusive process through a combination of textual and contextual analysis: a brief description of the film's overall structure and its historical significance as a famous Berlin film, followed by a detailed discussion of its representation of white-collar society and its critical reception in the Weimar press. In doing so, I seek to offer an alternative to readings that look at the film only in terms of mental maps or imaginary topographies, thus essentializing its formal principles as part of a technologically based urban imaginary entirely disconnected from the material conditions in Weimar Berlin and the struggles of the classes, collectivities, and multitudes that call the metropolis their home.

I. A City Symphony in Five Movements

In order to understand the filmic representation of the urban masses in *Berlin,* we must reconstruct the process of aestheticization that is evident already in the highly abstract opening sequence and the atmospheric images of the capital at dawn. The first movement begins with a series of quick dissolves that transport the viewer from several high-angle shots of the historic center to empty streets in a typical working-class neighborhood. When the church clock strikes five, the city still appears deserted, its uncanny stillness heightened by the slow editing. Several close-ups of machine parts, doors, and windows rely on anthropomorphisms to suggest a sleeping organism, a point picked up later in the repeated opening of blinds, shutters, and curtains. As if following a secret mechanism, the first workers emerge from the tenements and are soon joined by others at subway entrances and commuter train stations. Recognizable by their open collars and soft caps, they inundate the city's central squares and major transit stations, their highly choreographed movements interrupted only briefly by the appearance of marching soldiers. The animation of the inanimate world in the representation of urban buildings and technologies and the objectification of human beings in the scenes of mass transit and street life establish the conceptual binaries of natural versus cultural, organic versus mechanical, and circular versus linear that are channeled through the film's symphonic structure and eventually resolved through the leveling effects of cross section. The arrival of the workers in the factories is visu-

Fig. 7.2. *Berlin, die Sinfonie der Großstadt.* Frame enlargement. Courtesy of Deutsche Kinemathek Museum für Film und Fernsehen Berlin and Mrs. Eva Riehl, Munich.

alized by the setting into motion of several cranks and flywheels, a subtle reference also to the technology of cinema. Moving with rhythmical precision, the gigantic machines bring forth everything from milk bottles and loaves of bread to light bulbs and sheets of metal. Significantly, the tight framing excludes the workers from the scene of production. The privileging of form over function (in this case, of oblong shapes) and the fetishist focus on the machine present production as productivity without producers and give rise to a machine aesthetic unburdened by the conditions of production (fig. 7.2).

The second movement of the city symphony, which begins with the clock striking eight, is devoted to the world of business and commerce. Again, the principles of acceleration, mobilization, and synchronization prevail as countless office workers board double-decker busses, emerge from subway exits, and walk briskly toward office buildings. Among them, one finds a large number of fashionably dressed young women who move with the self-confidence of the emancipated New Woman. Now it is the spectacle of filing cabinets, typewriters, and telephones that, in a variation on the earlier factory scene, set into motion the modern bureaucracies. The big city traffic loses some of its purposeful, directed quality as more and more vehicles and pedestrians converge in the commercial center. The camera now seems omnipresent, stopping for the presentation of a street vendor, watching an elegantly dressed couple on an outing, lingering for a street brawl, observing one woman as she waits impatiently on a street corner, following another as she inspects window displays, and trailing a young man as he picks up an attractive woman, perhaps a prostitute, as some critics have suggested.[8] A series of dissolves on train destination plates and hotel marquees confirms Berlin's importance as the German capital and a favorite tourist destination. The camera records everything with the same indifferent attentiveness, whether a wedding party or a fallen horse, a procession of conservative fraternities or a leftist demonstration, a public appearance of Reich President Hindenburg or a sandwich man advertising Bullrich antacid.

Several close-ups of wheels coming to a standstill mark the beginning of the third movement. With its slower pacing, the lunchtime scenes allow Ruttmann to give some city dwellers individual traits. For the first time, the problem of urban poverty comes into view through the figures of a war cripple, an old beggar, and a destitute young woman with two small children. The three bearded (Jewish?) men in traditional dress and the two women (prostitutes?) leaning provocatively out of a window draw attention to the film's underlying mechanisms of exclusion, but any threatening otherness is contained through the formalistic approach to montage. Even the juxtaposition of day laborers eating their sandwiches in public parks and respectable burghers gathering in elegant restaurants and outdoor cafés only serves to underscore the integrative force of the cross-section principle. Reduced to variations on a theme, even the marginalized social types and ethnic groups end up confirming the homogenizing effects of modern mass society. In the restaurants, meanwhile, cooks, waiters, and dishwashers have taken the place of the factory workers at the conveyer belt, with an endless stream of filled plates and clean dishes announcing the triumph of the modern service economy. The metropolis, the frantic ending of the third movement suggests, may be a living organism, but it is above all a gigantic machine that never stops. More specifically, the city body/machine appears to run without purpose, propelled forward only by its own laws of movement, production, and consumption.

The livelier but also more disjointed fourth movement starts with a man's impatient call for his waitress and sleepy zoo animals rising from the ground. Leaving behind the spectacle of labor and industry, the film now turns its attention to the world of mass communication and mass entertainment. Close-ups of rotary presses printing the evening newspapers are followed by shots of newspaper boys selling papers on busy streets. Through trick photography, the front-page headlines disintegrate into isolated words like *crisis, murder, stock market,* and *marriage.* After the word *money* is repeated six times, the scene, quite literally, explodes during a roller-coaster ride in Lunapark, the famous amusement park near Kaiserdamm. The animated spiral in a shop window, signifying the vertigo induced by modern life, finds its human equivalent in the wide-open eyes of a terrified woman ready to jump off a bridge, presumably in response to the worsening economic situation suggested by the word *crisis.* This staged melodramatic scene, which quotes the visual conventions of the expressionist street film, briefly abandons the celebration of rhythm and tempo and allows for a rare acknowledgment of the shock of modernity and the violence of modernization (fig. 7.3). Yet already the next scene takes us back to the luxurious window displays on the Kurfürstendamm, an affirmation of the film's enormous debt to commodity aesthetics.

The halting of wheels and the image of birds flying free announce the end of the workday and the beginning of the fifth movement. With joyful anticipation, the white- and blue-collar workers leave their offices and factories for a wide range of recreational activities such as bicycling, rowing, swimming, and running. As darkness falls, the pursuit of visual pleasures becomes more pronounced. Nighttime brings out the beauty of the big city, beginning with the dramatic light effects created by the headlights of passing vehicles, the rows of street lights, and the flashing neon signs advertising Odol mouthwash, Dujardin cognac, Hildebrand chocolate, and Vox records. While some city dwellers attend a screening of Chaplin's *The Gold Rush,* others gather at the Scala's spectacular revues, complete with showgirls, acrobats, jugglers, and clowns. The close-up of a man and woman's legs climbing into a taxi, followed by one of a hotel sign, offers a not too subtle comment on the outcome of many a city night. For others, the search for excitement continues, as evidenced by a quick tour through the world of spectator sports, including the famous six-day races, and a survey of typical nightlife amusements, from an ordinary neighborhood dive to an elegant dining club. Yet even in the dimly lit cocktail bar, the dancers only repeat the mechanical movements trained at the workplace, with one small difference: now it is the Charleston, and not the machine,

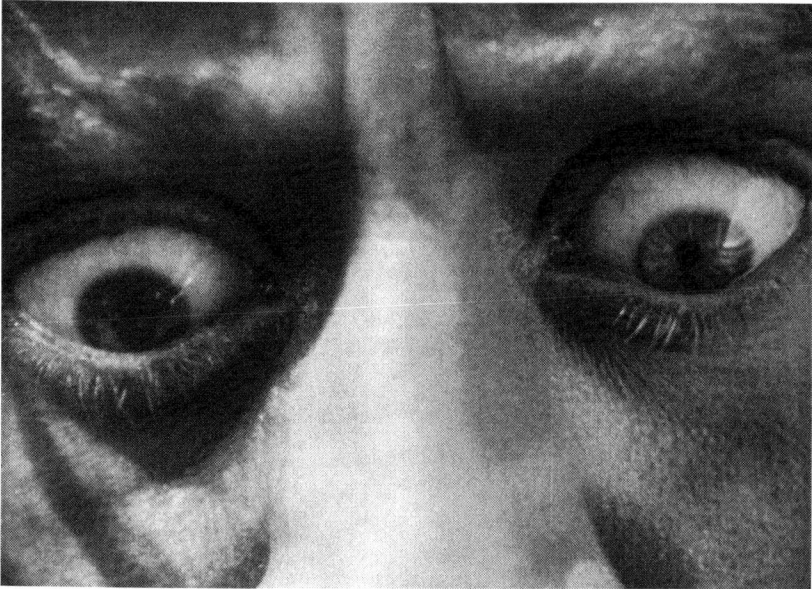

Fig. 7.3. *Berlin, die Sinfonie der Großstadt.* Frame enlargement. Courtesy of Deutsche Kinemathek Museum für Film und Fernsehen Berlin and Mrs. Eva Riehl, Munich.

that dictates the tempo and the rhythm. There is one last glance toward the neon sign of the famous Café am Zoo, before the logo begins a dizzying rotation until it turns into veritable fireworks, with the bright rays of the radio tower signaling the final chords of this "symphony of the big city."

Though originally conceived by the famous screenwriter Carl Mayer, *Berlin* was primarily the work of Walter Ruttmann who, with Baberske (and, possibly, Freund) responsible for the camerawork, focused on the editing process as the most important tool in visualizing the modern metropolis. In developing all formal relations out of the reality of fragmentation, he brought the aesthetic sensibilities of the historical avant-garde to a remarkable experiment in urban representation equally removed from the formal conventions of the feature film and the *Kulturfilm* (cultural film), a nonnarrative genre with documentary qualities and educational ambitions. Like Wagner who compared his work as an urban planner to that of a conductor, Ruttmann likened his approach to filmmaking to the act of composing. With his interest in film as a synaesthetic art form already evident in the *Opus* series (1918–23), his description of *Berlin* is filled with musical references: "The most delicate pianissimo had to be consistently moved toward fortissimo. Major and minor had to be logically transformed into, or sharply contrasted with, one another. A counterpoint had to emerge out of the rhythm of man and machine."[9] After mastering the visualization of sound in *Berlin,* Ruttmann turned subsequently to the acoustics of space in *Weekend* (1930), a radio play produced for the *Berliner Funk-stunde* program. Yet whereas his more experimental "symphony of sounds,"[10] to quote Lotte Eisner, benefited from the inherent tendency of sound toward abstraction, his city symphony remained subject to the laws of mimetic representation and failed to overcome the deep social, economic, and political divisions that haunted Berlin toward the end of the Weimar Republic.

Laying the ground for the tension between abstraction and representation that continues to define the critical reception of *Berlin,* Ruttmann in a polemic against the absolute film asserted that film is "not just an artistic matter . . . but above all a human and social matter! . . . Art means no longer abstraction but taking a stance (*Stellungnahme*)."[11] Yet what does taking a stance mean within the formal and thematic preoccupations of the city symphony? Does it refer to aesthetic or political commitments, a particular attitude or a set of beliefs? Ruttmann's later application of the cross-section principle to nonurban subjects suggests that he was not talking about the kind of committed art envisioned by Wagner, Taut, or Döblin. Demonstrating the compatibility of fascist and modernist aesthetics in the factuality, objectivity, and cool detachment of New Vision photography, after 1933 Ruttmann continued to work in the cross-section format but this time in industrial films for big corporations like Henkel and Mannesmann and the German armament industry during World War II.[12] His artistic biography illustrates in what ways both the aestheticization of politics, identified by Benjamin as a distinguishing mark of fascism, and the affirmative realism of New Objectivity can be read as formalized responses to experiences of conflict, crisis, and trauma. To what degree fascist culture moved beyond the "steely romanticism" of the Weimar years to harness premodern and antiurban fantasies of national community can be inferred from Ruttmann's decision in the infamous *Blut und Boden* (Blood and Soil, 1933) to use scenes from *Berlin* as evidence of the dangers of big city life during the reviled *Systemzeit* (i.e., the Weimar period). He also saw no problem in instrumentalizing the format of the city symphony for the celebration of *Heimat* (homeland) and *Volksgemeinschaft* (racial community) in two 1935 productions about Stuttgart and Düsseldorf, with the latter's title *Kleiner Film einer großen Stadt* (A Small Film about a Big City) announcing the genre's deterioration into picturesque vignettes and regionalist sentiments.

The opening sequence of *Berlin* directly thematizes the relationship between abstraction and representation that proves so central to the transformation of cross section into a conceptual and, ultimately, ideological tool. By establishing the terms of translatability and transferability, this sequence recalls Ruttmann's early abstract films and their constitutive tension between referentiality and nonreferentiality. The film opens on images of small waves that turn into graphic patterns: first several bright horizontal lines and, later, a rectangle and a half circle. These lines begin to pulsate, with the geometric forms dictating the rhythm, until two opposing lines metamorphose (through a match-dissolve) into the barriers of a railroad crossing and give rise to the suggestive equation of camera and train. With a sign announcing "Berlin 15 km," this rhythmic geometry continues

Fig. 7.4. *Berlin, die Sinfonie der Großstadt.* Frame enlargement. Courtesy of Deutsche Kinemathek Museum für Film und Fernsehen Berlin and Mrs. Eva Riehl, Munich.

in the graphic vocabulary of steam wheels, railroad tracks, power lines, and steel bridges. The sequence culminates in a powerful allegory of cinema, with the train windows and railroad tracks evoking the filmstrip as the conduit to a mobilized space and visual consciousness unburdened by physical reality (fig. 7.4). After the train's arrival at Anhalter Station, these self-reflexive references become an integral part of Ruttmann's filmic reconstruction of urban life, with movement and mobility (in the literal and figurative sense) as the defining traits of the New Berlin and its systems of circulation and exchange. The similarities between urban experience and filmic perception are acknowledged whenever the camera, mounted on a car, moves among other vehicles and passersby or tracks along sidewalks and shop windows, a technological extension of the modern flaneur and a training instrument for the mobilized consciousness of the urban masses. To what degree the convergence of cinema and urbanism involves processes of projections is alluded to in another allegorical scene as the camera, now placed at the front of a subway train, leaves the darkness of a tunnel and turns the bright outside into a blank screen waiting to be inscribed.

This radical expansion of time and space and this collapsing of image and perception is perhaps described best by Laszlo Moholy-Nagy, the author of an unrealized film script on *Dynamik der Großstadt* (Dynamics of the Big City, 1922), whose proposal to forge all visual elements into "a spatiotemporal whole and to involve the spectator actively in the city dynamic"[13] reads very much like a blueprint for the Ruttmann film. Moholy-Nagy's assertion that, through photography, film, and architecture, "we have attained an enlargement and sublimation of our appreciation of space, the comprehension of a new spatial culture"[14] establishes a clear connection between the new technologies of vision and the ideologies of space that promise to overcome the crisis of class society and modern subjectivity. However, where the constructivist method in Moholy-Nagy is predicated on the acceptance of fragmentation and abstraction as a constitutive part of modern life, the symphonic approach to editing in Ruttmann aims at the opposite effect: it reconciles all elements into a semblance of mimetic totality. His method of rhythmic cutting, with frame composition emphasizing verticals, horizontals, and diagonals and with individual shot sequences grouped according to the direction of movement within the frame (e.g., upward versus downward, leftward versus rightward), achieves a homogenizing effect that has profound implications for the understanding of Weimar Berlin as the center of the most radical experiments in modern art and culture and the object of extensive debates on the future of class society and mass society.

After all, what happens when such formalist techniques are applied to a place and space easily recognized by contemporary audiences as Berlin? Abstraction comes to serve as a vehicle for other meanings, with the composition of lines, triangles, and rectangles merging with the choreography of machines, workers, goods, and vehicles and with both paradigms announcing the rise of white-collar society and a consumption-driven, service-based economy. Analyzing this process through the relationship between place and space, Wolfgang Natter astutely describes *Berlin* "as a circulatory system, defined by accumulation and exchange, and as such, a materialization of the compression of the space-time perception associated with modernism."[15] To this should be added the establishment of cross section as the formal equivalent of the leveling effects of commodification in the urban economy.

II. Walter Ruttmann and the City Film

We have already alluded to the contribution of the historical avant-garde to the emancipation of urban representation from mimetic impulses and realist conventions. Yet what exactly were the filmic traditions challenged by Ruttmann when he set out to construct or, rather, compose *Berlin* as a city symphony? In what ways did the principle of cross section offer freedom from the illusionist strategies and identificatory patterns in the fiction film and the naive belief in verisimilitude fostered by the newsreel and the cultural film? What formal strategies allowed *Berlin* to move beyond the social distinctions and spatial divisions that organized dramatic conflicts in most city films of the period? Answering these questions requires at least a cursory look at the filmic representation of Berlin within the generic conventions of Weimar cinema and the representation of the metropolis in the international genre of the city symphony.

Ruttmann's *Berlin* and the city of Berlin must be described as an integral part of the discourse of cinema and urbanism that provided the strategies of representation in the so-called *Zeitfilm* (contemporary film) and that used filmic metaphors to discuss the problems of the metropolis in the feuilleton. Critics repeatedly turned to cinematic metaphors when reflecting on what they perceived as a dangerous blurring of reality and fantasy in urban consciousness, and film scholars have since made the relationship between cinema and urbanism a major subject of scholarly inquiry.[16] Clearly aware of the imaginary cityscapes built in the Ufa studios in Babelsberg, John Chancellor, in a Berlin guide for Englishmen, observed that the "sort of scenery which filmgoers saw in such German films as *The Cabinet of Dr. Caligari* is to be seen springing up in reality in many corners of Berlin."[17] Similarly, novelist Rudolf Stratz likened the area between *Scheunenviertel* and Schlesisches Tor to "a film set cordoned off with chains."[18] These two quotations—and many others could have been chosen in their place—confirm to what degree filmic sensibility and media consciousness were considered an integral part of urban experience. More specifically, the (often unfavorable) comparisons of famous Berlin streets and monuments to their filmic doubles point to widespread anxiety about the consequences of this fundamental transformation of the space of lived experience according to the rules of filmic identification and spectatorial desire. Many cultural critics reacted to what they perceived as the reinvention of Berlin as a mere *Kulissenstadt* (stage set city) with a mixture of cultural pessimism, moral outrage, and aesthetic revulsion. The conclusion of Alfred Polgar is very typical in this regard:

> Film occupies Berlin, deserters stream to it in masses, and the city's total capitulation is not far. For the stranger blinded by klieg lights, the real Berlin often looks like a film fantasy made of cardboard, with the real houses only put there to feign a little bit of "authentic city." One could also say: one single film strip embraces all peoples of Berlin. . . . Its inscription: Millions—be embraced.[19]

For the same reasons that the visual pleasures and illusionist effects of cinema changed the very terms of urban experience, the actual city became a recognizable presence in many contemporary dramas and comedies. Whereas the expressionist street films in the style of Karl Grune's *Die Straße* (The Street, 1923) staged their highly ambiguous relationship to the big city in psychologically charged interiors and exteriors, the romantic comedies, social dramas, and so-called *Zeitfilme* (topical films) produced in the late 1920s chose more realistic approaches to celebrate the attractions of urban life. Rejecting the bourgeois sensibilities of the expressionist street film as incompatible with the smooth surface aesthetics of New Objectivity, studio professionals like Joe May in *Asphalt* (1929) re-created their mobilized, animated, and virtual Berlin entirely on the modern sound stage. Others (once again) opened the studio doors to capture glimpses of social reality, relying heavily on on-location shooting to record contemporary moods and attitudes and organizing in short sequences what Ruttmann expanded into a totalizing vision of modern urbanity. Taking advantage of the location of the Ufa studios on the southwestern outskirts of Berlin, many mainstream productions organized their storylines around recognizable Berlin locations in the style of Ernst Laemmle's *Der Teufelsreporter* (A Hell of a Reporter, 1929) or Gerhard Lamprecht's *Emil und die Detektive* (Emil and the Detectives, 1931), to mention two examples that prominently feature the Kurfürstendamm. Every exuberant celebration of the freedom of movement produced its own counternarrative of anxiety and dread, however, which often culminated in the characters' difficulties in negotiating city traffic and making their way through the hustle and bustle of big city life. In two well-known films from the early 1930s, this counternarrative is built around the screen persona of Heinrich George, whose family in Werner Hochbaum's *Schleppzug M 17* (Barge M 17, 1933) literally breaks apart in their attempt to cross Potsdamer Platz, and whose own efforts to become a decent person are thwarted forever as soon as he returns to Alexanderplatz in the eponymous 1931 film adaptation of the Döblin novel. In both cases, the kinetic thrills of cinematic flanerie and the experience of what Max Osborn, in a different context, called "traffic psychosis,"[20] remain inseparable from the spatial trajectories of class identity, with some protagonists—the young, the ambitious, and the educated—adjusting perfectly to the accelerated urban tempo and with others—the old, the poor, and the unskilled—overwhelmed by the city's sheer size and intensity.

Like these narrative films, *Berlin* conceived of the metropolis as a set of recognizable locations, activities, and characters, relying heavily on the trope of traffic to reenact the effect of movement, circulation, and exchange on modern subjectivity. Yet by choosing real locations and actual people as his main protagonists and by replacing character identification with the disembodied gaze of the camera, Ruttmann modeled his organization of the material on the standards of factuality and objectivity associated primarily with nonnarrative forms. He developed further the tradition of the city symphony started by the Ufa cultural film department with *Die Stadt der Millionen: Ein Lebensbild Berlins* (The City of Millions: A Portrait of Berlin, 1925), directed by Adolf Trotz. One of the first featurelength cultural films made for commercial release, *The City of Millions* already used innovative techniques such as double exposure, time lapse photography, and associative montage to depict "a typical day in the life of a big city." Similarly, *Berlin*'s mixture of realistic street scenes and evocative urban metaphors can already be found in Leo Peukert's *Im Strudel des Verkehrs* (In the Vortex of Traffic, 1925), which offers a humorous commentary on the trope of big city traffic by having a golemlike monster trudge across Potsdamer Platz. Rejecting the didactic intentions and totalizing perspectives of these cultural films, more innovative filmmakers often focused on one particular location, activity, or social group to examine the contradictions of big city life. Famous examples include Ernö Metzner's *Überfall* (Assault, 1928), a surrealist exploration of crime, dream, and the urban uncanny; Wilfried Basse's atmospheric portrayal of a weekly farmers' market in *Markt am Nollendorfplatz* (Market on Nollendorfplatz, 1929); Moholy-Nagy's unjustly forgotten portrayal of social outsiders in *Großstadtzigeuner* (Big City Gypsies, 1930); and the collaboration between Robert Siodmak, Edgar Ulmer, Billy Wilder, and Fred Zinnemann on *Menschen am Sonntag* (People on a Sunday, 1930), featuring young Berliners engaged in their weekend activities.[21]

The filmic representation of social discrimination and political confrontation was nowhere more apparent than in the few Berlin films with a progressive political agenda. The most famous example, Slatan Dudow's *Kuhle Wampe, oder dem gehört die Welt?* (To Whom Does the World Belong? 1932) continued the critique of the tenement as the site of working-class misery started by Piel Jutzi in *Mutter Krausens Fahrt ins Glück* (Mother Krause's Journey to Happiness, 1929) and similar so-called Zille films, named after the photographer and artist Heinrich Zille, the famous pre–World War I chronicler of Berlin's urban poor. Rejecting the melodramatic tradition of the Zille films, which took a deterministic approach to social milieu, Dudow included extended documentary sequences (e.g., of a workers' sports festival and a street performance of the Red Megaphone theater group) to show the importance of class solidarity and the possibility of radical change. In his and in other films, working-class districts were no longer depicted as places only of poverty and suffering. In the short films produced by the leftist media organization Weltfilm, Berlin's famous buildings and streets also provided a perfect setting for the political empowerment of the modern masses, the dynamics of empty and filled space, crowds contained and unleashed, of multitudes assembling and the revolution on the march. In these films, proletarian districts such as Wedding and Kreuzberg appeared as hotbeds of communist activism from which the workers emerged to organize mass protests and political rallies in the city's historic center; hence the frequent return of KPD film crews to the Lustgarten as the site of the annual May Day celebrations. Significantly, their

May Day films relied on the same candid camera and tracking shots as Ruttmann, but this time to uncover the deep class divisions in the metropolis and to effect a very different kind of mobilization of the masses. Thus, in *Roter Pfingsten* (Red Whitsunday, 1928), *Der 1. Mai—Weltfeiertag der Arbeiterklasse* (May Day—International Workers' Day Celebration, 1929), and *Der 1. Mai in Berlin* (May Day in Berlin, 1930), the camera no longer has any interest in the commodities displayed in the shop windows. Instead the cameraman's assertive movements announce the conquest of the street by the revolutionary working class: a short-lived filmic dream, to be sure, and one that would soon be replaced by very different scenarios of social division and racial exclusion announced by a National Socialist propaganda film like *Kampf um Berlin* (The Battle for Berlin, 1929).

In its realistic portrayal of urban locations and social types, Ruttmann's city symphony shares many characteristics with the countless feature films, cultural films, and documentaries set in Weimar Berlin. Yet in terms of its formal qualities, *Berlin* has much more in common with the international genre of the city film. This started with Paul Strand and Charles Sheeler's *Manhatta* (1921) and Alberto Cavalcanti's Parisian *Rien que les heures* (Nothing But Time, 1926), continued with Mikhail Kaufman's *Moskva* (Moscow, 1927) and Dziga Vertov's *Chelovek s kino-apparatom* (Man with a Movie Camera, 1929), and traveled from the centers of global capitalism depicted in Robert Florey's New York *Skyscraper Symphony* (1929), to the edges of economic development in Adalberto Kemeny's *Sao Paolo—sinfonia da metropole* (Symphony of the Metropolis, 1929) and Kenji Mizoguchi's *Tokai kokyogaku* (Metropolitan Symphony, 1929).[22] All of these city symphonies use the spatiotemporal regimes of cinema to measure the leveling effect of capitalism or communism on the look and feel of individual cities. The worldwide appeal of city symphonies during the 1920s, a decade that brought the productive alliance of artistic modernism with a progressive mass culture but ended with the worldwide Depression and the rise of fascism, raises important questions about the function of the symphony as a principle of integration and leveling—or, more specifically, a leveling of geographic differences, local knowledges, social distinctions, and historical experiences through the imaginary topographies of cinema.

Significantly, none of these filmmakers quite share Ruttmann's ambivalence about the modern metropolis, believing either (like Cavalcanti) in the power of the city to maintain the proper balance between individual and collective, or developing (like Vertov) a form of montage that preserves the revolutionary potential of film. Using cross section to gloss over the underlying contradictions, *Berlin* subordinates all material to the principles of equivalence, repetition, and serialization established by capitalist commodity culture. Throughout, the universal principle of exchangeability functions as protection against the many signs of economic and social inequality. The emphasis on formal affinities and functional differentiations distracts from the power structures behind the seemingly natural choreography of producers, consumers, and commodities. By avoiding the question of causality altogether and by presenting contradictions as mere manifestations of diversity, the film's five movements are able to foreground the beautiful surface manifestations of the new consumer and entertainment culture. In light of the abstractness of cross section as an organizing principle, we might even want to agree with Walter Schobert, who describes *Berlin* as an abstract film "that merely takes its raw material from images of the city of Berlin"[23]—if it were not for the actual city dwellers who went to the movies to see themselves depicted on the screen and who reacted very differently to this symphonic treatment of their daily lives.

III. The Spectacle of White-Collar Culture

Like Wagner in his proposals for the New Berlin, Ruttmann in *Berlin* redefines the elements of the urban to envision a modern metropolis unburdened by spatial boundaries and social divisions. His city symphony not only simulates the acceleration and fragmentation of modern life but, through its formal characteristics, also trains the sensibilities most suited for the triumph of the commodity and the society of the spectacle. In achieving this effect, Ruttmann relies on the two most powerful technologies of social engineering available at the time: architecture and cinema. Through thematic choices, the film presents white-collar workers as the dominant new social class in late 1920s Berlin. Reducing traffic, labor, and industry to spectacular effects, *Berlin* conjures up a seductive vision of social harmony, but it is an illusory harmony based on external similarities and the leveling forces of movement, rhythm, and tempo. Like his fellow architects and city planners, Ruttmann organizes his modular elements according to the laws of differentiation, coordination, and functionality. With differences replaced by diversity, the spatial divisions and social distinctions of the prewar metropolis are easily absorbed into new paradigms of looking, and the familiar experiences of exclusion and containment dissolved into the spatiotemporal regimes of film as a laboratory of modern subjectivity.

Yet how were the historical spectators interpellated into this new sociospatial order? And how did the film produce its imaginary subject effects? The answers can be found in the filmic organization of the gaze, the equation of experience with spectatorship, and the ascendancy of vision in the making of urban mentality. By shifting the locus of agency from the city dweller to the film spectator, Ruttmann re-creates Weimar Berlin entirely within new paradigms of looking. The diegesis (i.e., the world of the film) is no longer a fictional space where urban realities can be examined critically. Instead the images become the raw material for new media-based identities and mentalities. In Ruttmann's *Berlin,* this momentous realignment in modern subjectivity is achieved through the difference between the anonymous protagonists in the diegesis and the ideal spectator inscribed into the film's formal structures.

Based on the sociological studies discussed in chapter 2, most of the people populating the streets and squares of Ruttmann's *Berlin* must be described as either young white-collar workers or members of the old and new middle classes. The industrial workers, though constituting half of the population, contribute little to his modern physiognomy of the metropolis; they disappear behind the machines and blend into the anonymous crowds. Trapped in factories and tenements, or too poor to participate in the rituals of consumption, they have little part in this triumphant self-presentation of Weimar culture. Yet even the representatives of the New Berlin, the chic young women and the energetic young men, appear to go about their daily business almost automatically, like cogs in a gigantic machine. With the actual city dwellers thus reduced to filmic raw material, identification in the traditional sense of character identification no longer takes place. Instead the imaginary subject, the implied spectator, of *Berlin* is constituted through the objects and settings associated with the new mobilized consciousness, creating a peculiar state of alertness and readiness thematized in the recurring motif of "crisis."

Ruttmann alludes to the underlying mechanisms of accommodation through repeated visual commentaries on the lack of individual agency and personal freedom. These commentaries are most pronounced in the animal metaphors used to characterize workers, women, and children. For instance, a shot of workers passing through the factory gate is followed by one of cows being herded to the slaughterhouse, a clear allusion to their

Fig. 7.5. *Berlin, die Sinfonie der Großstadt.* Frame enlargement. Courtesy of Deutsche Kinemathek Museum für Film und Fernsehen Berlin and Mrs. Eva Riehl, Munich.

shared fate. The comparison of female secretaries and telephone operators to screaming monkeys and barking dogs locates the conflicts of modern urban life in the presumed aggressiveness of working women. The many comparisons between human beings and mechanical dolls or mannequins achieve the same effect through more humorous means (fig. 7.5). Pedestrians struggle to cross a busy street, with their helpless attempts repeated by five small wooden dolls rocking back and forth in a window display advertising foot cream. Even before the first human being appears in the early morning sequence, a group of mannequins in a lingerie store is already introduced as the true inhabitants of Weimar Berlin, attesting to the pervasiveness of objectification and commodification.

Through cross section as the main principle of social leveling, *Berlin* also overcomes the conceptual divisions that dominated contemporaneous debates on the metropolis, beginning with the juxtaposition of city and country, society and community, linear and cyclical time, interior and exterior space, and so forth. The competing iconographies of the city as organism and machine, which we examined earlier in the montage sequences of *Berlin Alexanderplatz* and the city texts/textual cities of the literary feuilleton, function once again as the discursive hinge between the anti-urban, antimodern, and *völkisch* ideologies associated with the conservative revolution, on one hand, and the modernist, functionalist, and rationalist programs identified with the New Berlin, on the other. Ruttmann's film successfully reconciles these two seemingly incompatible models: the organicist/corporatist model of the city as living being, and the functionalist/rationalist model of the city as machine. Whereas the narrative of a typical day evokes biological functions and cyclical processes, the ubiquitous machine imagery presents mechanical processes and rational decisions as necessary to the organization of modern life. As a result, the nature scenes end up naturalizing culture, with the machine wheel as the ultimate symbol of the innate productivity, generativity, and life force of the modern metropolis. At the same time, the comparison of people to objects results in a leveling of the animate and inanimate worlds, that is, of worker and machine, and of consumer and commodity, with objectification confirmed as an inevitable consequence of capitalist development.

Ruttmann, to summarize the discussion thus far, translates the sociospatial dialectic into a filmic fantasy; therein lies the artistic significance and historical relevance of his *Berlin* film. Rather than duplicating the available city maps, with their recognizable coordinates and retraceable itineraries, his film aims at a deterritorialization of Weimar Berlin, a dissolution of the specific into the typical and the universal. This explains his surprising indifference to the actual built environment. While the Wilhelmine architecture of tenements, stores, and factories appears in almost all shots, the famous historical monuments included in most other filmic and photographic portraits of Berlin remain conspicuously absent—unlike the modernist provocation symbolized by Mendelsohn's Mossehaus project and the Babylon-Theater designed by Poelzig. The well-known locations to which the camera returns time and again are Potsdamer Platz, Friedrichstraße, and the Kurfürstendamm, all transit stations in the organization of new urban rituals and pleasures. In Ruttmann's conception of the metropolis, architecture thus functions primarily as an agent of mobility and change. The resultant apotheosis of transitoriness makes superfluous the need for permanence; and the desire for place, for settledness, is absorbed into the thrills of rhythm and speed.

The concept of white-collar society as the culmination of social mobility and economic progress finds foremost expression in traffic as the central metaphor of urban life. Especially the relationship between movement and spectatorship is explored through the constitutive tension between the images of traffic and the traffic in images. *Berlin* begins with the arrival of a train at Anhalter Station and, during the course of a typical day in spring or early summer, returns repeatedly to various train stations to show how travelers board trains, workmen repair tracks, and railroad signals give directions. In accordance with the city-as-organism metaphor, the streets and tracks are equated with the arteries, the offices and factories with the various organs, and the ubiquitous traffic signs and traffic cops—the latter a stand-in for the director—with the heart. Especially the late morning sequence takes full advantage of these physiological references. Perhaps it is the sudden lack of a human agent—people have arrived at work—that makes possible the subsequent celebration of streetcars, trains, bicycles, carriages, trucks, wagons, taxis, busses, and limousines as the main protagonists. Even Gleisdreieck, allegorized by Joseph Roth and others in suggestive essays on technology and modernity, is included in this filmic

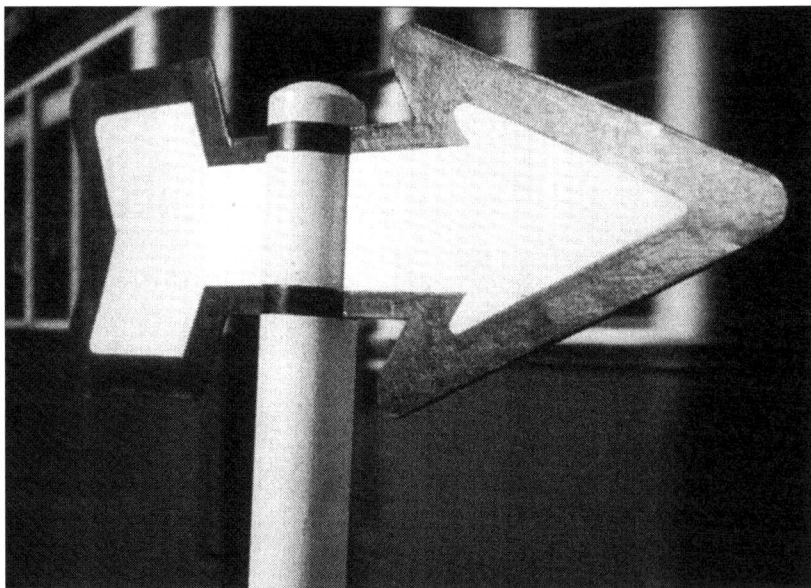

Fig. 7.6. *Berlin, die Sinfonie der Großstadt.* Frame enlargement. Courtesy of Deutsche Kinemathek Museum für Film und Fernsehen Berlin and Mrs. Eva Riehl, Munich.

apotheosis of traffic as a life force and model of modern society, as are several shots from the subway construction at Alexanderplatz.

In searching for an iconic representation for such relentless activity, the camera stops several times on an arrow-shaped traffic signal that alternately points to the left or right, guiding the flow of traffic but also revealing the arbitrary nature of such frantic movement (fig. 7.6). While the arrow stands for forward movement, and by implication, economic progress, the film uses another visual symbol, a spiral, to address the pervasive feeling of disorientation and confusion. In the same way that the traffic signs give direction to motorists and pedestrians, the animated spirals in the shop windows induce consumer vertigo in the film spectator. Combining the elements of spectatorship with the rituals of consumerism, these window displays—and by extension, the film as a whole—invite the spectator to both surrender to the image, with the spiral evoking the pleasures and dangers of passive looking, and reflect on the double framing of filmic perception as an integral part of daily life in the modern metropolis (fig. 7.7).

Not surprising given the frequent identification of massification with

Fig. 7.7. *Berlin, die Sinfonie der Großstadt.* Frame enlargement. Courtesy of Deutsche Kinemathek Museum für Film und Fernsehen Berlin and Mrs. Eva Riehl, Munich.

feminization, these two paradigms of urban experience are clearly organized along gendered lines. Control over the urban environment is asserted through the kind of directed activities and structured processes visualized by the arrow as a masculine principle. By contrast, surrender to the consumer attractions of the metropolis is indicated through circular and repetitive movements. The spiral either implies an excessively subjective perspective, for instance, during the roller-coaster ride, or it announces a dramatic transformation of the visible world that, in the animated sequences, assumes almost hallucinatory qualities. The breakdowns in the systems of urban perception, from the vertigo experienced in front of the shopwindow to the woman's (staged) suicide attempt described earlier, are invariably presented as feminine or feminizing, beginning with the first appearance of the animated spiral out of the keys of a woman's typewriter.

The close affinities between urbanism and cinema, acknowledged in the many framing devices (e.g., the windows of trains and busses, the iron structures of bridges and passageways), play a key role in the underlying process of specularization. Often the camera focuses on objects that are momentarily hidden from view by passing vehicles. With the casings of windows functioning like a filmstrip, these objects are then reframed and reanimated through the movement of the vehicle in the foreground, thus giving rise to a powerful allegory of cinema. The actual filmstrip moves through the projector at a speed high enough to produce an illusion of continuity; in *Berlin,* the camera reproduces this process through the interplay of frame and motion. In one typical scene that involves two vehicles moving at different speeds, the additional layer of frames creates almost abstract effects, with the windows of a passing trolley imposing their outlines on a slower moving hearse. With its ornately dressed window, the hearse in turn frames the building in the background, thereby duplicating the cinematic effect in a way that leaves no object, image, or perception untouched by this process of filmic self-reflection. Similarly, the revolving glass doors of high-class restaurants and grand hotels are transformed into a compelling metaphor of both the cinematic apparatus and the modern condition. Reminiscent of an endless loop, the doors continuously generate new images by framing the entrances and exits of people while remaining firmly in place: a telling reenactment of filmic spectatorship and modern subjectivity. This vacillation among different levels of representation—namely, mimesis, abstraction, and allegorization—makes *Berlin* a film not only about Weimar Berlin but also about ways of representing Weimar

Berlin; as a consequence, the technology of cinema, to paraphrase Michael Minden, is confirmed as an integral part of the metropolis.[24]

The role of film spectatorship as a model for urban perception is further explored in numerous window shots that serve as a constant reminder of the film's own conditions of production. In fact, much of the first movement is structured around the highly symbolic gesture of raising the shutters of small neighborhood stores and displaying the window decorations of butchers, tailors, and tobacconists. The first pedestrian to stop in front of a store window therefore becomes the ideal-typical spectator in, and of, the film. With the next shot, the camera ventures into the interior of an apartment, probably a bedroom, and the same scenario is repeated, now from the perspective of someone, presumably a woman, pulling up venetian blinds to reveal an inner courtyard. These two moments capture the two models of spectatorship and, by extension, subjectivity offered in the film: the pleasure of watching others, and identification with the camera and its changing viewpoints. Together these two configurations, looking into a window and looking out of a window, give rise to the myriad constellations made possible by the equation of urban experience with filmic spectatorship. Yet they also reveal newly evolving divisions between public and private space, and between the real and imaginary metropolis, that, throughout the 1920s, informed the particularly intense public responses to urban utopias enlivened by difference but devoid of conflict: reason enough, finally, to take a closer look at the critical reception of the Ruttmann film and consider its continued relevance to the filmic representation of postunification Berlin.

IV. Critical Reception and Filmic Reinterpretation

Berlin's affirmative representation of white-collar society played a key role in the countless reviews written after its release. Placed within larger debates on modernism, Americanism, and New Objectivity, the film allowed critics to assess the project of modernity in light of the economic and political crises of the late 1920s. Disagreements over the film were often expressed in the oppositional terms current in Weimar culture: critical versus affirmative, subversive versus conformist, and progressive versus reactionary. Much of the controversy in 1927 revolved around Ruttmann's use of montage to reconfigure the heterogeneous elements of urban life. Both panegyrics to dynamic editing and what some called "image music,"[25] and diatribes against formal experimentation and what others denounced as a "mechanical dismemberment,"[26] originated in a shared belief that the structure of traditional class society had fundamentally changed with the rise of white-collar society. Most contributions agreed that the broader implications for the film's politics of class had to be reassessed through cross section as construction principle, aesthetic effect, and ideological position. Those who emphasized the differences between montage and cross section naturally faulted the latter for its affirmative view of Weimar society. Thus, leftist critic Paul Friedländer acknowledged the film's artistic accomplishments but objected to its lack of a clear point of view: "The authors wanted to show things without tendency [i.e., an identifiable political position]. However, reality is materialized tendency. Berlin is a capitalist metropolis. Capitalism gives it its character, the pursuit of profit. Every minute in this city is filled with class difference and class struggle."[27] Even Willy Haas, who effusively praised Ruttmann's virtuoso application of filmic techniques, wanted "no transposition of symphonic-musical possibilities, no Wagnerism of the film of the future"[28]—a clear rejection of the totalizing effects of the cross-section principle.

Some reviewers were acutely aware of the innovative ways through which *Berlin* realigned urban representation with uniquely filmic modes of perception. Describing them as an almost physical sensation, Rudolf Kurtz observed: "The individual shots are organized according to the point of view of what kinetic sensations they arouse in the viewer until . . . one has the feeling of standing in the middle of a very busy intersection."[29] Imitating the acceleration and intensification of sensory stimuli in his choice of verbs, Alfred Kerr wrote: "But here objects rush by, line up, glow, rise, push, glide, move, wither, flow, swell, dawn: growing, bending, expanding, shrinking, rolling, narrowing, sharpening, separating, twisting, lifting, filling, emptying, inflating, reducing, thriving, and disappearing."[30] The formalism of *Berlin* caused some, like Kurt Pinthus, to emphasize the positive effects of defamiliarization: "Our retina, our nerves—lashing out at our consciousness . . . Suddenly we see what we don't see because we see it every day."[31] Others, like Béla Balázs, described the focus on perception in very different terms, namely, a flight from physical reality: "The camera is turned inward, as it were, and no longer records the appearances in the outside world, but their reflection in the consciousness. Not the thing as such, but its image in the psyche, is filmed by the camera."[32]

Did the divided critical reception of *Berlin* arise from what Benjamin calls the film's ability to uncover an "optical unconscious"? Or did it have to do with the filmmaker's ambition to project an image of Weimar Berlin that had little to do with the living conditions of the majority of its inhabitants? For Siegfried Kracauer, the answer was clear:

> Ruttmann, instead of penetrating his immense subject-matter with a true understanding of its social, economic, and political structure . . . records thousands of details without connecting them, or at best connects them through fictitious transitions which are void of content. His film may be based upon the idea of Berlin as the city of tempo and work; but this is a formal idea which does not imply content either and perhaps for that very reason intoxicates the German petite bourgeoisie in real life and literature. This symphony fails to point out anything, because it does not uncover a single significant context.[33]

According to Kracauer's reading of the film, *Berlin* was symptomatic of the entire stabilization period and its cult of surface phenomena. He later elaborated on what he denounced as the affirmative function of most Berlin films in a critical review of Jutzi's 1931 adaptation of *Berlin Alexanderplatz,* in which he accused the director of limiting Döblin's innovative use of montage to a few experimental big city sequences and of reducing the lower-class milieu around Alexanderplatz to a mere backdrop for the imposing screen persona of Heinrich George. Kracauer's conclusions about *Berlin Alexanderplatz* apply equally to the *Berlin* film, as they speak directly to a key concept in his evolving theory of film, namely, the betrayal of film's inherent realism and critical potential: "It is as if the camera roamed aimlessly back and forth between brand-new buildings of dubious provenance, workers, subway trains, and wooden fences. Movement has become an end in itself and neglects its most urgent task: to convey a position."[34] Perhaps it was this need for conceptual clarity that prompted Kracauer, after seeing the Ruttmann film, to move away from his earlier defense of white-collar culture as legitimate and progressive and address head-on the problem of accommodation and cooptation in the 1930 *Angestellten* study discussed in chapter 2.

Why not just disregard such readings as "speculative indoctrination, ideological propositions, and normative value judgments,"[35] as does David Macrae? Because Kracauer's critique of *Berlin* (and *Berlin Alexanderplatz*) must be seen in the larger context of his reevaluation of surface culture toward the end of the Weimar Republic; and because it bears witness to a deeper understanding of the ideology of form that formalist readings of the film are bound to miss (or find irrelevant). The same tension between mystification and enlightenment that animates the city texts discussed in chapter 4 informs Kracauer's approach to Weimar cinema and the emancipatory potential of modern mass culture, what Miriam Hansen in a different context has called "vernacular modernism."[36] For the critic of the *Frankfurter Zeitung*, film afforded contemporary audiences a sense of control that could no longer be attained in everyday life; hence its great significance "as a medium particularly equipped to promote the redemption of physical reality. Its imaginary permits us, for the first time, to take away with us the objects and occurrences that comprise the flow of material life."[37] Placed in the service of escapism and illusionism, the films of the late 1920s furthered a mentality, and a way of looking, that no longer had any use for critical illumination and physical redemption. With the medium's utopian potential enlisted in the preservation of the status quo, the filmic construction of urban reality became problematically linked to the imaginary constructions that organized social and spatial relations in the modern metropolis.

What, in the larger context of this book, accounts for the continued attraction of *Berlin, Symphony of a Big City*? The Ruttmann film, like the kind of mass mobilizations envisioned by Wagner and Hilberseimer and the spatial images and city texts analyzed by Kracauer and Hessel, evokes the utopian promise of a future unburdened by the distinctions of class. Like the Döblin novel, the film enlists the most advanced formal means to confront the dialectics of freedom and domination, progress and destruction—in short, of enlightenment and mystification—that sustained the urban imagination through the Weimar period. By combining avant-garde and documentary techniques, Ruttmann's city symphony conflates visual perception and social experience and establishes a model of urban experience based exclusively on spectatorial effects. By presenting the modern city as a perceptual rather than social space, the film reflects self-consciously on the formal possibilities of film and its affinities with mass society but does so from a position of full agreement with the consequences of commodification and medialization. Yet by repeating the leveling effect of mass culture in its formal strategies, *Berlin* also presents a view of the metropolis that is far more radical than that of any melodramatic street film or class-conscious milieu study. For in Ruttmann's vision of the metropolis, reification, mechanization, and the cult of functionality return as the essence of things; no longer externalized, they give rise to new pleasures and desires from the inside of alienation. Precisely these qualities distinguish *Berlin* from other Berlin films of the period, align it with the international avant-garde, and account for its continued appeal as a document of the modern urban imagination.

The qualities that made Ruttmann's *Berlin* film such a central text of Weimar mass culture and modernity have been recognized not only in its critical reception and academic scholarship; its formal strategies also live on in repeated attempts to revive the genre of the city symphony and utilize the principle of cross section for the continued remapping of the sociospatial dialectic. Given the overdetermined function of Berlin in the spatial imaginary of class and nation, the Ruttmann film was almost destined to inspire repeated remakes, with the first conceived during the Third Reich and the second produced after German unification. In the early 1940s, Ufa cameraman Leo de Laforgue planned a more conventional *Symphonie einer Weltstadt* (Symphony of a World City) in direct response to the modernist sensibilities of the Weimar original. With production interrupted by the bombing of the German capital, a truncated version of the film premiered in 1950 under the melancholy title *Berlin, wie es war* (Berlin, How It Was), denying the provocation of modernism but also confirming destruction as an integral part of urban history. More recently, documentary filmmaker Thomas Schadt conceived his *Berlin: Sinfonie der Großstadt* (Berlin Symphony, 2002) in direct dialogue with the 1927 precursor, a debt recognized by the filmmaker when he named his camera dolly "Walter." With its black-and-white film stock, narrative format of a typical day, original score, and, most important, symphonic approach to editing, Schadt's beautifully shot film references not only the formal qualities of cross section; it also makes new use of its ideological effects, and not always in unproblematic ways. Committed (like the New Objectivist films) to a documentary aesthetic without "tendency," the film explores the fluid connections between the postmodern architectures and virtual spaces of the global metropolis and, based on the visual regimes of the digital age and the urban topographies of a postnational Europe, celebrates postunification Berlin as a city "free of historical burdens and constraints."[38] Of course, in the context of this study, this also suggests a city without classes, a point that, given the many signs of economic crisis in the capital of the Berlin Republic, has been made by reviewers who, like Kracauer before them, remain committed to the program of critical realism and an emancipatory cinema.

Finally, and in ways that apply equally to the other texts discussed in this study, the continuing fascination with *Berlin* must be located in the central position of Weimar Berlin in the visual archives of German modernity and postmodernity. Ruttmann's city symphony, like the modernist buildings presented in chapter 3 and the urban photographs discussed in chapter 5, has become an integral part of the legacies of Weimar culture, forever recycled in television documentaries and book publications about the period and almost obsessively referenced in the architectural projects and urban reconstructions of the new Berlin Republic. Specifically, it is the film's ambivalent relationship to the project of mass culture and modernity that still haunts us, whether as a reminder that modernity remains an incomplete project, or a first inkling of the virtual scenarios that have fundamentally transformed urban culture and public life in the global world cities of today. Similarly, it is the focus on modern architecture and its symbolic force that reminds us of the power of space in defining identities and building societies. And it is the symptomatic function of the metropolis as a stage for the reconfiguration of class society that links contemporary pronouncements on the postmetropolis to the historical moment when the foundations of the modern metropolis, capitalism and class society, experienced their first serious crisis and moment of self-transformation.

Between the ambitious social and architectural projects of the Weimar Republic and the city's reemergence as the capital and the cultural center of a unified Germany, Berlin has undergone several dramatic transformations and now stands at the beginning of an even more ambitious urban experiment, testing its sustainability as a metropolis in the age of the postmetropolis and its viability as a national capital in the age of globalization. Throughout the twentieth century, Berlin has played a key role in the critical mapping of German modernity and its competing sociospatial narratives. Just as the capital of the Weimar Republic functioned as a laboratory for the reconfiguration and rearticulation of class, it provided the stage on which the forces of modernization and urbanization were in fact negotiated: in the rich and complex architectural culture that has served as the main theme and organizing device in the last seven chapters and through the central question of class that has functioned as a ubiquitous reference point in the ongoing negotiation of modern architecture and mass society.

Weimar Berlin is bound to remain an object of critical, sentimental, and nostalgic appropriation, with the desire for preservation of the past in the future nourished by that period's innovative modernisms, its bold architectural visions, its progressive mass culture, its alternative public sphere, its emancipatory movements, and its revolutionary working class.

From the perspective of this study, nostalgia for Weimar Berlin does not just mean sentimental attitudes or retrograde tastes; nostalgia also attests to the power of the past to remind us of the unredeemed possibilities in the present, a point worth remembering when it comes to the legacies of Weimar architectural culture and its relationship to the question of class. In the words of cultural theorist Elizabeth Wilson:

> Perhaps the real secret pleasure of nostalgia is that it allows us, as we look back at a past bathed in the rosy glow of melancholy beauty, at those lost corners of the old city, at the same time to measure the distance we have come—not in the sense necessarily of progress or improvement, but simply in the sense of experiencing the reality of change, the passage of time, and the existence of that great hinterland of "lost time" that yet somehow is still with us. It is the subtle pleasure of imaginatively experiencing the past from the detached standpoint of the present. . . . For it is only by embracing both the past and the future of our cities that we can fulfill their potential in the present, using the awareness that nostalgia brings in order to move beyond it into an acceptance of and an active engagement with change.[39]

Far from offering only "the rosy glow" of the old city, this sense of nostalgia also extends to the cool comforts of modern architecture whose social and spatial utopias are of equal relevance to future development as the remnants of the classical metropolis. It is in recognition of these utopian promises that we must view the nostalgic postcards of Weimar Berlin, the (completed or planned) reconstructions of the icons of New Building, the ongoing literary excursions into the topographies of modern urban culture, and the most recent filmic reenactments of Berlin as visual spectacle or virtual reality. All of these attempts attest to the powerful promise of social equality, and with it, of gender equality, inscribed in these visual and architectural reconstructions. They bear witness to the dream of social mobility and the belief in collective agency that is worked out in the aesthetic manifestations of architectural culture. They furthermore remind us of the violence inherent in the making of mass society and what remains hidden behind the tropes of massification, mapping as they do the movement from the rigid class divisions of the nineteenth century, to the more fluid social and ethnic demarcations of the twenty-first century. The existence of the urban masses, whether defined in the traditional terms of class or the more contemporary category of multitudes, continues to be displaced onto the kind of urban discourses that the book's seven chapters have analyzed from the perspective of architectural culture and its changing manifestations in critical, literary, photographic, and filmic terms.

If there is one aspect of urban discourses that these chapters have emphasized, it is how spatial and architectural solutions, and their representation in literature, photography, and film, deal with social hierarchies and divisions. It is this attempt by architects, urban planners, writers, critics, and filmmakers to imagine alternatives that keeps alive the creative dialogue between the Weimar Republic and the Berlin Republic. The reality of social and economic inequality originates, then as now, in the alliance of urbanism, capitalism, and class society that the sociospatial dialectic of Weimar will not allow us to forget. The category of class may have been marginalized in the identity politics of postmodern culture and the postnational culture of world cities, but hidden behind the new topographies of the multicultural or multiethnic metropolis and its culture of hybridity and migrancy, class remains the question that will not go away. The architectural culture and urban imaginary of Weimar Berlin remind us to take up that challenge and confront the utopian possibilities inscribed in buildings, texts, and films within the social and spatial configurations of today.

Notes

INTRODUCTION

1. The spatial turn in cultural studies has been an important source of inspiration for this study, especially the neo-Marxist work in social theory and urban geography. See Henri Lefebvre, *The Production of Space,* trans. Donald Nicholson-Smith (Oxford: Blackwell, 1991); David Harvey, *The Urban Experience* (Baltimore: Johns Hopkins University Press, 1989); and Edward Soja, *Postmetropolis: Critical Studies of Cities and Regions* (London: Blackwell, 2001). For a critical reading of Harvey and other urban geographers that raises important issues, see Kian Tajbakhsh, *The Promise of the City: Space, Identity, and Contemporary Social Thought* (Berkeley: University of California Press, 2001). On urban theory from Simmel and Benjamin to Harvey and Lefebvre, also see the overview by Andrew Merrifield, *Metromarxism* (London: Routledge, 2002).

2. Edward W. Soja, "The Socio-Spatial Dialectic," *Annals of the Association of American Geographers* 70, no. 2 (1980): 207.

3. I will refer to modern architecture when discussing architecture and design as part of more general and decidedly international formal innovations, artistic movements, and cultural trends. As two retroactively applied terms, neither *architectural modernism* nor *International Style* adequately capture the social and political project of New Building and its embeddedness in Weimar architectural culture.

4. The connection between Weimar culture and the crisis of classical modernity was established by Detlev J. K. Peukert in *The Weimar Republic: The Crisis of Classical Modernity,* trans. Richard Deveson (New York: Hill and Wang, 1989) and, since then, has become a critical commonplace, repeated even in popular accounts such as Günter Drommer, *Die ruhelose Republik: Alltag zwischen Gewalt und Hoffnung 1918–1933* (Hamburg: Schwartzkopff, 2004). Recent English-language studies on Weimar culture with a special emphasis on the metropolis (i.e., Berlin) include (in chronological order) Maria Tatar, *Lustmord: Sexual Murder in Weimar Germany* (Princeton: Princeton University Press, 1995); Katharina von Ankum, ed., *Women in the Metropolis: Gendered Urban Discourses of Weimar Germany* (Berkeley: University of California Press, 1996); Anke Gleber, *The Art of Taking a Walk: Flanerie, Literature, and Film in Weimar Culture* (Princeton: Princeton University Press, 1999); Bernd Widdig, *Culture and Inflation in Weimar Germany* (Berkeley: University of California Press, 2001); Janet Ward, *Weimar Surfaces: Urban Visual*

Culture in 1920s Germany (Berkeley: University of California Press, 2001); Peter Jelavich, *Berlin Alexanderplatz: Radio, Film, and the Death of Weimar Culture* (Berkeley: University of California Press, 2006); Kathleen Canning, Kerstin Barndt, and Kristin Mcguire, eds., *Weimar Publics / Weimar Subjects* (Oxford: Berghahn, 2008); and Stephen Webber, *Berlin in the Twentieth Century: A Cultural Topography* (Cambridge: Cambridge University Press, 2008).

5. Fredric Jameson, *Postmodernism or, The Cultural Logic of Late Capitalism* (Durham: Duke University Press, 1991), 37, 51. The notion of cognitive mapping has played a key role in recent studies on the modern metropolis such as Neil Leach, *The Hieroglyphics of Space: Reading and Experiencing the Modern Metropolis* (London: Routledge, 2001).

6. Jameson, "Architecture and the Critique of Ideology," in Joan Ockman, ed., *Architecture, Criticism, Ideology* (Princeton: Princeton Architectural Press, 1985), 51–87.

7. Francesco Dal Co, *Figures of Architecture and Thought: German Architecture Culture, 1880–1920*, trans. Stephen Sartarelli (New York: Rizzoli, 1990), 20.

8. Susan Buck-Morss, *Dreamworld and Catastrophe: The Passing of Mass Utopia in East and West* (Cambridge: MIT Press, 2000), ix.

9. Setting the tone for early studies on Weimar culture were Peter Gay, *Weimar Culture: The Outsider as Insider* (New York: Harper and Row, 1968); Jost Hermann and Reinhold Grimm, ed., *Die sogenannten Zwanziger Jahre* (Bad Homburg: Gehlen, 1970), and, from the GDR perspective, Bärbel Schrader and Jürgen Schebera, *Kunstmetropole Berlin* (Berlin: Aufbau, 1987). Since then, the myth of Weimar Berlin has been perpetuated in popular books such as Otto Friedrich, *Before the Deluge: A Portrait of Berlin in the 1920's* (New York: Fromm International, 1989); Thomas Friedrich, *Berlin: A Photographic Portrait of the Weimar Years, 1918–1933* (London: John Calmann and King, 1991); Manfred Görtemaker, *Weimar in Berlin* (Berlin: be.bra, 2002); and Rainer Metzger, *Berlin: Die 20er Jahre. Kunst und Kultur in der Weimarer Republik* (Vienna: Christian Branstätter, 2006). Weimar Berlin has played a central role in the architectural histories published around the 750-year celebration, most notably Josef Paul Kleinhues, ed., *750 Jahre Architektur und Städtebau in Berlin* (Stuttgart: Gerd Hatje, 1987), and in the architectural histories published since unification, most importantly Thorsten Scheer, Josef Paul Kleinhues, and Paul Kahlfeldt, eds., *City of Architecture, Architecture of the City: Berlin 1900–2000*, trans. from the German (Berlin: Nicolai, 2000). For the kind of local histories published as part of museum exhibitions, commemorative practices, and local initiatives (e.g., the creation of a Stiftung Scheunenviertel e.V.), see Horst Helas, *Juden in Berlin-Mitte: Biografien Orte Begegnungen* (Berlin: Trafo, 2001) or, with a greater topographical focus, Dieter Weigert, *Der Hackesche Markt: Kulturgeschichte eines Berliner Platzes* (Berlin: Haude und Spener, 1997). For an unabashedly touristic approach, see Michael Bienert and Elke L. Buchholz, *Die Zwanziger Jahre in Berlin: Ein Wegweiser durch die Stadt* (Berlin: Berlin-Story, 2005).

10. For English-language publications that have influenced my reading of Weimar architectural culture, see Manfredo Tafuri, *The Sphere and the Labyrinth: Avant-Gardes and Architecture from Piranesi to the 1970s*, trans. Pellegrino

d'Acierno and Robert Connolly (Cambridge: MIT Press, 1987); Fritz Neumeyer, *The Artless Word: Mies van der Rohe and the Building Art,* trans. Mark Jarzombek (Cambridge: MIT Press, 1991); Mitchell Schwarzer, *German Architectural Theory and the Search for Modern Identity* (Cambridge: Cambridge University Press, 1995); Stanford Anderson, *Peter Behrens and a New Architecture for the Twentieth Century* (Cambridge: MIT Press, 1999); Kathleen James-Chakraborty, *German Architecture for a Mass Audience* (London: Routledge, 2000); and, from a comparative perspective, Mari Hvattum and Christian Hermansen, eds., *Tracing Modernity: Manifestations of the Modern in Architecture and the City* (London: Taylor and Francis, 2002).

11. On this issue, see the insightful discussion of David Frisby, "The Metropolis as Text: Otto Wagner and Vienna's 'Second Renaissance,'" in Neil Leach, ed., *The Hieroglyphics of Space: Reading and Experiencing the Modern Metropolis* (London: Routledge, 2002), 15–30.

12. Lefebvre, *The Production of Space,* 1–67.

13. I am referring to Lefebvre's conceptual triad in *The Production of Space* of spatial practice, or perceived space; representations of space, or conceived space; and representational space, or lived space. In *Thirdspace: Journeys to Los Angeles and Other Real-and-Imagined Places* (Cambridge: Blackwell, 1996) Soja introduces the distinctions among the actual world of First Space, the virtual world of Second Space, and the social world of Third Space to develop a similar "trialectics of space."

14. On the difficulties of conceptualizing the relationship between modernism and modernity, see Peter Brooker, *Modernity and Metropolis: Writing, Film, and Urban Formations* (New York: Palgrave, 2002), especially the introduction (1–30). For poststructuralist explorations of spatiality and subjectivity within the discourses of the urban, see (in chronological order) Michael Keith and Steve Pile, eds., *Place and the Politics of Identity* (London: Routledge, 1993); Philip Kasinitz, ed., *Metropolis: Center and Symbol of Our Times* (New York: New York University Press, 1995); Anthony King, ed., *Re-presenting the City: Ethnicity, Capital, and Culture in the Twenty-first Century* (Basingstoke: Macmillan, 1996); Steve Pile, *Real Cities: Modernity, Space, and the Phantasmagoria of City Life* (London: Sage, 2005); and Christopher Linder, ed., *Urban Space and Cityscapes: Perspectives from Modern and Contemporary Culture* (London: Routledge, 2006). On recent shifts in the conceptualization of the city across the disciplines, see Nan Ellis, "Reconceiving the City and Culture," in *Postmodern Urbanism* (New York: Princeton Architectural Press, 1999), 241–69.

15. Christine M. Boyer, *The City of Collective Memory: Its Historical Imagery and Architectural Entertainments* (Cambridge: MIT Press, 1995), 5. On the centrality of memory and history to the debates on postunification Berlin, see Brian Ladd, *The Ghosts of Berlin: Confronting German History in the Urban Landscape* (Chicago: University of Chicago Press, 1996), Michael Z. Wise, *Capital Dilemma: Germany's Search for a New Architecture of Democracy* (Princeton: Princeton University Press, 1998), Andreas Huyssen, *Present Pasts: Urban Palimpsests and the Politics of Memory* (Stanford: Stanford University Press, 2003), Karen E. Till, *The New Berlin: Memory, Politics, Place* (Minneapolis: University of Minnesota Press,

2005), and Jennifer A. Jordan, *Structures of Memory: Understanding Urban Change in Berlin and Beyond* (Stanford: Stanford University Press, 2006).

16. Some of the arguments presented in this paragraph are adopted from the introduction of Tajbakhsh, *The Promise of the City*, 1–32.

17. See Andreas Gillen, *Berlin Electropolis: Shocks, Nerves, and German Modernity* (Berkeley: University of California Press, 2006).

18. Lefebvre, *The Production of Space*, 44.

CHAPTER 1

1. For historical overviews of architecture and urban planning in Weimar Berlin, see Norbert Huse, *Neues Bauen 1918–1933: Moderne Architektur in der Weimarer Republik* (Munich: Moos, 1975); Karl-Heinz Hüter, *Architektur in Berlin 1900–1933* (Stuttgart: Kohlhammer, 1988); Jochen Boberg, Tilman Fichter, and Eckhart Gillen, eds., *Die Metropole: Industriekultur in Berlin im 20. Jahrhundert* (Munich: C. H. Beck, 1986); and Tilman Buddensieg, ed., *Berlin 1900–1933: Architecture and Design* (New York: Cooper-Hewitt Museum, 1988). On Weimar Berlin in the larger context of urban history, see Doug Clelland, *Berlin: An Architectural History* (London: Academy Editions, 1983); Hans Reuther, *Die große Zerstörung Berlins: Zweihundert Jahre Stadtbaugeschichte* (Frankfurt am Main: Propyläen, 1985); Harald Bodenschatz, *Platz frei für das neue Berlin! Geschichte der Stadterneuerung seit 1871* (Berlin: Transit, 1987), and Josef Paul Kleinhues, ed., *750 Jahre Architektur und Städtebau in Berlin* (Stuttgart: Gerd Hatje, 1987).

2. Ernesto Laclau and Chantal Mouffe, *Hegemony and Socialist Strategy* (London: Verso, 1985), 77.

3. Karl Baedeker, *Berlin und Umgebung: Handbuch für Reisende* (Leipzig: Baedeker, 1923), 49. All translations are mine unless noted otherwise.

4. Baedeker, *Berlin und Umgebung: Handbuch für Reisende* (Leipzig: Baedeker, 1927), 30.

5. Iwan Heilbut, reprinted in Christian Jäger and Erhard Schütz, eds., *Glänzender Asphalt: Berlin im Feuilleton der Weimarer Republik* (Berlin: Fannei und Waltz, 1994), 96. On foreigner writers and artists in Berlin, see Klaus Kändler, Helga Karolewski, and Ilse Siebert, eds., *Berliner Begegnungen: Ausländische Künstler in Berlin 1918–1933* (Berlin: Dietz, 1987). On the strong Russian presence in particular, see Fritz Mierau, ed., *Russen in Berlin: Literatur Malerei Theater Film 1918–1933* (Leipzig: Philipp Reclam, 1990).

6. Amédé Ozenfant, "Weekend Berlin," *Der Querschnitt* 11 (1931): 298, and Jean Giradoux, "Berlin, nicht Paris!" *Der Querschnitt* 11 (1931): 295.

7. Stephen Spender, *World Within World* (New York: Harcourt, Brace, 1951), 113–14.

8. Stefan Großmann, *Ich war begeistert* (Berlin: S. Fischer, 1931), 208.

9. Julius Bab, reprinted in Klaus Strohmeyer, ed., *Berlin in Bewegung*, 2 vols. (Reinbek: Rowohlt, 1987), 2:86.

10. Leonhard Frank, *Links wo das Herz ist* (Munich: Nymphenburger, 1967), 81–82.

11. Hermann Kesser, reprinted in Jäger and Schütz, *Glänzender Asphalt*, 57–58.

12. Walter Curt Behrendt, "Berlin wird Weltstadt—Metropole im Herzen Europas," *Das Neue Berlin* 5 (1929): 98–101.

13. Egon Erwin Kisch, *Razzia auf der Spree: Berliner Reportagen* (Berlin: Aufbau, 1986), 104.

14. Joseph Roth, "Gleisdreieck," *Werke: Das journalistische Werk,* 3 vols., ed. Klaus Westermann (Cologne: Kiepenheuer und Witsch, 1989–91), 2:220–21.

15. On architecture and urban planning in Wilhelmine Berlin, see the groundbreaking study by Julius Posener, *Berlin auf dem Wege zu einer neuen Architektur: Das Zeitalter Wilhelm II* (Munich: Prestel, 1979), as well as Jochen Boberg, Tilman Fichter, and Eckhart Gillen, eds., *Exerzierfeld der Moderne: Industriekultur in Berlin im 19. Jahrhundert* (Munich: C. H. Beck, 1984) and Helmut Engel, *Berlin auf dem Weg zur Moderne* (Berlin: Jovis, 1997).

16. See Detlev J. K. Peukert, *The Weimar Republic: The Crisis of Classical Modernity,* trans. Richard Deveson (New York: Hill and Wang, 1993), xiii.

17. On the paradoxes of modernity in the context of modern mass housing, see Adelheid von Saldern, "'Instead of Cathedrals, Dwelling Machines': The Paradoxes of Rationalization under the Banner of Modernity," in *The Challenge of Modernity: German Social and Cultural Studies, 1890–1960,* trans. Bruce Little, intro. Geoff Eley (Ann Arbor: University of Michigan Press, 2002), 93–114.

18. David Blackbourn, *The Long Nineteenth Century: A History of Germany, 1780–1918* (New York: Oxford University Press, 1998), esp. 175–460.

19. On the important contribution of Peter Behrens, see Tilman Buddensieg and Henning Rogge, eds., *Industriekultur: Peter Behrens and die AEG,* trans. Iain Boyd Whyte (Cambridge: MIT Press, 1984) and Stanford Anderson, *Peter Behrens and a New Architecture for the Twentieth Century* (Cambridge: MIT Press, 1999).

20. On AEG in Berlin, see Peter Strunk, *Die AEG: Aufstieg und Niedergang einer Industrielegende* (Berlin: Nicolai, 2002). On Borsig in Berlin, see Manfred Birk and Helmut Engel, eds., *Borsig: Zwischen Tradition and Aufbruch* (Berlin: Jovis, 2000).

21. Fritz Neumeyer, "Im Schatten des mechanischen Haines. Versuchsanordnungen zur Metropole," in Karl Schwarz, ed., *Die Zukunft der Metropolen: Paris London New York Berlin,* 3 vols. (Berlin: Dietrich Reimer, 1984), 1:273.

22. Leyden, *Groß-Berlin,* 114.

23. On the history of the tenement, see Johann Friedrich Geist and Klaus Kürvers, *Das Berliner Mietshaus,* 3 vols. (Munich: Prestel, 2001).

24. Werner Hegemann, *Das steinerne Berlin: Geschichte der größten Mietskasernenstadt der Welt* (1930; Braunschweig: Vieweg, 1988), 16.

25. See Klaus Neukrantz, *Barrikaden am Wedding: Der Roman einer Straße aus den Berliner Maitagen 1929,* afterword by Walther Willmer (Berlin: Mackensen, 1988).

26. See Werner Sombart, *Liebe, Luxus und Kapitalismus: Über die Entstehung der modernen Welt aus dem Geiste der Verschwendung* (Berlin: Wagenbach, 1983).

27. For a publication from the period, see Leo Colze, *Berliner Warenhäuser* (1908; Berlin: Fannei und Walz, 1989).

28. Paul Westheim, "Architektur des 'juste milieu,'" *Das Kunstblatt* 8 (1924): 34.

For a survey of Hoffmann's work, see Wolfgang Ribbe, ed., *Baumeister Architekten Stadtplaner: Biographien zur baulichen Entwicklung Berlins* (Berlin: Stapp-Verlag, 1987), 287–300. A good historical overview of prewar city planning appears in Bodenschatz 198, 19–113. A useful summary of nineteenth-century debates can be found in Mitchell Schwarzer, *German Architectural Theory and the Search for Modern Identity* (Cambridge: Cambridge University Press, 1995).

29. Posener, *Berlin auf dem Weg zu einer neuen Architektur*, 107–26.

30. For the work of Sitte and its influence on later generations of city planners, see Camillo Sitte, *The Art of Building Cities*, trans. Charles T. Stewart (Westport: Hyperion, 1991). This is a translation of *Der Städtebau nach seinen künstlerischen Grundsätzen* (1889).

31. Martin Mächler, *Weltstadt Berlin: Schriften und Materialien*, ed. Ilse Balg (Berlin: Galerie Wannsee, 1986), 160.

32. Fredric Jameson, "Architecture and the Critique of Architecture," *Architecture Critique Ideology*, ed. Joan Ockman (Princeton: Princeton Architectural Press, 1985), 62.

33. Erwin Gutkind, "Vom städtebaulichen Problem der Einheitsgemeinde Berlin," *Erwin Gutkind 1886–1968. Architektur als Stadtraumkunst*, ed. Rudolf Hierl (Basel: Birkhäuser, 1992), 29.

34. For a historical overview of this tradition, see Vittorio Magnano Lampugnani and Romana Schneider, eds., *Moderne Architektur in Deutschland 1900 bis 1950: Reform und Tradition* (Stuttgart: Gerd Hatje, 1992).

35. Apart from Manfredo Tafuri, *The Sphere and the Labyrinth: Avant-Gardes and Architecture from Piranesi to the 1970s,* trans. Pellegrino d'Acierno and Robert Connolly (Cambridge: MIT Press, 1987), see Francesco Dal Co, *Figures of Architecture and Thought: German Architecture Culture, 1880–1920,* trans. Stephen Sartarelli (New York: Rizzoli, 1990), and Massimo Cacciari, *Architecture and Nihilism: On the Philosophy of Modern Architecture,* trans. Stephen Sartarelli, intro. Patrizia Lombardo (New Haven: Yale University Press, 1993). For a critical assessment of the Venice School and their work on modern German architecture, see Hilde Heynen, *Architecture and Modernity: A Critique* (Cambridge: MIT Press, 1999), 128–47.

36. Hugo Häring, "Baurat, nein—Bauherr," *Das Tagebuch* 6 (1925): 980.

37. See Martin Wagner, *Der sanitäre Grün der Städte: Ein Beitrag zur Flächentheorie* (Berlin: Carl Heymanns, 1915).

38. Stephen Graham and Simon Marvin, *Splintering Urbanism: Networked Infrastructures, Technological Mobilities, and the Urban Condition* (London: Routledge, 2001), 67.

39. Graham and Marvin, *Splintering Urbanism,* 68. On this point, also see Stiftung Bauhaus, ed., *Zukunft aus Amerika: Fordismus in der Zwischenkriegszeit* (Dessau: Stiftung Bauhaus, 1995).

40. Tafuri, "*Sozialpolitik* and the City in Weimar Germany," in *The Sphere and the Labyrinth,* 197–233. For a critique of Tafuri and his conviction that "there can be no qualitative change in any element of the older capitalist system—as, for instance in architecture or urbanism—without beforehand a total revolutionary and systemic transformation," see Fredric Jameson, "Architecture and the Critique of

Ideology," *The Ideologies of Theory,* vol. 2 (Minneapolis: University of Minnesota Press, 1988), 40.

41. Wagner, "Städtebauliche Probleme der Großstadt," in *Martin Wagner 1885–1957. Wohnungsbau und Weltstadtplanung: Die Rationalisierung des Glücks* (Berlin: Akademie der Künste, 1986), 102.

42. Wagner, "Das neue Berlin—die Weltstadt Berlin," in *Das Neue Berlin,* ed. Martin Wagner and Adolf Behne, pref. Julius Posener (Basel: Birkhäuser,1988), 5. Reprint of the 1929 volume of *Das Neue Berlin.*

43. For an administrative perspective, see Gustav Böß, *Berlin von heute: Stadtverwaltung und Wirtschaft* (Berlin: Gsellius, 1929), and Hans Brennert and Erwin Stein, eds., *Probleme der neuen Stadt Berlin* (Berlin: Deutscher Kommunal-Verlag, 1926).

44. Ernst Reuter, "Berliner Verkehr," *Das Neue Berlin* 11 (1929): 213–16.

45. Tafuri, *The Sphere and the Labyrinth,* 197–263.

46. See the exhibition catalogue *Martin Wagner 1885–1957. Wohnungsbau und Weltstadtplanung: Die Rationalisierung des Glücks* (Berlin: Akademie der Künste, 1986).

47. Ludovica Scarpa, *Martin Wagner und Berlin: Architektur und Städtebau in der Weimarer Republik* (Braunschweig: Vieweg, 1986), 65–76. On Wagner, also see David Frisby, *Cityscapes of Modernity: Critical Explorations* (Cambridge: Polity Press, 2001), 264–302.

48. Wagner, "Verkehr und Tradition," in *Das Neue Berlin* 7 (1929): 130. On this point, see Bodenschatz, *Platz frei für das neue Berlin!* 101.

49. Wagner, "Städtebauliche Probleme der Großstadt," in *Martin Wagner 1885–1957,* 105.

50. Wagner, "Der Platz der Republik," in *Das Neue Berlin* 4 (1929): 69.

51. On the history of the four most famous housing estates and their historical reconstruction in the 1980s, see Norbert Huse, ed., *Vier Berliner Siedlungen der Weimarer Republik: Britz • Onkel Toms Hütte • Siemensstadt • Weiße Stadt,* 2nd rev. ed. (Berlin: Argon, 1987). On Siemensstadt, also see Wolfgang Ribbe and Wolfgang Schächte, *Die Siemensstadt: Geschichte und Architektur eines Industriestandortes* (Berlin: Ernst, 1985).

52. Bruno Taut, quoted in Tilman Buddensieg, *Berlin 1900–1933: Architecture and Design. Architektur und Design* (Berlin: Gebr. Mann, 1987), 142–43.

53. Censorship card, quoted in Jeanpaul Goergen, "Urbanität und Idylle," in Klaus Kreimeier, Antje Ehmann, and Jeanpaul Goergen, eds., *Geschichte des dokumentarischen Films in Deutschland,* 3 vols. (Stuttgart: Philip Reclam, 2005), 2:162.

54. Tessenow expressed these ideas in *Handwerk und Kleinstadt,* ed. Otto Kindt (Berlin: Mann, 1972) and *Geschriebenes: Gedanken eines Baumeisters* (Braunschweig: Vieweg, 1982).

55. Wagner, "Die Reichsausstellungsstadt Berlin," in *Das Neue Berlin* 1 (1929): 10.

56. Wagner, "Zivilisation, Kultur, Kunst," *Wohnungswirtschaft* 3, no. 20–21 (1926): 165.

57. Peter Behrens, "Einfluß von Zeit- und Raumausnutzung auf moderne For-

mentwicklung," reprinted in Posener, *Berlin auf dem Wege zu einer neuen Architektur,* 236.

58. Behrens, "Einfluß von Zeit- und Raumausnutzung auf moderne Formentwicklung," 237.

59. Wagner, "Städtebauliche Probleme der Großstadt," 105.

60. Balg, in Mächler, *Weltstadt Berlin,* 363.

61. Franziska Bollerey, "Martin Wagners 'Polipolis' oder Berlin, die Metropole für Alle," in *Die Zukunft der Metropolen,* 1:365.

62. Mächler, *Weltstadt Berlin,* 348.

63. Mächler, *Weltstadt Berlin,* 52. On organicism in Mächler, see Balg, in Mächler, *Weltstadt Berlin,* 121. On the concept of *Demodynamik,* see Mächler, *Weltstadt Berlin,* 348–59. Unlike Wagner, and most of the other architects, writers, and critics discussed in this study, Mächler stayed in Germany after 1933.

64. Aerial photography was very popular in the 1920s. For example, see the image of Potsdamer Platz in "Verkehr von oben," *Die Woche* 27, no. 16 (1925): 354, or E. Ewald, *Im Flugzeug über Berlin: 48 Luftbilder* (Marburg: N. G. Elwer'sche Verlagsbuchhandlung, 1925), which contains impressive shots of Potsdamer Platz and Leipziger Platz (nos. 42, 43). On the continued fascination with aerial photography, see *Historische Luftaufnahmen von Berlin,* texts by Hans-Werner Klünner (Berlin: Verlag Jürgen Schacht, 1985), which is based on the *Luftbildplan* produced by the Hansa-Luftbildgesellschaft in 1928.

65. Alan Balfour, *Berlin: The Politics of Order, 1737–1989* (New York: Rizzoli, 1990), 250. On Potsdamer Platz, see Joachim Fischer and Michael Makropoulous, eds., *Potsdamer Platz: Soziologische Studien zu einem Ort der Moderne* (Munich: Fink, 2004).

66. Michael Makropoulos, "Ein Mythos massenkultureller Urbanität," in Fischer and Makropoulos, eds., *Potsdamer Platz,* 164. The reference is to Robert Musil's monumental *Der Mann ohne Eigenschaften* (The Man Without Qualities, 1930).

67. Franz Hessel, *Ein Flaneur in Berlin* (Berlin: Das Arsenal, 1984), 57.

68. Roth, "Betrachtung über den Verkehr," *Werke* 2:276.

69. Kesser, "Potsdamer Platz," *Die neue Rundschau* 40 (1929): 407.

70. Marcel Breuer, "Verkehrsarchitektur—ein Vorschlag zur Neuordnung des Potsdamer Platzes," in *Das Neue Berlin* 7 (1929): 136.

71. Breuer, "Verkehrsarchitektur," 141.

72. Kurt Tucholsky, "Berliner Verkehr," *Die Weltbühne* 22 (1926): 739.

73. Richard Korherr, "Berlin: Die neue Weltstadt," *Süddeutsche Monatshefte* 27 (1930): 378–79.

74. Endell, *Zauberland des Sichtbaren,* 107. Compare the very similar description in *Die Schönheit der großen Stadt* (Stuttgart: von Strecker und Schröder, 1908), 83–85. Endell's critical writings are collected in *Vom Sehen: Texte 1896–1925 über Architektur, Formkunst und "Die Schönheit der großen Stadt,"* ed. David Helge (Basel: Birkhäuser, 1995). On the larger intellectual and aesthetic context, see Lothar Müller, "The Beauty of the Metropolis: Toward an Aesthetic Urbanism in Turn-of-the-Century Berlin," in Charles W. Haxthausen and Heidrun Suhr, eds., *Berlin: Culture and Metropolis* (Minneapolis: University of Minnesota Press, 1990), 37–57.

CHAPTER 2

1. On the ongoing reassessment of Weimar discourse as crisis discourse, see Werner Möller, ed., *Die Welt spielt Roulette: Zur Kultur der Moderne in der Krise 1927–1932* (Frankfurt am Main: Campus, 2002); Moritz Föllmer and Rüdiger Graf, eds., *Die "Krise" der Weimarer Republik: Zur Kritik eines Deutungsmusters* (Frankfurt am Main: Campus, 2005); and, more generally, Walter Delabar, *Moderne-Studien: Beiträge zur literarischen Verarbeitung gesellschaftlicher Modernisierungen im frühen 20. Jahrhundert* (Berlin: Weidler, 2005).

2. Examples for the German context include Willi Bolle, *Physiognomik der modernen Metropole: Geschichtsdarstellung bei Walter Benjamin* (Cologne: Böhlau, 1994), and Klaus Scherpe, ed., *Die Unwirklichkeit der Städte: Großstadtdarstellungen zwischen Moderne und Postmoderne* (Rowohlt: Reinbek, 1988).

3. Louis Wirth, quoted in Anthony McElligott, *The German Urban Experience, 1900–1945: Modernity and Crisis* (London: Routledge, 2001), 1. Wirth, a German-Jewish immigrant, was a member of the Chicago School of Sociology.

4. David Harvey, *The Urban Experience* (Baltimore: Johns Hopkins University Press, 1989), 6.

5. Harvey, *The Urban Experience*, 230. For a similar concept in German, see Gottfried Korff, "Mentalität und Kommunikation in der Großstadt. Berliner Notizen zur 'inneren Urbanisierung'," in Theodor Kohlmann and Hermann Bausinger, eds., *Großstadt: Aspekte empirischer Kulturforschung* (Berlin: Staatliche Museen Preußischer Kulturbesitz, 1985), 343–61.

6. Siegfried Kracauer, "Aus dem Fenster gesehen," in *Schriften* 5, 3 vols., ed. Inka Mülder-Bach (Frankfurt am Main: Suhrkamp, 1990), 2:401.

7. Klaus Neukrantz, *Barrikaden am Wedding: Der Roman einer Straße aus den Berliner Maitagen 1929*, afterword by Walther Willmer (Berlin: Mackensen, 1988), 36, 37.

8. See the statistics presented by Ferdinand Leyden in *Groß-Berlin: Geographie der Weltstadt*, afterword by Hans-Werner Klünner (Berlin: Gebr. Mann, 1995), 212–14.

9. The numbers are taken from Erwin Gutkind, *Von städtebaulichen Problem der Einheitsgemeinde Berlin* (Berlin: Robert Engelmann, 1922), 16.

10. For studies on working-class Berlin, see Richard Bodek, *Proletarian Performance in Weimar Berlin: Agitprop, Chorus, and Brecht* (Columbia: Camden House, 1998); Pamela Swett, *Neighbors and Enemies: The Culture of Radicalism in Berlin, 1929–1933* (Cambridge: Cambridge University Press, 2004); and more generally, Willi Guttsmann, *Workers' Culture in Weimar Germany* (Oxford: Berg, 1990). On Moabit in particular, see Skyler J. Arndt-Briggs, "The Construction and Practice of Place in Weimar Republic Berlin (Germany)," Ph.D. dissertation, University of Massachusetts, Amherst, 2000. Sociospatial analyses from the early twentieth century include Ernst Hirschberg, *Die soziale Lage der arbeitenden Klassen in Berlin* (Berlin: Liebmann, 1897) and Oscar Stillich, *Die Lage der weiblichen Dienstboten in Berlin* (Berlin: Akademischer Verlag für soziale Wissenschaften, 1902). For ethnographic studies from the period, see Werner Sombart, *Das Proletariat* (Frankfurt am Main: Rütten und Loening, 1906) and Leo Schidrowitz, ed., *Sittengeschichte des Proletariats* (Vienna: Verlag für Kulturforschung, 1925).

11. On this point, see Eve Rosenhaft, "Working-Class Life and Working-Class Politics: Communists, Nazis, and the State in the Battle for the Street, Berlin, 1928–1932," in Richard J. Bessel and Edgar J. Feuchtwanger, eds., *Social Change and Political Development in Weimar Germany* (Totowa, NJ: Barnes and Noble, 1981), 207–40.

12. Benjamin von Brentano, *Wo in Europa ist Berlin? Bilder aus den zwanziger Jahren* (Frankfurt am Main: Suhrkamp, 1987), 96.

13. Leyden, *Groß-Berlin,* 103–5.

14. These questions continue to surface in recurring diagnoses on the disappearance of class into more fluid configurations, from Helmut Schelsky's postwar analysis of a leveled middle-class society to Ulrich Beck's concept of risk society and Niklas Luhmann's work on social differentiation. The references are to Helmut Schelsky, *Wandlungen der deutschen Familie in der Gegenwart* (Stuttgart: Enke, 1967); Ulrich Beck, *Risk Society: Towards a New Modernity,* trans. Mark Ritter (London: Sage, 1992); and Niklas Luhmann, *Social Systems,* trans. John Bednarz (Stanford: Stanford University Press, 1995), and *Observations on Modernity,* trans. William Whobrey (Stanford: Stanford University Press, 1998). On urban historiography from the perspective of systems theory, see Harry Jansen, *The Construction of an Urban Past: Narrative and System in Urban History* (Providence: Berg, 2001).

15. The numbers are taken from Hans Speier, *German White-Collar Workers and the Rise of Hitler* (New Haven: Yale University Press, 1986). Originally written in German and translated by the author himself, the study was completed in 1933 and first published in German in 1977.

16. Whereas the notion of class suggests economic determination and the kind of labor struggles embodied by the working class, the category of social stratum or group implies a degree of social mobility and individual agency usually associated with technocratic and managerial elites. The less frequently used notion of estate, finally, suggests the increasing significance of professional identities that cut across class lines and rely on markers of social status and prestige other than income alone.

17. Speier, *German White-Collar Workers,* 9.

18. Leyden, *Groß-Berlin,* 184.

19. Erich Fromm, *Arbeiter und Angestellte am Vorabend des Dritten Reiches: Eine sozialpsychologische Untersuchung,* ed. Wolfgang Bonß (Munich: dtv, 1983). Completed in American exile, the original English manuscript is called "German Workers 1929: A Survey, Its Methods and Results." The 1983 German version has been translated as *The Working Class in Weimar Germany: A Psychological and Sociological Study,* trans. Barbara Weinberger, ed. and intro. Wolfgang Bonss (Cambridge: Cambridge University Press, 1984).

20. Theodor Geiger, *Die soziale Schichtung des deutsches Volkes* (Stuttgart: Emke, 1932). For other empirical studies published during the Weimar period, see Gerhard Albrecht, ed., *Das soziale System des Kapitalismus,* vol. 9 of *Grundriss der Sozialökonomik* (Tübingen: J. C. B. Mohr, 1926) and the empirical study *Die wirtschaftliche und soziale Lage der Angestellten. Ergebnisse aus der großen sozialen Erhebung des Geswerkschaftsbundes der Angestellten* (Berlin: GDA, 1931).

21. Kracauer, *Die Angestellten* (Frankfurt am Main: Suhrkamp, 1977), 15. A

not entirely satisfactory English translation is available in *The Salaried Masses: Duty and Distraction in Weimar Berlin,* trans. Quitin Hoare, intro. Inka Mülder-Bach (London: Verso, 1998). A comprehensive analysis of the *Angestellten* study can be found in Henry Band, *Mittelschichten und Massenkultur: Siegfried Kracauers publizistische Auseinandersetzung mit der populären Kultur und der Kultur der Mittelschichten in der Weimarer Republik* (Berlin: Lukas, 1999), 125–223. Also see Inka Mülder, "Soziologie als Ethnographie: Siegfried Kracauers Studie 'Die Angestellten'," in Christine Holste, ed., *Kracauers Blick: Anstöße zu einer Ethnographie des Städtischen* (Hamburg: Philo and Philo Fine Arts, 2006), 37–62.

22. Walter Benjamin, "Politisierung der Intelligenz," reprinted in Kracauer, *Die Angestellten,* 118.

23. Kracauer, *Die Angestellten,* 16.

24. Kracauer, *Die Angestellten,* 12.

25. Kracauer, *Die Angestellten,* 91.

26. Kracauer, "Cult of Distraction," *The Mass Ornament: Weimar Essays,* ed., trans., and intro. Thomas Y. Levin (Cambridge: Harvard University Press, 1995), 325.

27. Kracauer, "Cult of Distraction," 328.

28. Kracauer, "Cult of Distraction," 328.

29. On this point, see the excellent overview in Jochen Meyer, ed., *Berlin Provinz: Literarische Kontroversen um 1930* (Marbach am Neckar: Deutsche Schillergesellschaft, 1988).

30. For references, see Friedrich Nietzsche, *Thus Spoke Zarathustra: A Book for All and None,* trans. Adrian Del Caro (Cambridge: Cambridge University Press, 2006); Walther Rathenau, *The New Society,* trans. Arthur Windham (New York: Harcourt, Brace, 1921); Max Weber, *The City,* ed. and trans. Don Martindale and Gertrud Neuwirth (New York: Free Press, 1958); Werner Sombart, *Luxury and Capitalism,* intro. Philip Siegelman, trans. W. R. Dittmar (Ann Arbor: University of Michigan Press, 1967); Ferdinand Tönnies, *Community and Civil Society,* ed. Jose Harris, trans. Harris and Margaret Hollis (Cambridge: Cambridge University Press, 2001); Oswald Spengler, *The Decline of the West,* 2 vols., trans. Charles Francis Atkinson (New York: Alfred Knopf, 1939); Julius Langbehn, *Rembrandt als Erzieher: Von einem Deutschen* (Leipzig: Hirschfeld, 1890); and Georg Lukács, *Theory of the Novel: A Historico-Philosophical Essay on the Forms of Great Epic Literature,* trans. Anna Bostock (Cambridge: MIT Press, 1975).

31. Walther Rathenau, *Zur Kritik der Zeit* (Berlin: S. Fischer, 1912), 15.

32. Kracauer, "Analysis of a City Map," *The Mass Ornament,* 43–44.

33. Karl Scheffler, *Berlin—Ein Stadtschicksal* (Berlin: Erich Reiss, 1910), 267, and Scheffler, *Berlin: Wandlungen einer Stadt* (Berlin: Bruno Cassirer, 1931), 240. The first book has been reprinted with an afterword by Detlef Bluhm as *Berlin—Ein Stadtschicksal* (Berlin: Fannei und Walz, 1989).

34. Heinrich Mann, "Berlin," *Essays* (Hamburg: Claassen,1960), 441.

35. Richard Hülsenback, "Berlin—Endstation," in Herbert Günther, ed., *Hier schreibt Berlin* (1929; Berlin: Fannei und Walz, 1989), 310.

36. Wilhelm Hausenstein, "Berliner Eindrücke," *Die neue Rundschau* 40 (1920): 83, 90.

37. Von Brentano, *Wo in Europa ist Berlin?* 11.

38. Joseph Roth, "Das steinerne Berlin," in *Werke: Das journalistische Werk,* 3 vols., ed. Klaus Westermann (Cologne: Kiepenheuer und Witsch, 1988, 1990, 1991), 3:228.

39. Lion Feuchtwanger, "Herr B.W. Smith besichtigt die Leipziger Straße," in Gunther, ed., *Hier schreibt Berlin,* 73.

40. Alfred Kantorowicz, "Gerechtigkeit für Berlin," *Das Tage-Buch* 12 (1931): 1563.

41. Wilhelm von Schramm, "Berlin als geistiger Kriegsschauplatz," *Süddeutsche Monatshefte* 28 (1931): 513. On the position of Weimar intellectuals within the city-country divide, see Wolfgang Bialas and Burkhard Stenzel, eds., *Die Weimarer Republik zwischen Metropole und Provinz: Intellektuellendiskurse zur politischen Kultur* (Cologne: Böhlau, 1996).

42. Wilhelm Stapel, "Der Geistige und sein Volk. Eine Parole," *Deutsches Volkstum* 12 (1930): 8.

43. Hermann Korherr, "Berlin: Die neue Weltstadt," *Süddeutsche Monatshefte* 27 (1930): 371.

44. In the Bible, these are the mysterious words written on the wall at Belshazzar's feast. Korherr, "Berlin: Die neue Weltstadt," 412.

45. Kurt Tucholsky, "Berlin! Berlin!" *Gesammelte Werke in zehn Bänden,* ed. Mary Gerold- Tucholsky and Fritz J. Raddatz (Reinbek: Rowohlt, 1987), 5: 185.

46. Edwin Hoernle, "Das Recht auf die Straße," quoted in Manfred Görtemaker and Bildarchiv Preußischer Kulturbesitz, ed., *Weimar in Berlin: Porträt einer Epoche* (Berlin: be.bra, 2002), 194.

47. Hermann Ullmann, *Flucht aus Berlin?* (Jena: Eugen Diederichs, 1932), 120. Also see the semiautobiographical novel by Joseph Goebbels, *Der Kampf um Berlin* (Munich: Franz Eher Nachf., 1933).

48. See Ulrich Linse, "Antiurbane Bestrebungen in der Weimarer Republik," in Peter Alter, ed., *Im Banne der Metropolen: Berlin und London in den zwanziger Jahren* (Göttingen: Vandenhoeck und Ruprecht, 1993), 314–44. On the conservative revolution, see Herff, *Reactionary Modernism,* 18–48.

49. Alfred Weber, *Die Großstadt und ihre sozialen Probleme* (Leipzig: Quelle und Meyer, 1908), 2. Alfred Weber was the older brother of Max Weber.

50. For a contemporary analysis of the crisis of the traditional middle class, see Kracauer, "Revolt of the Middle Classes: An Examination of the *Tat* Circle," in *Mass Ornament,* 107–27.

51. See Andrew Lees, "Berlin and Modern Urbanity in German Discourse, 1845–1945," *Journal of Urban History* 17 (1991): 153–80, and Mitchell Schwarzer, *German Architectural Theory and the Search for Modern Identity* (Cambridge: Cambridge University Press, 1995).

52. On reactionary tendencies in Weimar architecture, see Barbara Miller Lane, *Architecture and Politics in Germany, 1918–1945,* 2nd ed. (Cambridge: Harvard University Press, 1985).

53. Theodor Fischer, *Sechs Vorträge über Stadtbaukunst,* 2nd ed. (Munich and Berlin: R. Oldenbourg, 1922), 9.

54. Fischer, *Sechs Vorträge über Stadtbaukunst*, 92.

55. The terms are taken from Jeffrey Herff, *Reactionary Modernism: Technology, Culture, and Politics in Weimar and the Third Reich* (Cambridge: Cambridge University Press, 1984).

56. Kracauer, "The Mass Ornament," *The Mass Ornament*, 76. On the mass ornament as an important trope in Kracauer's writings, see Henrik Reeh, *Ornaments of the Metropolis: Siegfried Kracauer and Modern Urban Culture*, trans. from Danish (Cambridge: MIT Press, 2004).

57. Gutkind, *Vom städtebaulichen Problem der Einheitsgemeinde Berlin*, 80. On Gutkind, who built apartment complexes in Berlin-Staaken, Lankwitz, Lichtenberg, and Reinickendorf, see *Erwin Gutkind 1886–1968. Architektur als Stadtraumkunst*, ed. Rudolf Hierl (Basel: Birkhäuser, 1992), 28.

58. Scheffler, *Berlin—Ein Stadtschicksal*, 200.

59. August Endell, *Die Schönheit der großen Stadt* (Stuttgart: von Strecker und Schröder, 1908), 23.

60. Scheffler, *Berlin—Ein Stadtschicksal*, 203.

61. Scheffler, *Berlin—Ein Stadtschicksal*, 258.

62. Scheffler, *Die Architektur der Großstadt* (Berlin: Bruno Cassirer, 1913), 130. Reprinted with an afterword by Helmut Geisert (Berlin: Gebr. Mann, 1998).

63. Scheffler, "Die Zukunft der Großstädte und die Großstädte der Zukunft," *Die neue Rundschau* 37 (1926): 529.

64. Scheffler, "Die Zukunft der Großstädte," 536.

65. Scheffler, *Berlin: Wandlungen einer Stadt*, 187.

66. Geiger, *Die Masse und ihre Aktion: Ein Beitrag zur Soziologie der Revolutionen* (Stuttgart: Ferdinand Enke, 1926), 73–74.

67. For a comprehensive definition of the term, see Eckart Panocke, "'Masse, Massen,'" in Joachim Ritter, ed., *Historisches Wörterbuch der Philosophie* (Darmstadt: Wissenschaftliche Buchgesellschaft, 1977–), 5:825–32; Johannes Papalekas, "Masse," in Erwin von Beckerath et al., eds., *Handwörterbuch der Sozialwissenschaften*, 12 vols. (Göttingen: Vanderhoeck und Ruprecht, 1956–68), 7:220–26; Werner Conze, "Proletariat, Pöbel, Pauperismus," in Otto Brunner et al., eds., *Geschichtliche Grundbegriffe: Historisches Lexikon zur politisch-sozialen Sprache in Deutschland* (Stuttgart: Klett, 1972), 5:27–68. For general overviews, see Norbert Krenzlin, ed., *Zwischen Angstmetapher und Terminus: Theorien der Massenkultur seit Nietzsche* (Berlin: Akademie, 1992), and Ulrich Lappenküper, Joachim Scholtyseck, and Christoph Studt, eds., *Masse und Macht im 19. und 20. Jahrhundert* (Munich: Oldenbourg, 2003). On mass discourse in the context of the modernist aesthetics, also see Markus Bernauer, *Die Ästhetik der Masse* (Basel: Wiese, 1990), 61–94.

68. Friedrich Engels and Karl Marx, *Die heilige Familie oder Kritik der kritischen Vernunft*, in *Marx-Engels Gesamtausgabe* (Berlin: Dietz, 1990) 2:89.

69. See Kathleen James-Chakraborty, *German Architecture for a Mass Audience* (London: Routledge, 2000), especially the introduction.

70. On this historical and intellectual configuration, see Lothar Müller, "Modernität, Nervosität und Sachlichkeit. Das Berlin der Jahrhundertwende als Hauptstadt der 'neuen Zeit,'" in Eberhard Knödler-Bunte, ed., *Mythos Berlin: Zur*

Wahrnehmungsgeschichte einer industriellen Metropole (Berlin: Ästhetik und Kommunikation, 1987), 79–92.

71. David Frisby, *Sociological Impressionism: A Reassessment of Georg Simmel's Social Theory,* 2nd ed. (London: Routledge, 1992), 68. On Simmel and the connections between the "Großstadt" essay and *The Philosophy of Money,* also see his *Cityscapes of Modernity: Critical Explorations* (Cambridge: Polity, 201), 100–158.

72. Not surprisingly, Simmel's contribution to theories of modernity has played a central role in the emergence of the metropolis as a critical topos in cultural studies and urban studies. For instance, see David Frisby, *Fragments of Modernity: Theories of Modernity in the Work of Simmel, Kracauer, and Benjamin* (Cambridge: MIT Press, 1986), 38–108. On Simmel and architectural culture, compare Massimo Cacciari, *Architecture and Nihilism: On the Philosophy of Modern Architecture,* trans. Stephen Sartarelli, intro. Patrizia Lombardo (New Haven: Yale University Press, 1993), 3–22.

73. Simmel, "The Metropolis and Mental Life," *On Individuality and Social Forms,* ed. and intro. Donald L. Levine (Chicago: University of Chicago Press, 1971), 326. The nervous life of modernity also plays a central role in Andreas Killen, *Electropolis: Shock, Nerves, and German Modernity* (Berkeley: University of California Press, 2006).

74. Karl Joël, quoted by Lothar Müller, "Die Großstadt als Ort der Moderne," in Klaus Scherpe, ed., *Die Unwirklichkeit der Städte: Großstadtdarstellungen zwischen Moderne und Postmoderne* (Rowohlt: Reinbek, 1988), 22.

75. Werner Sombart, reprinted in McElligott, *The German Urban Experience,* 10.

76. Harvey, *The Urban Experience,* 231.

77. Simmel, "Soziologie des Raumes," *Schriften zur Soziologie,* ed. and intro. Heinz-Jürgen Dahme and Otthein Rammstaedt (Frankfurt am Main: Suhrkamp, 1983), 222.

78. See Frisby, *Cityscapes of Modernity,* 124–30.

79. Martin Lindner, *Leben in der Krise: Zeitromane der neuen Sachlichkeit und die intellektuelle Mentalität der klassischen Moderne* (Stuttgart: Metzler, 1994), 5–144.

80. Gustav Hartlaub, "Zur Einführung," *Die Neue Sachlichkeit* (Mannheim: Kunsthalle, 1925), 3. Useful introductions to New Objectivity in the context of literature can be found in Sabina Becker, *Neue Sachlichkeit,* 2 vols. (Cologne: Böhlau, 2000); for the visual arts, see Wieland Schmid, *Der kühle Blick: Realismus der Zwanziger Jahre in Europa und Amerika* (Munich: Hypo-Stiftung, 2001). The classic English-language study on the subject is John Willet, *The New Sobriety, 1917–1933: Art and Politics in the Weimar Period* (London: Thames and Hudson, 1987).

81. Wilhelm Michel, quoted by Wieland Schmid, "Die neue Wirklichkeit: Surrealismus und Sachlichkeit," in Neue Nationalgalerie, ed., *Tendenzen der zwanziger Jahre* (Berlin: Dietrich Reimers, 1977), 4/24.

82. Béla Balázs, "Sachlichkeit und Sozialismus," *Schriften zum Film,* ed. Helmut H. Diederichs and Wolfgang Gersch, 2 vols. (Munich: Carl Hanser, 1984),

2:236–39, and Georg Lukács, Reportage or Portrayal?" in *Essays on Realism* (Cambridge: Harvard University Press, 1981), 45–75.

83. Helmut Lethen, *Neue Sachlichkeit 1924–1932: Studien zur Literatur des "Weißen Sozialismus"* (Stuttgart: Metzler, 1970), 8.

84. Lethen, *Neue Sachlichkeit,* 32.

85. Jost Hermand, "Unity within Diversity? The History of the Concept 'Neue Sachlichkeit,'" in Keith Bullivant, ed., *Culture and Society in the Weimar Republic* (Manchester: Manchester University Press, 1977), 178.

86. Frank Matzke, *Jugend bekennt: So sind wir!* (Leipzig: Reclam, 1930), 41.

87. Peter Sloterdijk, *Kritik der zynischen Vernunft,* 2 vols. (Frankfurt am Main: Suhrkamp, 1983), 2:697–927.

88. See Helmut Lethen, *Cool Conduct: The Culture of Distance in Weimar Germany,* trans. Don Renau (Berkeley: University of California Press, 1998).

CHAPTER 3

1. H[einrich] de Vries, "Ansprache an eine imaginäre Versammlung der jungen Architekten," *Das Kunstblatt* 4 (1920): 65. On de Vries, see Roland Jaeger, *Heinrich de Vries und sein Beitrag zur Architekturpublizistik der zwanziger Jahre* (Berlin: Gebr. Mann, 2001).

2. Paul Zucker, "Architektur," *Die neue Rundschau* 33 (1922): 1218.

3. Mies van der Rohe, reprinted in Ulrich Conrads, ed., *Programs and Manifestos on 20th Century Architecture* (Cambridge: MIT Press, 1970), 304.

4. Mies, reprinted in Fritz Neumeyer, *The Artless Word: Mies van der Rohe on the Building Art,* trans. Mark Jarzombek (Cambridge: MIT Press, 1991), 245. Mies remained the great exception among Weimar architects, with his bold individual vision subsumable to neither the rationalist nor the functionalist side and instead driven by the belief that "beauty in architecture . . . can only be attained if in building we have more than the immediate purpose in mind" (307).

5. Bruno Taut, reprinted in *Programs and Manifestos on 20th Century Architecture,* 38.

6. Adolf Rading, *Bauten, Entwürfe und Erläuterungen,* ed. Peter Pfankuch (Berlin: Gebr. Mann, 1970), 11.

7. Rading, "Stadt, Form, Architekt," in Felix Schwarz and Frank Gloor, eds., *"Die Form." Stimme des Deutsches Werkbundes 1925–1934* (Gütersloh: Bertelsmann, 1969), 115.

8. Hugo Häring, "Der Platz der Republik," *Das Neue Berlin* 4 (1929): 70.

9. Arthur Holitscher, "Utopische Architektur," *Das Kunstblatt* 4 (1920): 240.

10. The most readable German-language survey on modern architecture in Weimar Berlin remains Karl-Heinz Hüter, *Architektur in Berlin 1900–1933* (Stuttgart: Kohlhammer, 1988).

11. Frank-Bertolt Raith, *Der heroische Stil: Studien zur Architektur am Ende der Weimarer Republik* (Berlin: Verlag für Bauwesen, 1997), 7. On the differences between New Building and International Style, see Torsten Scheer, "Where Diversity Rules Cities: Architecture and Urban Design in Berlin between 1900 and 2000," in

Torsten Scheer, Josef Paul Kleinhues, and Paul Kahlfeldt, eds., *City of Architecture—Architecture of the City* (Berlin: Nicolai, 2000), 11.

12. Hilde Heynen, *Architecture and Modernity: A Critique* (Cambridge: MIT Press, 1999), 3.

13. Elisabeth Hajos and Leopold Zahn, *Berliner Architektur 1919 bis 1929: 10 Jahre Architektur der Moderne,* afterword by Michael Neumann (Berlin: Gebr. Mann, 1996), viii. Originally published in 1928 under the title *Berliner Architektur der Nachkriegszeit.* For surveys written by practicing architects, see Walter Gropius, *Internationale Architektur* (Munich: Albert Langen, 1925), and Bruno Taut, *Die neue Baukunst in Europa und Amerika* (Stuttgart: Hoffmann, 1929).

14. Manfredo Tafuri, *Architecture and Utopia: Design and Capitalist Development,* trans. Barbara Luigia La Penta (Cambridge: MIT Press, 1976), 100.

15. Tafuri, *Architecture and Utopia,* 48.

16. Alexander Schwab (pseud. Albert Sigrist), *Das Buch vom Bauen* (Berlin: Verlag "Der Bücherkreis," 1930), 211.

17. On rationalization in the context of Americanization, see Mary Nolan, *Visions of Modernity: American Business and the Modernization of Germany* (New York and Oxford: Oxford University Press, 1994). On Americanism and Fordism in relation to urban practices, see the anthology *Zukunft aus Amerika: Fordismus in der Zwischenkriegszeit. Siedlung Stadt Raum* (Dessau: Stiftung Bauhaus, 1995).

18. For early debates on the *Turmhaus,* see Rainer Stommer, *Hochhaus: Der Beginn in Deutschland* (Marburg: Jonas, 1990), and Dietrich Neumann, *Die Wolkenkratzer kommen: Deutsche Hochhäuser der zwanziger Jahre. Debatten Projekte Bauten* (Wiesbaden: Vieweg, 1995), esp. 39–61. On the most famous competition for a high-rise in Berlin, see Florian Zimmermann, ed., *Der Schrei nach dem Turmhaus: Der Ideenwettbewerb Hochhaus am Bahnhof Friedrichstraße, Berlin 1921/22* (Berlin: Argon, 1988).

19. Walther Rathenau, *Nachgelassene Schriften* (Berlin: S. Fischer, 1928), 329.

20. See Taut, *The Crystal Chain Letters: Architectural Fantasies by Bruno Taut and His Circle,* ed. and trans. Iain Boyd Whyte (Cambridge: MIT Press, 1985). The original Taut text was published as *Die Stadtkrone* (Jena: Eugen Diederichs, 1919) and reprinted in 2003 by Gebr. Mann Verlag. On Taut's social vision, see Kurt Junghanns, *Bruno Taut 1880–1938: Architektur und sozialer Gedanke* (Leipzig: Seemann, 1998).

21. Iain Boyd Whyte, *Bruno Taut and the Architecture of Activism* (Cambridge: Cambridge University Press, 1982), 46–48.

22. Theodor W. Adorno, "Functionalism Today," in Neil Leach, ed., *Rethinking Architecture: Reader in Cultural Theory* (London: Routledge, 1997), 14.

23. On Behne, see the introduction by Rosemarie Haag Bletter to *The Modern Functional Building,* 1–83 (see fn. 24) and the biographical essay by Magdalena Bushart, "Adolf Behne, 'Kunst-Theoretikus,'" in *Adolf Behne: Essays zu seiner Kunst- und Architektur-Kritik,* ed. Magdalena Bushart (Berlin: Gebr. Mann, 2000), 11–88.

24. Adolf Behne, *Der moderne Zweckbau* (Berlin: Drei Masken, 1926), 10. In English as *The Modern Functional Building,* intro. Rosemarie Haag Bletter, trans.

Michael Robinson (Santa Monica: Getty Research Institute, 1996). For a critical assessment of *Der moderne Zweckbau,* see the contributions by Bernd Nicolai, "Der 'Moderne Zweckbau' und die Architekturkritik Adolf Behnes," 173–96, and Jochen Meyer, "Adolf Behne und das Problem der Form," 197–228. On the contradictions within Behne's architectural discourse, also see, in the same volume, Frederic C. Schwartz, "Form Follows Fetish: Adolf Behne and the Problem of 'Sachlichkeit,'" 229–72.

25. Behne, "Ludwig Hoffmann oder zum Thema Architektur-Kritik" (1925), reprinted in Haila Ochs, ed., *Adolf Behne: Architekturkritik in der Zeit und über die Zeit hinaus. Texte 1913–1946* (Basel: Birkhäuser, 1994), 146. The original German reads: "Dekoration ist immer mit einem Bein im Krieg."

26. Behne, "Neue Kräfte in unserer Architektur" (1921), reprinted in *Adolf Behne,* 66.

27. Behne, "'Kollektiv'—und 'En gros'" (1926), reprinted in *Adolf Behne,* 161.

28. Behne, *Neues Wohnen—Neues Bauen* (Leipzig: Hesse und Becker, 1927), 34.

29. Behne, *Eine Stunde Architektur* (Stuttgart: Fritz Wedekind, 1928), 61.

30. Behne, *Eine Stunde Architektur,* 152.

31. Werner Hegemann, "Bauausstellung, Städtebau and 'Kapitalismus'," *Die neue Rundschau* 42 (1931): 236. Behne also wrote about a very different exhibition opening on Köpenicker Straße, "Proletarische Bauausstellung. Mitten in die Welt des Proletariats gestellt," *Die Welt am Abend,* 10 June 1931.

32. Behne, "Kunstausstellung Berlin," *Das Neue Berlin* 5 (1929), 150. On the functionalist façade, especially in relation to commodity culture, see Janet Ward, *Weimar Surfaces: Urban Visual Culture in 1920s Germany* (Berkeley: University of California Press, 2001), 45–92. Published in *Das neue Frankfurt,* Behne's "picture reports" (*Bilderberichte*) from Berlin take his characterization of the city as exhibition space to its logical conclusion. Thus a picture report from 1928 presents the constitutive elements of the big city under headings such as "The Building," "The Shop Window," "The Light Advertisement," "The Poster," "The Illustrated Magazine," and, announced by a film still from Ruttmann's famous city symphony, "The Film." See Behne, "Berlin—Bilderbericht," in Heinz Hirdina, ed., *Neues Bauen. Neues Gestalten. Das Neue Frankfurt: Die neue Stadt. Eine Zeitschrift zwischen 1926 und 1933* (Dresden: Verlag der Kunst, 1991), 220–21, 233–34.

33. Behne, "Kunstausstellung Berlin," 151.

34. Behne, *Der moderne Zweckbau,* 10.

35. Gropius, reprinted in *Programs and Manifestos on 20th Century Architecture,* 96.

36. Gropius, quoted by Hüter, *Architektur in Berlin 1900–1933,* 91.

37. Gropius, quoted by Hüter, *Architektur in Berlin 1900–1933,* 124.

38. Hannes Meyer, reprinted in Kristina Hartmann, ed., *Trotzdem modern: Die wichtigsten Texte zur Architektur in Deutschland 1919–1933* (Braunschweig: Vieweg, 1994), 147.

39. Rading, "Stadt, Form, Architekt" (1925), reprinted in Felix Schwarz and Frank Gloor, eds., *"Die Form." Stimme des Deutsches Werkbundes 1925–1934* (Gütersloh: Bertelsmann, 1969), 115–21.

40. Häring, "Wege zur Form," *Die Form* I (1925–26): 3.

41. Hain uses Martin Buber's distinction between the occidental type and oriental type and their very different perception- and movement-based conception of experience to point to the considerable influence of East European culture—and by extension, Jewish culture—on New Building especially during its early utopian phase. See "'Ex oriente lux'. Deutschland und der Osten," in Vittorio Magnago and Romana Schneider, eds., *Moderne Architektur in Deutschland 1900 bis 1950. Expressionismus und Neue Sachlichkeit* (Stuttgart: Gerd Hatje, 1994), 133–59.

42. On both projects, see Kathleen James, "'No Stucco Pastries for Potemkin and Scapa Flow.' Metropolis Architecture in Berlin: The WOGA Complex and the Universum Theater," 110–19, and Regina Stephan, "'We Believe in Berlin!' The Metal Workers' Union Building, the Columbushaus, and Other Office Buildings in Berlin," 120–41, both in Regina Stephan, ed., *Eric Mendelsohn Architect 1887–1953: Gebaute Welten: Arbeiten für Europa, Palestina und Amerika* (Ostfildern-Ruit: Hatje, 1998).

43. Alan Balfour, *Berlin: The Politics of Order, 1737–1989* (New York: Rizzoli, 1990), 250. Balfour confuses Columbushaus with Columbiahaus, a former military prison on Columbiadamm near Tempelhof Airport. On its history during the Third Reich, see Hans-Norbert Burkert, Klaus Matußek, and Wolfgang Wippermann, *"Machtergreifung" Berlin 1933* (Berlin: Hentrich, 1982), 65.

44. Otto Rudolf Salvisberg, quoted by Hierl, *Erwin Gutkind 1886–1968*, 94.

45. Rading, quoted by Hüter, *Architektur in Berlin 1900–1933*, 183.

46. Erich Mendelsohn, "Das Problem einer neuen Baukunst" (1919), *Das Gesamtschaffen des Architekten: Skizzen Entwürfe Bauten* (Berlin: Rudolf Mosse, 1930), 7. For a very useful introduction to Mendelsohn, see Kathleen James, *Erich Mendelsohn and the Architecture of German Modernism* (Cambridge: Cambridge University Press, 1997), esp. 88–102 (on Mossehaus).

47. Mendelsohn, "Das Problem einer neuen Baukunst," 21.

48. Mendelsohn, "Die internationale Übereinstimmung des neuen Baugedankens oder Dynamik und Funktion," *Das Gesamtschaffen des Architekten,* 26.

49. Ernst Bloch, "Berlin: Functions in Hollow Space," *Heritage of Our Times,* trans. Neville Plaice and Stephen Plaice (Berkeley: University of California Press, 1990), 195.

50. Bloch, "Berlin, as Viewed from the Landscape," *Literary Essays,* trans. Andrew Joron (Stanford: Stanford University Press, 1998), 370, 371.

51. Bloch, "Berlin: Functions in Hollow Space," 199.

52. Bloch, "Building in Empty Spaces," *The Utopian Function of Art and Literature: Selected Essays,* trans. Jack Zipes and Frank Mecklenburg (Cambridge: MIT Press, 1988), 186.

53. Despite its ubiquity as an adjective in cultural debates (i.e., as a synonym for *innovative, provocative,* or *unconventional*), the term *avant-garde* continues to resist easy explanation and classification. From the beginning, the historical avant-gardes have led a peculiar existence as the uncanny double of the modernist movement, articulating its most radical demands and extreme visions but also highlighting its conceptual shortcomings and ideological failures. As has been noted by Paul

Mann, the distinction between modernism and the avant-garde complicates the conceptual oppositions—continuity versus change, tradition versus innovation, creation versus destruction, and compliance versus resistance—that are usually evoked to describe the struggle of the modern against the forces of tradition. Consequently, the avant-garde cannot be consigned to the second term in any of these binaries, for "it must be seen as the means by which the polarity as such is articulated." In Paul Mann, *The Theory Death of the Avant-garde* (Bloomington: Indiana University Press, 1991), 86.

54. Ludwig Hilberseimer, *Berliner Architektur der 20er Jahre*, afterword by H. M. Wingler (Mainz: Florian Kupferberg, 1967), 19.

55. Häring, "Eine physiognomische Studie, zugleich ein Beitrag zur Problematik des Städtebaus," *Die Form* 1, no. 1 (1925–26): 172.

56. On Mies, see Fritz Neumeyer, *The Artless Word: Mies van der Rohe and the Building Art*, trans. Mark Jarzombek (Cambridge: MIT Press, 1991). On the difference between Hilberseimer's and Mies's approach to city planning, see Christine Mengin in Vittorio Magnano Lampugnani and Romana Schneider, eds., *Moderne Architektur in Deutschland 1900 bis 1950: Expressionismus und Neue Sachlichkeit* (Stuttgart: Gerd Hatje, 1994), 185–203.

57. K. Michael Hays, *Modernism and the Posthumanist Subject: The Architecture of Hannes Meyer and Ludwig Hilberseimer* (Cambridge: MIT Press, 1995), 153.

58. Richard Pommer, "'More a Necropolis than a Metropolis.' Ludwig Hilberseimer's Highrise City and Modern City Planning," in Richard Pommer, David Spaeth, and Kevin Harrington, eds., *In the Shadow of Mies: Ludwig Hilberseimer. Architect, Educator, and Urban Planner* (Chicago: Art Institute of Chicago, 1988), 36. On Hilberseimer's unrealized Berlin projects, also see Dietrich Neumann, "The Unbuilt City of Modernity," in *City of Architecture—Architecture of the City*, 161–73.

59. Pommer, "'More a Necropolis than a Metropolis'," 27.

60. Hays, *Modernism and the Posthumanist Subject*, 7.

61. Hilberseimer, *Großstadtarchitektur* (1927; Stuttgart: Julius Hoffmann, 1978), 13.

62. Hilberseimer, "Der Wille zur Architektur," *Das Kunstblatt* 7 (1923): 139.

63. Hilberseimer, *Großstadtarchitektur*, 1–2.

64. Hilberseimer, *Großstadtarchitektur*, 103.

65. Hilberseimer, *Großstadtarchitektur*, 98.

66. Hilberseimer, *Entfaltung einer Planungsidee* (Berlin: Ullstein, 1963), 22.

67. Walter Benjamin, "Experience and Poverty," in *Selected Writings, vol. 2, 1927–1934*, ed. Michael W. Jennings, Howard Eiland, and Gary Smith, trans. Rodney Livingstone and others (Cambridge: Harvard University Press, 1999), 732.

68. Benjamin, "Experience and Poverty," 734.

69. Benjamin, "The Destructive Character," in *Selected Writings*, 2:541. Michael Müller has examined the "bad new" in Benjamin for its significance to the critical assessment of architectural modernism; see his *Architektur und Avantgarde: Ein vergessenes Projekt der Moderne?* (Frankfurt am Main: Athenäum, 1984), 93–147.

CHAPTER 4

1. Michel de Certeau, "Walking in the City," *The Practice of Everyday Life,* trans. Steven Rendall (Berkeley: University of California Press, 1984), 93.

2. On Berlin in the Weimar feuilleton, see Christian Jäger and Erhard Schütz, eds., *Glänzender Asphalt: Berlin im Feuilleton der Weimarer Republik* (Berlin: Fannei und Waltz, 1994), 100. For a similar study published in the GDR, compare Hermann Kähler, *Berlin—Asphalt und Licht: Die große Stadt in der Literatur der Weimarer Republik* (Berlin: Dietz, 1986). On the literary representation of Berlin more generally, see Silvio Vietta, ed., *Das literarische Berlin im 20. Jahrhundert* (Reclam: Stuttgart, 2001). On coffeehouse culture in particular, see Jürgen Schebera, *Damals im Romanischen Café: Künstler und ihre Lokale im Berlin der zwanziger Jahre* (Leipzig: Büchergilde Gutenberg, 1988).

3. Michael Keith, quoted by Sallies Westwood and John Williams, eds., *Imagining Cities: Scripts, Signs, Memory* (London: Routledge, 1997), 8.

4. Eugen Szatmari, *Das Buch von Berlin: Was nicht im Baedecker steht* (1927; Leipzig: Connewitzer Verlagsbuchhandlung, 1997), 36.

5. For a cultural history of Kurfürstendamm, see Karl-Heinz Metzger and Ulrich Dunker, eds., *Der Kurfürstendamm: Leben und Mythos des Boulevards in 100 Jahren deutscher Geschichte* (Berlin: Konopka, 1986), esp. 101–56; Ernest Wichner and Herbert Wiesner, eds., *Industriegebiet der Intelligenz: Literatur im Neuen Berliner Westen der 20er und 30er Jahre* (Berlin: Literaturhaus. Stürichow, 1990); and Regina Stürichow, *Der Kurfürstendamm: Gesichter einer Straße* (Berlin: arani, 1995), esp. 79–128.

6. Curt Moreck, *Führer durch das lasterhafte Berlin* (Berlin: Nicolaische Buchhandlung, 1996), 38. Facsimile reprint of the 1931 edition.

7. Christian Bouchholtz, *"Kurfürstendamm"* (Berlin: Juncker, 1921), 112, 115.

8. See Rudolf Weilbier, "Die City-Filiale im Westen," *Vossische Zeitung,* 16 June 1926.

9. See Miriam Hansen, "America, Paris, the Alps: Kracauer (and Benjamin) on Cinema and Modernity," in Leo Charney and Vanessa R. Schwartz, eds., *Cinema and the Invention of Modern Life* (Berkeley: University of California Press, 1995), 362–402, and, by the same author, "The Mass Production of the Senses: Classical Cinema as Vernacular Modernism," in Christine Gledhill and Linda Williams, eds., *Reinventing Film Studies* (London: Arnold, 2000), 332–50.

10. Heinz Pollack, "Zwiegespräch über Berlin," *Die Weltbühne* 19 (1923): 595.

11. On *Lichtarchitektur* and surface culture, see Janet Ward, *Weimar Surfaces: Urban Visual Culture in 1920s Germany* (Berkeley: University of California Press, 2001), 92–141. On the genealogy of *Lichtarchitektur* in the context of the historical avant-gardes, also see Werner Oechslin, "Light Architecture: A New Term's Genesis," 28–34, and Dietrich Neumann, "Lichtarchitektur and the Avantgarde," 36–51, both in Dietrich Neumann, ed., *Architecture of the Night: The Illuminated Building* (Munich: Prestel, 2002).

12. Wilhelm Hausenstein, "Berliner Eindrücke," *Die neue Rundschau* 40 (1929): 82–83.

13. Wilhelm Schnarrenberger, "Reklame architekturbildend," *Die Form* 3 (1928):

271. On the metropolis and the history of electrification, see Joachim Schlör, *Nachts in der großen Stadt: Paris, Berlin, London 1840–1930* (Munich: Artemis und Winkler, 1991), 72–161, and Wolfgang Schivelbusch, *Disenchanted Night: The Industrialization of Light in the Nineteenth Century,* trans. Angela Davies (Berkeley: University of California Press, 1988). The perceived dangers of light advertising were discussed in Hans H. Reinsch, "Psychologie der Lichtreklame," *Das Neue Berlin* 8 (1929): 154.

14. Ernst Reinhardt, "Gestaltung der Lichtreklame," *Die Form* 4 (1929): 74.

15. Roth, "Der Kurfürstendamm," 99.

16. Walter Riezler, "Umgestaltung der Fassaden," *Die Form* 2 (1927): 40.

17. Riezler, "Organisierte Lichtreklame," *Die Form* 4 (1929): 238.

18. Hermann Sinsheimer, "Mitten im Kurfürstendamm," reprinted in Jäger and Schütz, eds., *Glänzender Asphalt,* 100.

19. Erhard Schütz, "'Kurfürstendamm' oder Berlin als geistiger Kriegsschauplatz. Das Textmuster 'Berlin' in der Weimarer Republik," in Klaus Siebenhaar, ed., *Das poetische Berlin: Metropolenkultur zwischen Gründerzeit und Nationalsozialismus* (Wiesbaden: Deutscher Universitäts-Verlag, 1992), 181.

20. Friedrich Hussong, *"Kurfürstendamm": Zur Kulturgeschichte des Zwischenreiches* (Berlin: Scherl, 1934).

21. Walter Benjamin, *The Arcades Project,* trans. Howard Eiland and Kevin McLaughlin, 2 vols. (Cambridge: Harvard University Press, 1999), 2:803.

22. Alfred Polgar, "Kurfürstendamm," in *Kleine Schriften,* 6 vols., ed. Marcel Reich-Ranicki, with Ulrich Weinzierl (Reinbek: Rowohlt, 1983), 2:345.

23. Szatmari, *Das Buch von Berlin,* 35.

24. Walther Kiaulehn, *Berlin—Lob der stillen Stadt* (Berlin: Fannei und Walz, 1989), 10.

25. Otto Flake, reprinted in Jäger and Schütz, eds., *Glänzender Asphalt,* 49.

26. Rudolf G. Binding, "Menschen- und Straßengeplauder," in *Menschen auf der Straße: Vierundzwanzig Variationen über ein einfaches Thema* (Stuttgart: J. Engelhorns Nachf., 1931), 19.

27. Kracauer, "Ein paar Tage Paris," *Schriften* 5, ed. Inka Mülder-Bach (Frankfurt am Main: Suhrkamp, 1990), 2:298.

28. See "Dichterstafette auf dem Autobus," *Berliner Tageblatt,* 1 January 1929, 4. Beiblatt.

29. Benjamin von Brentano, *Wo in Europa ist Berlin? Bilder aus den zwanziger Jahren* (Frankfurt am Main: Suhrkamp, 1987), 76.

30. Arthur Eloesser, *Die Straße meiner Jugend: Berliner Skizzen* (1919; Berlin: Das Arsenal, 1987), 33.

31. Polgar, "Von oben," *Kleine Schriften,* 1:429.

32. Alfons Paquet, "Reise-Beschreibung. Kultur und Landschaft," *Frankfurter Zeitung,* 7 June 1931.

33. On the problems with such an anachronistic stance, compare Rüdiger Severin, *Spuren des Flaneurs in deutschsprachiger Prosa* (Frankfurt am Main: Peter Lang, 1988), 198.

34. For a typical anthology, see Keith Tester, ed., *The Flâneur* (London: Routledge, 1994). For examples of the appropriation of the flaneur by postmodern discourse, see Anne Friedberg, *Window Shopping: Cinema and the Postmodern* (Berke-

ley: University of California Press, 1993), and Rolf Goebel, *Benjamin heute: Postmodernität und Flanerie zwischen den Kulturen* (Munich: Judicium, 2001), esp. the chapter on Hessel and Benjamin (69–85).

35. Anke Gleber, "Criticism or Consumption of Images? Franz Hessel and the Flâneur in Weimar Culture," *Journal of Communication Inquiry* 13, no. 1 (1989): 82. For a confirmation of this point, see Peter Sprengel, ed., *Berlin-Flaneure: Stadt-Lektüren in Roman und Feuilleton 1910–1930* (Berlin: Weidler, 1998). Using the flaneur for more theoretical explorations, Gerwin Zohlen reads the flaneur texts as the incunabula of classical modernity and its legacies (in Kessler and Levin 1990, 123). Emphasizing questions of modern subjectivity, Dietmar Voss focuses on the "the phantasmagoric dimension of *flanerie*" (1988, 37), especially in relation to unresolved fantasies of power and the affinities with eroticism and intoxication. Arguing for a more precise social typology, Hanns-Josef Ortheil distinguishes the flaneur "who, through his gaze, brings the things to a standstill" from the passerby who "wants to disappear by nestling against the things" (1988, 30–31). Insisting on greater attention to questions of gender, Sigrid Weigel draws attention to the complicated dynamics of gender, writing, and the metropolis in the textual flaneries of Hessel and Kracauer (1988, 194–95). The calls for greater historical and topographical specificity in the scholarship on flanerie are most pronounced in the contributions by Michael Bienert (1992, 78–83) and Joachim Schlör (1991, 238–41). For full bibliographical references, see Gerwin Zohlen, "Schmugglerpfad. Siegfried Kracauer, Architekt und Schriftsteller," in Michael Kessler and Thomas Y. Levin, eds., *Siegfried Kracauer: Neue Interpretationen* (Tübingen: Stauffenburg, 1990), 325–44; Dietmar Voss, "Die Rückseite der Flanerie. Versuch über ein Schlüsselphänomen der Moderne," in Klaus Scherpe, ed., *Die Unwirklichkeit der Städte: Großstadtdarstellungen zwischen Moderne und Postmoderne* (Rowohlt: Reinbek, 1988), 37–60; Hanns-Josef Ortheil, "Der lange Abschied vom Flaneur," *Merkur* 40 (1988): 30–42; Sigrid Weigel, "'Die Städte sind weiblich und nur dem Sieger hold.' Zur Funktion des Weiblichen in Gründungsmythen und Städtedarstellungen," in Sigrun Anselm and Barbara Beck, eds., *Triumph und Scheitern in der Metropole: Zur Rolle der Weiblichkeit in der Geschichte Berlins* (Berlin: Dietrich Reimer, 1987), 207–27; and Michael Bienert, *Die eingebildete Metropole: Berlin im* Feuilleton *der Weimarer Republik* (Stuttgart: Metzler, 1992).

36. Bienert, *Die eingebildete Metropole,* 82.

37. Oswald Spengler, *The Decline of the West,* trans. Charles Francis Atkinson (New York: Knopf, 1980), 90.

38. Franz Hessel, *Ein Flaneur in Berlin* (Berlin: Arsenal, 1984), 145. The original 1929 title was *Spazierengehen in Berlin.* For an introduction to Hessel, see Michael Opitz and Jörg Plath, eds., *Genieße froh, was du nicht hast: Der Flaneur Franz Hessel* (Würzburg: Königshausen und Neumann, 1997). The strong autobiographical dimension of *Ein Flaneur in Berlin* becomes apparent in the many textual overlaps with Hessel's Berlin novel, *Heimliches Berlin* (Frankfurt am Main: Suhrkamp, 1987).

39. Benjamin, "Berlin Chronicle," *Selected Writings* 2:600. On Benjamin and Berlin, see the collection of relevant texts published in *Beroliniana,* afterword by Sebastian Kleinschmidt (Munich: Koehler und Amelang, 2001). For a critical dis-

cussion, see Willi Bolle, *Physiognomik der modernen Metropole: Geschichtsdarstellung bei Walter Benjamin* (Cologne: Böhlau, 1994), and Nicolas Whybroth, *Street Scenes: Brecht, Benjamin, and Berlin* (Bristol: Intellect, 2005).

40. Hessel, *Ein Flaneur in Berlin,* 145.

41. Hessel, "Die Kunst spazieren zu gehn," in *Ermunterungen zum Genuß: Kleine Prosa,* ed. Karin Grund and Bernd Witte (Berlin: Das Arsenal, 1987), 108. Published in an earlier version under the title "Von der schwierigen Kunst spazieren zu gehen" and reprinted in Hessel, *Ermunterung zum Genuß: Kleine Prosa,* ed. Karin Grund and Bernd Witte (Berlin: Brinkmann und Bose, 1988), 53–61.

42. Hessel, *Ein Flaneur in Berlin,* 245.

43. Hessel, "Die Kunst spazieren zu gehn," 107.

44. Hessel, "Die Kunst spazieren zu gehn," 108.

45. Hessel, *Ein Flaneur in Berlin,* 7.

46. Hessel, "Die Kunst spazieren zu gehn," 108 and 111.

47. Hessel, "Von der schwierigen Kunst spazieren zu gehen," *Ermunterung zum Genuß,* 59.

48. Hessel, *Ein Flaneur in Berlin,* 12.

49. Hessel, *Ein Flaneur in Berlin,* 15.

50. Hessel, *Ein Flaneur in Berlin,* 193.

51. Hessel, *Ein Flaneur in Berlin,* 32–33.

52. Hessel, *Ein Flaneur in Berlin,* 21.

53. Hessel, *Ein Flaneur in Berlin,* 23.

54. Hessel, *Ein Flaneur in Berlin,* 266.

55. Hessel, "Die Kunst spazieren zu gehn," 107.

56. Bernd Witte, afterword in Hessel, *Ermunterung zum Genuß,* 247.

57. Benjamin, "The Return of the *Flâneur,*" *Selected Writings* 2:264.

58. Benjamin, "The Return of the *Flâneur,*" 263.

59. Benjamin, "The Return of the *Flâneur,*" 264.

60. Gudrun Klatt, "Berlin—Paris bei Walter Benjamin," in Peter Wruck, ed., *Literarisches Leben in Berlin 1871–1933* (Berlin: Akademie, 1987), 292.

61. Hessel, "Die größte Mietskasernenstadt der Welt," *Die literarische Welt* 6, no. 46 (1930): 6. Not surprisingly, given the many affinities between flanerie and photography, Hessel reviewed the two most famous Berlin photo-books from the period, Mario von Bucovich's *Berlin 1928: Das Gesicht der Stadt* (1928) and Sasha Stone's *Berlin in Bildern* (1929), to be discussed in chapter 5.

62. Benjamin, "Ein Jakobiner von heute. Zu Werner Hegemanns *Das steinerne Berlin,*" *Gesammelte Schriften,* 12 vols., ed. Rolf Tiedemann and Hermann Schweppenhäuser (Frankfurt am Main: Suhrkamp, 1974), 8:264.

63. Kracauer, "Erinnerung an eine Pariser Straße," *Schriften* 5.2:243.

64. Kracauer, "Einer, der nichts zu tun hat," *Schriften* 5.2:155.

65. Köhn, *Straßenrausch,* 238.

66. Frisby, "Deciphering the Hieroglyphics of Weimar Berlin: Siegfried Kracauer," in Charles W. Haxthausen and Heidrun Suhr, eds., *Berlin: Culture and Metropolis* (Minneapolis: University of Minnesota Press, 1990), 154.

67. Kracauer, "Die Unterführung," *Schriften* 5.3:41.

68. For a different reading that focuses on agoraphobia as "a central metaphor for the more generalized psychological interpretation of modern space," compare Anthony Vidler, "Spaces of Passage: The Architecture of Estrangement: Simmel, Kracauer, Benjamin," *Warped Space: Art, Architecture, and Anxiety in Modern Culture* (Cambridge: MIT Press, 2000), 67.

69. Kracauer, "Ein paar Tage Paris," *Schriften* 5.2:298.

70. Kracauer, "Ginster," *Schriften* 7, ed. Karsten Witte (Frankfurt am Main: Suhrkamp, 1973), 23.

71. Kracauer, "Georg," *Schriften* 7:490.

72. Kracauer, quoted by Zohlen, Editorial, in *Straßen in Berlin und anderswo* (Berlin: Das Arsenal, 1987), 121.

73. Kracauer, "Der Kurfürstendamm als Siegesallee," *Schriften* 5.2:318.

74. Kracauer, "Straße ohne Erinnerung," *Schriften* 5.3:173. On this point, see Elizabeth Wilson, "Looking Backward: Nostalgia and the City," in Westwood and Williams, eds., *Imagining Cities,* 129.

75. Kracauer, "Straße ohne Erinnerung," 170.

76. Kracauer, "Cult of Distraction," *The Mass Ornament: Weimar Essays,* ed., trans., and intro. Thomas Y. Levin (Cambridge: Harvard University Press, 1995), 327.

77. Kracauer, "Wiederholung," *Schriften* 5.3:71.

78. Kracauer, "Er ist ein guter Junge," *Schriften* 5.3:13.

79. Kracauer, "Langeweile," *Schriften* 5.1:278–79.

80. On the *Straßenbuch* project, see Graeme Gilloch, "Impromptus of a Great City: Siegfried Kracauer's *Strassen in Berlin und anderswo,*" in Mari Hvattum and Christian Hermansen, eds., *Tracing Modernity: Manifestations of the Modern in Architecture and the City* (London: Taylor and Francis, 2002), 291–306. *Straßen in Berlin und anderswo* was first published in 1987.

81. Michael Schröter, "Weltzerfall und Rekonstruktion. Zur Physiognomik Siegfried Kracauer," *Text + Kritik* 68 (1980): 32.

82. Zohlen, "Schmugglerpfad. Siegfried Kracauer, Architekt und Schrift-steller," 342.

83. Anthony Vidler, "Agoraphobia: Spatial Estrangement in Georg Simmel and Siegfried Kracauer," *New German Critique* 54 (1991): 33.

84. David Frisby, *Fragments of Modernity: Theories of Modernity in the Work of Simmel, Kracauer, and Benjamin* (Cambridge: MIT Press, 1986), 117–26. On this point, compare Bienert, *Die eingebildete Metropole,* 163–74.

85. Martin Jay, "The Extraterritorial Life of Siegfried Kracauer," *Salmagundi* 31–32 (1976): 57.

86. Kracauer, *Die Angestellten: Aus dem neuesten Deutschland* (Frankfurt am Main: Suhrkamp, 1971), 16.

87. See Zohlen, "Schmugglerpfad. Siegfried Kracauer, Architekt und Schrift-steller," in Kessler and Levin, eds., *Siegfried Kracauer,* 325–44. For a recent contribution, see Christine Holste, "'Wenn der Mensch aus dem Glas steigt'—Siegfried Kracauer als Vermittler einer neuen Formensprache der Architektur," in Christine Holste, ed., *Kracauers Blick: Anstöße zu einer Ethnographie des Städtischen* (Hamburg: Philo and Philo Fine Arts, 2006), 103–58.

88. Kracauer, "'Er ist ein guter Junge.' Berliner Betrachtung," *Schriften* 5.3:13.

89. Kracauer, *Die Angestellten,* 96. For a highly suggestive reflection on architecture and forgetting, see "Farewell to the Linden Arcade," *The Mass Ornament,* 337–42.

90. Kracauer, "Kleine Patrouille durch die Bauausstellung," *Schriften* 5.2: 329.

91. Kracauer, "Guckkasten-Bilder," *Schriften* 5.3:79.

92. Kracauer, "Das neue Bauen," *Schriften* 5.2:74.

93. Kracauer, "Tessenow baut das Berliner Ehrenmal," *Schriften* 5.2: 211.

94. Kracauer, "Das Berliner Ehrenmal. Vorläufige Bemerkungen," *Frankfurter Zeitung,* 19 July 1930.

95. Kracauer, "Über Arbeitsnachweise," *Schriften* 5.2:185–86.

96. Kracauer, "The Little Shopgirls Go to the Movies," *The Mass Ornament,* 292.

97. Kracauer, "Aus dem Fenster gesehen," *Schriften* 5.2:401.

98. Kracauer, "Aus dem Fenster gesehen," 399.

99. Kracauer, "Schreie auf der Straße," *Schriften* 5.2:206.

100. Kracauer, "Ginster," 7:22.

101. Kracauer, "Ginster," 130, 196.

102. Kracauer, "The Mass Ornament," 75.

103. Henrik de Reeh, *Ornaments of the Metropolis: Siegfried Kracauer and Modern Urban Culture* (Cambridge: MIT Press, 2004), 195. A translation of a 1991 Danish monograph, the book does not take into account any of the Kracauer scholarship published in the last fifteen years.

104. Reeh, *Ornaments,* 204.

105. Kracauer, "Proletarische Schnellbahn," *Schriften* 5.2:180.

106. Kracauer, "Der neue Alexanderplatz," *Schriften* 5.3:150, 151.

CHAPTER 5

1. Bertolt Brecht, "The Threepenny Lawsuit," *Bertolt Brecht on Film and Radio,* ed. and trans. Marc Silberman (London: Methuen, 2000), 164. For overviews of Weimar photography, see Ute Eskildsen and Jan-Christopher Horak, eds., *Film und Foto in den zwanziger Jahren* (Stuttgart: Gerd Hatje, 1979), and Herbert Molderings, *Fotografie in der Weimarer Republik* (Berlin: Dirk Nishen, 1988).

2. Walter Benjamin, "The Author as Producer," in *Selected Writings, vol. 2, 1927–1934,* ed. Michael W. Jennings, Howard Eiland, and Gary Smith, trans. Rodney Livingstone and others (Cambridge: Harvard University Press, 1999), 775.

3. On this point, see Allan Sekula, "Reading an Archive," in Brian Wallis and Marcia Tucker, eds., *Blasted Allegories* (Cambridge: MIT Press, 1991), 114–28.

4. Thomas Friedrich, *Berlin in Bildern: Über 300 zeitgenössische Photographien* (Munich: Heyne, 1991). In English as *Berlin: A Photographic Portrait of the Weimar Years, 1918–1933* (London: I. B. Tauris, 1991). Other examples include *So war Berlin,* preface by Christian Wolsdorff (Weingarten: Weingarten, 1997), with texts in German, English, and French; also see Antonia Meiners, ed., *Berlin: Photographie 1900–1930* (Berlin: Nicolai, 2002), with texts in five languages. For a book

with a greater architectural focus, see *Berlin: Bilder der dreißiger Jahre. Historische Photographien der Berliner Innenstadt und des Neuen Westens* (Berlin: Jürgen Schacht, 1995).

5. Sekula, "On the Invention of Photographic Meaning," in Victor Burgin, ed., *Thinking Photography* (London: Macmillan, 1982), 85.

6. The term is taken from Beatrice Colomina, *Privacy and Publicity: Modern Architecture as Mass Media* (Cambridge: MIT Press, 1994).

7. The numbers are taken from Thomas Friedrich, "Die Berliner Zeitungslandschaft am Ende der Weimarer Republik," in Diethart Kerbs and Henrick Stadt, eds., *Berlin 1932. Das letzte Jahr der ersten deutschen Republik: Politik, Symbole, Medien* (Berlin: edition Hentrich, 1992), 56–68.

8. On the illustrated press and the central role of photography in the politicization of Weimar urban culture, see Diethart Kerbs, "Die illustrierte Presse am Ende der Weimarer Republik," in *Berlin 1932,* 68–89, and Bernd Weise, "Photojournalism from the First World War to the Weimar Republic," in Klaus Honeff and Karin Thomas, eds., *Nichts als Kunst: Schriften zur Kunst und Photographie* (Cologne: Dumont, 1997), 58–67. For an English-language account, see Hanno Hardt, "The Site of Reality: Constructing Press Photography in Weimar Germany, 1928–33," *Communication Review* 1, no. 3 (1996): 373–402.

9. Siegfried Kracauer, "Photography," *The Mass Ornament: Weimar Essays,* ed., trans., and intro. Thomas Y. Levin (Cambridge: Harvard University Press, 1995), 58.

10. See Erich Salomon, *Berühmte Zeitgenossen in unbewachten Augenblicken* (Stuttgart: Engelhorns Nachf., 1931) and Felix H. Man (i.e., Hans Baumann), "Kurfürstendamm bei Nacht," *BIZ* 30, no. 5 (1929). The genre of night photography has been explored in Jürgen Sembach and Janos Frecot, *Berlin im Licht: Photographien der nächtlichen Stadt* (Berlin: Nicolai, 2002).

11. The contribution of New Vision photographers should not be ignored in this context. Laszlo Moholy-Nagy and Otto Umbehr (Umbo) repeatedly explored the spectacle of the crowd and the mysteries of the street through the technical possibilities of the camera and the defamiliarization effect of skewed angles and unusual perspectives. Celebrating the modern uncanny, Umbo's 1928 look out of an apartment window in the surrealist "Mysterium der Straße" and Moholy-Nagy's 1928 bird's-eye view in "Vom Funkturm" can be described as iconic images of Weimar modernism.

12. The references are "Ein Vormittag Unter den Linden," *BIZ* 28, no. 14 (1919): 107; "Ein Tag in der Wilhelmstraße," *BIZ* 39, no. 25 (1930): 1101; and "Großstadt in der Morgendämmerung zwischen 4 und 6 Uhr," *BIZ* 41, no. 32 (1932): 1064, with photographs by Herbert Hoffmann.

13. See "Die Kunst zu fallen," *BIZ* 38, no. 5 (1929): 195–96.

14. See "Jeder einmal in Berlin," *BIZ* 40, no. 12 (1931): 477.

15. See Leo Hirsch, "2 Minuten Film auf dem Potsdamer Platz," *Weltspiegel* 50 (1929): 4–5.

16. Enno Kaufhold, *Heinrich Zille: Photograph der Moderne,* ed. Photographische Sammlung der Berlinischen Galerie (Munich: Schirmer-Mosel, 1995), plate 9. For a comparative perspective on Berlin photography before World War I,

see Miriam Paeslack, "Fotografie Berlin 1871–1914. Eine Untersuchung zum Darstellungswandel, den Medieneigenschaften, den Akteuren und Rezipienten von Stadtfotografien im Prozeß der Großstadtbildung," Ph.D. dissertation, University of Freiburg, 2003.

17. Janos Frecot, "Der Flaneur mit dem Fotoapparat," in Bildarchiv Preußischer Kulturbesitz, ed., *Der faszinierende Augenblick: Fotografien von Friedrich Seidenstücker* (Berlin: Nicolaische Verlagsbuchhandlung, 1987), 82. Driving was a popular narrative device in photo reportages; for a humorous variation on the theme, see Hermann Nöll, "Mit der grünen Minna durch Berlin," *Der Querschnitt* 11 (1931): 692–97.

18. Edwin Hoernle, "Das Auge des Arbeiters," *Der Arbeiter-Fotograf* 4, no. 7 (1930): 154.

19. On publishing in Weimar Berlin, see Peter de Mendelssohn, *Zeitungsstadt: Menschen und Mächte in der deutschen Presse* (Frankfurt am Main: Ullstein, 1982), 312–409, and Torsten Palmér and Hendrik Neubauer, *Die Weimarer Zeit in Pressefotos und Fotoreportagen* (Cologne: Könemann, 2000). On the role of mass publishing in the development of urban consciousness before World War I, compare Peter Fritzsche, *Reading Berlin 1900* (Cambridge: Harvard University Press, 1996).

20. Willi Münzenberg, cited by Hanno Hardt and Karin B. Ohrn, "The Eyes of the Proletariat: The Worker-Photography Movement in Weimar," *Studies in Visual Communication* 7, no. 3 (1981): 49. On *Der Arbeiter-Fotograf*, see Joachim Büthe, Thomas Kuchenbuch, Günther Lier, Friedhelm Roth, Jan-Thom Prikker, Alois Weber, and Richard Weber, eds., *Der Arbeiter-Fotograf: Dokumente und Beiträge zur Arbeiterfotografie 1926–1932* (Cologne: Prometh, 1977); Heinz Willman, *Geschichte der Arbeiter-Illustrierten Zeitung 1921–1930* (Cologne: Dietz, 1975); and W. Körner and J. Stüber, "Die Arbeiterfotografenbewegung 1926–33," in Verband Arbeiterfotografie, ed., *Arbeiterfotografie* (Berlin: Elefanten-Press, 1976), 25–68.

21. See, for instance, the cover of *Der rote Stern* 5, no. 1 (1928).

22. Franz Höllering, "Die Eroberung der beobachtenden Maschinen," *Arbeiter-Fotograf* 11, no. 10 (1928): 3.

23. Walter Nettelbeck, "Reportagen," *Der Arbeiter-Fotograf* 12, no. 1 (1929): 3–4. For the heated debates on photomontage in the communist press, also see Franz Höllering, "Fotomontage," *Der Arbeiter-Fotograf* 11, no. 8 (1928): 3–4, and Heinz Luedecke, "Bild—Wort—Montage," *Der Arbeiter-Fotograf* 5, no. 9 (1931): 211–13.

24. Egon Erwin Kisch, "Großstadt Berlin," *AIZ* 8, no. 7 (1929): 8.

25. See Kisch, "Berlin bei der Arbeit," *AIZ* 6, no. 25 (1927): 8–9, and "Nächtliche Arbeits-Symphonie der Großstadt," *AIZ* 8, no. 18 (1929): 6. His focus on road construction is also evident in the subway construction images of "U-Bahn Bau," *AIZ* 7, no. 49 (1928): 8–9.

26. Kisch, "Ankunft in Berlin," *AIZ* 9, no. 24 (1930): 464–65.

27. Alfred Eisenstaedt, "Januskopf Berlin," *Weltspiegel* 34 (1932): 8–9.

28. See Traut Hajdu, "Meyershof—eine Stadt in der Stadt," *AIZ* 8, no. 19 (1929): n.p. Compare the typical evocation of milieu in the photo reportage in *Weltspiegel* 26 (1929): 4–5 by Neudatschin and Joffe under the heading "Ackerstraße 132/33 lädt zum Ball." Also see the contribution by Walter Petry (with photos by

R. Horlemann), "Ackerstraße 132 'Meyers-Hof,'" in the special Zille issue of *Das neue Berlin* 10 (1929): 199–200, and "Die Kaserne," in *Volk und Zeit* 40 (1930). The inhabitants of the "Zille-Burg" returned to the news in 1932 because of their participation in several tenant strikes. See Erwin Vulpius, "Bilderjagd in der Wanzenburg," *Arbeiter-Fotograf* 6, no. 11 (1932): 231–32. On the negative effects of gentrification, see "Das Berliner Scheunenviertel," *AIZ* 8, no. 23 (1929): 7; on makeshift solutions to the housing crisis, also see "Auf der Laube," *AIZ* 8, no. 7 (1929): 6.

29. See "Querschnitt durch Berliner Mietskasernen," *AIZ* 5, no. 15 (1926): 4, and Felix H. Man, "Querschnitt durch ein Haus. Eins von hunderttausend Berliner Mietshäusern," *BIZ* 40, no. 3 (1932): 61–63.

30. Other publications that featured Mossehaus include Hans Brennert and Erwin Stein, eds., *Probleme der neuen Stadt Berlin* (Berlin-Friedenau: Deutscher Kommunal-Verlag, 1926), 280, and Max Osborn, *Berlin 1870–1929: Der Aufstieg zur Weltstadt* (Berlin: Gebr. Mann, 1994), 198. The latter was first published in 1926 in Leipzig.

31. One Web site about the recent 1992–93 renovation of Mossehaus by Peter Kolb, Bernd Kemper, and Dieter Schneider states that the original building was damaged during World War I. See http://www.galinsky.com/buildings/mossehaus/.

32. Manfredo Tafuri, *Architecture and Utopia: Design and Capitalist Development*, trans. Barbara Luigia La Penta (Cambridge: MIT Press, 1988), 100.

33. While a series of bad business decisions forced Lachmann-Mosse to sell his almost bankrupt company to Max Winkler's infamous Cautio GmbH in 1932, Mendelsohn felt increasingly marginalized within the architectural profession and, in 1933, had no choice but to leave Berlin, first for Istanbul and Tel Aviv, and eventually for Southern California. On the Mosse project, see Regina Stephan, "'Thinking from Day to Day, where History Takes Great Turns, Leaving Hundreds of Thousands Unsatisfied.' Early Expressionist Buildings in Luckenwalde, Berlin, and Gleiwitz," in *Erich Mendelsohn Architekt 1887–1953: Gebaute Welten: Arbeiten für Europa, Palestina und Amerika* (Berlin: Hatje, 1998), 48–52.

34. For an account of these revolutionary days, see *Die Revolution in Berlin November–Dezember 1918* (Berlin: Dirk Nishen, 1989). On Römer, whose Photothek was among the most influential photo agencies of the Weimar Republic, see Diethart Kerbs, ed., *Auf den Straßen von Berlin: Der Fotograf Willy Römer 1887–1979* (Bönen/Westfalen: Kettler, 2004).

35. See, for instance, the cover of *BIZ* 38, no. 2 (1929).

36. See the cover of *Der rote Stern* 6, no. 1 (1929).

37. See "Auf den Dächern von Berlin," *Weltspiegel* 26 (1929): 2, and "Zeugen der Nacht," *Weltspiegel* 17 (1929): 4.

38. See the covers of "Berlin as Welt- und Fremdenstadt," *Weltspiegel* 34 (1926), and "Berlin, die Weltstadt der Arbeit," *Weltspiegel* 43 (1927).

39. Erich Mendelsohn, *Amerika: Bilderbuch eines Architekten* (Berlin: Rudolf Mosse, 1926). In English as *Erich Mendelsohn's "Amerika,"* trans. Stanley Appelbaum (Toronto: Dover, 1993). About half of the photographs were taken by Mendelsohn; the others seem to have been either taken by friends or reprinted from other publications.

40. Mendelsohn, *Russland–Europa–Amerika* (Berlin: Rudolf Mosse, 1929), n.p. The book was advertised in *Weltspiegel* 30 (1930).

41. This is the title of an article by Johannes Molzahn, "Nicht mehr Lesen! Sehen!" *Das Kunstblatt* 12, no. 3 (1928): 78–83.

42. Benjamin, "Little History of Photography," in *Selected Writings* 2:527.

43. Mendelsohn, "Die internationale Übereinstimmung des Neues Baugedankens oder Dynamik und Funktion" (1923), in *Das Gesamtschaffen des Architekten: Skizzen Entwürfe Bauten* (Berlin: Rudolf Mosse, 1930), 28. Translation adapted from Regina Stephan. Reprinted in 1988 by the Braunschweig-based Vieweg-Verlag. For a critical review that takes issue with the arrangement of the photographs, see Adolf Behne, *Das Neue Berlin* 12 (1929): 245.

44. Heinz Johannes, *Neues Bauen in Berlin: Ein Führer mit 168 Bildern* (Berlin: Deutscher Kunstverlag, 1931), 16.

45. Elisabeth M. Hajos and Leopold Zahn, *Berliner Architektur 1919 bis 1929,* afterword by Michael Neumann (Berlin: Gebr. Mann, 1996), 125. First published in 1929 by Albertus Verlag in Berlin. The quotation is apparently from Mendelsohn himself.

46. Edwin Redslob, Introduction, in Hajos and Zahn, *Berliner Architektur 1919 bis 1929,* vii.

47. See Leesa L. Rittelmann, "Constructed Identities: The German Photo Book from Weimar to the Third Reich," Ph.D. dissertation, University of Pittsburgh, 2002.

48. Franz Hessel, reviews of Stone, *Berlin in Bildern, Literarische Welt* 5, no. 13–14 (1929): 8, and von Bucovich, *Berlin, Literarische Welt* 4, no. 46 (1928): 6.

49. Alfred Döblin, Preface to Mario von Bucovich, *Berlin 1928: Das Gesicht der Stadt,* afterword by Hans-Werner Klünner (Berlin: Nicolaische Verlag, 1992), 5, 7. A reprint of the 1928 edition, the book contains 107 of the original 254 photographs. Compare Döblin's statement in an unpublished prologue to the novel that "there are two ways in this world: a visible one and an invisible one." Reprinted in Matthias Prangel, ed., *Materialien zu Alfred Döblin "Berlin Alexanderplatz"* (Frankfurt am Main: Suhrkamp, 1975), 26.

50. Adolf Behne, Introduction to Sasha Stone, *Berlin in Bildern,* afterword by Michael Neumann (Berlin: Gebr. Mann, 1998), 8. On Stone, see Eckhardt Köhn, ed., *Sasha Stone: Fotografien 1925–1939* (Berlin: Dirk Nishen, 1990).

51. Karl Vetter, Introduction to Laszlo Willinger, *100 x Berlin,* afterword by Helmut Geisert (Berlin: Gebr. Mann, 1997), xxv.

52. On architectural photography, see Rolf Sachsse, *Photographie als Medium der Architekturinterpretation: Studien zur Geschichte der deutschen Architekturphotographie im 20. Jahrhundert* (Munich: Saur, 1984).

53. Willy Pragher, *Berliner Verkehrsgewühl,* ed. Alfred Gottwaldt (Berlin: Museum für Verkehr und Technik, 1992), 33.

54. von Bucovich, *Berlin 1928,* 35.

55. Willinger, *100 x Berlin,* xxx; image, 15.

56. Rudolf Arnheim, "Berlin in Bildern," *Die Weltbühne* 25 (1929): 111. For other reviews of *Berlin in Bildern,* see Bernhard von Brentano, *Frankfurter Zeitung,* 6 February 1929; Paul Westheim, *Das Kunstblatt* 11–12 (1928); and Fritz Hellwag, *Die Form* 1, no. 4 (1929): 24.

57. Stone, "Photo-Kunstgewerblereien," *Das Kunstblatt* 3 (1928): 86. The articles appeared together with a retouched photograph of Tauentzienstraße and Auguste-Viktoria-Platz (today Breitscheidplatz) without the Kaiser Wilhelm Memorial Church.

58. Stone, "Zurück zur Fotografie," *Die Form* 7 (1929): 168.

59. Published in *BIZ* 37, no. 51 (1928), *Die Form* 9 (1929), and *Die Dame* 14 (1928).

60. See his cover to Alfred Döblin and Oskar Loerke, *Alfred Döblin: Im Buch—Zu Haus—Auf der Straße* (Berlin: S. Fischer, 1928), and Walter Benjamin, *Einbahnstraße* (Berlin: Rowohlt, 1928).

61. Max Missmann, *Das große Berlin: Photographien 1899–1935,* ed. Wolfgang Gottschalk (Berlin: Argon, 1991), 15, 16–17. On Missmann, see Wolfgang Gottschalk, Janos Frecot, Ludwig Hoerner, and Michael Rutschky, eds., *Max Missmann: Photograph für Architektur, Industrie, Illustration, Landschaft und Technik* (Berlin: Berlinische Galerie, 1989). For other photographers from the prewar period, see Harald Brost and Laurenz Demps, *Berlin wird Weltstadt: Photographien von F. Albert Schwartz Hof-Photograph* (Berlin: Brandenburgisches Verlags-Haus, 1997) and Archiv für Kunst und Geschichte, ed., *Berlin um 1900: Photographiert von Lucien Levy,* with descriptions by Herbert Kraft (Munich: Max Hueber, 1986); both books include several images of Alexanderplatz.

62. Michael Bienert and Erhard Senf, *Berlin wird Metropole: Fotografien aus dem Kaiser-Panorama* (Berlin: be.bra, 2000), 25.

63. Public pride about the new Alexanderplatz continued after 1933, as evidenced by Robert von Wahlert, ed., *Berlin in Bildern* (Berlin: Scherl, 1942), 71.

64. See the exhibition catalogue by Neue Gesellschaft für Bildende Kunst, ed., *Revolution und Fotografie Berlin 1918/19* (Berlin: Dirk Nishen, 1989). For a historical survey, see *Illustrierte Geschichte der deutschen Revolution* (Frankfurt am Main: Neue Kritik, 1968). Reprint of the 1929 edition.

65. Benjamin, "Little History of Photography," 512.

66. Benjamin, "Little History of Photography," 510.

67. Benjamin, "On the Concept of History," *Selected Writings* 4:390.

CHAPTER 6

1. Anon., "Berlin-Alexanderplatz," *BIZ* 41, no 37: 1232–33.

2. Eugen Szatmari, *Das Buch von Berlin: Was nicht im Baedecker steht* (Leipzig: Connewitzer Verlagsbuchhandlung, 1997), 195–206.

3. Alfred Döblin, *Berlin Alexanderplatz,* trans. Eugene Jolas (New York: Frederick Ungar, 1992), 4. Hereafter all references to the English translation of the novel (*BA*) will appear in the text in parentheses.

4. Döblin, "Nachwort zu einem Neudruck," *Berlin Alexanderplatz: Die Geschichte vom Franz Biberkopf* (Olten: Walter, 1977), 508. Given the gendered nature of this struggle, my use of the male pronoun is intentional here.

5. In the extensive scholarship on *Berlin Alexanderplatz,* many critics read the novel's distinct style as a reenactment of the chaos of modern urban life through

narrative, thematic, and formal means (Martini 1956, 358–59; Ziolkowski 1969, 110–11). Some point to Döblin's double role of detached monteur and omniscient narrator in the creation of the city text (Klotz 1969, 379), while others insist that the city tells itself without the presence of a mediating figure (Schöne 1965, 323). More recent contributions have questioned the narratability of the city from within a modernist framework (Scherpe 1989) or introduced poststructuralist concepts to analyze the city text in terms of its decentered textuality (Freisfeld 1982; Jähner 1984) and urban discursivity (Keller 1990). Feminist readings of the metropolis as a gendered space have played a key role in the remapping of urban spatiality and subjectivity (Scholvin 1985; Tatar 1995). For full bibliographical references, see Fritz Martini, *Das Wagnis der Sprache: Interpretationen deutscher Prosa von Nietzsche bis Benn* (Stuttgart: Ernst Klett, 1956); Theodore Ziolkowski, *Dimensions of the Modern Novel* (Princeton: Princeton University Press, 1969); Volker Klotz, *Die erzählte Stadt: Ein Sujet als Herausforderung des Romans von Lesage bis Döblin* (Munich: Hanser, 1969); Albrecht Schöne, "Alfred Döblin: 'Berlin Alexanderplatz,'" in Benno von Wiese, ed., *Der deutsche Roman: Vom Barock bis zur Gegenwart: Struktur und Geschichte*, 2 vols. (Düsseldorf: August Bagel, 1965), 2:291–325; Andreas Freisfeld, *Das Leiden an der Stadt: Spuren der Verstädterung in deutschen Romanen des 20. Jahrhunderts* (Cologne and Vienna: Böhlau, 1982); Harald Jähner, *Erzählter, montierter, soufflierter Text: Zur Konstruktion des "Berlin Alexanderplatz" von Alfred Döblin* (Frankfurt am Main: Peter Lang, 1984); Klaus Scherpe, "The City as Narrator: The Modern Text in Alfred Döblin's 'Berlin Alexanderplatz,'" trans. Max Reinhart and Mark Anderson, in Andreas Huyssen and David Bathrick, eds., *Modernity and the Text: Revisions of German Modernism* (New York: Columbia University Press, 1989), 162–79; Otto Keller, *Döblins "Berlin Alexanderplatz": Die Großstadt im Spiegel ihrer Diskurse* (Berne: Peter Lang, 1990); Ulrike Scholvin, *Döblins Metropolen: Über reale und imaginäre Städte und die Travestie der Wünsche* (Weinheim and Basel: Beltz, 1985), 98–105; and Maria Tatar, *Lustmord: Sexual Murder in Weimar Germany* (Princeton: Princeton University Press, 1995), 132–52. One of the few discussion of *Berlin Alexanderplatz* in terms of mass discourse can be found in Bernd Widdig, *Männerbünde und Massen: Zur Krise männlicher Identität in der Literatur der Moderne* (Opladen: Westdeutscher Verlag, 1992), 144–77.

6. Walter Benjamin, "The Crisis of the Novel," *Selected Writings*, 4 vols., ed. Howard Eiland and Michael W. Jennings, trans. Edmund Jephcott and others (Cambridge: Harvard University Press, 2003), 2:300.

7. Heinrich Mendelsohn, "Die Stadt am Alexanderplatz," *Das Neue Berlin* 5 (1929): 104. Compare Ulf Dietrich, "Der Alexanderplatz in Berlin," *Städtebau* 24 (1929): 570–72, and Walter Riezler, "Die Bebauung des Alexanderplatzes," *Die Form* 4 (1929): 129–32.

8. See Sammy Gronemann, *Tohuwaboru*, afterword by Joachim Schlör (Leipzig: Reclam, 2000), and Martin Beradt, *Die Straße der kleinen Ewigkeit*, with an essay by Eike Geisel (Frankfurt am Main: Eichborn, 2001). On Jewish life in the *Scheunenviertel*, see Horst Helas, *Juden in Berlin–Mitte: Biografien Orte Begegnungen* (Berlin: Trafo, 2001). For a history of the area, also see the publication by the

Verein Stiftung Scheunenviertel: *Das Scheunenviertel: Spuren eines verlorenen Berlins* (Berlin: Haude und Spener, 1996), which includes a discussion of the first pogroms on 5 and 6 November 1923.

9. Ludwig Hilberseimer, "Das Formproblem eines Welstadtplatzes," *Das Neue Berlin* 2 (1929): 39.

10. On the history of Alexanderplatz, see Gernot Jochheim, *Der Berliner Alexanderplatz* (Berlin: Links, 2006). On the 1929 competition and the ongoing debate on reconstruction and restoration, see Hans-Joachim Pysall, ed., *Das Alexanderhaus. Der Alexanderplatz* (Berlin: Jovis, 1998).

11. Döblin, *Berlin Alexanderplatz: Die Geschichte vom Franz Biberkopf. Anhang. Entwürfe und Reste von Frühfassungen,* ed. Anthony W. Riley (Düsseldorf: Olten, 1996), 818.

12. For a history of the central slaughterhouse, see Susanne Schindler-Reinisch, ed., *Berlin–Central–Viehhof: Eine Stadt in der Stadt* (Berlin: Aufbau, 1996). Even Hessel made a rare excursion to Landsberger Allee in "Nach Osten," *Ein Flaneur in Berlin* (Berlin: Das Arsenal, 1984), 214.

13. Benjamin, "The Crisis of the Novel," 301. Compare Ulf Zimmermann, "Benjamin and 'Berlin Alexanderplatz': Some Notes towards a View of Literature and the City," *Colloquia Germanica* 12 (1979): 256–72.

14. I borrow this term from Fred Evans and his forthcoming study *The Multi-Voiced Body: Society, Communication, and the Age of Diversity* (New York: Columbia University Press, 2008).

15. Hans Sochacwer, "Der neue Döblin," reprinted in Matthias Prangel, ed., *Materialien zu Alfred Döblin "Berlin Alexanderplatz"* (Frankfurt am Main: Suhrkamp, 1975), 58. Prangel contributes to the debate on the city novel in "Vom dreifachen Umgang mit der Komplexität der Großstadt: Alfred Döblins *Berlin Alexanderplatz,*" in Jattie Enklaar and Hans Ester, ed., *Das Jahrhundert Berlins: Eine Stadt in der Literatur* (Amsterdam: Rodopi, 2000), 51–65.

16. Karl Marx and Friedrich Engels, *The Communist Manifesto* (1848), trans. Samuel Moore (London: Penguin, 1967), 92. Of course, the meaning and function of lumpenproletariat as a historical category is much more complicated; for an illuminating discussion, see "The Lumpenproletariat and the Proletarian Unnamable," in Nicholas Thoburn, *Deleuze, Marx, and Politics* (London: Routledge, 2002), 47–68.

17. Ignaz Jezower, review of Döblin's *Berlin Alexanderplatz, Das Neue Berlin* 12 (1929): 255.

18. Gottfried Korff, "Mentalität und Kommunikation in der Großstadt. Berliner Notizen zur 'inneren Urbanisierung,'" in Theodor Kohlmann and Hermann Bausinger, eds., *Großstadt: Aspekte empirischer Kulturforschung* (Berlin: Staatliche Museen Preußischer Kulturbesitz, 1985), 343–61.

19. Armin Kesser, "Ein Berliner Roman," reprinted in Prangel, *Materialien,* 55.

20. Klaus Neukrantz, review of *Berlin Alexanderplatz, Die Linkskurve* 1, no. 5 (1929): 31.

21. Neukrantz, *Barrikaden am Wedding: Der Roman einer Straße aus den Berliner Maitagen 1929,* afterword by Walther Willmer (Berlin: Mackensen, 1988), 56.

22. Karl Schröder, *Klasse im Kampf* (Berlin: Büchergilde Gutenberg, 1932), 20–21.

23. Alexander Stenbock-Fermor, reprinted in Anthony McElligott, *The German Urban Experience, 1900–1945: Modernity and Crisis* (London: Routledge, 2001), 187.

24. For an overview of the relevant debates, see David Midgley, *Writing Weimar: Critical Realism in German Literature, 1918–1933* (London: Oxford University Press, 2000).

25. j-s, "Ist das unser Alex," reprinted in Prangel, *Materialien,* 70.

26. Johannes R. Becher, "Einen Schritt weiter!" reprinted in Prangel, *Materialien,* 93.

27. Otto Biha, "Herr Döblin verunglückt in einer 'Linkskurve,'" reprinted in Prangel, *Materialien,* 99. The reference is to the BPRS journal *Linkskurve.*

28. For instance by Kurt Reinhold, "Hier schreibt Berlin. Parodiert von . . . " *Der Querschnitt* 10 (1930): 119–20.

29. For a comparative analysis of the motif of walking in the modern city novel, compare Peter I. Barta, *Bely, Joyce, and Döblin: Peripatetics in the City Novel* (Gainesville: University of Florida Press, 1996).

30. On these adaptations, see Peter Jelavich, *Berlin Alexanderplatz: Radio, Film, and the Death of Weimar Culture* (Berkeley: University of California Press, 2006).

31. Julius Bab, review of *Berlin Alexanderplatz,* in Ingrid Schuster and Ingrid Bode, eds., *Alfred Döblin im Spiegel der zeitgenössischen Kritik* (Berne: Francke, 1973), 210.

32. Wilhelm Westecker, review of *Berlin Alexanderplatz,* reprinted in Schuster and Bode, eds., *Alfred Döblin im Spiegel der zeitgenössischen Kritik,* 238.

33. Benjamin von Brentano, review of *Berlin Alexanderplatz,* reprinted in Schuster and Bode, eds., *Alfred Döblin im Spiegel der zeitgenössischen Kritik,* 213.

34. Döblin, "Wissenschaft und moderne Literatur," *Schriften zu Ästhetik, Politik und Literatur,* ed. Erich Kleinschmidt (Olten: Walter, 1989), 215.

35. Döblin, quoted by Klaus Müller-Salget, *Alfred Döblin: Werk und Entwicklung,* 2nd ed. (Bonn: Bouvier, 1988), 108.

36. Harald Jähner, *Erzählter, montierter, soufflierter Text: Zur Konstruktion des "Berlin Alexanderplatz" von Alfred Döblin* (Frankfurt am Main: Peter Lang, 1984), 38–60.

37. Andreas Freisfeld, *Das Leiden an der Stadt: Spuren der Verstädterung in deutschen Romanen des 20. Jahrhunderts* (Cologne: Böhlau, 1982), 166–67.

38. Döblin, "Altes Berlin," *Schriften zu Leben und Werk,* ed. Erich Kleinschmidt (Olten: Walter, 1986), 219. Also see "Ankunft in Berlin," 110–11, in the same volume.

39. Döblin, "Östlich um den Alexanderplatz," *Kleine Schriften,* 2 vols. (Olten: Walter, 1990), 2:298–302.

40. Döblin, "Vorstoß nach dem Westen," *Kleine Schriften* 2:325–28.

41. Döblin, "Berlin und die Künstler," *Schriften zu Leben und Werk,* 38.

42. Döblin, "Zur Physiologie des dichterischen Schaffens," *Schriften zu Leben und Werk,* 179.

43. Döblin, quoted in Jochen Meyer, ed., *Alfred Döblin 1878–1978* (Marbach am Neckar: Deutsches Literaturarchiv im Schiller-Nationalmuseum, 1978), 214.

44. David B. Dollenmayer, *The Berlin Novels of Alfred Döblin: "Wadzek's Battle with the Steam Engine," "Berlin Alexanderplatz," "Men Without Mercy," and "November 1918"* (Berkeley: University of California Press, 1988), 51.

45. Döblin, "Östlich um den Alexanderplatz," *Die Zeitlupe: Kleine Prosa,* ed. Walter Muschg (Olten: Walter, 1962), 60.

46. Döblin, "An Romanautoren und ihre Kritiker: Berliner Programm," *Schriften zu Ästhetik, Politik und Literatur,* ed. Erich Kleinschmidt (Olten: Walter, 1989), 121–22.

47. Döblin, "Der Bau des epischen Werks," *Neue Rundschau* 40 (1929): 527–51.

48. Döblin, "An Romanautoren und ihre Kritiker," 121.

49. Döblin, "An Romanautoren und ihre Kritiker," 122.

50. Döblin, "Der Geist des naturalistischen Zeitalters," *Schriften zu Ästhetik, Politik und Literatur,* 178.

51. Döblin, "Der Geist des naturalistischen Zeitalters," 188–89.

52. Döblin, "Der Geist des naturalistischen Zeitalters," 189.

53. Döblin, "Großstadt und Großstädter," *Die Zeitlupe: Kleine Prosa,* ed. Walter Muschg (Olten: Walter, 1962), 227.

54. Döblin, *Das Ich über der Natur* (Berlin: S. Fischer, 1927), 239.

55. Döblin, "Der Geist des naturalistischen Zeitalters," 182.

56. Döblin, "Der Geist des naturalistischen Zeitalters," 180.

57. Döblin, "Großstadt und Großstädter," 229.

58. Döblin, *Unser Dasein,* ed. Walter Muschg (Olten: Walter, 1964), 20.

59. Döblin, "Großstadt und Großstädter," 225.

60. Döblin, Interview, *Lichtbildbühne,* 7 October 1931.

61. Herbert Ihering, *Von Reinhardt bis Brecht: Vier Jahrzehnte Theater und Film,* 3 vols. (Berlin: Aufbau, 1961), 3:367.

62. For instance, Ekkehard Kaemmerling equates Döblin's narrative strategies with filmic techniques such as framing, shot sizes, point of view, shot/counter shot, parallel editing, and so forth. See "Die filmische Schreibweise," in Helmut Schwimmer, ed., *Materialien zu Alfred Döblin "Berlin Alexanderplatz"* (Munich: R. Oldenbourg, 1973), 185–98.

CHAPTER 7

1. Walter Benjamin, "The Work of Art in the Age of Mechanical Reproducibility," in *Walter Benjamin: Selected Writings,* 4 vols., ed. Howard Eiland and Michael Jennings, trans. Edmund Jephcott and others (Cambridge: Harvard University Press, 2003), 4:265.

2. Interestingly, these photomontages include no Berlin landmarks. Many of the buildings are New York or Chicago skyscrapers, a comment on the frequent characterization of Weimar Berlin as an American city. For further discussion, see Herbert Molderings, *Umbo: Otto Umbehr 1902–1980* (Düsseldorf: Richter, 1995), 89–90. Moldering's discussion of parataxis as the organizing principle in these photomontages applies equally to the cross-section film.

3. Siegfried Kracauer, *From Caligari to Hitler: A Psychological History of the German Film,* ed. Leonardo Quaresima (Princeton: Princeton University Press, 2004), 187.

4. This openness to often contradictory readings is reflected in the various English translations for the German title (e.g., *Symphony of a Great City, A Symphony of the Big City*). The film's affinities with the avant-garde aesthetics of New Vision, its connection to the mentality of New Objectivity, and its position between documentary, avant-garde film, and narrative film has opened up a space for formalist readings that either praise its avant-garde elements, question its documentary ethos, uncover its narrative tendencies, or emphasize its purely visual elements (Kolaja 1965; Chapman 1971; Bernstein 1984; Weihsmann 1988). An indication of the productive tensions within the reconceptualization of urban experience, *Berlin* continues to serve as an important test case for comparative studies on the European city film (Minden 1985) and critical challenges to Kracauer's sociopsychological reading of Weimar cinema (Macrae 2003). The film also plays a key role in historical overviews of the self-representation of Weimar Berlin (Prümm 1989) and the tradition of the documentary film (Zimmermann et al. 2005), and theoretical reflections on the slippage between cinematic space and social space (Natter 1994), the productive relationship between urbanity and femininity (Gleber 1997), the role of urban modernity in the experience of spatial displacement (Kaes 1998), and the ambivalence toward modernization (Hillard 2004). More recently, *Berlin* has allowed some scholars to challenge Kracauer's sociopsychological reading of Weimar culture (Macrae 2004; Hillard 2005). For the respective references (in chronological order), see Jiri Kolaja and Arnold W. Foster, "'Berlin, the Symphony of a City' as a Theme of Visual Rhythm," *Journal of Aesthetics and Art Criticism* 23 (1965): 353–58; Matthew Bernstein, "Visual Style and Spatial Articulations in 'Berlin, Symphony of a City' (1927)," *Journal of Film and Video* 36, no. 4 (1984): 5–12; Helmut Weihsmann, *Gebaute Illusionen: Architektur im Film* (Vienna: Promedia, 1988); Jay Chapman, "Two Aspects of the City: Cavalcanti and Ruttmann," in *The Documentary Tradition,* ed. Jay Leyda (New York: W. W. Norton, 1971), 37–42; Michael Minden, "The City in Early Cinema," in Edward Timms and David Kelley, eds. *Unreal City: Urban Experience in Modern European Literature and Art* (New York: St. Martin's Press, 1985), 193–213; Karl Prümm, "'Dynamik der Großstadt.' Berlin-Bilder im Film der Zwanziger Jahre," in Gerhard Brunn and Jürgen Reulecke, eds., *Berlin . . . Blicke auf die deutsche Metropole* (Essen: Reimar Hobbing, 1989), 105–23; Wolfgang Natter, "The City as Cinematic Space: Modernism and Place in 'Berlin, Symphony of a City,'" in Stuart C. Aitken and Leo E. Zonn, eds., *Place, Power, Situation, and Spectacle: A Geography of Film* (Lanham, MD: Rowman and Littlefield, 1994), 203–27; Anke Gleber, "Women on the Screens and Streets of Modernity: In Search of the Female Flaneur," in Dudley Andrew, ed., *The Image in Dispute: Art and Cinema in the Age of Photography* (Austin: University of Texas Press, 1997), 55–85; Anton Kaes, "Leaving Home: Film, Migration, and the Urban Experience," *New German Critique* 74 (1998): 179–92; David Macrae, "Ruttmann, Rhythm, and 'Reality': A Response to Siegfried Kracauer's Interpretation of *Berlin: The Symphony of a Great City,*" in Dieter Scheunemann, ed., *Expressionist Film: New Perspectives* (Rochester: Camden House, 2003), 251–70; Derek Hillard, "Walter Ruttmann's Janus-Faced View of Modernity: The

Ambivalence of Description in *Berlin. Die Sinfonie der Großstadt,*" *Monatshefte* 96, no. 1 (2004): 78–92; and Karl Prümm, "Symphonie contra Rhythmus. Widersprüche und Ambivalenzen in Walter Ruttmanns Berlin-Film," in Peter Zimmermann and Kay Hoffmann, eds., *Geschichte des dokumentarischen Films in Deutschland,* 3 vols. (Stuttgart: Philip Reclam, 2005), 3:411–34. For yet another contribution, see Andrew Webber, "Symphony of a City: Motion Pictures and Still Lives in Weimar Berlin," in Andrew Webber and Emma Wilson, eds., *The Modern Metropolis and the Moving Image* (London: Wallflower, 2007).

5. Derek Hillard, "Walter Ruttmann's Janus-Faced View of Modernity," 85, 90.

6. Advance promotion of the film by Fox Europe in *Film-Kurier,* 10 July 1927.

7. Antje Ehmann, "Wie Wirklichkeit erzählen? Methoden des Querschnittfilms," in Klaus Kreimeier, Antje Ehmann, and Jeanpaul Goergen, eds., *Geschichte des dokumentarischen Films in Deutschland,* 2:581. The ideological underpinnings of New Vision photography and cinematography are discussed by Norbert M. Schmitz, "Zwischen 'Neuem Sehen' und 'Neuer Sachlichkeit,'" in Michael Esser, ed., *Gleißende Schatten: Kamerapioniere der zwanziger Jahre* (Berlin: Henschel, 1994), 79–95, and further elaborated in "Der Film der Neuen Sachlichkeit," in *Einübung des dokumentarischen Blicks. Fiction Film und Non Fiction Film. Film zwischen Wirklichkeitsanspruch und expressiver Sachlichkeit 1895–1945* (Marburg: Schüren, 2001), 147–68. Also see Hermann Kappelhoff, "Die neue Gegenständlichkeit. Die Bildidee der Neuen Sachlichkeit und der Film," in Thomas Koebner, ed., *Diesseits der 'Dämonischen Leinwand.' Neue Perspektiven auf das späte Weimarer Kino* (Munich: edition text + kritik, 2003), 119–38.

8. For such interpretations, see Uricchio, "Ruttmann's 'Berlin' and the City Film to 1930," 260, and Minden, "The City in Early Cinema," 203.

9. Ruttmann, quoted in Ludwig Greve, Margot Pehle, and Heidi Westhoff, eds., *Hätte ich das Kino! Die Schriftsteller und der Stummfilm* (Stuttgart: Kösel, 1976), 378. For an excellent introduction to Ruttmann, see Jeanpaul Goergen, ed., *Walter Ruttmann: Eine Dokumentation* (Berlin: Freunde der Deutschen Kinemathek, 1989).

10. Lotte Eisner, "Walter Ruttmann schneidet ein Film-Hörspiel, "*Film-Kurier,* 1 March 1930.

11. Ruttmann, "Die 'absolute' Mode," reprinted in Goergen, *Walter Ruttmann,* 82.

12. A point made in the case of Ruttmann by Heinz-B. Heller, "Stählerne Romantik und Avantgarde. Beobachtungen und Anmerkungen zu Ruttmanns Industriefilmen," in Zimmermann und Hoffmann, eds., *Die Einübung des dokumentarischen Blicks,* 105–18, and, more generally, by Leonardo Quaresima, "Der Film in Dritten Reich. Moderne, Amerikanismus, Unterhaltungsfilm," *montage a/v* 3, no. 2 (1994): 5–22.

13. Laszlo Moholy-Nagy, *Painting Photography Film,* trans. Janet Seligman (Cambridge: MIT Press, 1969), 120.

14. Moholy-Nagy, reprinted in Richard Kostelanetz, ed., *Moholy-Nagy: An Anthology* (New York: Praeger, 1970), 53–54.

15. Natter, "The City as Cinematic Space," 204. On film as part of a more per-

vasive dynamization and mobilization of space, see Mitchell Schwarzer, *Zoom-scape: Architecture in Motion and Media* (New York: Princeton Architectural Press, 2004).

16. The contribution of Berlin to the evolution of the city film is confirmed by Guntram Vogt, ed., *Die Stadt im Kino: Deutsche Spielfilme 1900–2000* (Marburg: Schüren, 2001), which includes a large number of feature films set in Berlin, including Ruttmann's *Berlin* film (167–84).

17. John Chancellor, *How to Be Happy in Berlin* (London: Arrowsmith, 1929), 49–50.

18. Rudolf Stratz, *Karussel Berlin* (Berlin: August Scherl, 1931), 123.

19. Alfred Polgar, *Kleine Schriften*, 6 vols., ed. Marcel Reich-Ranicki, with Ulrich Weinzierl (Reinbek: Rowohlt, 1982), 5:341.

20. Max Osborn, *Berlin 1870–1929. Der Aufstieg zur Weltstadt*, afterword by Thomas Friedrich (Berlin: Gebr. Mann, 1994), 155–56.

21. On the German city film, see Goergen, "Urbanität und Idylle. Städtefilme zwischen Kommerz und Kulturpropaganda," in Kreimeier et al., eds., *Geschichte des dokumentarischen Films in Deutschland*, 2:151–72. A growing number of films were produced to promote the ideas of New Building, from films such as *Sozialistisches Bauen—neuzeitliches Wohnen* (Socialist Building—Contemporary Living, 1929) about the Horseshoe Estate to Maximilian von Goldbeck's and Erich Kotzer's *Die Stadt von morgen* (The City of Tomorrow, 1930), which, with the help of Svend Noldan's famous trick animation, presents the separation of urban functions as the only valid solution to the ills of the tenement city.

22. In fact, the formal similarities between *Berlin* and *Sao Paolo* suggest that Kemeny and Rudolf Lex Lustig, who had worked in the Ufa studios in Berlin in the mid-1920s, must have known the Ruttmann film.

23. Walter Schobert, "'Painting in Time' and 'Visual Music': On German Avant-garde Films of the 1920s," in Scheunemann, ed., *Expressionist Film*, 243.

24. Minden, "The City in Early Cinema," 201.

25. Herbert Ihering, *Von Reinhardt bis Brecht: Vier Jahrzehnte Theater und Film*, 3 vols. (Berlin: Aufbau, 1961), 2:539–40.

26. Anon., "Filmrhythmus und Filmgestaltung," reprinted in Goergen, *Walter Ruttmann*, 119.

27. Paul Friedländer, review of *Berlin*, reprinted in Gertraude Kühn, Karl Tümmler, and Walter Wimmer, eds., *Film und revolutionäre Arbeiterbewegung in Deutschland 1918–1932: Dokumente und Materialien zur Erweiterung der Filmpolitik der revolutionären Arbeiterbewegung und zu den Anfängen einer sozialistischen Filmkunst in Deutschland*, 2 vols. (Berlin: Henschel, 1975), 1:195.

28. Willy Haas, review of *Berlin*, reprinted in Goergen, *Walter Ruttmann*, 117.

29. Rudolf Kurtz, review of *Berlin*, reprinted in Goergen, *Walter Ruttmann*, 30.

30. Alfred Kerr, review of *Berlin*, reprinted in *Hätte ich das Kino!* 377.

31. Kurt Pinthus, review of *Berlin*, reprinted in *Hätte ich das Kino!* 380.

32. Béla Balázs, *Schriften*, 2 vols., ed. Helmut H. Diederichs and Wolfgang Gersch (Munich: Carl Hanser, 1984), 2:127.

33. Kracauer, *From Caligari to Hitler*, 187–88. Compare his earlier review of

Ruttmann's *Berlin* film in "Film 1928," *The Mass Ornament: Weimar Essays,* ed., trans., and intro. Thomas Y. Levin (Cambridge: Harvard University Press, 1995), 318.

34. Kracauer, review of *Berlin Alexanderplatz,* in *Von Caligari bis Hitler,* trans. Ruth Baumgarten and Karsten Witte (Frankfurt am Main: Suhrkamp, 1979), 509. Not included in the English translation of the book.

35. Macrae, "Ruttmann, Rhythm, and 'Reality,'" 253.

36. Miriam Hansen, "The Mass Production of the Senses: Classical Cinema as Vernacular Modernism," in Christine Gledhill and Linda Williams, eds., *Reinventing Film Studies* (London: Arnold, 2000), 332–50, and "America, Paris, the Alps: Kracauer (and Benjamin) on Cinema and Modernity," in Leo Charney and Vanessa R. Schwartz, eds., *"Cinema and the Invention of Modern Life* (Berkeley: University of California Press, 1995), 362–402.

37. Kracauer, *Theory of Film: The Redemption of Physical Reality* (New York: Oxford University Press, 1960), 299.

38. Thomas Schadt, "Berlin. Sinfonie einer Großstadt. Eine Wiederverfilmung," *Filmgeschichte* 15 (2001), 65. After the release of the Berlin film, Schadt published a photo book, *Berlin: Sinfonie einer Großstadt* (Berlin: Nicolaische Verlagsbuchhandlung, 2002) and *Das Gefühl des Augenblicks: Zur Dramaturgie des Dokumentarfilms* (Bergisch Gladbach: Bastei Lübbe, 2003). On the film, see Evelyn Preuss, "The Collapse of Time: German History and Identity in Hubertus Siegert's *Berlin Babylon* (2001) and Thomas Schadt's *Berlin: Sinfonie einer Großstadt* (2002)," in Carol Anne Costabile-Heming, Rachel J. Halverson, and Kristie A. Foell, eds., *Berlin: The Symphony Continues: Orchestrating Architectural, Social, and Artistic Change in Germany's New Capital* (Berlin: Walter de Gruyter, 2004), 119–42. A similar argument about the echoes of Weimar Berlin films in postunification Berlin films is made by Sunka Simon in "Weimar Project(ions) in Post-Unification Cinema," 301–19, in the same anthology.

39. Elizabeth Wilson, "Looking Backward, Nostalgia and the City," in Sally Westwood and John Williams, eds., *Imagining Cities: Scripts, Signs and Memories* (London: Routledge, 1997), 138–39.

Index of Names

313

Index of Places

Index of Titles